PREFACE

This is the first edition of this book which has not been prepared by its progenitors, Professor Sir Rupert Cross and Mr. Philip Asterley Jones. The success of their venture is shown by the fact that this book has already passed through five editions. I hope that this edition does not fall far short of the standards which they set.

Those who have used previous editions of this book will note that its title has been changed from *Cases on Criminal Law* to *Cases and Statutes on Criminal Law* to reflect the increased amount of statutory material which I have incorporated. I have retained and extended the former practice of providing the occasional note or comment on a case. This book is read most profitably in conjunction with Cross and Jones, *Introduction to Criminal Law*, which is at present in its eighth edition, and, because of this, I have normally refrained from detailed comments on matters dealt with adequately in that book. Many of the comments and notes which I have inserted refer to cases reported after the last edition of the *Introduction to Criminal Law* and, to this extent, this book can be regarded as up-dating the *Introduction*.

This edition is about twenty per cent longer than its predecessor. The greatest expansion is in the chapter on offences under the Theft Act 1968 which has nearly doubled in length as a result of a number of important cases which have been reported since the last edition. I have deleted the chapter on bigamy because I consider that, in the light of the content of most courses on criminal law, the space which it occupied was better devoted to other matters. The chapter on sentencing has also been eliminated for the same reason and also because sentencing is not dealt with in the *Introduction to Criminal Law*. With a few exceptions the materials in this book follow the same order as in the *Introduction*.

The judgments in all cases have been copied from the reports mentioned at the beginning of the case and I would like to thank the proprietors of these reports for kind permission to publish the extracts. I also wish to thank my wife and Mr. David Few who assisted in checking the proofs, and finally the publishers for compiling the tables of statutes and cases and the index.

R.C.

1st *March*, 1977

TABLE OF CONTENTS

TABLE OF STATUTES

References in this Table to "*Statutes*" are to Halsbury's Statutes of England (Third Edition) showing the volume and page at which the annotated text of the Act will be found. Page references printed in bold type indicate where the Act is set out in part or in full.

TABLE OF CASES

In the following Table references are given where applicable to the
English and Empire Digest where a digest of the case will be found.
The numbers in bold type indicate where a case is set out in the text.

PAGE

CHAPTER 1
CRIMINAL LIABILITY

Preliminary Notes

The notes between this page and page 16 have been inserted in order to explain and put into context the extracts from, and references to, cases on these pages. For a fuller discussion of these matters, see Cross and Jones, *Introduction to Criminal Law*, 8th ed., Ch. 3.

The criminal liability of an accused person depends on whether he has committed the *actus reus* (i.e. legally blameworthy conduct) of a particular offence with the necessary *mens rea* (i.e. legally blameworthy state of mind).[1]

The *actus reus* of each offence is derived from its definition, whether statutory or common law. Normally, the central requirement of the *actus reus* is an act, but sometimes in statutory offences the mere existence of an event will suffice (e.g. the offence of unauthorised possession of controlled drugs) and sometimes an omission to do something is penalised expressly by statute, or, in certain offences and provided that the accused was under a legal duty to act (see *Instan, infra*), suffices instead of an act.

A mere act, omission or event is rarely, if ever, sufficient for criminal liability. The definitions of offences invariably specify, expressly or impliedly, surrounding circumstances, e.g. of time and place, which are essential to render conduct criminal. Sometimes, the definition of an offence also requires a consequence to result from an act or omission, e.g. death in murder and manslaughter, in order to constitute the *actus reus* of that offence.

---

[1] It is a cardinal rule of criminal liability that the accused's *mens rea* must exist at the time of his prohibited conduct. See, for instance, *Fagan* v. *Metropolitan Police Commissioner*, p. 138, *infra*. For exceptions to the rule, see *A.-G. for Northern Ireland* v. *Gallagher*, p. 118, *infra*, and *Thabo Meli* v. *R*, pp. 181 and 182, *infra*.

R. v. INSTAN
[1893] 1 Q.B. 450

If a person dies in consequence of another person's failure to perform a duty recognised by the criminal law, such other person may be convicted of manslaughter.[1]

The accused lived with her aunt aged 73. The evidence was that the aunt was suffering from a disease and that, during the last ten days of her life, she was not supplied with food or medical attendance by the accused, and that her death had thereby been accelerated. The accused was convicted of manslaughter, but a case was stated for the opinion of the Court for Crown Cases Reserved who were of opinion that the conviction was correct.

Extract from the Judgments of the Court for Crown Cases Reserved

Lord Coleridge, C.J.—
". . . It would not be correct to say that every moral obligation involves a legal duty; but every legal duty is founded on a moral obligation. A legal common law duty is nothing else than the enforcing by law of that which is a moral obligation without legal enforcement. There can be no question in this case that it was the clear duty of the prisoner to impart to the deceased so much as was necessary to sustain life of the food which she from time to time took in, and which was paid for by the deceased's own money for the purpose of the maintenance of herself and the prisoner; it was only through the instrumentality of the prisoner that the deceased could get the food. There was, therefore, a common law duty imposed upon the prisoner which she did not discharge.

Nor can there be any question that the failure of the prisoner to discharge her legal duty at least accelerated the death of the deceased, if it did not actually cause it. There is no case directly in point; but it would be a slur upon and a discredit to the administration of justice in this country if there were any doubt as to the legal principle, or as to the present case being within it. The prisoner was under a moral obligation to the deceased from which arose a legal duty

---

[1] Cf. *Lowe*, [1973] 1 All E.R. 805, p. 239, *infra*.

towards her; that legal duty the prisoner has wilfully and
deliberately left unperformed, with the consequence that
there has been an acceleration of the death of the deceased
owing to the non-performance of that legal duty. It is
unnecessary to say more than that upon the evidence this
conviction was most properly arrived at."

CONVICTION AFFIRMED.

The mental element in crime varies from offence to offence,
see Stephen, J., in *Tolson*, p. 31, *infra*. It must also be admitted
that a person can be convicted of certain offences despite the fact
that he lacked *mens rea* as to an element or elements of the offence
(see pp. 40–71, *infra*); such offences are known as offences of
strict liability.

As the next two cases show *mens rea* has nothing necessarily
to do with notions of an evil mind or knowledge of the wrongfulness
of one's act.

R. v. SHARPE
(1857), 7 Cox C.C. 214

The motive, however laudable, of an accused is no defence.

Sharpe's mother was buried in a cemetery belonging
to a congregation of Protestant dissenters. After the death
of his father Sharpe obtained entry to the cemetery and
removed his mother's corpse in order to bury it with his
father's in a churchyard some miles away. It was undisputed
that Sharpe had been actuated by motives of affection for
his mother and of religious duty. He was convicted of
removing a corpse from a burying-ground without lawful
authority but the judge reserved the case for consideration
by the Court for Crown Cases Reserved.

Extracts from the Judgment of the Court for Crown Cases Reserved

Erle, J.—
"The evidence for the prosecution proved the misdemeanour, unless there was a defence. We have considered
the grounds relied on in that behalf, and although we all feel
sensible of the estimable motives on which the defendant
acted, namely, filial affection and religious duty, still neither
authority nor principle would justify the position that the

wrongful removal of a corpse was no misdemeanour, if the motive for the act deserved approbation. . . . The result is, the conviction will stand, and, as the Judge states, the sentence should be a nominal fine of one shilling."

CONVICTION AFFIRMED.

R. v. BAILEY
(1800), Russ. & Ry. 1

Ignorance of the criminal law is no defence.

Bailey, the captain of a ship, fired without justification at another ship on the high seas and wounded a sailor on the other ship. He was charged under an Act which made such a shooting on the high seas triable in England and was tried before Lord Eldon at the Admiralty Sessions.

Extracts from the Summing-up of Lord Eldon

"It was then insisted that the prisoner could not be found guilty of the offence with which he was charged, because the Act of 39 Geo. 3, c. 37 upon which (together with [a previous statute]) the prisoner was indicted at this Admiralty Sessions, . . . only received the Royal Assent on 10th of May, 1799, and the fact charged in the indictment happened on 27th of June, in the same year, when the prisoner could not know that any such Act existed (his ship, the 'Langley', being at the time upon the coast of Africa).

Lord Eldon told the jury that he was of opinion that he was, in strict law, guilty within the statutes, taken together, if the facts laid were proved, though he could not then know that the Act of 39 Geo. 3, c. 37, had passed, and that his ignorance of that fact, could in no otherwise affect the case, than that it might be the means of recommending him to a merciful consideration elsewhere should he be found guilty. . . ."

VERDICT, GUILTY. THE ACCUSED WAS SUBSEQUENTLY PARDONED.

Of the various types of *mens rea* known to the law, the following are particularly noteworthy: intention and recklessness in relation to the consequences of an *actus reus*, guilty knowledge in relation to its circumstances, and negligence.

The definition of intention is particularly difficult since that word is used in various senses in different offences and contexts. One thing is clear, a person can always be said to intend something if he falls within the definition of intention given in the following case.

R. v. MOHAN
[1975] 2 All E.R. 193

A person who decides to bring about a consequence so far as it lies within his power, intends that consequence, whether he desired that consequence of his act or not.

Mohan, who was driving a car, was signalled to stop by a police officer. The car slowed down but, when about ten yards away from the officer, accelerated hard and was driven straight at the officer who moved out of its way in order to avoid being knocked down. Mohan was charged, *inter alia*, with attempting by wanton driving to cause bodily harm to the officer. The jury were directed that the Crown had to prove that Mohan had deliberately driven the vehicle wantonly and that he must have realised at the time that, unless he were to stop or there were some other intervening factor, such driving was likely to cause bodily harm, or that he was reckless as to whether bodily harm was caused. It was not necessary, they were told, to prove an intention actually to cause bodily harm. Mohan was convicted and appealed to the Court of Appeal.

Extracts from the Judgment of the Court of Appeal

James, L.J.—
    "This appeal is about the question what state of mind, *mens rea*, is required to be proved as an ingredient of the offence of attempting to commit a crime. . . .
    Counsel's argument for the Crown was that the judge was right in his direction that the Crown did not have to prove . . . any intention in the mind of the appellant. His argument was that where the attempt charged is an attempt to commit a crime which itself involves a specific state of mind, then to prove the attempt the Crown must prove that the accused had that specific state of mind, but where the attempt relates to a crime [such as the one here] which does not involve a specific state of mind, the offence of attempt

is proved by evidence that the accused committed an act
or acts proximate to the commission of the complete offence
and which unequivocally point to the completed offence
being the result of the act or acts committed. . . .

The attraction of this argument is that it presents a
situation in relation to attempts to commit crime which is
simple and logical, for it requires in proof of the attempt
no greater burden in respect of *mens rea* than is required in
proof of the completed offence. The argument in its extreme
form is that an attempt to commit a crime of strict liability
is itself a strict liability offence. . . .

Counsel for [the appellant's] . . . argument was expressed
in words which he cited from Smith and Hogan's Criminal
Law[1]:

> 'Whenever the definition of the crime requires that some
> consequence be brought about by [the defendant's] con-
> duct, it must be proved, on a charge of attempting to
> commit that crime, that [the defendant] intends that
> consequence; and this is so even if, on a charge of commit-
> ting the complete crime, recklessness as to that consequence
> —or even some lesser degree of *mens rea*—would suffice.'

That, counsel argued, is an accurate statement of the law.

In support of his argument he cited the words of Lord
Goddard, C.J., in *R.* v. *Whybrow*:[2]

> 'Therefore, if one person attacks another, inflicting a
> wound in such a way that an ordinary, reasonable person
> must know that at least grievous bodily harm will result,
> and death results, there is the malice aforethought suffi-
> cient to support the charge of murder. But, if the charge
> is one of attempted murder, the intent becomes the
> principal ingredient of the crime. It may be said that the
> law, which is not always logical, is somewhat illogical in
> saying that, if one attacks a person intending to do grievous
> bodily harm, and death results, that is murder, but that if
> one attacks a person and only intends to do grievous
> bodily harm, and death does not result, it is not attempted
> murder, but wounding with intent to do grievous bodily
> harm. It is not really illogical because, in that particular
> case, the intent is the essence of the crime while, where the
> death of another is caused, the necessity is to prove
> malice aforethought, which is supplied in law by proving
> intent to do grievous bodily harm.'

---

[1] 3rd ed., p. 191.
[2] (1951), 35 Cr. App. Rep. 141, at p. 146.

. . . In our judgment it is well established law that intent (*mens rea*) is an essential ingredient of the offence of attempt. This principle does not seem to have presented any problems, such as those related to the character of the act relied on as constituting the attempt, in the earlier cases. Insofar as the learned judge directed the jury that it was not necessary to prove any intent . . . he fell into error.

That does not, however, dispose of this appeal. . . . It has been necessary . . . to consider whether taken as a whole the directions did, by the words 'he must have realised . . . that such driving, unless it were to stop . . . was likely to cause bodily harm if he went on, or he was reckless as to whether bodily harm was caused' include the need for proof of the element of *mens rea*. The first question we have to answer is: what is the meaning of 'intention' when that word is used to describe the *mens rea* in attempt? It is to be distinguished from 'motive' in the sense of an emotion leading to action; it has never been suggested that such a meaning is appropriate to 'intention' in this context. It is equally clear that the word means what is often referred to as 'specific intent' and can be defined as 'a decision to bring about a certain consequence' or as the 'aim'.

In *Hyam* v. *Director of Public Prosecutions*[1] Lord Hailsham of St. Marylebone cited with approval the judicial interpretation of 'intention' or 'intent' applied by Asquith, L.J., in *Cunliffe* v. *Goodman*:[2]

> 'An "intention" to my mind, connotes a state of affairs which the party "intending"—I will call him X.—does more than merely contemplate. It connotes a state of affairs which, on the contrary, he decides, so far as in him lies, to bring about, and which, in point of possibility, he has a reasonable prospect of being able to bring about, by his own act of volition.'

If that interpretation of 'intent' is adopted as the meaning of *mens rea* in the offence of attempt, it is not wide enough to justify the direction in the present case. The direction, taken as a whole, can be supported as accurate only if the necessary *mens rea* included not only specific intent but also the state of mind of one who realises that, if his conduct continues, the likely consequence is the commission of the complete offence and who continues his conduct in that realisation, or the state of mind of one who,

---

[1] [1975] A.C. 55, at p. 74; [1974] 2 All E.R. 41, at pp. 51, 52; p. 197, *infra*.
[2] [1950] 2 K.B. 237, at p. 253; [1950] 1 All E.R. 720, at p. 724.

knowing that continuation of his conduct is likely to result in the commission of the complete offence, is reckless as to whether or not that is the result.

[James, L.J., then considered the other speeches in *Hyam's* case, see pp. 194, *infra*, and continued:]

We do not find in the speeches of their Lordships in *Hyam* anything which binds us to hold that *mens rea* in the offence of attempt is proved by establishing beyond reasonable doubt that the accused knew or correctly foresaw that the consequences of his act unless interrupted would 'as a high degree of probability', or would be 'likely' to, be the commission of the complete offence. Nor do we find authority in that case for the proposition that a reckless state of mind is sufficient to constitute the *mens rea* in the offence of attempt.

An attempt to commit crime is itself an offence. Often it is a grave offence which is attempted but not in fact committed. Nevertheless it falls within the class of conduct which is preparatory to the commission of a crime and is one step removed from the offence which is attempted. The court must not strain to bring within the offence of attempt conduct which does not fall within the well-established bounds of the offence. The bounds are presently set requiring proof of specific intent, a decision to bring about, insofar as it lies within the accused's power, the commission of the offence which it is alleged the accused attempted to commit, no matter whether the accused desired that consequence of his act or not.

In the present case the . . . direction was bad in law. Not only did the judge maintain the exclusion of 'intent' as an ingredient of the offence [of attempt], but he introduced an alternative basis for a conviction which did not and could not constitute the necessary *mens rea*."

APPEAL AGAINST CONVICTION FOR ATTEMPTING, BY WANTON DRIVING, TO CAUSE BODILY HARM ALLOWED.

Intention of the type defined in *Mohan* is often called direct intention, to distinguish it from oblique intention. It is generally agreed that if a person foresees a particular consequence resulting from his act but goes on to do the act in order to achieve some other objective he can be said in law to have intended (oblique intention) that consequence. However, there is dispute as to whether it is enough that the consequence should be foreseen as a probable or highly probable result or whether it must be foreseen as substantially certain to result. This difference of opinion has even existed in the House of Lords as reference to the extracts from the speeches in *Hyam* v. *Director of Public Prosecutions*, p. 194, *infra*, shows. The majority of the House of Lords seemed to take the view that a consequence is intended when it is foreseen as a probable, or highly probable, result of one's act. Lord Hailsham, however, favoured a narrower view, namely that the consequence must have been foreseen as "morally certain" to result from one's act.

The controversy as to whether foresight of probability should, like foresight of certainty, be described as intention is unimportant in practice because, whatever terminology is used, it is difficult if not impossible to point to a decided case which suggests that there may be liability where the prohibited consequence (which is not aimed at) is foreseen as certain, but not where it is foreseen as probable.

As *Steane, infra*, shows, there are some offences where, the courts have held, only a direct intention suffices; oblique intention being insufficient. Examples are attempt to commit an offence (see *Mohan, supra*), offences where the accused's act is required expressly to be done "with intent" to achieve the particular consequence of the *actus reus* (see *Belfon*, p. 170, *infra*) and offences requiring a further (or ulterior) intent (see *Belfon*). "Further intention" describes a requisite intention which does not relate to a consequence required for the *actus reus* of the offence charged but instead relates to something ulterior to the *actus reus*, e.g. the intention to permanently deprive which an appropriator of another's property must have in the offence of theft or the intent to steal or to commit certain other offences in the building which a person who enters it as a trespasser must have in the offence of burglary (see pp. 251, 273, *infra*).

R. v. STEANE
[1947] K. B. 997

The offence of doing acts likely to assist the enemy with intent to assist the enemy required proof of a direct intention to assist the enemy.

Steane was charged under Reg. 2 (a)[1] of the Defence (General) Regulations 1939 with "doing acts likely to assist the enemy, with intent to assist the enemy". He had been employed as a film actor in Germany for some time before the outbreak of the war of 1939–45, and he was then residing in Germany with his wife and children.

---

[1] Since revoked.

Shortly after the outbreak of the war, he had an interview with representatives of the German government at which he was knocked down and told to say "Heil Hitler!" In consequence of threats subsequently made against himself, his wife and children, he broadcast news for the Germans between January and April 1940. Subsequently, and after further threats were made against himself and his family, he returned to work for his former employer, and assisted in the preparation of films until 1945.

He swore that, throughout, he had no intention or idea of assisting the enemy, and that his sole object had been to save his wife and children from trouble.

Henn-Collins, J., in effect directed the jury that, if they were satisfied that the accused had done acts which were likely to assist the enemy, the intent to do so might be presumed, and Steane was convicted.

He appealed to the Court of Criminal Appeal against his conviction, which was quashed on the ground of misdirection of the jury.

Extracts from the Judgment of the Court of Criminal Appeal

Lord Goddard, C.J.—

". . . While no doubt the motive of a man's act and his intention in doing the act are, in law, different things, it is, none the less, true that in many offences a specific intention is a necessary ingredient and the jury have to be satisfied that a particular act was done with that specific intent, although the natural consequences of the act might, if nothing else were proved, be said to show the intent for which it was done. To take a simple illustration, a man is charged with wounding with intent to do grievous bodily harm. It is proved that he did severely wound the prosecutor. Nevertheless, unless the Crown can prove that the intent was to do the prosecutor grievous bodily harm, he cannot be convicted of that felony. It is always open to the jury to negative by their verdict the intent and to convict only of the misdemeanour of unlawful wounding. . . . No doubt, if the prosecution prove an act the natural consequence of which would be a certain result and no evidence or explanation is given, then a jury may, on a proper direction, find that the prisoner is guilty of doing the act with the intent alleged, but if on the totality of the evidence there is room for more than one view as to the intent of the prisoner, the jury should be directed that it is for the prosecution to prove the intent to the jury's satisfaction, and if, on a review of the whole evidence, they either think that the intent did not exist or they are left in doubt as to the intent, the prisoner is entitled to be acquitted. . . .

In this case the court cannot but feel that some confusion arose with regard to the question of intent by so much being said in the case with regard to the subject of duress. Duress is a matter of defence where a prisoner is forced by fear of violence or imprisonment to do an act which in itself is criminal. . . . But here again, before any question of duress arises, a jury must be satisfied that the prisoner had the intention which is laid in the indictment. . . .

Now, another matter which is of considerable importance in this case, but does not seem to have been brought directly to the attention of the jury, is that very different considerations may apply where the accused at the time he did the acts is in subjection to an enemy power and where he is not . . . if invasion had unhappily taken place, British subjects who might have been set to work by the enemy digging trenches would undoubtedly be doing acts likely to assist the enemy. It would be unnecessary surely in their cases to consider any of the niceties of the law relating to duress, because no jury would find that merely by doing this work they were intending to assist the enemy."

APPEAL ALLOWED.

Many offences where oblique intention suffices can also be committed recklessly, in the subjective sense of that term. "Recklessness" has been used by the judges in two senses: subjective and objective. Objective recklessness is a species of negligence and is discussed later. Subjective recklessness as to a consequence of his act exists where the accused foresees that that consequence may possibly result from his act yet goes on to take the risk of it occurring, that risk being unjustified. In the recent case of *Briggs*[1] the Court of Appeal approved the following formula:

"A man is reckless in the [subjective] sense . . . when he carries out a deliberate act knowing that there is some risk of [whatever the relevant consequence is] resulting from that act but nevertheless continues in the performance of that act."

---

[1] [1977] 1 All E.R. 475.

Also see *Cunningham*, p. 166, *infra*. While the formula in *Briggs* is adequate where it is unjustifiable to take any risk of the relevant consequence resulting, the additional question of whether an unjustifiable risk was taken should be left to the jury if, in the particular case, it may have been justifiable for the accused to take the risk of the relevant consequence resulting.

It must be emphasised that intention and recklessness as to the consequence of one's act is only required to extend to the consequence defined for the *actus reus* of the offence in question, the particular victim or way in which that consequence occurs need not be aimed at or foreseen. Thus, if A fires at B wanting to kill him, or foreseeing that he may very probably do so, and misses B but kills C, A is guilty of murder since he has *mens rea* for that offence—an intention to kill a human being. One authority for this principle follows:

R. v. LATIMER
(1886), 17 Q.B.D. 359

Provided that the prosecution prove that the accused had the necessary mens rea, it is irrelevant that the actual victim or object of his conduct was unforeseen.

Latimer was charged with unlawfully and maliciously wounding a barmaid by a blow with a belt. The evidence was that he had become involved in a quarrel with one Chapple in a public house, and that, after going into the yard for a short time, he returned to the room in which Chapple was sitting, and aimed a blow at him with a belt which he had in his hand as he passed the place where Chapple was sitting. The belt struck and cut the face of the barmaid.

The jury found that he hit the barmaid accidentally. A verdict of guilty was entered, but a case was stated for the opinion of the Court for Crown Cases Reserved who were of opinion that the conviction was correct.

Extracts from the Judgments of the Court for Crown Cases Reserved

Lord Coleridge, C.J.—

"We are of opinion that this conviction must be sustained. It is common knowledge that a man who has an unlawful and malicious intent against another, and, in attempting to carry it out, injures a third person, is guilty of what the law deems malice against the person injured, because the offender is doing an unlawful act, and has that which the judges call general malice, and that is enough. Such would be the case if the matter were *res integra*; but it is not so, for *R*. v. *Hunt*[1] is an express authority on the point. There a man intended to injure A, and said so, and, in the course of doing it, stabbed the wrong man, and had clearly malice in fact, but no intention of injuring the man who was stabbed. . . . So, but for *R*. v. *Pembliton*,[2] there would not have been the slightest difficulty. Does that case make any difference? I think not, and on consideration, that it was quite rightly decided. But it is clearly distinguishable, because the indictment in *R*. v. *Pembliton*[2] was on the Act making unlawful and malicious injury to property a statutory offence punishable in a certain way, and the jury expressly negatived, and the facts expressly negatived, any intention to do injury to property, and the Court held that under the Act making it an offence to injure any property there must be an intent to injure property. *R*. v. *Pembliton*,[2] therefore, does not govern the present case and on no other ground is there anything to be said for the prisoner."

CONVICTION AFFIRMED.

Mens rea in relation to the circumstances of the *actus reus* is known as "guilty knowledge".

ROPER v. TAYLOR'S CENTRAL GARAGES (EXETER), LTD.
[1951] 2 T.L.R. 284

There are three kinds of guilty knowledge known to the criminal law.

The defendants were convicted by a magistrates' court on an information charging them with having permitted the operation of a coach in contravention of s. 72 of the Road

---

[1] (1825), 1 Mood. C.C. 93.
[2] (1874), L.R. 2 C.C.R. 119; where a stone aimed at another person smashed a window.

Traffic Act 1930,[1] which prohibited the use of a vehicle as a stage carriage except under a road service licence. The coach had been hired to a Mr. Hartnell, ostensibly to carry a band to an engagement, but, unknown to the defendants, the hirer had advertised to the general public that they could be conveyed on the coach to the hotel where the band was to perform, thereby making the coach a stage carriage on that occasion.

The Divisional Court allowed the defendant's appeal against conviction because the magistrates had wrongly taken into consideration certain evidence which had been given against the hirer, who had been convicted of using the coach in contravention of s. 72 of the Road Traffic Act 1930,[1] immediately beforehand, in order to save repetition of the evidence. However, in his judgment, Devlin, J., went on to make some further observations.

Extract from the Judgments of the Divisional Court

Devlin, J.—
"The other thing which I desire to say is that it seems to me to be very important, in cases of this sort, that the prosecution, where the burden [of proof] lies on the prosecution, should explain to lay justices . . . exactly what sort of knowledge the prosecution desires to be found. There are, I think, three degrees of knowledge which it may be relevant to consider in cases of this kind. The first is actual knowledge,[2] which the justices may find because they infer it from the nature of the act done, for no man can prove the state of another man's mind; and they may find it even if the defendant gives evidence to the contrary. They may say, 'We do not believe him; we think that that was his state of mind.' They may feel that the evidence falls short of that, and if they do they have then to consider what might be described as knowledge of the second degree; whether the defendant was, as it has been called, shutting his eyes to an obvious means of knowledge. Various expressions have been used to describe that state of mind. I do not think it necessary to look further, certainly not in cases of this type, than the phrase which Lord Hewart, C.J., used in a case under this

---

[1] Subsequently re-enacted by Road Traffic Act 1960, s. 134.
[2] Where a person has actual knowledge of the circumstances in which he is acting he is said to act intentionally in relation to them.

section, *Evans* v. *Dell*[1], where he said: ' . . . the respondent deliberately refrained from making inquiries the results of which he might not care to have.'[2]

The third kind of knowledge is what is generally known in the law as constructive knowledge: it is what is encompassed by the words 'ought to have known' in the phrase 'knew or ought to have known'. It does not mean actual knowledge at all; it means that the defendant had in effect the means of knowledge. When, therefore, the case of the prosecution is that the defendant fails to make what they think were reasonable inquiries it is, I think, incumbent on them to make it plain which of the two things they are saying. There is a vast distinction between a state of mind which consists of deliberately refraining from making inquiries, the result of which the person does not care to have, and a state of mind which is merely neglecting to make such inquiries as a reasonable and prudent person would make. If that distinction is kept well in mind I think that justices will have less difficulty than this case appears to show they have had in determining what is the true position. The case of shutting the eyes is actual knowledge in the eyes of the law; the case of merely neglecting to make inquiries is not knowledge at all—it comes within the legal conception of constructive knowledge, a conception which, generally speaking, has no place in the criminal law."

APPEAL ALLOWED.

A person can act negligently in relation to a circumstance or consequence of an *actus reus*. Negligence as to circumstance is the "constructive knowledge" or "knowledge of the third degree" referred to by Devlin, J., in *Roper* v. *Taylor's Garages*, *supra*, and, as he indicated, is only a basis of liability in exceptional offences or contexts. Negligence as to consequence is the "objective recklessness" referred to previously. A person is negligent with regard to a consequence of his conduct when, although he did not realise the risk of it occurring, he ought to have done so, and would have avoided it if he had acted reasonably. The only important instance of negligence as to consequence as a basis of criminal liability is manslaughter, which can be committed by someone who is grossly negligent, in the sense that he fails to comply with

---

[1] [1937] 1 All E.R. 349, at p. 353.
[2] Knowledge of the second degree, or "wilful blindness" as it is usually called, is a species of recklessness with reference to surrounding circumstances.

a low standard of care in relation to a reasonably foreseeable risk of death or, possibly, grievous bodily harm to another, which he would have foreseen if he had been moderately careful.

Proposals for the reform of the law concerning the mental element in crime are contained in Law Commission Working Paper No. 31, *The Mental Element in Crime*, which is summarised in Cross and Jones, *Introduction to Criminal Law*, 8th ed., para. 3.31.

WOOLMINGTON v. DIRECTOR OF PUBLIC PROSECUTIONS
[1935] A.C. 462

Subject to the exceptional case of the defence of insanity,[1] *and to certain statutory exceptions, the onus of proving beyond reasonable doubt that the accused not only committed the guilty act, but also did so with the guilty mind requisite to constitute the crime charged, rests upon the prosecution throughout a criminal charge, and never shifts to the defence; in particular, the guilty mind will not of necessity be presumed from the fact that the accused committed the guilty act.*

Woolmington was charged with the murder of his wife. He did not deny that he had shot her, but he stated that the gun had gone off accidentally while he was endeavouring to induce her to return to live with him by theatening to shoot himself.

Swift, J., directed the jury that, once it is shown that death was caused by the act of the accused, the law presumes malice until the contrary is proved, and the jury returned a verdict of guilty.

Woolmington appealed against his conviction to the Court of Criminal Appeal, and that court affirmed the conviction and dismissed the appeal on the ground that the direction to the jury was supported by authority.

Woolmington appealed to the House of Lords, who allowed the appeal and quashed the conviction after an exhaustive review of the authorities which had been said to support the summing up.

---

[1] *M'Naghten's Case* (1843), 10 Cl. & Fin. 200; p. 74 *infra*.

Extracts from Speeches of the House of Lords

Viscount Sankey, L.C.—

". . . if it is proved that the conscious act of the prisoner killed a man and nothing else appears in the case, there is evidence upon which the jury may, not must, find him guilty of murder. It is difficult to conceive so bare and meagre a case, but that does not mean that the onus is not still on the prosecution.

If at any period of a trial it was permissible for the judge to rule that the prosecution had established its case and that the onus was shifted on the prisoner to prove that he was not guilty and that unless he discharged that onus the prosecution was entitled to succeed, it would be enabling the judge in such a case to say that the jury must in law find the prisoner guilty and so make the judge decide the case and not the jury, which is not the common law. . . . Just as there is evidence on behalf of the prosecution so there may be evidence on behalf of the prisoner which may cause a doubt as to his guilt. In either case, he is entitled to the benefit of the doubt. But while the prosecution must prove the guilt of the prisoner, there is no such burden laid on the prisoner to prove his innocence and it is sufficient for him to raise a doubt as to his guilt; he is not bound to satisfy the jury of his innocence. . . .

Throughout the web of the English Criminal Law one golden thread is always to be seen, that it is the duty of the prosecution to prove the prisoner's guilt subject to what I have already said as to the defence of insanity[1] and subject also to any statutory exception. If, at the end of and on the whole of the case, there is a reasonable doubt, created by the evidence given by either the prosecution or the prisoner, as to whether the prisoner killed the deceased with a malicious intention, the prosecution has not made out the case and the prisoner is entitled to an acquittal. No matter what the charge or where the trial, the principle that the prosecution must prove the guilt of the prisoner is part of the common law of England and no attempt to whittle it down can be entertained. When dealing with a murder case the Crown must prove (a) death as the result of a voluntary act of the accused and (b) malice of the accused.

---

[1] His Lordship had already treated *M'Naghten's Case* (1843), 10 Cl. & Fin. 200, p. 74, *infra*, as exceptional so far as the onus of proof is concerned, [1935] A.C. 462, at p. 475.

It may prove malice either expressly or by implication. For malice may be implied where death occurs as the result of a voluntary act of the accused which is (i) intentional and (ii) unprovoked. When evidence of death and malice has been given (this is a question for the jury) the accused is entitled to show, by evidence or by examination of the circumstances adduced by the Crown that the act on his part which caused death was either unintentional or provoked. If the jury are either satisfied with his explanation or, upon a review of all the evidence, are left in reasonable doubt whether, even if his explanation be not accepted, the act was unintentional or provoked, the prisoner is entitled to be acquitted [sic].[1] It is not the law of England to say, as was said in the summing up in the present case; 'if the Crown satisfy you that this woman died at the prisoner's hands then he has to show that there are circumstances to be found in the evidence which has been given from the witness-box in this case which alleviate the crime so that it is only manslaughter or which excuse the homicide altogether by showing it was a pure accident.' . . ."

APPEAL ALLOWED.

Comment on Director of Public Prosecutions v. Woolmington

There is a third exception to the general rule enunciated in *Woolmington's* case, although it is not referred to there. Where a a statute on its true construction prohibits the doing of an act save in specified circumstances or by persons of specified classes or with specified qualifications or with the licence or permission of specified authorities, the onus of proving such an exemption is on the accused. This rule is provided in the case of summary proceedings by s. 81 of the Magistrates' Courts Act 1952 and applies in the case of trials on indictment as the result of the decision of the Court of Appeal in *Edwards*[2] where a number of authorities were reviewed.

Where the accused bears the burden of proof he only has to

---

[1] As was pointed out in *Mancini* v. *Director of Public Prosecutions*, [1942] A.C. 1, at p. 13, the sentence should have concluded not with the word "acquitted" but with the words "the prisoner is entitled to the benefit of the doubt." This is because when there is provocation, a verdict of manslaughter instead of murder may be returned but the prisoner is not entitled to be acquitted.

[2] [1975] Q.B. 27; [1974] 2 All E.R. 1085. Cf. *Tynan* v. *Jones*, [1975] R.T.R. 465.

prove the exculpating fact on the balance of probabilities, not beyond reasonable doubt.[1]

CRIMINAL JUSTICE ACT 1967

"*Section 8.—Proof of criminal intent*
    A court or jury, in determining whether a person has committed an offence,—
    (*a*) shall not be bound in law to infer that he intended or foresaw a result of his actions by reason only of its being a natural and probable consequence of those actions; but
    (*b*) shall decide whether he did intend or foresee that result by reference to all the evidence, drawing such inferences from the evidence as appear proper in the circumstances."

R. v. GILL
[1963] 2 All E.R. 688

The burden of adducing evidence of duress is borne by the accused; but the ultimate burden of disproving it is borne by the prosecution.

Gill was convicted of conspiracy and larceny. So far as the charge of larceny was concerned his defence was that, having entered into a conspiracy to steal a lorry and its load from his employers, he repented and told his fellow conspirators that he would not go through with the conspiracy. The fellow conspirators then threatened him with physical violence, producing a crow bar and a bottle of petrol. The accused thereupon drove the lorry into a lay-by on the M.1 having, after the threats, gone to collect it from his employer's yard. The trial judge used language which, taken by itself, might have led the jury to suppose that the ultimate burden of proving duress was borne by the accused; but the Court of Criminal Appeal held on the accused's appeal against the conviction on the larceny count, that, read as a whole, the trial judge's summing-up did not amount to a misdirection with regard to the burden of proof.

---

[1] *Sodeman* v. *R.*, [1936] 2 All E.R. 1128; *Carr Briant* [1943] K.B. 607; [1943] 2 All E.R. 156.

Extract from the Judgment of the Court of Criminal Appeal

Edmund Davies, J.—

"The third and most interesting point taken relates only to the larceny count, it being submitted that the learned deputy-chairman wrongly directed the jury that it was for the appellant to establish that he was acting under duress. The account given by the appellant himself makes it very doubtful whether such a defence was strictly open to him, inasmuch as there was a time after the alleged threats when, having been left outside his employer's yard and having then entered it, he could presumably have raised the alarm and so wrecked the whole criminal enterprise. In *M'Growther's Case*[1] Lee, L.C.J., directed the jury that, to establish a plea of duress, the defendant must have resisted or fled from the wrongdoer if that were possible. Seemingly, the position under American law is the same, as appears from the statement in Professor Rollin Perkins' *Criminal Law* that,

'The excuse (of compulsion) is not available to someone who had an obviously safe avenue of escape before committing the prohibited act.'

The issue of duress was, nevertheless, left to the jury in the present case, and that may well have been the prudent course. Having been left, did the burden rest on the Crown conclusively to destroy this defence, in the same way as it is required to destroy such other defences as provocation or self-defence? For the latter view, reliance was placed on the judgement of Lord Goddard, C.J., in *R. v. Steane*[2] in the course of which he said:

'. . . before any question of duress arises, a jury must be satisfied that the prisoner had the intention which is laid in the indictment. Duress is a matter of defence and the onus of proving it is on the accused. As we have already said, where intent is charged in the indictment, it is for the prosecution to prove it, so the onus is the other way.'

On the other hand, in *R. v. Purdy*[3] where a British prisoner of war was charged with treason, Oliver, J., directing the jury on the defence of duress, said:

---

[1] (1746), 18 State Tr. 391.
[2] [1947] K.B. 997, at p. 1005; [1947] 1 All E.R. 813, at p. 817; p. 9, *supra.*
[3] (1946), 10 J.C.L. 182, at p. 186.

'If you believe, or if you think that it might be true, that he only did that because he had the fear of death upon him, then you will acquit him on that charge, because to act in matters of this sort under threat of death is excusable.'

Similarly, in *R. v. Shiartos*[1] where duress was relied on by an accused charged with arson, Lawton, J., directed the jury that: 'If, in all the circumstances of this case, you are satisfied that what he did he did at pistol point and in fear of his life, he is entitled to be acquitted. If, although you are not satisfied, you think it might well be that he was forced at pistol point to do what he had to do, then again you should acquit him, because the prosecution would not have made you feel sure that what he did he did maliciously.'

In our judgment, the law on this matter is to be found correctly stated in Dr. Glanville Williams' *Criminal Law* (2nd Edn.), p. 762, para. 247, in this way: '. . . alhough it is convenient to call duress a "defence", this does not mean that the ultimate (persuasive) burden of proving it is on the accused. . . . But the accused must raise the defence by sufficient evidence to go to the jury; in other words, the evidential burden is on him.'

The Crown are not called on to anticipate such a defence and destroy it in advance. The accused, either by the cross-examination of the prosecution witnesses or by evidence called on his behalf, or by a combination of the two, must place before the court such material as makes duress a live issue and proper to be left to the jury. But, once he has succeeded in doing this, it is then for the Crown to destroy that defence in such a manner as to leave in the jury's minds no reasonable doubt that the accused cannot be absolved on the grounds of the alleged compulsion. It is true that this approach appears to conflict with the literal reading of the passage from Lord Goddard, C.J.'s judgment in *R. v. Steane*. It is to be observed, however, that that passage was *obiter*, in that the real decision there was that it was for the Crown to prove the specific intent laid and that, in the particular circumstances of that case, an inference could not be drawn that the appellant intended the natural consequences of his act. We agree with Dr. Glanville Williams that the *dictum* must be read as relating only to what the author calls the 'evidential' burden cast on the accused, and not to the ultimate (or 'persuasive') burden placed on

---

[1] (1961), unreported September 19th, Central Criminal Court.

the Crown of destroying the defence of duress where it has been substantially raised."

APPEAL DISMISSED.

Note

As indicated in *Gill* the same rule as to proof as was enunciated in that case applies to other defences which the accused may raise, such as provocation (on a murder charge) or self-defence or non-insane automatism. For another authority on this matter the reader is referred to *Bratty* v. *A.-G. for Northern Ireland*, p. 91, *infra*.

DIRECTOR OF PUBLIC PROSECUTIONS v. MORGAN

[1975] 2 All E.R. 347

A person cannot be convicted of an offence if he acts under a mistaken belief which negatives the subjective mental element which the prosecution must prove in the first instance, even though his mistake is not based on reasonable grounds.

Morgan invited the three other appellants to come to his house and have sexual intercourse with his wife. He assured them that his wife would be willing but would probably simulate reluctance for her own pleasure. The three men agreed and accompanied Morgan to his house. Mrs. Morgan was asleep but they woke her and forcibly took her into another bedroom, where each of the three men had intercourse with her while the others restrained her and committed indecent acts on her body. The three men were charged with raping Mrs. Morgan and, together with Morgan, with aiding and abetting the rapes by the others. The judge directed the jury that the prosecution had to prove that the men intended to have intercourse with Mrs. Morgan without her consent and that if they had believed she was consenting they should be acquitted provided that their belief was a reasonable one. Morgan and the other three men were convicted. The Court of Appeal dismissed their appeals but granted them leave to appeal to the House of Lords.

Extracts from the Speeches of the House of Lords

Lord Hailsham of St. Marylebone—

". . . The question certified as being of general public

importance by the Court of Appeal, and the only point of principle raised on [the appellants'] behalf is:

'Whether, in rape, the defendant can properly be convicted notwithstanding that he in fact believed that the woman consented if such belief was not based on reasonable grounds.'

The certified question arises because counsel for the appellants raised the question whether, even if the victim consented, the appellants may not have honestly believed that she did. As I have pointed out, the question was wholly unreal, because if there was reasonable doubt about belief, the same material must have given rise to reasonable doubt about consent and vice-versa. But presumably because, at that stage, the jury's view of the matter had not been sought, the matter was left to them, as the appellants complain, in a form which implied that they could only acquit if the mistaken belief in consent was reasonable, and it was not enough that it should be honest. . . . The learned judge said:

'. . . Further, the prosecution have to prove that each defendant intended to have sexual intercourse with this woman without her consent. Not merely that he intended to have intercourse with her but that he intended to have intercourse without her consent. Therefore if the defendant believed or may have believed that Mrs. Morgan consented to him having sexual intercourse with her, then there would be no such intent in his mind and he would be not guilty of the offence of rape, but such a belief must be honestly held by the defendant in the first place. He must really believe that. And, secondly, his belief must be a reasonable belief; such a belief as a reasonable man would entertain if he applied his mind and thought about the matter. It is not enough for a defendant to rely upon a belief, even though he honestly held it, if it was completely fanciful; contrary to every indication which could be given which would carry some weight with a reasonable man. And, of course, the belief must be not a belief that the woman would consent at some time in the future, but a belief that at the time when intercourse was taking place or when it began that she was then consenting to it.'

No complaint is made . . . by the appellants of the judge's first proposition describing the mental element.

It is on the second proposition about the mental element that the appellants concentrate their criticism. An honest belief in consent, they contend, is enough. It matters not whether it be also reasonable. No doubt a defendant will wish to raise argument or lead evidence to show that this belief was reasonable, since this will support its honesty. No doubt the prosecution will seek to cross-examine or raise arguments or adduce evidence to undermine the contention that the belief is reasonable, because, in the nature of the case, the fact that a belief cannot reasonably be held is a strong ground for saying that it was not held honestly at all. Nonetheless, the appellants contend, the crux of the matter, the factum probandum, or rather the fact to be refuted by the prosecution, is honesty and not honesty plus reasonableness. In making reasonableness as well as honesty an ingredient in this 'defence' the judge, say the appellants, was guilty of a misdirection.

My first comment on this direction is that the propositions described 'in the first place' and 'secondly' in the above direction as to the mental ingredient in rape are wholly irreconcilable. . . . If it is true, as the learned judge says 'in the first place' that the prosecution have to prove that 'each defendant intended to have sexual intercourse without her consent. Not merely that he intended to have intercourse with her but that he intended to have intercourse without her consent', the defendant must be entitled to an acquittal if the prosecution fail to prove just that. The necessary mental ingredient will be lacking and the only possible verdict is 'not guilty'. If, on the other hand, as is asserted in the passage beginning 'secondly', it is necessary for any belief in the woman's consent to be a 'reasonable belief' before the defendant is entitled to an acquittal, it must either be because the mental ingredient in rape is not 'to have intercourse and to have it without her consent' but simply 'to have intercourse' subject to a special defence of 'honest and reasonable belief', or alternatively to have intercourse without a reasonable belief in her consent. Counsel for the respondent argued for each of these alternatives, but in my view each is open to insuperable objections of principle. No doubt it would be possible, by statute, to devise a law by which intercourse, voluntarily entered into, was an absolute offence, subject to a 'defence' of belief whether honest or honest and reasonable, of which the 'evidential' burden is primarily on the defence and the 'probative' burden on the prosecution. But in my opinion such is not the crime of rape as it has hitherto been understood. The prohibited act in rape is to have intercourse without the victim's consent. The minimum *mens rea* or guilty mind in most common law offences, including rape, is the intention to do the prohibited act, and that is correctly stated in the proposition stated 'in the first place' of the judge's direction. In murder the situation is different,because the murder is only complete when the victim dies, and an intention to do really serious bodily harm has been held to be enough in such a case.

The only qualification I would make to the direction of the learned judge's 'in the first place' is the refinement for which, as I shall show, there is both Australian and English authority, that if the intention of the accused is to have intercourse nolens volens, that is recklessly and not caring whether the victim be a consenting party or not, that is equivalent on ordinary principles to an intent to do the prohibited act without the consent of the victim. . . .

The beginning of wisdom in all the *'mens rea'* cases to which our attention was called is, as was pointed out by Stephen, J., in *R.* v. *Tolson*[1], that *'mens rea'* means a number of quite different things in relation to different crimes. Sometimes it means an intention, e.g. in murder, 'to kill or to inflict really serious injury'. Sometimes it means a state of mind or knowledge, e.g. in receiving or handling stolen goods 'knowing them to be stolen'. Sometimes it means both an intention and a state of mind, e.g. 'Dishonestly and without a claim of right made in good faith with intent permanently to deprive the owner thereof'. Sometimes it forms part of the essential ingredients of the offence without proof of which the prosecution, as it were, withers on the bough. Sometimes, it is a matter, of which, though the 'probative' burden may be on the Crown, normally the 'evidential' burden may usually (though not always) rest on the defence, e.g. 'self-defence' and 'provocation' in murder, though it must be noted that if there is material making the issue a live one, the matter must be left to the jury even if the defence do not raise it. In statutory offences the range is even wider since, owing to the difficulty of proving a negative, Parliament quite often expressly puts the burden on the defendant to negative a guilty state (see per Lord Reid in *Sweet* v. *Parsley*[2]) or inserts words like 'fraudulently', 'negligently', 'knowingly', 'wilfully', 'maliciously', which import special types of guilty mind, or even imports them by implication by importing such word as 'permit' (cf. Lord

---

[1] (1889), 23 Q.B.D., at p. 185; [1886–90] All E. R. Rep., at p. 36; p. 34, *infra*.
[2] [1970] A.C., at p. 150; [1969] 1 All E.R., at p. 351.

Diplock[1] in the same case) or as in *Warner* v. *Metropolitan Police Comr.*[2] prohibit the 'possession' of a particular substance, or as, in *Sweet* v. *Parsley*[3] itself, leaves the courts to decide whether a particular prohibition makes a new 'absolute' offence or provides an escape by means of an honest, or an honest and reasonable belief. Moreover of course, a statute can, and often does, create an absolute offence without any degree of *mens rea* at all. It follows from this, surely, that it is logically impermissible, as the respondent sought to do in this case, to draw a necessary inference from decisions in relation to offences where *mens rea* means one thing, and cases where it means another, and in particular from decisions on the construction of statutes, whether these be related to bigamy, abduction or the possession of drugs, and decisions in relation to common law offences. It is equally impermissible to draw direct or necessary inferences from decisions where the mens rea is, or includes, a state of opinion, and cases where it is limited to intention (a distinction I referred to in *Hyam* v. *Director of Public Prosecutions*)[4], or between cases where there is a special 'defence', like self-defence or provocation, and cases where the issue relates to the primary intention which the prosecution has to prove.

Once one has accepted, what seems to me to be abundantly clear, that the prohibited act in rape is non-consensual sexual intercourse, and that the guilty state of mind is an intention to commit it, it seems to me to follow as a matter of inexorable logic that there is no room either for a 'defence' of honest belief or mistake, or of a defence of honest and reasonable belief and mistake. Either the prosecution proves that the accused had the requisite intent, or it does not. In the former case it succeeds, and in the latter it fails. Since honest belief clearly negatives intent, the reasonableness or otherwise of that belief can only be evidence for or against the view that the belief and therefore the intent was actually held, and it matters not whether, to quote Bridge, J.[5], [in the Court of Appeal]: 'the definition of a crime includes no specific element beyond the prohibited act' . . .

By contrast, the appellants invited us to overrule the

---

[1] [1970] A.C., at p. 162; [1969] 1 All E.R., at p. 361; p. 66, *infra*.
[2] [1969] 2 A.C. 256; [1968] 2 All E.R. 356; p. 59, *infra*.
[3] [1970] A.C. 132; [1969] 1 All E.R. 347; p. 63, *infra*.
[4] [1975] A.C. 55; [1974] 2 All E.R. 41; p. 194, *infra*.
[5] [1975] 1 All E.R., at p. 14.

bigamy cases from *R. v. Tolson*[1] onwards and perhaps also
R. v. Prince[2] (the abduction case) as wrongly decided at
least insofar as they purport to insist that a mistaken belief
must be reasonable. . . .

Although it is undoubtedly open to this House to
reconsider *R. v. Tolson* and the bigamy cases, and perhaps
R. v. Prince which may stand or fall with them, I must
respectfully decline to do so in the present case. Nor is it
necessary that I should. I am not prepared to assume that
the statutory offences of bigamy or abduction are necessarily
on all fours with rape, and before I was prepared to undermine a whole line of cases which have been accepted as law
for so long, I would need argument in the context of a case
expressly relating to the relevant offences. I am content to
rest my view of the instant case on the crime of rape by
saying that it is my opnion that the prohibited act is and
always has been intercourse without consent of the victim
and the mental element is and always has been the intention
to commit that act, or the equivalent intention of having
intercourse willy-nilly not caring whether the victim consents or no. A failure to prove this involves an acquittal
because the intent, an essential ingredient, is lacking. It
matters not why it is lacking if only it is not there, and in
particular it matters not that the intention is only lacking
because of a belief not based on reasonable grounds. I should
add that I myself am inclined to view *R. v. Tolson*[3] as a
narrow decision based on the construction of a statute, which
prima facie seemed to make an absolute statutory offence,
with a proviso, related to the seven year period of absence,
which created a statutory defence. The judges in *R. v. Tolson*
decided that this was not reasonable, and, on general
jurisprudential principles, imported into the statutory
offence words which created a special 'defence' of honest and
reasonable belief of which the 'evidential' but not the
probative burden lay on the defence. I do not think it is
necessary to decide this conclusively in the present case. But
if this is the true view there is a complete distinction between
R. v. Tolson and the other cases based on statute and the
present.

. . . [T]hough I get some support for what I have been
saying from the reasoning of the decision in *R. v. Smith*[4],

---

[1] (1889), 23 Q.B.D. 168; [1886–90] All E.R. Rep. 26; p. 31, *infra*.
[2] (1875), L.R. 2 C.C.R. 154; [1874–80] All E.R. Rep. 881; p. 40, *infra*.
[3] (1889), 23 Q.B.D. 168; [1886–90] All E.R. Rep. 26; p. 31, *infra*.
[4] [1974] Q.B. 354; [1974] 1 All E.R. 632; p. 313, *infra*.

I nevertheless regard that case as a decision on the Criminal Damage Act 1971 rather than a decision covering the whole law of criminal liability.

For the above reasons I would answer the question certified in the negative, but would apply the proviso to s. 2 (1) of the Criminal Appeal Act 1968 on the ground that no miscarriage of justice has or conceivably could have occurred. In my view, therefore, these appeals should be dismissed."

Lord Fraser of Tullybelton—

"My Lords, the answer to the general question raised in this case depends, in my opinion, on the nature of the *mens rea* or mental element in the definition of the crime of rape. Most offences, whether at common law or under statute, include some mental element, but the description of the offence normally refers only to the prohibited act, leaving the mental element to be implied. Thus, the definition of rape in East's Pleas of the Crown[1] is as follows: 'Rape is the unlawful carnal knowledge of a woman by force and against her will.' The nature of the mental element differs in different offences, as was explained by Stephen, J., in *R. v. Tolson*, and he said:[2]

'The full definition of every crime contains expressly or by implication a proposition as to a state of mind. Therefore, if the mental element of any conduct alleged to be a crime is proved to have been absent in any given case, the crime so defined is not committed; or, again, if a crime is fully defined, nothing amounts to that crime which does not satisfy that definition.'

That passage was quoted in *Sweet v. Parsley*[3] by Lord Diplock who went on to say:

'Where the crime consists of doing an act which is prohibited by statute, the proposition as to the state of mind of the doer which is contained in the full definition of the crime must be ascertained from the words and subject-matter of the statute.'

Rape being a crime at common law, the proposition as to the state of mind of the doer which is contained in the full

---

[1] (1803), 1 P.C. 434.
[2] (1889), 23 Q.B.D. 168, at p. 187; [1886–90] All E.R. Rep. 26, at p. 37; p. 34, *infra*.
[3] [1970] A.C. 132, at p. 162; [1969] 1 All E.R. 347, at p. 361; p. 66, *infra*.

definition has to be collected from such judicial dicta or other authoritative statements of law as are available.

... It seems to me that the meaning of the [trial judge's] direction, and of the earlier dicta, is that the *mens rea* of rape is an intention to have intercourse with a non-consenting woman or to have non-consensual intercourse. If that is so, then the logical difficulty of requiring a belief in the woman's consent to be based on reasonable grounds arises sharply. If the effect of the evidence as a whole is that the defendant believed, or may have believed, that the woman was consenting, then the Crown has not discharged the onus of proving commission of the offence as fully defined and, as it seems to me, no question can arise whether the belief was reasonable or not. Of course, the reasonableness or otherwise of the belief will be important as evidence tending to show whether it was truly held by the defendant but that is all.

... We were invited to overrule *R.* v. *Tolson* but, as it has stood for over 80 years, and has been followed in many later cases, I would not favour that course. But in my opinion the case is distinguishable from the present. Bigamy was a statutory offence under the Offences against the Person Act 1861, s. 57. So far as appears from the words of the section, bigamy was an absolute offence, except for one defence set out in the proviso, and it is clear that the mental element in bigamy is quite different from that in rape. In particular, bigamy does not involve any intention except the intention to go through a marriage ceremony, unlike rape in which I have already considered the mental element. So, if a defendant charged with bigamy believes that his spouse is dead, his belief does not involve the absence of any intent which forms an essential ingredient in the offence, and is thus not comparable to the belief of a defendant charged with rape that the woman consents. The difficulty of arguing by analogy from one offence to another is strikingly illustrated by reference to *R.* v. *Prince*[1]. That case dealt with abduction of a girl under the age of 16, an offence created by s. 55 of the 1861 Act. Lord Bramwell, with whom five other judges concurred, held that a mistaken and reasonable belief by the defendant that the abducted girl was aged 16 or more was no excuse, because abduction of a young girl was immoral as well as illegal, although a mistaken and reasonable belief by the defendant that he had the consent of the girl's father would have been an excuse. If such differences

---

[1] (1875), L.R. 2 C.C.R. 154; [1874–80] All E.R. Rep. 881; p. 40, *infra*.

can exist about mistaken beliefs of different facts in one offence, it is surely dangerous to argue from one offence to another...

For these reasons, I am of the opinion that there is no authority which compels me to answer the question in this case in what I would regard as an illogical way. I would therefore answer the question in the negative—that is in favour of the appellants. But for the reasons stated by my noble and learned friends, Lord Hailsham and Lord Edmund-Davies, I would apply the proviso to the Criminal Appeal Act 1968, s. 2(1), and I would refuse the appeal."

APPEAL DISMISSED.

Note on Director of Public Prosecutions v. Morgan

The decision in *Morgan's* case concerning mistakes negativing the subjective *mens rea* which the prosecution must prove is of particular importance where the mistake negatives *mens rea* as to a circumstance of the *actus reus*, since the terms of s. 8 of the Criminal Justice Act 1967[1] had already suggested that a mistake negativing *mens rea* as to a consequence of the *actus reus* need not be reasonable to excuse the accused.

In relation to the offence of rape the actual decision in *Morgan's* case has now been put into statutory effect by the Sexual Offences (Amendment) Act 1976. Section 1(1) states that a man commits rape if he has unlawful sexual intercourse with a woman who at the time of intercourse does not consent to it, knowing that she does not consent to the intercourse or reckless as to whether she consents to it. Section 1(2) is a declaratory provision applying whenever a jury at a trial for rape has to consider whether the accused believed that the woman was consenting to sexual intercourse at the time of the alleged offence. It emphasises that the presence or absence of reasonable grounds for an alleged belief in the woman's consent is a factor which the jury is to take into account in conjunction with any other relevant evidence in considering whether the accused had such a belief. These provisions, of course, do not make *Morgan's* case any less important in respect of the general statements made in it concerning the reasonableness of a mistake.

The rest of the Act of 1976 reforms the rules relating to evidence and procedure in rape trials. Section 2 contains provisions (aimed at preventing character assassination) which seek to reduce the occasions on which the defence can legitimately

---

[1] P. 19, *supra*.

cross-examine or adduce evidence about the sexual history of the complainant with men other than the accused. The Act also provides that, exceptional circumstances apart, complainants shall be anonymous, as shall defendants, unless and until they are convicted (ss. 4–6). A detailed discussion of these other provisions is outside the scope of this book.

R. v. TOLSON
(1889), 23 Q.B.D. 168

A reasonable belief in the death of the first spouse is a defence to a charge of bigamy, although he or she has not been continuously absent from the accused for seven years.

Mrs. Tolson was charged with bigamy contrary to s. 57 of the Offences against the Person Act 1861, under which "whosoever, being married, shall marry any other person during the life of the former husband or wife shall be guilty of felony. . . . Provided that nothing in this section shall extend to any person marrying a second time whose husband or wife shall have been continually absent from such person for the space of seven years last past and shall not have been known by such person to have been living within that time or shall extend to any person who, at the time of such second marriage, shall have been divorced from the bond of the first marriage, or to any person whose former marriage shall have been declared void by the sentence of any court of competent jurisdiction."

Mrs. Tolson was married to Mr. Tolson on the 11th of September 1880, and was deserted by her husband on the 13th of December 1881. As a result of enquiries made on her behalf by her father, she was led to believe that her husband had been drowned on his way to America, and, on the 10th of January 1887, she went through a second ceremony of marriage. Mr. Tolson returned from America at the end of 1887.

In response to a question put to them by Stephen, J., who was the trial judge, the jury found that, at the time she went through the second ceremony of marriage, Mrs. Tolson believed in good faith, and upon reasonable grounds, that her first husband was dead.

As there had been conflicting decisions of Courts of first instance on the point, Stephen, J., directed the jury that this was no defence to the charge, in order that he might reserve the case for the opinion of the Court for Crown Cases Reserved on the point of law involved. Mrs. Tolson was accordingly found guilty, and sentenced to a day's imprisonment.

The Court for Crown Cases Reserved, of which Stephen, J., was a member in accordance with a practice which was then common, quashed the conviction by a majority of nine to five judges.

Extracts from Judgments of the Court for Crown Cases Reserved

Cave, J.—

". . . At common law an honest and reasonable belief in the existence of circumstances, which, if true, would make the act for which a prisoner is indicted an innocent act has always been held to be a good defence. This doctrine is embodied in the somewhat uncouth maxim *'actus non facit reum, nisi mens sit rea'*. Honest and reasonable mistake stands in fact on the same footing as absence of the reasoning faculty, as in infancy, or perversion of that faculty, as in lunacy. Instances of the existence of this common law doctrine will readily occur to the mind. So far as I am aware it has never been suggested that these exceptions do not equally apply in the case of statutory offences unless they are excluded expressly or by necessary implication. . . . It is argued, however, that, assuming the general exception to be as stated, yet the language of the Act (24 & 25 Vict. c. 100, s. 57), is such that that exception is necessarily excluded in this case. Now it is undoubtedly within the competence of the legislature to enact that a man shall be branded as a felon and punished for doing an act which he honestly and reasonably believes to be lawful and right; just as the legislature may enact that a child or a lunatic shall be punished criminally for an act which he has been led to commit by the immaturity or perversion of his reasoning faculty. But such a result seems so revolting to the moral sense that we ought to require the clearest and most indisputable evidence that such is the meaning of the Act. It is said that this inference necessarily arises from the language of the section in question, and particularly of the proviso. The section (omitting immaterial parts) is in these words: 'Whosoever being married shall marry any other person during the life of the former husband or wife shall be guilty of felony: provided that nothing in this section contained shall extend to any person marrying a second time whose husband or wife shall have been continually absent from such person for the space of seven years then last past and shall not have been known by such person to be living within that time.' It is argued that the first part is expressed absolutely; but, surely, it is not contended that the language admits of no exception, and therefore that a lunatic who, under the influence of a delusion, marries again, must be convicted; and, if an exception is to be admitted where the reasoning faculty is perverted by disease, why is not an exception equally to be admitted where the reasoning faculty, although honestly and reasonably exercised, is deceived? But it is said that the proviso is inconsistent with the exception contended for; and, undoubtedly, if the proviso covers less ground or only the same ground as the exception, it follows that the legislature has expressed an intention that the exception shall not operate until after seven years from the disappearance of the first husband. But if, on the other hand, the proviso covers more ground than the general exception, surely it is no argument to say that the legislature must have intended that the more limited defence shall not operate within the seven years because it has provided that a less limited defence shall only come into operation at the expiration of those years.

What must the accused prove to bring herself within the general exception? She must prove facts from which the jury may reasonably infer that she honestly and on reasonable grounds believed her first husband to be dead before she married again. What must she prove to bring herself within the proviso? Simply that her husband has been continually absent for seven years; and, if she can do that, it will be no answer to prove that she had no reasonable grounds for believing him to be dead or that she did not honestly believe it. Unless the prosecution can prove that she knew her husband to be living within the seven years she must be acquitted. The honesty or reasonableness of her belief is no longer in issue. Even if it could be proved that she believed him to be alive all the time, as distinct from knowing him to be so, the prosecution must fail. The proviso, therefore, is far wider than the general exception, and the intention of the legislature, that a wider and more easily established defence should be open after seven years from the disappearance of the husband, is not necessarily inconsistent with the intention that a different defence, less extensive and more difficult of proof, should be open within the seven years. . . "

Stephen, J.—

". . . My view of the subject is based upon a particular application of the doctrine usually, though I think not happily, described by the phrase *'non est reus, nisi mens sit rea.'* Though this phrase is in common use, I think it most unfortunate, and not only likely to mislead, but actually misleading, on the following grounds. It naturally suggests that, apart from all particular definitions of crimes, such a thing exists as a *'mers rea,'* or 'guilty mind', which is always expressly or by implication involved in every definition. This is obviously not the case, for the mental elements of different crimes differ widely. *'Mens rea'* means in the case of murder, malice aforethought; in the case of theft, an intention to steal; in the case of rape, an intention to have forcible connection with a woman without her consent; and in the case of receiving stolen goods, knowledge that the goods were stolen. In some cases it denotes mere inattention. For instance, in the case of manslaughter by negligence it may mean forgetting to notice a signal. It appears confusing to call so many dissimilar states of mind by one name. It seems contradictory indeed to describe a mere absence of mind as a *'mens rea,'* or guilty mind. The expression again is likely to and often does mislead. To an unlegal mind it suggests that by the law of England no act is a crime which is done from laudable motives, in other words, that immorality is essential to crime. . . .

The principle involved appears to me, when fully considered, to amount to no more than this. The full definition of every crime contains expressly or by implication a proposition as to a state of mind. Therefore, if the mental element of any conduct alleged to be a crime is proved to have been absent in any given case, the crime so defined is not committed; or, again, if a crime is fully defined, nothing amounts to that crime which does not satisfy that definition. Crimes are in the present day much more accurately defined by statute or otherwise than they formerly were. The mental element of most crimes is marked by one of the words 'maliciously,' 'fraudulently,' 'negligently,' or 'knowingly,' but it is the general—I might, I think, say, the invariable—practice of the legislature to leave unexpressed some of the mental elements of crime. In all cases whatever, competent age, sanity, and some degree of freedom from some kinds of coercion are assumed to be essential to criminality, but I do not believe they are ever introduced into any statute by which any particular crime is defined.

The meanings of the words 'malice,' 'negligence,' and 'fraud' in relation to particular crimes has been ascertained by numerous cases. Malice means one thing in relation to murder, another in relation to the Malicious Mischief Act, and a third in relation to libel, and so of fraud and negligence.

With regard to knowledge of fact, the law, perhaps, is not quite so clear, but it may, I think, be maintained that in every case knowledge of fact is to some extent an element of criminality as much as competent age and sanity. To take an extreme illustration, can any one doubt that a man who, though he might be perfectly sane, committed what would otherwise be a crime in a state of somnabulism, would be entitled to be acquitted? And why is this? Simply because he would not know what he was doing. A multitude of illustrations of the same sort might be given. I will mention one or two glaring ones. *Levett's Case*[1] decides that a man who, making a thrust with a sword at a place where, upon reasonable grounds, he supposed a burglar to be, killed a person who was not a burglar, was held not to be a felon, thought he might be (it was not decided that he was) guilty of killing *per infortunium*, or possibly, *se defendendo*, which then involved certain forfeitures. In other words, he was in the same situation as far as regarded the homicide as if he had killed a burglar. In the decision of the judges in *M'Naghten's Case*[2] it is stated that if under an insane delusion one man killed another, and if the delusion was such that it would, if true, justify or excuse the killing, the homicide would be justified or excused. This could hardly be if the same were not law as to a sane mistake. . . .

It is said, first, that the words of 24 & 25 Vict. c. 100, s. 57, are absolute, and that the exceptions which that section contains are the only ones which are intended to be admitted, and this it is said is confirmed by the express proviso in the section—an indication which is thought to negative any tacit exemption. It is also supposed that the case of *R. v. Prince*,[3]

---

[1] (1639), 1 Hale P.C. 474.
[2] (1843), 10 Cl. & Fin. 200; p. 74, *infra*.
[3] (1875), L.R. 2 C.C.R. 154; p. 40, *infra*.

decided on s. 55, confirms this view. I will begin by saying how far I agree with these views. First, I agree that the case turns exclusively upon the construction of s. 57 of 24 & 25 Vict. c. 100. . . . Of course, it would be competent to the legislature to define a crime in such a way as to make the existence of any state of mind immaterial. The question is solely whether it has actually done so in this case.

In the first place I will observe upon the absolute character of the section. It appears to me to resemble most of the enactments contained in the Consolidation Acts of 1861, in passing over the general mental elements of crime which are presupposed in every case. Age, sanity, and more or less freedom from compulsion, are always presumed, and I think it would be impossible to quote any statute which in any case specifies these elements of criminality in the definition of any crime. It will be found that either by using the words wilfully and maliciously, or by specifying some special intent as an element of particular crimes, knowledge of fact is implicitly made part of the statutory definition of most modern definitions of crimes, but there are some cases in which this cannot be said. Such are s. 55, on which *R.* v. *Prince*[1] was decided, s. 56, which punishes the stealing of 'any child under the age of fourteen years,' s. 49, as to procuring the defilement of any 'woman or girl under the age of twenty-one,' in each of which the same question might arise as in *R.* v. *Prince*;[1] to these I may add some of the provisions of the Criminal Law Amendment Act of 1885. Reasonable belief that a girl is sixteen or upwards is a defence to the charge of an offence under ss. 5, 6 and 7 but this is not provided for as to an offence against s. 4, which is meant to protect girls under thirteen.

It seems to me that as to the construction of all these sections the case of *R.* v. *Prince*[1] is a direct authority. It was the case of a man who abducted a girl under sixteen, believing, on good grounds, that she was above that age. Lord Esher, then Brett, J., was against the conviction. His judgment establishes at much length, and, as it appears to me, unanswerably, the principle above explained, which he states as follows: 'That a mistake of facts on reasonable grounds, to the extent that, if the facts were as believed, the acts of the prisoner would make him guilty of no offence at all, is an excuse, and that such an excuse is implied in every criminal charge and every criminal enactment in England.'

---

[1] (1875), L.R. 2 C.C.R. 154; p. 40, *infra.*

Lord Blackburn, with whom nine other judges agreed, and Lord Bramwell, with whom seven others agreed, do not appear to me to have dissented from this principle, speaking generally; but they held that it did not apply fully to each part of every section to which I have referred. Some of the prohibited acts they thought the legislature intended to be done at the peril of the person who did them, but not all.

The judgment delivered by Lord Blackburn proceeds upon the principle that the intention of the legislature in s. 55 was 'to punish the abduction unless the girl was of such an age as to make her consent an excuse.'

Lord Bramwell's judgment proceeds upon this principle; 'The legislature has enacted that if any one does this wrong act he does it at the risk of her turning out to be under sixteen. This opinion gives full scope to the doctrine of the *mens rea*. If the taker believed he had her father's consent, though wrongly, he would have no *mens rea*; so if he did not know she was in any one's possession nor in the care or charge of anyone. In those cases he would not know he was doing the act forbidden by the statute.'

All the judges therefore in *R.* v. *Prince*[1] agreed on the general principle, though they all, except Lord Esher, considered that the object of the legislature being to prevent a scandalous and wicked invasion of parental rights (whether it was to be regarded as illegal apart from the statute or not) it was to be supposed that they intended that the wrongdoer should act at his peril.

As another illustration of the same principle, I may refer to *R.* v. *Bishop*.[2] The defendant in that case was tried before me for receiving more than two lunatics into a house not duly licensed, upon an indictment on 8 & 9 Vict. c. 100, s. 44. It was proved that the defendant did receive more than two persons, whom the jury found to be lunatics, into her house, believing honestly, and on reasonable grounds, that they were not lunatics. I held that this was immaterial, having regard to the scope of the Act, and the object for which it was apparently passed, and this Court upheld that ruling.

The application of this to the present case appears to me to be as follows. The general principle is clearly in favour of the prisoners, but how does the intention of the legislature appear to have been against them? It could not be the

[1] (1875), L.R. 2 C.C.R. 154.
[2] (1880), 5 Q.B.D. 259.

object of parliament to treat the marriage of widows as an act to be if possible prevented as presumably immoral. The conduct of the women convicted[1] was not in the smallest degree immoral, it was perfectly natural and legitimate. Assuming the facts to be as they supposed, the infliction of more than a nominal punishment on them would have been a scandal. Why, then, should the legislature be held to have wished to subject them to punishment at all. . . .

It is argued that the proviso that a re-marriage after seven years' separation shall not be punishable, operates as a tacit exclusion of all other exceptions to the penal part of the section. It appears to me that it only supplies a rule of evidence which is useful in many cases, in the absence of explicit proof of death. But it seems to me to shew not that belief in the death of one married person excuses the marriage of the other only after seven years' separation, but that mere separation for that period has the effect which reasonable belief of death caused by other evidence would have at any time. It would to my mind be monstrous to say that seven years separation should have a greater effect in excusing a bigamous marriage than positive evidence of death, sufficient for the purpose of recovering a policy of assurance or obtaining probate of a will, would have . . . or in others which might be even stronger."

CONVICTION QUASHED.

R. v. HIBBERT

(1869), L.R. 1 C.C.R. 184

A person cannot be convicted of the statutory offence of taking a girl out of the possession and against the will of her parent or guardian in the absence of evidence that he knew or had reason to believe that she had a father.

The accused met a girl called Elizabeth Ann Oldham in the street. He took her to another place where he seduced her and then took her back to the place where he had met her. The girl was fourteen years old and the accused made no inquiry as to whether she had a father.

---

[1] Another case involving the identical point had also been reserved.

He was charged with and found guilty of unlawfully taking a girl under 16 out of the possession and against the will of her father contrary to s. 55 of the Offences against the Person Act 1861 (substantially re-enacted by s. 20 of the Sexual Offences Act 1956) but a case was reserved for the opinion of the Court for Crown Cases Reserved who quashed the conviction.

Extract from the Judgments of the Court for Crown Cases Reserved

Bovill, C.J.—

". . . In the present case there is no statement of any finding of fact that the prisoner knew or had reason to believe that the girl was under the lawful care or charge of her father, mother, or of any other person. Still less is there any statement that the prisoner knew that she was under the care of her father as charged in this indictment. In some cases, as, for instance, if the girl were a girl of the town, there would be a probability that the person taking her away had no reason to believe that he was taking her out of the possession of her father or other person. In other cases, again, the surrounding circumstances might be such as to satisfy a jury that he had knowledge that he was taking the girl from the possession of those who lawfully had charge of her. In the absence, however, of any finding of fact on this point the conviction cannot be supported. The decision at which we have arrived is quite in accordance with *R.* v. *Green*,[1] where the facts resembled those of the present case. Martin, B., there said, 'There must be a taking out of the possession of the father; here the prisoners picked up the girl in the streets, and for anything that appeared, they might not have known that the girl had a father. The essence of the offence was the taking the girl out of the possession of the father. The girl was not taken out of the possession of any one. . . . The act of the prisoners was scandalous, but it was not any legal offence.' Under these circumstances, therefore, the conviction must be quashed."

CONVICTION QUASHED.

---

[1] (1862), 3 F. & F. 274.

R. v. PRINCE
(1875), L.R. 2 C.C.R. 154

A mistaken belief, even though based on reasonable grounds, that the girl is over sixteen is no defence to a charge of the statutory offence of taking a girl under sixteen out of the possession and against the will of her parent or guardian.

Prince was charged with having unlawfully taken an unmarried girl under the age of sixteen out of the possession and against the will of her father contrary to s. 55 of the Offences against the Person Act 1861 (substantially re-enacted by s. 20 of the Sexual Offences Act 1956).

It was proved that he took a girl named Annie Phillips out of the possession and without the consent of her father, but that he believed her on reasonable grounds to be of the age of eighteen.

On these facts, a case was reserved for the opinion of the Court for Crown Cases Reserved, and Prince was convicted, sentence being deferred pending the statement of the opinion of the Court for Crown Cases Reserved as to the correctness of the conviction.

By a majority of fifteen to one, the Court was of opinion that Prince's conviction was correct.

Extracts from Judgments of the Court for Crown Cases Reserved

Blackburn, J.—

". . . we are of opinion that the intention of the legislature sufficiently appears to have been to punish the abduction, unless the girl, in fact, was of such an age as to make her consent an excuse, irrespective of whether he knew her to be too young to give an effectual consent, and to fix that age at sixteen. The section in question is one of a series of enactments, beginning with s. 48, and ending with s. 55, forming a code for the protection of women, and the guardians of young women.[1] . . .

Sect. 50 enacts, that whosoever shall 'unlawfully and carnally know and abuse any girl under the age of ten

---

[1] The code, with different age limits, is now contained in the Sexual Offences Act 1956.

years,' shall be guilty of felony. Sect. 51, whoever shall
'unlawfully and carnally know and abuse any girl being
above the age of ten years, and under the age of twelve
years,' shall be guilty of a misdemeanour.

It seems impossible to suppose that the intention of the
legislature in those two sections could have been to make
the crime depend upon the knowledge of the prisoner of the
girl's actual age. It would produce the monstrous result that
a man who had carnal connection with a girl, in reality not
quite ten years old, but whom he on reasonable grounds
believed to be a little more than ten, was to escape altogether.
He could not, in that view of the statute, be convicted of the
felony, for he did not know her to be under ten. He could not
be convicted of the misdemeanour, because she was in fact
not above the age of ten.[1] It seems to us that the intention
of the legislature was to punish those who had connection
with young girls, though with their consent, unless the girl
was in fact old enough to give a valid consent. The man who
has connection with a child, relying on her consent, does it
at his peril, if she is below the statutable age.

The 55th section, on which the present case arises, uses
precisely the same words as those in ss. 50 and 51, and must
be construed in the same way. . . ."

Bramwell, B.—

". . . the question is, has the prisoner taken an unmarried girl under the age of sixteen out of the possession of
and against the will of her father? In fact, he has; but it
is said not within the meaning of the statute, and that that
must be read as though the word 'knowingly,' or some
equivalent word, was in; and the reason given is, that as a
rule the *mens rea* is necessary to make any act a crime or
offence, and that if the facts necessary to constitute an
offence are not known to the alleged offender, there can be
no *mens rea*. . . . What the statute contemplates, and what
I say is wrong, is the taking of a female of such tender years
that she is properly called a *girl*, can be said to be in another's
possession, and in that other's *care or charge*. No argument
is necessary to prove this; it is enough to state the case.

---

[1] This point owes its validity to the fact that offences under s. 50 and
s. 51 of the Act of 1861 were defined exclusively. S. 6 of the Sexual Offences
Act 1956 (as amended by the Criminal Law Act 1967) punishes intercourse
with girls under 16 and thus overlaps with s. 5, punishing intercourse with
girls under 13.

The legislature has enacted that if anyone does this wrong act, he does it at the risk of her turning out to be under sixteen. This opinion gives full scope to the doctrine of the *mens rea*. If the taker believed he had the father's consent, though wrongly, he would have no *mens rea*; so if he did not know she was in anyone's possession, nor in the care or charge of anyone.[1] In those cases he would not know he was doing the *act* forbidden by the statute—an act which, if he knew she was in possession and in care or charge of anyone, he would know was a crime or not, according as she was under sixteen or not. He would not know he was doing an act wrong in itself, whatever was his intention, if done without lawful cause.

In addition to these considerations, one may add that the Statute does use the word 'unlawfully,' and does not use the words 'knowingly' or 'not believing to the contrary.' If the question was whether his act was unlawful, there would be no difficulty, as it clearly was not lawful.

This view of the section, to my mind, is much strengthened by a reference to other sections of the same statute. Sect. 50 makes it a felony to unlawfully and carnally know a girl under the age of ten. Sect. 51 enacts when she is above ten and under twelve to unlawfully and carnally know her is a misdemeanour. Can it be supposed that in the former case a person indicted might claim to be acquitted on the ground that he had believed the girl was over ten though under twelve, and so that he had only committed a misdemeanour; or that he believed her over twelve, and so had committed no offence at all; or that in a case under s. 51 he could claim to be acquitted, because he believed her over twelve. In both cases the act is intrinsically wrong; for the statute says if 'unlawfully' done.[2] The act done with a *mens rea* is unlawfully and carnally knowing the girl, and the man doing that act does it at the risk of the child being under the statutory age. It would be mischievous to hold otherwise. So s. 56, by which, whoever shall take away any child under fourteen with intent to deprive parent or guardian of the possession of the child, or with intent to steal any article upon such child, shall be guilty of felony. Could a prisoner say, 'I did take away the child to steal its clothes, but I believed it to be over fourteen?' If not, then neither could

---

[1] See *Hibbert*, p. 38, *supra*.
[2] For the present position see footnote to Blackburn, J.'s judgment on the same point.

he say, 'I did take the child with intent to deprive the parent of its possession, but I believed it over fourteen.' Because if words to that effect cannot be introduced into the statute where the intent is to steal the clothes, neither can they where the intent is to take the child out of the possession of the parent. But if those words cannot be introduced in s. 56, why can they be in s. 55?

The same principle applies in other cases. A man was held liable for assaulting a police officer in the execution of his duty, though he did not know he was a police officer.[1] Why? because the act was wrong in itself. . . .''

Denman, J.—

". . . In the present case the jury find that the defendant believed the girl to be eighteen years of age; even if she had been of that age, she would have been in the lawful care and charge of her father, as her guardian by nature: see Co. Litt. 88, b, n. 12, 19th ed., recognized in *R.* v. *Howes.*[2] Her father had a right to her personal custody up to the age of twenty-one, and to appoint a guardian by deed or will, whose right to her personal custody would have extended up to the same age. The belief that she was eighteen would be no justification to the defendant for taking her out of his possession, and against his will. By taking her, even with her own consent, he must at least have been guilty of aiding and abetting her in doing an unlawful act, viz. in escaping against the will of her natural guardian from his lawful care and charge. This, in my opinion, leaves him wholly without lawful excuse or justification for the act he did, even though he believed that the girl was eighteen, and therefore unable to allege that what he has done was not unlawfully done, within the meaning of the clause. In other words, having knowingly done a wrongful act, viz. in taking the girl away from the lawful possession of her father against his will, and in violation of his rights as guardian by nature, he cannot be heard to say that he thought the girl was of an age beyond that limited by the statute for the offence charged against him. He had wrongfully done the very thing contemplated by the legislature: he had wrongfully and knowingly violated the father's rights against the father's will. And he cannot set up a legal defence by merely proving that he thought he

---

[1] *Forbes and Webb* (1865), 10 Cox C.C. 362. See also *Kenlin* v. *Gardiner*, [1967] 2 Q.B. 510; [1966] 3 All E.R. 931; p. 147, *infra*.
[2] (1860), 3 E. & E. 332.

was committing a different kind of wrong from that which in fact he was committing."

CONVICTION AFFIRMED.

Comment on R. v. Hibbert and R. v. Prince

One way in which the student may approach the artificial task of reconciling these two cases is to imagine that the accused was being questioned in the presence of the other parties. If Hibbert had been asked whether he intended to take Elizabeth Ann Oldham out of the possession of her father, Mr. Oldham, he could truthfully have said "No", and might have been able to add "I have never seen, or thought about him before". On the other hand, if Prince had been asked whether he intended to take Annie Phillips out of the possession of Mr. Phillips, he would have been constrained to say "Yes", as he was, at all material times, aware that the girl had a father. The artificiality of the distinction is shown by the fact that if, in either case, the accused had been asked whether he intended to take a girl under 16 away from her father, the answer would have been in the negative, although for different reasons. Such artificiality appears to be inevitable once the Courts depart from the ordinary doctrine of *mens rea*.

SHERRAS v. DE RUTZEN
[1895] 1 Q.B. 918

Even in the case of a modern statutory offence the accused will normally be entitled to be acquitted if he did not know of the facts which the prosecution must prove in order to convict him of the offence charged.

The appellant, a licensed victualler, was convicted before a magistrate of supplying liquor to a constable on duty, without the authority of his superior officer, contrary to s. 16 (2) of the Licensing Act 1872.[1] The constable was served by the appellant's daughter in his presence, and no questions were asked as to whether he was on duty, because he had removed his armlet which, to the knowledge of the appellant, was worn by constables in the locality of his public house, when they were on duty. The magistrate found as a fact that the appellant did not know the constable to be on duty.

---

[1] Re-enacted by s. 178 (*b*) of the Licensing Act 1964.

The appellant's conviction was confirmed by Quarter Sessions, and a case was stated for the opinion of the Divisional Court, who were of opinion that the conviction should be quashed.

Extracts from the Judgments of the Divisional Court

Day, J.—

". . . An argument has been based on the appearance of the word 'knowingly' in sub-s. 1 of s. 16, and its omission in sub-s. 2. In my opinion the only effect of this is to shift the burden of proof. In cases under sub-s. 1 it is for the prosecution to prove the knowledge, while in cases under sub-s. 2 the defendant has to prove that he did not know. That is the only inference I draw from the insertion of the word 'knowingly' in the one sub-section and its omission in the other.

It appears to me that it would be straining the law to say that this publican, acting as he did in the *bona fide* belief that the constable was off duty, and having reasonable grounds for that belief, was nevertheless guilty of an offence against the section, for which he was liable both to a penalty and to have his licence indorsed."

Wright, J.—

". . . There is a presumption that *mens rea*, an evli intention, or a knowledge of the wrongfulness of the act, is an essential ingredient in every offence; but that presumption is liable to be displaced either by the words of the statute creating the offence or by the subject-matter with which it deals, and both must be considered: *Nichols* v. *Hall*.[1] One of the most remarkable exceptions was in the case of bigamy. It was held by all the judges, on the statute 1 Jac. 1, c. 11, that a man was rightly convicted of bigamy who had married after an invalid Scotch divorce, which had been obtained in good faith, and the validity of which he had no reason to doubt: *Lolley's* Case.[2] Another exception, apparently grounded on the language of a statute, is *Prince's* Case,[3] where it was held by fifteen judges against one that a man was guilty of abduction of a girl under sixteen, although he believed, in good faith and on reasonable grounds, that she was over that age. Apart from isolated and extreme

---

[1] (1873), L.R. 8 C.P. 322.
[2] (1812), Russ. & Ry. 237.
[3] (1875), L.R. 2 C.C.R. 154; p. 40, *infra*.

cases of this kind, the principal classes of exceptions may perhaps be reduced to three. One is a class of acts which, in the language of Lush, J., in *Davies* v. *Harvey*,[1] are not criminal in any real sense, but are acts which in the public interest are prohibited under a penalty. Several such instances are to be found in the decisions on the Revenue Statutes, *e.g.*, *Attorney General* v. *Lockwood*,[2] where the innocent possession of liquorice by a beer retailer was held an offence. So under the Adulteration Acts, *R.* v. *Woodrow*[3] as to innocent possession of adulterated tobacco; *Fitzpatrick* v. *Kelly*[4] and *Roberts* v. *Egerton*[5] as to the sale of adulterated food. So under the Game Acts, as to the innocent possession of game by a carrier: *R.* v. *Marsh.*[6] So as to the liability of a guardian of the poor, whose partner, unknown to him, supplied goods for the poor: *Davies* v. *Harvey.*[1] To the same head may be referred *R.* v. *Bishop*,[7] where a person was held rightly convicted of receiving lunatics in an unlicensed house, although the jury found that he honestly and on reasonable grounds believed that they were not lunatics. Another class comprehends some, and perhaps all, public nuisances: *R.* v. *Stephens*[8] where the employer was held liable on indictment for a nuisance caused by workmen without his knowledge and contrary to his orders; and so in *R.* v. *Medley*[9] and *Barnes* v. *Ackroyd.*[10] Lastly, there may be cases in which, although the proceeding is criminal in form, it is really only a summary mode of enforcing a civil right: see *per* Williams and Willes, JJ., in *Morden* v. *Porter*,[11] as to unintentional trespass in pursuit of game; *Lee* v. *Simpson*,[12] as to unconscious dramatic piracy; and *Hargreaves* v. *Diddams*,[13] as to a *bona fide* belief in a legally impossible right to fish. But, except in such cases as these, there must in general be guilty knowledge on the part of the defendant, or of some one whom he has put in his place to

---

[1] (1874), L.R. 9 Q.B. 433.
[2] (1842), 9 M. & W. 378.
[3] (1846), 15 M. & W. 404.
[4] (1873), L.R. 8 Q.B. 337.
[5] (1874), L.R. 9 Q.B. 494.
[6] (1824), 2 B. & C. 717.
[7] (1880), 5 Q.B.D. 259.
[8] (1866), L.R. 1 Q.B. 702.
[9] (1834), 6 C. & P. 292.
[10] (1872), L.R. 7 Q.B. 474.
[11] (1860), 7 C.B. (N.S.) 641.
[12] (1847), 3 C.B. 871.
[13] (1875), L.R. 10 Q.B. 582.

act for him, generally, or in the particular matter, in order to constitute an offence. It is plain that if guilty knowledge is not necessary, no care on the part of the publican could save him from a conviction under s. 16, sub-s. 2, since it would be as easy for the constable to deny that he was on duty when asked, or to produce a forged permission from his superior officer, as to remove his armlet before entering the public-house. I am, therefore, of opinion that this conviction ought to be quashed."

CONVICTION QUASHED.

Note on Sherras v. De Rutzen

Day, J.'s, statement that the absence of "knowingly" from the provision in question shifted the burden of proof so that it was for the defence to prove lack of knowledge was doubted by Devlin, J., in *Roper* v. *Taylor's Central Garages (Exeter), Ltd.*[1] Devlin, J., said:

"There are some statutes where the burden of proof is expressly shifted. . . . But where the statute contains no express provision, that is, where it does not contain the word 'knowingly', the first thing is to examine the statute to see whether the ordinary presumption that *mens rea* is required applies or not. If it is found that it does not apply, the mere doing of the act is itself an offence and guilty knowledge is irrelevant. If it does apply, I should have thought that the natural result would be that the prosecution must discharge the burden of showing guilty knowledge. All that the word 'knowingly' does is to say expressly what is normally implied, and if the presumption that the statute requires *mens rea* is not rebutted I find difficulty in seeing how it can be said that the omission of the word 'knowingly' has, as a matter of construction, the effect of shifting the burden of proof from the prosecution to the defence."

CUNDY v. LE COCQ
(1884), 13 Q.B.D. 207

The absence of a word such as "knowingly" in the statutory provision in question and its presence in other provisions in the statute may cause the offence to be construed as one of strict liability.[2]

---

[1] [1951] 2 T.L.R. 284.
[2] But this will not necessarily be the effect of such absence, cf. *Sherras* v. *De Rutzen*, p. 44, *supra*.

The appellant, a licensed victualler, was convicted of unlawfully selling liquor to a drunken person, contrary to s. 13 of the Licensing Act 1872[1]. The magistrate found that the person to whom the liquor was supplied was drunk, but that the appellant was not aware of this fact, and the appellant unsuccessfully appealed to the Divisional Court by way of case stated.

Extract from the Judgments of the Divisional Court

Stephen, J.—

". . . I am of opinion that the words of the section amount to an absolute prohibition of the sale of liquour to a drunken person, and that the existence of a *bona fide* mistake as to the condition of the person served is not an answer to the charge, but is a matter only for mitigation of the penalties that may be imposed. I am led to that conclusion both by the general scope of the Act, which is for the repression of drunkenness, and from a comparison of the various sections under the head 'offences against public order'. Some of these contain the word 'knowingly', as for instance s. 14, which deals with keeping a disorderly house, and s. 16, which deals with the penalty for harbouring a constable. Knowledge in these and other cases is an element in the offence; but the clause we are considering says nothing about the knowledge of the state of the person served. I believe the reason for making this prohibition absolute was that there must be a great temptation to a publican to sell liquor without regard to the sobriety of the customer, and it was thought right to put upon the publican the responsibility of determining whether his customer is sober. Against this view we have had quoted the maxim that in every criminal offence there must be a guilty mind; but I do not think that maxim has so wide an application as it is sometimes considered to have. In old time, and as applicable to the common law or to earlier statutes, the maxim may have been of general application; but a difference has arisen owing to the greater precision of modern statutes. It is impossible now, as illustrated by the cases of *R.* v. *Prince*[2] and *R.* v. *Bishop*[3], to apply the maxim generally to all statutes, and the substance of all the reported cases is that it is necessary to look

---

[1] Re-enacted by s. 172 (3) of the Licensing Act 1964.
[2] (1875), L.R. 2 C.C.R. 154; p. 40, *supra.*
[3] (1880), 5 Q.B.D. 259.

at the object of each Act that is under consideration to see whether and how far knowledge is of the essence of the offence created. Here, as I have already pointed out, the object of this part of the Act is to prevent the sale of intoxicating liquor to drunken persons, and it is perfectly natural to carry that out by throwing on the publican the responsibility of determining whether the person supplied comes within that category.

I think, therefore, the conviction was right and must be affirmed."

APPEAL DISMISSED.

GRAYS HAULAGE CO., LTD. v. ARNOLD
[1966] 1 All E.R. 896

Generally,[1] a person is not guilty of permitting unless he either has actual knowledge of the relevant facts or else shuts his eyes to the obvious.

The appellants were charged with permitting one of their drivers to drive for continuous periods amounting in the aggreggte to more than eleven hours in twenty four, contrary to s. 73(1) (ii) of the Road Traffic Act 1960.[2] It was not disputed that the driver had driven for continuous periods of more than eleven hours, but the appellants contended that they had no knowledge of this fact. The justices nonetheless convicted them on the footing that they could have taken more precautions to prevent the driving for excessive periods. A case was stated for the opinion of the Divisional Court who were of opinion that no offence had been committed by the appellants.

Extract from the Judgments of the Divisional Court

Lord Parker, C.J.—

"The prosecution case was that the appellants were guilty of permitting in that they had failed to take certain

---

[1] In some offences the courts have held that "permitting" does not require actual knowledge or wilful blindness as to a particular relevant fact, see *Lyons* v. *May*, [1948] 2 All E.R. 1062; *Baugh* v. *Crago*, [1975] R.T.R. 453.

[2] Replaced by s. 96(1) of the Transport Act 1968.

steps which they might have taken which would or might
have prevented the driver from acting as he did. Those
that were referred to, which admittedly the appellants had
not carried out, were the supply of staff at their yard to
check the coming in of the vehicle, devices on the vehicle,
an arrangement whereby the driver could telephone to them
during the journey by reverse charges, and matters of that
sort. The justices, in convicting the appellants said: 'We were
of opinion that the appellants had failed to take adequate
steps to prevent their driver driving for continuous periods
amounting as alleged', and accordingly convicted them.

In my judgment, there is a tendency today to impute
knowledge in circumstances which really do not justify
knowledge being imputed. It is of the very essence of the
offence of permitting someone to do something that there
should be knowledge. The case that is always referred to in
this connexion is *James & Sons, Ltd.* v. *Smee, Green* v.
Burnett,[1] where in giving judgment, I pointed out that
knowledge is really of two kinds, actual knowledge, and
knowledge which arises either from shutting one's eyes to
the obvious, or, what is very much the same thing but put
in another way, failing to do something or doing something
not caring whether contravention takes place or not. Here,
there is no question of actual knowledge at all, nor is it a
case where there is a shutting of eyes to the obvious as,
for instance, refraining from looking at the records which
had to be kept of hours of work showing that the driver
was not complying with the statute. This, of course, goes
very much further, because it is said that the mere fact that
they did not take steps which would have prevented the
driver from doing this, amounts to a permitting. A similar
case, *Fransman* v. *Sexton*,[2] came before this court recently
on July 8, 1965. In that case I tried to limit the tendency
that there is today for extending imputing knowledge in
this way. The justices there had said that knowledge could
be imputed when a man fails 'to take adequate steps to
prevent defects occurring by an adequate system of maintenance of vehicles'. I said:

'For myself I very much doubt whether those words
really do properly define what I may call the third category of
knowledge (it is really part of the second category of know-

---

[1] [1955] 1 Q.B. 78; [1954] 3 All E.R. 273.
[2] [1965] Crim. L.R. 556.

ledge). If they are meaning merely this, that knowledge
was being imputed to the appellant because in fact he had
failed to discover the defect and might have taken steps
which would have revealed a defect, then in my judgment the
test is completely wrong. Knowledge is not imputed by mere
negligence but by something more than negligence, something which one can describe as reckless, sending out a car
not caring what happens.'

So here, it seems to me, there was no knowledge and
no *prima facie* evidence that the appellants had actual
knowledge or knowledge of circumstances which fixed them,
as it were, with a suspicion or knowledge of circumstances
so that it could be said that they had shut their eyes to the
obvious, or had allowed something to go on, not caring
whether an offence was committed or not."

APPEAL ALLOWED.

ALPHACELL, LTD. v. WOODWARD
[1972] 2 All E.R. 475

*The offence of causing poisonous, noxious or polluting
matter to enter a stream created by s. 2(1) of the Rivers (Prevention of Pollution) Act 1951, is one of strict liability.*

Alphacell, Ltd. prepared manilla fibres for paper on
premises adjoining a river. The water in which the fibres
were washed was polluted and, in order to prevent it from
flowing into the river, Alphacell, Ltd. installed pumps in
the cleansing tank. On one occasion these pumps, designed
to work automatically, did not do so owing to the fact that
the rose was blocked by brambles. Alphacell, Ltd. were
charged with causing polluting matter to enter the river
contrary to s. 2 of the Rivers (Prevention of Pollution) Act
1951.[1] They were convicted by the Magistrates although
there was no finding that they knew of the defect in the
pumps or that they were negligent. Alphacell, Ltd. unsuccessfully appealed to a Divisional Court and to the House
of Lords.

---

[1] "A person commits an offence if he causes or knowingly permits to
enter a stream any poisonous, noxious or polluting matter."

Extracts from the Speeches of the House of Lords

Lord Salmon.—

"The appellants contend that even if they caused the pollution still they should succeed since they did not cause it intentionally or knowingly or negligently. Section 2(1) (a) of the Rivers (Prevention of Pollution) Act 1951 is undoubtedly a penal section. It follows that if it is capable of two or more meanings then the meaning most favourable to the subject should be adopted. Accordingly, so the argument runs, the words 'intentionally' or 'knowingly' or 'negligently' should be read into the section immediately before the word 'causes'. I do not agree. It is of the utmost public importance that our rivers should not be polluted. The risk of pollution, particularly from the vast and increasing number of riparian industries, is very great. The offences created by the 1951 Act seem to me to be prototypes of offences which 'are not criminal in any real sense, but are acts which in the public interest are prohibited under a penalty': *Sherras* v. *De Rutzen*,[1] *per* Wright, J., referred to with approval by my noble and learned friends, Lord Reid and Lord Diplock, in *Sweet* v. *Parsley*.[2] I can see no valid reason for reading the word, 'intentionally', 'knowingly' or 'negligently' into s. 2(1) (a) and a number of cogent reasons for not doing so. In the case of a minor pollution such as the present, when the justices find that there is no wrongful intention or negligence on the part of the defendant, a comparatively nominal fine will no doubt be imposed. This may be regarded as a not unfair hazard of carrying on a business which may cause pollution on the banks of a river. The present appellants were fined £20 and order to pay in all £24 costs. I should be surprised if the costs of pursuing this appeal to this House were incurred to the purpose of saving these appellants £43.

If this appeal succeeded and it were held to be the law that no conviction could be obtained under the 1951 Act unless the prosecution could discharge the often impossible onus of proving that the pollution was caused intentionally or negligently, a great deal of pollution would go unpunished and undeterred to the relief of many riparian factory owners. As a result, many rivers which are now filthy would become filthier still and many rivers which are now clean would lose

---

[1] [1895] 1 Q.B. 918, at p. 922; [1895–99] All E.R. 1167, at p. 1169; p. 46, *supra*.
[2] [1970] A.C. 132, at pp. 149, 162; [1969] 1 All E.R. 347, at pp. 350, 360.

their cleanliness. The legislature no doubt recognised that as a matter of public policy this would be most unfortunate. Hence s. 2(1)(a) which encourages riparian factory owners not only to take reasonable steps to prevent pollution but to do everything possible to ensure that they do not cause it.

I do not consider that the appellants can derive any comfort (as they seek to do) from the inclusion in s. 2(1)(a) of the words 'knowingly permits'. . . . The inclusion of the word 'knowingly' before 'permits' is probably otiose and, if anything, is against the appellants, since it contrasts with the omission of the word 'knowingly' before the word 'causes'."

APPEAL DISMISSED.

LIM CHIN AIK v. R.
[1963] 1 All E.R. 223

Before a regulation is construed so as to impose strict liability, it is generally necessary inter alia for the court to be satisfied that the imposition of strict liability will assist the enforcement of the regulation.

The appellant was charged with entering and remaining in Singapore as a prohibited person contrary to the Singapore Immigration Ordinance. The evidence was that an order had been made prohibiting his entry into Singapore, and that he entered Singapore after the order had been made. There was, however, no evidence that the order had been served on the appellant, or that it had been published, or that he was aware of its existence. The trial judge and the Court of Appeal of Singapore nonetheless convicted the appellant of the offence. The appellant successfully appealed to the Privy Council.

Extract from the Advice of the Privy Council
Lord Evershed.—
    "Where the subject-matter of the statute is the regulation for the public welfare of a particular activity—statutes regulating the sale of food and drink are to be found among the earliest examples—it can be and frequently has been inferred that the legislature intended that such activities should be carried out under conditions of strict liability.

The presumption is that the statute or statutory instrument can be effectively enforced only if those in charge of the relevant activities are made responsible for seeing that they are complied with. When such a presumption is to be inferred, it displaces the ordinary presumption of *mens rea*. Thus sellers of meat may be made responsible for seeing that the meat is fit for human consumption and it is no answer for them to say that they were not aware that it was polluted. If that were a satisfactory answer, then as Kennedy, L.J., pointed out in *Hobbs* v. *Winchester Corporation*[1] the distribution of bad meat (and its far-reaching consequences) would not be effectively prevented. So a publican may be made responsible for observing the condition of his customers, *Cundy* v. *Le Cocq*.[2]

But it is not enough in their Lordships' opinion merely to label the statute as one dealing with a grave social evil and from that to infer that strict liability was intended. It is pertinent also to inquire whether putting the defendant under strict liability will assist in the enforcement of the regulations. That means that there must be something he can do, directly or indirectly, by supervision or inspection, by improvement of his business methods or by exhorting those whom he may be expected to influence or control, which will promote the observance of the regulations. Unless this is so, there is no reason in penalising him, and it cannot be inferred that the legislature imposed strict liability merely in order to find a luckless victim. This principle has been expressed and applied in *Reynolds* v. *G. H. Austin & Sons, Ltd.*[3] and *James & Sons, Ltd.* v. *Smee, Green* v. *Burnett*.[4] Their Lordships prefer it to the alternative view that strict liability follows simply from the nature of the subject-matter and that persons whose conduct is beyond any sort of criticism can be dealt with by the imposition of a nominal penalty. This latter view can perhaps be supported to some extent by the dicta of Kennedy, L.J., in *Hobbs* v. *Winchester Corporation* and of Donovan, J., in *R.* v. *St. Margaret's Trust, Ltd.*[5] But though a nominal penalty may be appropriate in an individual case where exceptional lenience is called for, their Lordships cannot, with respect, suppose

---

[1] [1910] 2 K.B. 471, at pp. 482–485.
[2] (1884), 13 Q.B.D. 207; p. 47, *supra*.
[3] [1951] 2 K.B. 135; [1951] 1 All E.R. 606.
[4] [1955] 1 Q.B. 78; [1954] 3 All E.R. 273.
[5] [1958] 2 All E.R. 289, at p. 293.

that it is envisaged by the legislature as a way of dealing with offenders generally. Where it can be shown that the imposition of strict liability would result in the prosecution and conviction of a class of persons whose conduct could not in any way affect the observance of the law, their Lordships consider that, even where the statute is dealing with a grave social evil, strict liability is not likely to be intended."

APPEAL ALLOWED.

HARDING v. PRICE
[1948] 1 K.B. 695

Where a statute requires a positive act to be done on the occurrence of a specified event, a person ought not to be convicted of failing to do the act if he was unaware of the occurrence of the event.

The appellant was convicted by the magistrates of having failed to report an accident contrary to s. 22(2) of the Road Traffic Act 1930, which re-enacted a similar provision in the Motor Car Act 1903, with the difference that the word "knowingly" was omitted from the definition of the offence.[1]

The vehicle which he was driving was a mechanical horse with a trailer attached to it, and it collided with a stationary car. The magistrates found as a fact that, owing to the noise made by the vehicle which he was driving, the appellant was unaware that an accident had occurred and, on being requested to do so by the appellant, they stated a case for the opinion of the Divisional Court who quashed the conviction.

Extracts from the Judgments of the Divisional Court

Lord Goddard, C.J.—

". . . I venture to repeat what I said in *Brend* v. *Wood*[2]; 'it is of the utmost importance for the protection of the liberty of the subject that a court should always bear in mind that, unless a statute either clearly or by necessary implication rules out *mens rea* as a constituent part of a

---

[1] See now Road Traffic Act 1972, s. 25.
[2] (1946), 62 T.L.R. 462, at p. 463.

crime, the court should not find a man guilty of an offence against the criminal law unless he has a guilty mind.' In these days when offences are multiplied by various regulations and orders to an extent which makes it difficult for the most law-abiding subjects in some way or at some time to avoid offending against the law, it is more important than ever to adhere to this principle. The presumption is always liable to be displaced either by the words of the statute, or by the subject matter with which it deals; *per* R. S. Wright, J., in *Sherras* v. *De Rutzen*.[1] . . .

If, apart from authority, one seeks to find a principle applicable to this matter it may be thus stated: if a statute contains an absolute prohibition against the doing of some act, as a general rule *mens rea* is not a constituent of the offence; but there is all the difference between prohibiting an act and imposing a duty to do something on the happening of a certain event. Unless a man knows that the event has happened, how can he carry out the duty imposed? If the duty be to report, he cannot report something of which he has no knowledge. . . . Any other view would lead to calling on a man to do the impossible.

I should, however, add that the authorities show that, even where the statute imposes what is apparently an absolute prohibition, an absence of guilty knowledge may in some cases be a defence; *Sherras* v. *De Rutzen*[2] is one instance, *R.* v. *Sleep*[3] and *Hearne* v. *Garton and Stone*[4] are others. Such cases depend on the wording and purpose of the particular statute, and it is unnecessary to consider them in detail.

In deciding whether *mens rea* is excluded as a necessary constituent of a crime, it is, in my opinion, always necessary to consider whether the offence consists in doing a prohibited act or in failing to perform a duty which only arises if a particular state of affairs exists. It must not be thought that this decision provides an easy defence to motorists, who fail to report an accident. The number of cases in which a motor car driver is ignorant that he has been involved in an accident must be small; where he in fact has no knowledge, it may well be, though I do not mean it was so in the present case, that the appropriate charge would be driving without proper care and attention. . . ."

CONVICTION QUASHED.

---

[1] [1895] 1 Q.B. 918, at p. 921; p. 45, *supra*.
[2] [1895] 1 Q.B. 918; p. 44, *supra*.
[3] (1861), 30 L. J. (M.C.) 170.
[4] (1859), 2 E. & E. 66.

R. v. GOSNEY
[1971] 3 All E.R. 220

The offence of driving in a manner dangerous to the public is not one of strict liability.

Mrs. Gosney was stopped by the police when driving in the wrong direction down a dual carriageway. She had turned right into the road with which she was unfamiliar, and she contended that there was nothing to indicate that the turn was prohibited. The trial judge would not allow her to adduce evidence in support of her contention because he took the view that driving in a manner dangerous to the public was an absolute offence. Mrs. Gosney was convicted, but she successfully appealed to the Court of Appeal.

Extracts from the Judgment of the Court of Appeal

Megaw, L.J.—

"The deputy chairman appears to have accepted that on that [the respondent's] view of the law a driver would be guilty of dangerous driving even if the fact were that he had been positively directed, by a road sign which had been turned the wrong way round, to travel in the wrong direction. It would mean (to use as an illustration the facts of an actual case in which some years ago one member of this court was concerned as counsel, in the civil jurisdiction) that a driver would be guilty of dangerous driving where, as a result of an obstruction in the highway, he had been affirmatively directed by a police officer to travel on the wrong carriageway and there, without any lack of care on his part, collided with a car travelling in the opposite direction, the police having omitted to stop or warn traffic coming from that direction.

It may well be thought that, if that is indeed the law, while it may lead towards certainty, it offends the sense of justice. The deputy chairman dealt with that aspect by saying: 'The practical answer is that there would be no prosecution.' That is not much comfort to the accused if a prosecution is brought and he is precluded from proving the facts by cross-examination or direct evidence. By way of background, it may also be said that in an enactment designed primarily to promote safe and careful driving it is unlikely that Parliament intended to subject to the risk of conviction a driver who is doing nothing contrary to the standard of a competent and careful driver.

CRIMINAL LIABILITY

As has been said, the deputy chairman's ruling excluding the evidence was founded on what was said in *R.* v. *Ball, R.* v. *Loughlin. . . .*[1] In that case these words were used:[2]

'It has been held time and again that an offence under this section is an absolute offence . . . it is a liability on the driver which he cannot get rid of, and if the result of his driving produced what the jury consider to be a dangerous situation, a dangerous manoeuvre, then even though he had been completely blameless, he can be held liable.'

A little later this was said:[3]

'The case of *Evans*[4] now sets out quite clearly that the test is a purely objective one and it matters not why the dangerous situation was caused or the dangerous manoeuvre executed.'

With very great respect, we disagree with both those passages. We do not think that they represent correctly the law as it had been previously stated in the authorities. We do not accept that the offence of dangerous driving is 'an absolute offence'. We do not accept that a driver who has been completely blameless can be held guilty. We do not accept that 'it matters not why the dangerous situation was caused. . . .'

We would state briefly what in our judgment the law was and is on this question of fault in the offence of driving in a dangerous manner. It is not an absolute offence. In order to justify a conviction there must be, not only a situation which, viewed objectively, was dangerous, but there must also have been some fault on the part of the driver, causing that situation. 'Fault' certainly does not necessarily involve deliberate misconduct or recklessness or intention to drive in a manner inconsistent with proper standards of driving. Nor does fault necessarily involve moral blame. Thus there is fault if an inexperienced or a naturally poor driver, while straining every nerve to do the right thing, falls below the standard of a competent and careful driver. Fault involves a failure; a falling below the care or skill of a competent and experienced driver, in relation to the manner of the driving and to the relevant circumstances of the case. A fault in that sense, even though it might be slight, even

---

[1] (1966), 50 Cr. App. Rep. 266.
[2] (1966), 50 Cr. App. Rep., at p. 270.
[3] (1966), 50 Cr. App. Rep., at p. 270.
[4] [1963] 1 Q.B. 412; [1962] 3 All E.R. 1086.

though it be a momentary lapse, even though normally no danger would have arisen from it, is sufficient."

APPEAL ALLOWED.

WARNER v. METROPOLITAN POLICE COMMISSIONER
[1968] 2 All E.R. 356

Although the offence created by s. 1 of the Drugs (Prevention of Misuse) Act 1964 was absolute, a person in control of a package did not have possession of its contents within the meaning of the section unless he was aware of their general nature; but it was unnecessary for the prosecution to show that the accused knew that the contents consisted of prohibited drugs.[1]

Warner sold scent as a sideline to his normal occupation of floor-layer. He was stopped by the police when driving a mini-van containing boxes, one of which was found to contain twenty thousand tablets of amphetamine sulphate, a substance the possession of which was, subject to irrelevant exceptions, prohibited by the Drugs (Prevention of Misuse) Act 1964. Warner was charged with being in possession of the tablets contrary to the provisions of the statute. His defence was that he believed the box in question to contain scent as did another box which he picked up together with it from a café.

The jury were directed that it was sufficient for the prosecution to prove that the accused was in control of the box containing the tablets and that his ignorance of the nature of the contents of the box was no defence. Warner was convicted and appealed unsuccessfully to the Court of Appeal. His appeal to the House of Lords was also dismissed on the ground that there had been no miscarriage of justice, but a majority of three to two was of opinion that the direction to the jury had been incorrect as a person cannot possess the contents of a package without at least being aware of their general nature.

---

[1] The past tense is used in the headnote and statement of facts because the Act of 1964 was repealed by the Misuse of Drugs Act 1971 (see comment on pp. 70–71, *infra*).

Extracts from the Speeches of the House of Lords

Lord Reid.—

"There is no doubt that for centuries *mens rea* has been an essential element in every common law crime or offence. Equally there is no doubt that Parliament, being sovereign, can create absolute offences if so minded; but we were referred to no instance where Parliament in giving statutory form to an old common law crime has or has been held to have excluded the necessity to prove *mens rea*. There are a number of statutes going back for over a century where Parliament in creating a new offence has transferred the onus of proof so that, once the facts necessary to constitute the crime have been proved, the accused will be held to be guilty unless he can prove that he had no *mens rea*. We were not referred, however, to any except quite recent cases in which it was held that it was no defence to a charge of a serious and truly criminal statutory offence to prove absence of *mens rea*.

On the other hand there is a long line of cases in which it has been held with regard to less serious offences that absence of *mens rea* was no defence. Typical examples are offences under public health, licensing and industrial legislation. If a person sets up as say a butcher, a publican, or a manufacturer and exposes unsound meat for sale, or sells drink to a drunk man or certain parts of his factory are unsafe, it is no defence that he could not by the exercise of reasonable care have known or discovered that the meat was unsound, or that the man was drunk or that his premises were unsafe. He must take the risk and when it is found that the statutory prohibition or requirement has been infringed he must pay the penalty. This may well seem unjust, but it is a comparatively minor injustice and there is good reason for it as affording some protection to his customers or servants or to the public at large. . . .

The only thing that makes me hesitate about this case ·s the severity of the penalty and the fact that this would be ιegarded as a truly criminal and disgraceful offence, so that a stigma would attach to a person convicted of it. Applicants for employment, permits or other advantages are often asked whether they have been convicted of any offence. Admission of a conviction of an ordinary offence of this class ought not to be too seriously regarded—and the conviction might be of the man's company and not of the man himself. A man who had, however, to admit a conviction with regard to dangerous drugs might be at a grave disadvantage, and this might not be removed by an explanation that he had only suffered a small penalty. He might even be dismissed by his employer. This makes me hesitate to impute to Parliament an intention to deprive persons accused of these offences of the defence that they had no *mens rea*. I would think it difficult to convince Parliament that there was any real need to convict a man who could prove that he had neither knowledge of what was being done nor any grounds for suspecting that there was anything wrong.

I dissent emphatically from the view that Parliament can be supposed to have been of the opinion that it could be left to the discretion of the police not to prosecute, or that if there was a prosecution justice would be served by only a nominal penalty being imposed. . . .

The object of this legislation is to penalise possession of certain drugs. So if *mens rea* has not been excluded what would be required would be the knowledge of the accused that he had prohibited drugs in his possession. It would be no defence, though it would be a mitigation, that he did not intend that they should be used improperly. And it is a commonplace that, if the accused had a suspicion but deliberately shut his eyes, the court or jury is well entitled to hold him guilty. Further, it would be pedantic to hold that it must be shown that the accused knew precisely which drug he had in his possession. Ignorance of the law is no defence and in fact virtually everyone knows that there are prohibited drugs. So it would be quite sufficient to prove facts from which it could properly be inferred that the accused knew that he had a prohibited drug in his possession. That would not lead to an unreasonable result. In a case like this Parliament, if consulted, might think it right to transfer the onus of proof so that an accused would have to prove that he neither knew nor had any reason to suspect that he had a prohibited drug in his possession; I am unable to find sufficient grounds for imputing to Parliament an intention to deprive the accused of all rights to show that he had no knowledge or reason to suspect that any prohibited drug was on his premises or in a container which was in his possession."

Lord Pearce.—

"My Lords, the illicit drug traffic is a very serious evil. Parliament intended by the Act of 1964 to prevent it so far as possible by penalising the unauthorised possession of certain drugs. There are three methods, broadly speaking, by which Parliament may have intended to achieve its purpose. The first (for which the appellant contends) is this. Parliament, it is said, intended that the word 'possession' should connote some knowledge of the thing possessed and of its quality. It also intended that a defendant should only be convicted if he had a guilty mind. The extent of the knowledge and the exact nature of the guilty mind are problems which obviously overlap. The second possible view (for which the Crown contend) is that Parliament intended that the defendant, even if innocent of any knowledge of the nature of the drug or any guilty knowledge, must be convicted when once it was shown that he had to his knowledge physical control of a thing which (whether he knows it or not) is or contains unlawful drugs. Thirdly, Parliament may have intended what was described as a 'half-way' house in the full and able argument by counsel on both sides. Each acknowledged its possibility and certain obvious advantages, but neither felt able to give it any very solid support. By this method the mere physical possession of drugs would be enough to throw on a defendant the onus of establishing his innocence, and unless he did so (on a balance of probabilities) he would be convicted. The Explosive Substances Act 1883 produces this fair and sensible result but it does so by express words ('Unless he can show that he had it in his possession for a lawful object'). . . .

Unfortunately I do not find the half-way house reconcilable with the speech of Viscount Sankey, L.C., in *Woolmington* v. *Director of Public Prosecutions*.[1] Reluctantly, therefore, I am compelled to the decision that it is not maintainable. Ultimately the burden of proof is always on the prosecution, unless it has been shifted by any statutory provision. If, therefore, there is initially in the crime an element of knowledge or guilty mind, the jury must at the end of the case acquit, if they are left in doubt. . . .

Lord Parker, C.J., in *Lockyer* v. *Gibb*[2] was right (and this is conceded by both sides) in taking the view that a person did not have possession of something which has been 'slipped into his bag' without his knowledge. One may, therefore, exclude from the 'possession' intended by the Act of 1964 the physical control of articles which have been 'planted' on him without his knowledge; but how much further is one to go? If one goes to the extreme length of requiring the prosecution to prove that 'possession' implies

1 [1935] A.C. 462, at p. 481; [1935] 1 All E.R. Rep. 1, at p. 8.
2 [1967] 2 Q.B. 243; [1966] 2 All E.R. 653.

a full knowledge of the name and nature of the drug concerned, the efficacy of the Act is seriously impaired, since many drug pedlars may in truth be unaware of this. I think that the term 'possession' is satisfied by a knowledge only of the existence of the thing itself and not its qualities, and that ignorance or mistake as to its qualities is not an excuse. This would comply with the general understanding of the word 'possess'. Though I reasonably believe the tablets which I possess to be aspirin, yet if they turn out to be heroin I am in possession of heroin tablets. This would be so I think even if I believed them to be sweets. It would be otherwise if I believed them to be something of a wholly different nature. At this point a question of degree arises as to when a difference in qualities amounts to a difference in kind. That is a matter for a jury who would probably decide it sensibly in favour of the genuinely innocent but against the guilty."

APPEAL DISMISSED.

SWEET v. PARSLEY
[1969] 1 All E.R. 347

The offence created by s. 5(b) of the Dangerous Drugs Act 1965 of being, as occupier, concerned in the management of premises used for the purpose of smoking cannabis was not absolute.

Miss Sweet was the sub-lessee of a farmhouse. She let the rooms in the house, but retained possession of one room which she occasionally used when visiting the house in order to collect the rents. Cigarette ends containing cannabis were found in the kitchen and boxes of cannabis and LSD were hidden in the garden, but there was no evidence that Miss Sweet knew that cannabis was being smoked on the premises. She was none the less charged with being concerned in the management of premises used for the purpose of smoking cannabis contrary to s. 5(b) of the Dangerous Drugs Act 1965.[1]

---

[1] "If a person (a) being the occupier of any premises, permits those premises to be used for the purpose of smoking cannabis or cannabis resin, or of dealing in cannabis or cannabis resin (whether by sale or otherwise); or (b) is concerned in the management of any premises used for any such purpose as aforesaid; he shall be guilty of an offence against this Act." (For the position under the Misuse of Drugs Act 1971 see p. 70, *infra*.)

Miss Sweet unsuccessfully appealed to a Divisional Court, but her appeal to the House of Lords succeeded.

Extracts from the Speeches of the House of Lords

Lord Pearce.—

". . . Before the court will dispense with the necessity for *mens rea* it has to be satisfied that Parliament so intended. The mere absence of the word 'knowingly' is not enough. But the nature of the crime, the punishment, the absence of social obloquy, the particular mischief and the field of activity in which it occurs, and the wording of the particular section and its context, may show that Parliament intended that the act should be prevented by punishment regardless of intent or knowledge.

Viewing the matter on these principles, it is not possible to accept the respondent's contention. Even granted that this were in the public health class of case, such as, for instance, are offences created to ensure that food shall be clean, it would be quite unreasonable. It is one thing to make a man absolutely responsible for all his own acts and even vicariously liable for his servants if he engages in a certain type of activity. But it is quite another matter to make him liable for persons over whom he has no control. The innocent hotel-keeper, the lady who keeps lodgings or takes paying guests, the manager of a cinema, the warden of a hostel, the matron of a hospital, the housemaster and matron of a boarding school, all these, it is conceded, are on the respondent's argument liable to conviction the moment that irresponsible occupants smoke cannabis cigarrettes. . . .

If, therefore, the words creating the offence are as wide in their application as the respondent contends, Parliament cannot have intended an offence to which absence of knowledge or *mens rea* is no defence.

Parliament might, of course, have taken what was conceded in argument to be a fair and sensible course. It could have said, in appropriate words, that a person is to be liable unless he proves that he had no knowledge or guilty mind. Admittedly, if the prosecution have to prove a defendant's knowledge beyond reasonable doubt, it may be easy for the guilty to escape. But it would be very much harder for the guilty to escape if the burden of disproving *mens rea* or knowledge is thrown on the defendant. And if that were done, innocent people could satisfy a jury of their innocence on a balance of probabilities. It has been said that a jury might

be confused by the different nature of the onus of satisfying
'beyond reasonable doubt' which the prosecution have to discharge and the onus 'on a balance of probabilties' which lies
on a defendant in proving that he had no knowledge or guilt.
I do not believe that this would be so in this kind of case.
Most people can easily understand rules that express in greater
detail that which their own hearts and minds already feel to
be fair and sensible. What they find hard to understand is
rules that go 'against the grain' of their own common sense...

If it were possible in some so-called absolute offences to
take this sensible half-way house, I think that the courts
should do so. This has been referred to in *Warner's* case.[1] I
see no difficulty in it apart from the opinion of Lord Sankey,
L.C., in *Woolmington* v. *Director of Public Prosecutions*.[2] But,
so long as the full width of that opinion is maintained, I see
difficulty. There are many cases where the width of that
opinion has caused awkward problems. But before reducing
that width, your Lordships would obviously have to consider
all the aspects of so far-reaching a problem. In the present
case, counsel for the appellant was wisely loth to involve
herself in this when she had easier and surer paths to pursue.

The Australian High Court, founding on Cave, J.,[3] and
Wills, J.,[4] in *R. v. Tolson,*[5] have evolved a defence of reasonable mistake of fact and the burden of proving this on a
balance of probabilities rests on the defendant. . . . Being
concerned in the management of premises used for the purpose of smoking cannabis necessarily imports some knowledge
of the use of the premises for the purpose. Admittedly the
appellant had no knowledge.

I appreciate that this limitation will, as the respondent
contends, rob s. 5(*b*) of the Act of 1965 of much of its force.
If a wider application or efficiency were desired, it could be
achieved by a change of onus and a consideration of what
exactly *is* being required of landladies and the like. They
cannot reasonably be branded with guilt whenever there
happens to be on their premises someone who without their
knowledge or assent smokes cannabis."

Lord Diplock.—
"The expression 'absolute offence' used in the first

---

[1] [1969] 2 A.C. 256; [1968] 2 All E.R. 356; p. 59, *supra*.
[2] [1935] A.C. 462; [1935] All E.R. Rep. 1; p. 16, *supra*.
[3] (1889), 23 Q.B.D., at p. 181; [1886–90] All E.R. Rep., at p. 34.
[4] (1889), 23 Q.B.D., at p. 175; [1886–90] All E.R. Rep., at pp. 30, 31.
[5] (1889), 23 Q.B.D. 168; [1886–90] All E.R. 26; p. 31, *supra*.

question is an imprecise phrase currently used to describe
an act for which the doer is subject to criminal sanctions,
even though when he did it he had no *mens rea*; but *mens rea*
itself also lacks precision and calls for closer analysis than is
involved in its mere translation into English by Wright, J.,
in *Sherras* v. *De Rutzen*[1] as 'evil intention, or a knowledge of
the wrongfulness of the act'—a definition which suggests a
single mental element common to all criminal offences and
appears to omit thoughtlessness which, at any rate if it
amounted to a reckless disregard of the nature or consequences of an act, was a sufficient mental element in some
offences at common law. A more helpful exposition of the
nature of *mens rea* in both common law and statutory offences
is to be found in the judgment of Stephen, J., in *R.* v. *Tolson*:[2]

> 'The full definition of every crime contains expressly
> or by implication a proposition as to a state of mind. There-
> fore, if the mental element of any conduct alleged to be a
> crime is proved to have been absent in any given case, the
> crime so defined has not been committed; or, again, if a
> crime is fully defined, nothing amounts to that crime which
> does not satisfy that definition.'

Where the crime consists of doing an act which is
prohibited by statute, the proposition as to the state of mind
of the doer which is contained in the full definition of the
crime must be ascertained from the words and subject-matter
of the statute. The proposition, as Stephen, J., pointed out,[3]
may be stated explicitly by the use of such qualifying adverbs
as 'maliciously', 'fraudulently', 'negligently' or 'knowingly'—
expressions which in relation to different kinds of conduct
may call for judicial exegesis. And even without such
adverbs the words descriptive of the prohibited act may
themselves connote the presence of a particular mental
element. Thus, where the prohibited conduct consists in
permitting a particular thing to be done the word 'permit'
connotes at least knowledge or reasonable grounds for suspicion on the part of the permittor that the thing will be
done and an unwillingness to use means available to him to
prevent it and, to take a recent example, to have in one's
'possession' a prohibited substance connotes some degree

[1] [1895] 1 Q.B. 918, at p. 921; [1895–99] All E.R. Rep. 1167, at p. 1169;
p. 45, *supra.*
[2] (1889), 23 Q.B.D. 168, at p. 187; [1886–90] All E.R. Rep. 26, at p. 37.
[3] (1889), 23 Q.B.D., at p. 187; [1886–90] All E.R. Rep., at p. 37.

of awareness of that which was within the possessor's physical control (*Warner* v. *Metropolitan Police Comr.*[1])

But only too frequently the actual words used by Parliament to define the prohibited conduct are in themselves descriptive only of a physical act and bear no connotation as to any particular state of mind on the part of the person who does the act. Nevertheless, the mere fact that Parliament has made the conduct a criminal offence gives rise to *some* implication about the mental element of the conduct proscribed. . . .

But where the subject-matter of a statute is the regulation of a particular activity involving potential danger to public health, safety or morals, in which citizens have a choice whether they participate or not, the court may feel driven to infer an intention of Parliament to impose, by penal sanctions, a higher duty of care on those who choose to participate and to place on them an obligation to take whatever measures may be necessary to prevent the prohibited act, without regard to those considerations of cost or business practicability which play a part in the determination of what would be required of them in order to fulfil the ordinary common law duty of care. But such an inference is not lightly to be drawn, nor is there any room for it unless there is something that the person on whom the obligation is imposed can do directly or indirectly, by supervision or inspection, by improvement of his business methods or by exhorting those whom he may be expected to influence or control, which will promote the observance of the obligation. (See *Lim Chin Aik* v. *R.*[2])

The numerous decisions in the English courts since R. v. *Tolson*[3] in which this later inference has been drawn rightly or, as I think, often wrongly, are not easy to reconcile with others where the court has failed to draw the inference, nor are they always limited to penal provisions designed to regulate the conduct of persons who choose to participate in a particular activity as distinct from those of general application to the conduct of ordinary citizens in the course of their everyday life. It may well be that, had the significance of R. v. *Tolson*[3] been appreciated here, as it was in the High Court of Australia, our courts, too, would have been less ready to infer an intention of Parliament to create offences for

---

[1] [1969] 2 A.C. 256; [1968] 2 All E.R. 356; p. 59, *supra*.
[2] [1963] A.C. 160, at p. 174; [1963] 1 All E.R. 223, at p. 228; p. 54, *supra*.
[3] (1889), 23 Q.B.D. 168; [1886–90] All E.R. Rep. 26; p. 31. *supra*.

which honest and reasonable mistake was no excuse. Its importance as a guide to the construction of penal provisions in statutes of general applications was recognized by Dixon, J., in *Maher* v. *Musson*,[1] and by the majority of the High Court of Australia in *Thomas* v. *R*.[2] It is now regularly adopted in Australia as a general principle of construction of statutory provisions of this kind.

By contrast, in England the principle laid down in *R.* v. *Tolson*[3] has been overlooked until recently (see *R.* v. *Gould*[4]) partly because the *ratio decidendi* was misunderstood by the Court of Criminal Appeal in *R.* v. *Wheat, R.* v. *Stocks*,[5] and partly, I suspect, because the reference in *R.* v. *Tolson*[6] to the mistaken belief as being a 'defence' to the charge of bigamy was thought to run counter to the decision of your Lordships' House in *Woolmington* v. *Director of Public Prosecutions*.[7] That expression might have to be expanded in the light of what was said in *Woolmington's* case,[7] though I doubt whether a jury would find the expansion much more informative than describing the existence of the mistaken belief as a defence to which they should give effect unless they felt sure either that the accused did not honestly hold it or, if he did, that he had no reasonable grounds for doing so.

Woolmington's case[7] affirmed the principle that the onus lies on the prosecution in a criminal trial to prove all the elements of the offence with which the accused is charged. It does not purport to lay down how that onus can be discharged as respects any particular elements of the offence. This, under our system of criminal procedure, is left to the common sense of the jury. *Woolmington's* case, did not decide anything so irrational as that the prosecution must call evidence to prove the absence of any mistaken belief by the accused in the existence of facts which, if true, would make the act innocent, any more than it decided that the prosecution must call evidence to prove the absence of any claim of right in a charge of larceny. The jury is entitled to presume that the accused acted with knowledge of the facts, unless there is some evidence to the contrary originating from the accused who alone can know on what belief he acted and on

---

[1] (1934), 52 C.L.R. 100, at p. 104.
[2] (1937), 59 C.L.R. 279.
[3] (1889) 23 Q.B.D. 168; [1886–9] All E.R. Rep. 26, p. 31, *supra*.
[4] [1968] 2 Q.B. 65; [1968] 1 All E.R. 849.
[5] [1921] 2 K.B. 119; [1921] All E.R. Rep. 602.
[6] (1889), 23 Q.B.D. 168; [1886–90] All E.R. Rep. 26.
[7] [1935] A.C. 462; [1935] All E.R. Rep. 1; p. 16, *supra*.

what ground the belief if mistaken was held. What *Wool-mington's* case[1] did decide is that, where there is any such evidence, the jury, after considering it and also any relevant evidence called by the prosecution on the issue of the exist-ence of the alleged mistaken belief, should acquit the ac-cused unless they feel sure that he did not hold the belief or that there were no reasonable grounds on which he could have done so. This, as I understand it, is the approach of Dixon, J., to the onus of proof of honest and reasonable mistaken belief as he expressed it in *Proudman* v. *Dayman*.[2] Unlike the position where a statute expressly places the onus of proving lack of guilty knowledge on the accused, the accused does not have to prove the existence of mistaken belief on the balance of probabilities; he has to raise a reasonable doubt as to its non-existence.

It has been objected that the requirement laid down in *R.* v. *Tolson*[3] and the *Bank of New South Wales* v. *Piper*[4] that the mistaken belief should be based on reasonable grounds introduces an objective mental element into *mens rea*. This may be so, but there is nothing novel in this. The test of the mental element of provocation which distinguishes manslaughter from murder has always been at common law and now is by statute the objective one of the way in which a reasonable man would react to provocation. There is nothing unreasonable in requiring a citizen to take reasonable care to ascertain the facts relevant to his avoiding doing a prohibited act. . . .

In my opinion, in the compound phrase 'is concerned in the management of premises used for the purpose of smoking cannabis', etc., the purpose described must be the purpose of the person concerned in the management of the premises. But at its highest against the appellant, the words of the paragraph are ambiguous as to whose is the relevant purpose. That ambiguity in a penal statute which, on the alternative construction that it would be sufficient if the purpose to use the premises for smoking cannabis were that of anyone who in fact smoked cannabis, would render her liable, despite lack of any knowledge or acquiescence on her part, should be unhesitatingly resolved in her favour."

APPEAL ALLOWED.

---

[1] [1935] A.C. 462; [1935] All E.R. Rep. 1.
[2] (1941), 67 C.L.R. 536, at p. 541.
[3] (1889), 23 Q.B.D. 168; [1886–90] All E.R. Rep. 26.
[4] [1897] A.C. 383.

Note on Warner v. Metropolitan Police Commissioner and Sweet v. Parsley

The statutory provisions on which these two cases turned are repealed by the Misuse of Drugs Act, 1971. Section 28(2) provides that, on a prosecution, for possession *inter alia*, of a controlled drug,

> ". . . it shall be a defence for the accused to prove that he neither knew nor suspected nor had reason to suspect the existence of some fact alleged by the prosecution which it is necessary for the prosecution to prove if he is to be convicted of the offence charged."

Under s. 28(3) it is necessary for the accused to prove not merely that he was unaware or did not suspect or have reason to suspect that the controlled drug he possessed was that alleged by the prosecution; he must show further either that he did not know or suspect or have reason to suspect that it was a controlled drug at all, or else that he believed it to be a controlled drug which he was entitled to possess. Section 28(2) and (3) also apply to offences concerned with the production or supply of controlled drugs and to certain other offences under the Act.

Section 8 of the Act of 1971 not only redrafts the offence with which Miss Sweet was charged but also makes it clear, by the insertion of "knowingly", that guilty knowledge is required to constitute the offence. Section 8 provides:

> "A person commits an offence if, being the occupier or concerned in the management of any premises, he knowingly permits or suffers any of the following activities to take place on those premises, that is to say—
>
> (a) producing or attempting to produce a controlled drug in contravention of section 4(1) of this Act;
> (b) supplying or attempting to supply a controlled drug to another in contravention of section 4 (1) of this Act, or offering to supply a controlled drug to another in contravention of section 4 (1);
> (c) preparing opium for smoking;
> (d) smoking cannabis, cannabis resin or prepared opium."

Clearly, the *rationes decidendi* of the above two cases are now of little importance. However, extracts from the speeches in the House of Lords have been included because of their importance in relation to strict liability generally. The majority of these speeches confirm the modern trend of the decisions against strict liability although *Alphacell, Ltd.* v. *Woodward*,[1] decided after *Sweet* v. *Parsley* shows that the House of Lords is prepared to construe a statute in such a way as to impose strict liability. If the proposals contained in Law Commission Working Paper No. 31, *The Mental Element in Crime*,[2] are adopted, it will be necessary for the prosecution to prove negligence even in the case of a statutory offence such as that with which *Alphacell, Ltd.* v. *Woodward* was concerned, although negligence will be presumed in the absence of evidence to the contrary, *i.e.* the accused will bear the burden of adducing evidence of due care.

Section 28 of the Misuse of Drugs Act 1971 produces the "half-way" house canvassed by Lord Pearce in *Warner's* case since it places the burden of proving ignorance, lack of suspicion, or of reason to suspect on the accused.[3] There is no doubt that the accused would be held to have discharged the burden by proof on a preponderance of probability, but the fact would remain that, once possession was proved, the onus of establishing his innocence would rest on the accused. In this respect the English statutory solution of some of the problems of strict liability tends to be less favourable to the accused than the Australian solution as explained by Lord Diplock in *Sweet* v. *Parsley*.[4]

---

[1] P. 51, *supra.*

[2] See Cross and Jones, *Introduction to Criminal Law*, 8th edn., para. 6.11.

[3] *Jayasena* v. *R.*, [1970] A.C. 618; [1970] 1 All E.R. 219.

[4] The Australian decisions are sometimes construed in such a way as to place the burden of proving reasonable mistake, as opposed to the burden of adducing evidence of it, on the accused. The statement with regard to the burden of proof by Dixon, J., in *Proudman* v. *Dayman* ((1941), 67 C.L.R. 536, at p. 541) is cast in indefinite terms.

CHAPTER 2
CAPACITY

Children
CHILDREN AND YOUNG PERSONS ACT 1933

"Section 50.—Age of criminal responsibility
It shall be conclusively presumed that no child under the age of [ten] years can be guilty of any offence."

Note

At common law the age of criminal responsibility was seven years. This section, as originally enacted, raised that age to eight years, but it was raised again to ten years by the Children and Young Persons Act 1963, s. 16.

R. v. GORRIE
(1919) 83 J.P. 136

A child aged between ten and fourteen is rebuttably presumed incapable of committing an offence. This presumption is rebutted if the prosecution prove that the child had a mischievous discretion.

Gorrie, who was aged thirteen, and three other schoolboys were playing near their homes. Gorrie had a penknife, with which he was cutting a piece of wood. Something was said in fun about Germans, and Gorrie chased one of the boys. The penknife, which Gorrie happened to have open in his hand at the time, occasioned a trifling wound in the boy's buttock. The boy did not report the wound and consequently died later of septic poisoning. Gorrie was charged with manslaughter.

Extracts from the report of the Summing-up of Salter, J.

"In the case of persons under fourteen years of age, the law presumed that they were not criminally responsible; they were not supposed to have that discretion which would make them criminally responsible. But in any particular case, if the prosecution could show that although the accused was under fourteen the act was done with what was called mischievous discretion, then they could rebut the presumption that the child was not responsible. Therefore the jury should first of all consider whether it would be their duty to find him guilty if he were over fourteen, and then consider whether mischievous disrection deprived him of the shelter he would otherwise have. . . . If it was an intentional stab, then, however sorry he might be, it would be manslaughter. Then they came to the second point. The boy was under fourteen, and the law presumed that he was not responsible criminally; and if the prosecution sought to show that he was responsible although under fourteen, they must give them very clear and complete evidence of what was called mischievous discretion; that meant that they must satisfy the jury that when the boy did this he knew that he was doing what was wrong—not merely what was wrong, but what was gravely wrong, seriously wrong. It was for the jury to say whether there was any evidence that this boy when, as alleged, he 'jabbed' the other with the knife in this horseplay, had any consciousness that he was doing that which was gravely wrong."

NOT GUILTY.

B. v. R.
(1960), 44 Cr. App. Rep. 1

The evidence in rebuttal of the presumption of incapability may consist of proof that the child is well brought up and comes from a good home.

B, aged eight (and therefore at that time over the age of criminal responsibility), had been convicted of housebreaking. After entering a house with another boy he had later returned with other boys and ransacked it. He had been properly brought up in a good home, and when questioned by the police he had made a very frank statement of all that had happened. The appeal committee of quarter sessions had rejected B's appeal and he then appealed to the Divisional Court on the ground that the evidence was insufficient to rebut the presumption that he did not know that what he was doing was wrong.

Extracts from the Judgments of the Divisional Court

Lord Parker, C.J.—

". . . There is no doubt in the case of a child between the age of eight and fourteen that there is a presumption that the child is [incapable of committing an offence] and it is to be observed that, the lower the child is in the scale between eight and fourteen, the stronger the evidence necessary to rebut that presumption, because in the case of a child under eight it is conclusively presumed he is inacpable of committing crime. . . . It may be that the case was rather 'thin', but I cannot say that there was no evidence on which the magistrates could say that the presumption was rebutted. Indeed, there are features which point very strongly that way. Here is a child who has had apparently every opportunity in life, coming from a respectable family and properly brought up, who, one would think, would know in the ordinary sense the difference between good and evil and what he should do and what he should not do. Here he is taking part, first, in the testing of the house at the back and front, climbing through the window, and on leaving taking the key and returning later with a gang, completely wrecking the house and taking certain articles. For my part, I cannot say there was no evidence on which the magistrates could come to the conclusion that this boy had guilty knowledge, and I would dismiss this appeal."

APPEAL DISMISSED.

Insanity

M'NAGHTEN'S CASE

(1843), 10 Cl. & Fin. 200

In order to be exempt from criminal responsibility on the ground of insanity, the accused must prove that, owing to a defect of reason, due to a disease of the mind, he did not know the nature and quality of his act, or, if he did know this, that he did not know that he was doing wrong.

M'Naghten was indicted for murder and acquitted on the ground of insanity. In consequence debates took place in the House of Lords, and it was decided to take the opinion of the judges as to the nature and extent of the unsoundness of mind which would excuse the commission of a felony of this sort. Five questions were put to the judges in the terms set out in the following extract from their opinions.

Extract from Opinion of the Judges

Lord Chief Justice Tindal.—

". . . The first question proposed by your Lordships is this: 'What is the law respecting alleged crimes committed by persons afflicted with insane delusion in respect of one or more particular subjects or persons: as, for instance, where at the time of the commission of the alleged crime the accused knew he was acting contrary to law, but did the act complained of with a view, under the influence of insane delusion, of redressing or revenging some supposed grievance or injury, or of producing some supposed public benefit?'

In answer to which question, assuming that your Lordships' inquiries are confined to those persons who labour under such partial delusions only, and are not in other respects insane, we are of opinion that, notwithstanding the party accused did the act complained of with a view, under the influence of insane delusion, of redressing or revenging some supposed grievance or injury, or of producing some public benefit, he is nevertheless punishable according to the nature of the crime committed, if he knew at the time of committing such crime that he was acting contrary to law; by which expression we understand your Lordships to mean the law of the land.

Your Lordships are pleased to inquire of us, secondly, 'What are the proper questions to be submitted to the jury where a person alleged to be afflicted with insane delusion respecting one or more particular subjects or persons, is charged with the commission of a crime (murder, for example), and insanity is set up as a defence?' And, thirdly, 'In what terms ought the question to be left to the jury as to the prisoner's state of mind at the time when the act was committed?' And as these two questions appear to us to be more conveniently answered together, we have to submit our opinion to be, that the jurors ought to be told in all cases that every man is to be presumed to be sane, and to possess a sufficient degree of reason to be responsible for his crimes, until the contrary be proved to their satisfaction; and that to establish a defence on the ground of insanity, it must be clearly proved that, at the time of the committing

of the act, the party accused was labouring under such a
defect of reason, from disease of the mind, as not to know the
nature and quality of the act he was doing; or, if he did know
it, that he did not know he was doing what was wrong.
The mode of putting the latter part of the question to the
jury on these occasions has generally been, whether the
accused at the time of doing the act knew the difference
between right and wrong: which mode, though rarely, if
ever, leading to any mistake with the jury, is not, as we
conceive, so accurate when put generally and in the abstract,
as when put with reference to the party's knowledge of right
and wrong in respect to the very act with which he is charged.
If the question were to be put as to the knowledge of the
accused solely and exclusively with reference to the law of
the land, it might tend to confound the jury, by inducing
them to believe that an actual knowledge of the law of the
land was essential in order to lead to a conviction; whereas
the law is administered upon the principle that everyone
must be taken conclusively to know it, without proof that he
does know it. If the accused was conscious that the act was one
which he ought not to do, and if that act was at the same
time contrary to the law of the land, he is punishable;
and the usual course therefore has been to leave the question
to the jury, whether the party accused has a sufficient
degree of reason to know that he was doing an act that
was wrong: and this course we think is correct, accompanied
with such observations and explanations as the circumstances
of each particular case may require.

The fourth question which your Lordships have proposed to us is this:—'If a person under an insane delusion
as to existing facts, commits an offence in consequence
thereof, is he thereby excused?' To which question the
answer must of course depend on the nature of the delusion:
but, making the same assumption as we did before, namely,
that he labours under such partial delusion only, and is not
in other respects insane, we think he must be considered in
the same situation as to responsibility as if the facts with
respect to which the delusion exists were real. For example,
if under the influence of his delusion he supposes another
man to be in the act of attempting to take away his life, and
he kills that man, as he supposes, in self-defence, he would
be exempt from punishment. If his delusion was that the
deceased had inflicted a serious injury to his character and
fortune, and he killed him in revenge for such supposed
injury, he would be liable to punishment.

The question lastly proposed by your Lordships is:—
'Can a medical man conversant with the disease of insanity,
who never saw the prisoner previously to the trial, but who
was present during the whole trial and the examination of
all the witnesses, be asked his opinion as to the state of the
prisoner's mind at the time of the commission of the alleged
crime, or his opinion whether the prisoner was conscious at
the time of doing the act that he was acting contrary to law,
or whether he was labouring under any and what delusion
at the time?' In answer thereto, we state to your Lordships,
that we think the medical man, under the circumstances
supposed, cannot in strictness be asked his opinion in the
terms above stated, because each of those questions involves
the determination of the truth of the facts deposed to, which
it is for the jury to decide, and the questions are not mere
questions upon a matter of science, in which case such
evidence is admissible. But where the facts are admitted or
not disputed, and the question becomes substantially one of
science only, it may be convenient to allow the question to
be put in that general form, though the same cannot be
insisted on as a matter of right."

R. v. CLARKE
[1972] 1 All E.R. 219

*A diabetic's temporary fit of absent-mindedness due to sugar
deficiency is not a defect of reason within the meaning of the
M'Naghten rules.*

Mrs. Clarke was charged with theft. While shopping in a
supermarket, she had removed goods for which she had not
paid from the market's basket to her own. Her defence was
that she had no intention to steal, having acted in a moment
of absent-mindedness caused by a diabetic depression brought
on by sugar deficiency. She called a psychiatrist who spoke
of her condition as a 'mental illness'. The assistant recorder
said that he would treat the defence as one of insanity
whereupon Mrs. Clarke pleaded guilty on legal advice. She
appealed to the Court of Appeal who quashed the conviction.

Extract from the Judgment of the Court of Appeal
Ackner, J.—
"It may be that on the evidence in this case the assistant

recorder was entitled to the view that the appellant suffered from a disease of the mind but we express no concluded view on that. However, in our judgment the evidence fell very far short either of showing that she suffered from a defect of reason or that the consequences of that defect in reason, if any, were that she was unable to know the nature and quality of the act she was doing. The *M'Naghten* rules relate to accused persons who by reason of a disease of the mind are deprived of the power of reasoning. They do not apply and never have applied to those who retain the power of reasoning but who in moments of confusion or absent-mindedness fail to use their powers to the full. The picture painted by the evidence was wholly consistent with this being a woman who retained her ordinary powers of reason but who was momentarily absent-minded or confused and acted as she did by failing to concentrate properly on what she was doing and by failing adequately to use her mental powers.

Because the assistant recorder ruled that the defence put forward had to be put forward as a defence of insanity, although the medical evidence was to the effect that it was absurd to call anyone in the appellant's condition insane, defending counsel felt constrained to advise the appellant to alter her plea from not guilty to guilty so as to avoid the disastrous consequences of her defence, as wrongly defined by the assistant recorder, succeeding."

APPEAL ALLOWED

R. v. KEMP
[1956] 3 All E.R. 249

A disease of physical origin which affects the mind is a "disease of the mind" within the M'Naghten rules and a person who suffers a temporary defect of reason because of such a disease is to be found not guilty by reason of insanity.

The accused was charged with causing grievous bodily harm to his wife. It was common ground that he hit her over the head with a hammer without any apparent motive, and that at the time he was unaware of the nature and quality of his act. There was evidence that the accused was suffering from arteriosclerosis which interfered with the flow of blood to his brain. The sole issue was whether the accused was suffering from a disease of the mind in which case the proper verdict would have been "guilty but insane" (now not guilty on the ground of insanity) or whether the disease was not a disease of the mind in which case the proper verdict would be a complete acquittal.

Extracts from the Judgment given before Directing the Jury

Devlin, J.—

"It is not merely a question of his striking his wife when in some mental derangement, not appreciating that what he was doing was wrong, but in the view of all three doctors it is a case in which the accused was not conscious that he picked up the hammer or that he was striking his wife with it. In those circumstances if the presumption that a man is sane continues to govern the case and if the jury accept the evidence to which I have referred, they would have to return a verdict of not guilty on the basis that the man was not responsible for his acts and did not know what he was doing and therefore could not have had the necessary guilty intent. That, indeed, was what happened in *R. v. Charlson*[1] where the facts were somewhat similar. In that case the doctors were apparently agreed that the accused was not suffering from any disease of the mind which would render him insane at the time of the commission of the acts. The present case is in my judgment entirely different, because here the doctors are not so agreed[2] and the whole question that I have to determine, which was not considered in that case, is what is meant by 'disease of the mind' within the meaning of the M'Naghten rules?. . .

The broad submission that was made to me on behalf of the defence was that this is a physical disease and not a mental disease, that arteriosclerosis is primarily a physical not a mental condition. . . . I should think that it would probably be recognised by medical men that there are mental diseases which have an organic cause; that there are disturbances of the brain which can be traced to some hardening of the arteries, to some degeneration of the brain

---

[1] [1955] 1 All E.R. 859.

[2] *Charlson* and *Kemp* are not so easily reconciled. The question of whether the accused is suffering from a disease of the mind is a question of law to be decided by the judge and not a medical question to be decided by medical witnesses, *Bratty* v. *A.-G. for Northern Ireland*, [1963] A.C. 386, at p. 412; [1961] 3 All E.R. 523, at p. 534. *Charlson* was doubted by Lord Denning in that case, p. 93, *infra*.

cells or to some physical condition which accounts for mental derangement. It would probably be recognised that there are diseases functional in origin about which it is not possible to point to any physical cause but simply to say that there has been a mental derangement of the functioning of the mind, such as melancholia, schizophrenia and many other of those diseases which are primarily handled by psychiatrists. . . . The distinction between the two categories is irrelevant for the purposes of the law, which is not concerned with the origin of the disease or the cause of it but simply with the mental condition which has brought about the act. It does not matter, for the purposes of the law, whether the defect of reasoning is due to a degeneration of the brain or to some other form of mental derangement. . . .

[The law] is not in any way concerned with the brain but with the mind, in the sense that the term is ordinarily used when speaking of the mental faculties of reasoning, memory and understanding. . . . If one read for 'disease of the mind' 'disease of the brain' it would follow that in many cases pleas of insanity would not be established because it would not be established that the brain had been affected either by degeneration of the cells or in any other way. In my judgment the condition of the brain is irrelevant and so is the question whether the disease is curable or incurable, or whether it is temporary or permanent. There is no warranty for introducing those considerations into the definition of the M'Naghten rules. Either temporary or permanent insanity is sufficient to satisfy them.

The prime thing is to determine what is admitted in the present case, namely, whether or not there is a defect of reasoning, and in my judgment the words 'from disease of the mind' are not to be construed as if they were put in for the purposes of distinguishing between diseases of the mind and diseases of the body, diseases which had mental or physical origin, but they were put in primarily for the purpose of limiting the effect of the words 'defect of reason'. A defect of reason is by itself normally enough to make the act irrational and therefore to deny responsibility in law, but it was not intended by that rule that it should apply to defects of reason which were caused simply by brutish stupidity without rational power. It was not intended that the law should say of a person: 'Although with a healthy mind he nevertheless had been brought up in such a way that he had never learned to exercise his reason, and therefore he is suffering from a defect of reason'. The main object,

in my judgment, was that it should be decided whether there
was a defect of reason which had been caused by a disease
affecting the mind; if it were so decided, then there would be
insanity within the meaning of the rule in M'*Naghten's*
case[1]. The hardening of the arteries is a disease which is
shown on the evidence to be capable of affecting the mind
in such a way as to cause a defect, temporarily or permanently, of its reasoning and understanding, and is thus a
disease of the mind within the meaning of the rule."

GUILTY BUT INSANE[2].

R. v. QUICK AND PADDISON
[1973] 3 All E.R. 347

*"Disease of the mind" within the M'Naghten rules
connotes a malfunctioning of the mind caused by disease.*
See p. 95, *infra*.

R. v. WINDLE
[1952] 2 Q.B. 826

*The trial judge may withdraw a plea of insanity from
the jury where there is no evidence that the accused did not
know that what he was doing was legally wrong.*

Windle was charged with murdering his wife with whom
he had led an unhappy life for some time, on account of the
fact that she was probably certifiably insane, and constantly
complained of her unhappiness. Windle was accustomed to
discuss his domestic troubles with his workmates, one of
whom said "give her a dozen aspirins", in order to stop
further conversation on the subject. Shortly afterwards,
Windle gave his wife a hundred aspirins, and she died in
consequence of the dose. He admitted that he had administered it, and said that he supposed that he would hang for
it. There was some evidence that he was suffering from a
form of communicated insanity, but Devlin, J., before whom
the case was tried, refused to leave the question of insanity
to the jury.

---

[1] (1843), 10 Cl. & Fin. 200; p. 74, *supra*.
[2] The verdict would now be an acquittal on the ground of insanity
under the Criminal Procedure (Insanity) Act 1964.

Windle appealed against conviction to the Court of Criminal Appeal who held that the course adopted by Devlin, J., was correct.

Extracts from the Judgment of the Court of Criminal Appeal

Lord Goddard, C.J.—

". . . If the only question in this case had been whether the appellant was suffering from a disease of the mind, I should say that that was a question which must have been left to the jury. That, however, is not the question.

As I endeavoured to point out in giving the judgment of the court in *R. v. Rivett*,[1] in all cases of this kind, the real test is responsibility. A man may be suffering from a defect of reason, but if he knows that what he is doing is 'wrong' and by 'wrong' is meant contrary to law, he is responsible. . . .

In the opinion of the court there is no doubt that in the M'Naghten rules 'wrong' means contrary to law and not 'wrong' according to the opinion of one man or of a number of people on the question whether a particular act might or might not be justified. In the present case, it could not be challenged that the appellant knew that what he was doing was contrary to law. . . .

In these circumstances what evidence was there to leave to the jury which could suggest that the appellant was entitled to a verdict of guilty but insane—that is, that he was guilty of the act, but that when he committed it he was insane so as not to be responsible according to law? If there was no such evidence, the judge was entitled to withdraw the case from the jury and was, I think, right in doing so."

APPEAL DISMISSED.

ATTORNEY-GENERAL FOR THE STATE OF SOUTH AUSTRALIA v. BROWN

[1960] A.C. 432

The law does not recognise irresistible impulse as a symptom from which the jury may, without evidence, infer insanity within the M'Naghten rules.

---

[1] (1950), 34 Cr. App. Rep. 87.

Brown shot and killed his employer without motive or provocation. His defence to a charge of murder was insanity. There was medical evidence that he was a schizoid personality and the submission made on his behalf was that he did not know that he was doing wrong. Brown said that he felt he could not help doing what he did, but admitted that he would not have shot at the deceased if a policeman had been present. The trial judge directed the jury that, if the true explanation of the accused's conduct was that he was unable to control his impulse to kill his employer, he had no defence to the charge. Brown was convicted and unsuccessfully appealed to the Full Court of the Supreme Court of South Australia. He succeeded on an appeal to the High Court of Australia on the ground that the jury should have been directed to consider whether his inability to control his impulse to kill the deceased prevented him from knowing that what he was doing was wrong. The Attorney-General for South Australia successfully appealed to the Privy Council.

Extract from the Advice of the Privy Council:

Lord Tucker.—

"At various times in the past attempts have been made to temper the supposed harshness or unscientific nature of the M'Naghten rules. These attempts were supported by the high authority of Sir James Fitzjames Stephen, but in the end the rules remain in full force[1] and their harshness has in this country been to some extent alleviated by the recent legislative enactment affording the defence of diminished responsibility.[2] While the High Court, of course, fully recognise the binding force of the M'Naghten rules, their Lordships think that the directions which they have indicated as appropriate for use by trial judges would in effect make a very considerable inroad into those rules as hitherto interpreted. Moreover, unless the law is presumed to take cognisance of irresistible impulse as a symptom of legal insanity,

---

[1] The courts have refused to add to the law as to insanity laid down in *M'Naghten's case*, p. 74, *supra*, a rule to the effect that where a man knew that he was doing wrong, but was forced to do the act charged by an irresistible impulse induced by disease of the mind he is entitled to a verdict of not guilty by reason of insanity. See *Sodeman* v. *R.*, [1936] 2 All E.R. 1138, P.C.

[2] P. 86, *infra*.

whence does the judge derive his knowledge of these matters, it not being permissible for him to make use of what he may have learned from evidence given in other cases?

Their Lordships must not, of course, be understood to suggest that in a case where evidence has been given (and it is difficult to imagine a case where such evidence would be other than medical evidence) that irresistible impulse is a symptom of the particular disease of the mind from which a prisoner is said to be suffering and as to its effect on his ability to know the nature and quality of his act or that his act is wrong it would not be the duty of the judge to deal with the matter in the same way as any other relevant evidence given at the trial.

Sodeman v. *R*[1] is an Australian example of such a case. The actual decision in thar case related to the burden of proof in cases where the defence of insanity is raised and to the sufficiency of the trial judge's direction thereon, but in the course of the judgments references were made to 'irresistible impulse' and its possible bearing on the defence raised by the medical evidence in that case to the effect that if a man has an obsession and if he gives way to that obsession and does the thing which is always before his mind as the thing he wants to do, then in doing it he does not know the quality of his act, he does not know what he is doing, and does not know whether it is right or wrong. (*Vide* the judgment of Latham, C.J.[2]) The learned Chief Justice used these words:[3] 'But, on the other hand, it should be remembered that, as already stated, the law recognises that mentai disease manifested in, for example, what is called 'uncontrollable impulse', may also be manifested in lack of knowledge, or incapacity to have knowledge, of the nature and quality of an act or of its character as a wrong act. Such an impulse may be evidence of this very lack or incapacity. *Indeed, that was the effect of the medical opinions given in evidence in this case, and this aspect of the case was definitely put to the jury by the judge.*'

This passage must be read in the light of the concluding sentence now italicised. So read, their Lordships would not question it. But if the word 'recognises' in the first sentence is construed to mean that the words which follow are matters of law which must or may be accepted and acted upon by

---

[1] (1936), 55 C.L.R. 192; affirmed, [1936] 2 All E.R. 1138, P.C.
[2] (1936), 55 C.L.R. 192, at p. 203.
[3] *Ibid.*, at p. 205.

juries without evidence it would not in their Lordships'
opinion be an accurate statement of the law. The word
'recognises' would seem to have been used in contrast to
the rejection of irresistible impulse *per se* and means no
more than that the law will not refuse to listen to evidence
to the effect stated whereas it will refuse to listen to evidence
of irresistible impulse *per se*.

The presumption that the law takes note of such matters
without evidence is implicit in the language of the High
Court's judgment in the present case. It is this that their
Lordships with great respect feel unable to accept."

APPEAL ALLOWED.[1]

Comment on A.-G. for South Australia v. Brown and the defence of insanity in some other parts of the British Commonwealth

Before *Brown's* case the Australian courts had approached
the M'Naghten rules in a different way from the English courts.
According to the Australian courts "wrong" in the rules means
"morally wrong", and "know" means "rationally appreciate".
Hence someone suffering from seriously impaired self control
could be said to come within the rules because he would be unable
to reason about what he was doing with a moderate degree of
composure.[2] From the point of view of the Australian courts
a classic summing-up is that of Dixon, J., in *Porter*:[3]

"The question is whether he was able to appreciate the
wrongness of the particular act he was doing at the particular
time. Could this man be said to know in this sense whether his
act was wrong if through a disease or defect or disorder of the
mind he would not think rationally of the reasons which to
ordinary people make that act right or wrong? If through the
disordered condition of the mind he could not reason about the
matter with a moderate degree of sense and composure it may be
said that he could not know that what he was doing was wrong."

This is very like letting the so-called plea of irresistible
impulse in at the back door, but the approach was formerly
favoured by Sir James Stephen in England. He said, "The
absence of the power of self control would involve an incapacity

---

[1] There is no equivalent to the Homicide Act 1957 in South Australia.
The Judicial Committee considered that Brown might well have been
entitled to a verdict of manslaughter on the grounds of diminished responsibility in this country.

[2] See the judgment of Dixon, C.J., in *Stapleton* v. *R.* (1952), 86 C.L.R.
358.

[3] (1933), 55 C.L.R. 182, at p. 189.

to know right from wrong."[1] Stephen's view failed to gain favour in England, but it is doubtful whether *Brown's* case means the end of it in Australia for all that the decision requires is that there should be medical evidence bearing on the accused's impaired self control through disease of the mind and its effect on his knowledge that his conduct was wrong. The Privy Council made no pronouncement on the meaning of "wrong".

The Butler Committee on Mentally Abnormal Offenders[2] has made proposals for the radical reform of the law relating to the criminal liability of mentally abnormal offenders. These proposals are summarised in Cross and Jones, *Introduction to Criminal Law*, 8th ed., para. 5. 17.

Diminished Responsibility
HOMICIDE ACT 1957

"Section 2.—Persons suffering from diminished responsibility

(1) Where a person kills, or is a party to the killing of another, he shall not be convicted of murder if he was suffering from such abnormality of mind (whether arising from a condition of arrested or retarded development of mind or any inherent causes or induced by disease or injury) as substantially impaired his mental responsibility for his acts or omissions in doing or being a party to the killing.

(2) On a charge of murder, it shall be for the defence to prove that the person charged is by virtue of this section not liable to be convicted of murder.

(3) A person who but for this section would be liable, whether as principal or as accessory, to be convicted of murder shall be liable instead to be convicted of manslaughter. . . ."

R. v. BYRNE
[1960] 2 Q.B. 396

The fact that the accused's powers or self control were seriously impaired is evidence that he was suffering from diminished responsibility within the meaning of s. 2 (1) of the Homicide Act 1957.

---

[1] *History of Criminal Law* Vol. 2, p. 171.
[2] Cmnd. 6244 (1975).

Byrne strangled a girl and mutilated her dead body. He was a sexual psychopath and there was evidence that he found it difficult, if not impossible, to control himself at the material time. The trial judge directed the jury that, even if this had been the case, it was insufficient to establish the plea of diminished responsibility. Byrne was convicted of murder and successfully appealed to the Court of Criminal Appeal who substituted a verdict of manslaughter, but did not alter the sentence of imprisonment for life.

Extract from the Judgment of the Court of Criminal Appeal

Lord Parker, C.J.—

" 'Abnormality of mind', which has to be contrasted with the time-honoured expression in the M'Naghten rules 'defect of reason', means a state of mind so different from that of ordinary human beings that the reasonable man would term it abnormal. It appears to us to be wide enough to cover the mind's activities in all its aspects, not only the perception of physical acts and matters, and the ability to form a rational judgment as to whether an act is right or wrong, but also the ability to exercise will power to control physical acts in accordance with that rational judgment. The expression 'mental responsibility for his acts' points to a consideration of the extent to which the accused's mind is answerable for his physical acts which must include a consideration of the extent of his ability to exercise will power to control his physical acts.

Whether the accused was at the time of the killing suffering from any 'abnormality of mind' in the broad sense which we have indicated above is a question for the jury. On this question medical evidence is no doubt of importance, but the jury are entitled to take into consideration all the evidence, including the acts or statements of the accused and his demeanour. They are not bound to accept the medical evidence if there is other material before them which, in their good judgment, conflicts with it and outweighs it.

The aetiology of the abnormality of mind (namely, whether it arose from a condition of arrested or retarded development of mind or any inherent causes, or was induced by disease or injury) does, however, seem to be a matter to be determined on expert evidence.

Assuming that the jury are satisfied on the balance of probabilities that the accused was suffering from 'abnorm-

ality of mind' from one of the causes specified in the parenthesis of the subsection, the crucial question nevertheless
arises: was the abnormality such as substantially impaired
his mental responsibility for his acts in doing or being a
party to the killing? This is a question of degree and essentially one for the jury. Medical evidence is, of course,
relevant, but the question involves a decision not merely
as to whether there was some impairment of the mental
responsibility of the accused for his acts but whether such
impairment can properly be called 'substantial', a matter
upon which juries may quite legitimately differ from doctors.

Furthermore, in a case where the abnormality of mind
is one which affects the accused's self control the step between
'he did not resist his impulse' and 'he could not resist his
impulse' is, as the evidence in this case shows, one which is
incapable of scientific proof. *A fortiori* there is no scientific
measurement of the degree of difficulty which an abnormal
person finds in controlling his impulses. These problems
which in the present state of medical knowledge are scientific-
ally insoluble, the jury can only approach in a broad,
common-sense way. This court has repeatedly approved
directions to the jury which have followed directions given
in Scots cases where the doctrine of diminished responsibility
forms part of the common law. We need not repeat them.
They are quoted in *R.* v. *Spriggs.*[1] They indicate that such
abnormality as 'substantially impairs his mental responsibility' involves a mental state which in popular language
(not that of the M'Naghten rules) a jury would regard as
amounting to partial insanity or being on the border-line
of insanity.

It appears to us that the judge's direction to the jury
that the defence under section 2 of the Act was not available
even though they found the facts set out in Nos. 2 and 3 of
the judge's summary,[2] amounted to a direction that difficulty
or even inability of an accused person to exercise will power
to control his physical acts could not amount to such abnormality of mind as substantially impairs his mental
responsibility. For the reasons which we have already
expressed we think that this construction of the Act is wrong.
Inability to exercise will power to control physical acts,

---

[1] [1958] 1 All E.R. 300. See comment on p. 89, *infra*.
[2] These were that Byrne found it difficult or impossible to resist
putting his perverted desires into practice and that the act of killing was
done under such an impulse or urge.

provided that it is due to abnormality of mind from one of the causes specified in the parenthesis in the subsection is, in our view, sufficient to entitle the accused to the benefit of the section; difficulty in controlling his physical acts depending on the degree of difficulty, may be. It is for the jury to decide on the whole of the evidence whether such inability or difficulty has, not as a matter of scientific certainty but on the balance of probabilities, been established, and in the case of difficulty whether the difficulty is so great as to amount in their view to a substantial impairment of the accused's mental responsibility for his acts. The direction in the present case thus withdrew from the jury the essential determination of fact which it was their province to decide."

APPEAL ALLOWED.

Comment on R. v. Byrne

The Scots cases mentioned in the judgment of Lord Goddard, C.J., in *Spriggs* were *H.M. Advocate* v. *Braithwaite*,[1] *H.M. Advocate* v. *Savage*[2] and *Muir* v. *H.M. Advocate*.[3] The following is an extract from the charge to the jury by Lord Cooper, Lord Justice-Clerk in *H. M. Advocate* v. *Braithwaite*:

"Now I have got to give you the most accurate instruction I can in this delicate question. The Solicitor-General read to you a passage from the charge of the Lord Justice-Clerk in the case of *H.M. Advocate* v. *Savage*,[2] and I am going to read a sentence or two again, because it seems to me to give as explicit and clear a statement of the sort of thing which you have to look for as I can find. He says; 'It is very difficult to put it in a phrase' and I respectfully agree, 'but it has been put in this way; that there must be aberration or weakness of mind; that there must be some form of mental unsoundness; there must be a state of mind which is bordering on, though not amounting to, insanity; that there must be a mind so affected that responsibility is diminished from full responsibility to partial responsibility—in other words, the prisoner in question must be only partially accountable for his actions.' And then he adds: 'And I think one can see running through the cases that there is implied . . . that there must be some form of mental disease'. The matter has been put in different words by other judges. I notice in a later case[3] that the condition was referred to for short as 'partial insanity'; and that this was explained as meaning 'that weakness or great peculiarity

---

[1] 1945 J.C. 55.
[2] 1923 J.C. 49, at p. 51.
[3] 1933 J.C. 46, at p. 49.

of mind which the law has recognised as possibly differentiating a case of murder from one of culpable homicide.'[1] And finally to give you one last test, the question as put by the late Lord Clyde in the same case, quoting from a charge to a jury by Lord Moncrieff, was stated thus (1933 J.C. 46, at p. 48): 'Was he, owing to his mental state, of such inferior responsibility that his act should have attributed to it the quality not of murder but of culpable homicide?' You will see, ladies and gentlemen, the stress that has been laid in all these formulations upon weakness of intellect, aberration of mind, mental unsoundness, partial insanity, great peculiarity of mind, and the like. I am emphasising that just now because I shall have to refer to it when I come to say a word about the evidence we have heard today from Dr. Harrowes; but meantime, with those passages in your mind, I can only say to you that this is the sort of thing you have got to look for in the evidence in support of this defence. If you can find enough to justify such a conclusion, your verdict should be one of culpable homicide only. If on the other hand you cannot find enough in the evidence to justify such a conclusion then I have to tell you that so far as this issue is concerned, you must steel yourselves to do your full duty by returning a verdict of guilty of murder."

On the question of the propriety of directing juries to consider whether someone pleading diminished responsibility was, at at the material time, on the border-line of insanity, the following statement by Lord Tucker in the Privy Council in *Rose* v. *R.*,[2] should be borne in mind:

"There may be cases in which the abnormality of mind relied on cannot readily be related to any of the generally recognised types of insanity. If, however, insanity is to be taken into consideration, as undoubtedly will usually be the case, the word must be used in its broad, popular sense. It cannot too often be emphasised that there is no formula that can be safely used in every case—the direction to the jury must always be related to the particular evidence that has been given, and there may be cases where the words 'border-line' and 'insanity' may not be helpful."

The Butler Committee on Mentally Abnormal Offenders[3] has made a number of proposals for the reform of the defence of diminished responsibility. These proposals are summarised in Cross and Jones, *Introduction to Criminal Law*, 8th ed., para. 5.20.

---

[1] The Scots equivalent to manslaughter.
[2] [1961] A.C. 496, at pp. 507, 508; [1961] 1 All E.R. 859, at pp. 863–864.
[3] Cmnd. 6244 (1975).

Automatism

R. v. KEMP
[1956] 3 All E.R. 249

Automatism is a defence to a criminal charge, but if the automatism of a person tried on indictment was due to a disease of the mind the special verdict of not guilty by reason of insanity must be returned.

See p. 78, *supra.*

BRATTY v. ATTORNEY-GENERAL FOR NORTHERN IRELAND
[1961] 3 All E.R. 523

(1) *Where the only cause alleged for an involuntary act is a defect of reason due to disease of the mind the judge need not direct the jury on the issue of automatism in addition to that of insanity.* (2) *The burden of disproving automatism which is not due to insanity is borne by the prosecution.*

Bratty was charged with the murder of a girl. It was not disputed that he had strangled her, but he said that a feeling of blackness came over him when he was with the girl and there was some evidence that he was suffering from psychomotor epilepsy. Bratty's counsel asked, *inter alia*, for an acquittal on the ground of automatism or a verdict of "guilty but insane". The trial judge directed the jury fully on the issue of insanity, but he did not say that, even if the jury should conclude that Bratty was not insane within the meaning of the M'Naghten rules, they might yet return a verdict of "not guilty" on the ground of automatism due to some cause other than insanity. Bratty was convicted and he unsuccessfully appealed first to the Northern Irish Court of Criminal Appeal and thence to the House of Lords.

Extracts from the Speeches of the House of Lords

Lord Denning.—

"My Lords, in *Woolmington* v. *Director of Public Prosecutions*[1] Viscount Sankey, L.C., said: 'When dealing

---

[1] [1935] A.C. 462; [1935] All E.R. Rep. 1; p. 16, *supra.*

with a murder case the Crown must prove (a) death as the result of a voluntary act of the accused and (b) malice of the accused.' The requirement that it should be a voluntary act is essential, not only in a murder case, but also in every criminal case. No act is punishable if it is done involuntarily: and an involuntary act in this context—some people nowadays prefer to speak of it as 'automatism'—means an act which is done by the muscles without any control by the mind such as a spasm, a reflex action or a convulsion; or an act done by a person who is not conscious of what he is doing such as an act done whilst suffering from concussion or whilst sleepwalking. The point was well put by Stephen, J., in 1889: ' . . . can anyone doubt that a man who, though he might be perfectly sane, committed what would otherwise be a crime in a state of somnambulism, would be entitled to be acquitted? And why is this? Simply because he would not know what he was doing'; see *R.* v. *Tolson.*[1] The term 'involuntary act' is, however, capable of wider connotations: and to prevent confusion it is to be observed that in the criminal law an act is not to be regarded as an involuntary act simply because the doer does not remember it. When a man is charged with dangerous driving, it is no defence for him to say 'I don't know what happened. I cannot remember a thing': see *Hill* v. *Baxter.*[2] Loss of memory afterwards is never a defence in itself, so long as he was conscious at the time; see *Russell* v. *H.M. Advocate*;[3] *R.* v. *Podola.*[4] Nor is an act to be regarded as an involuntary act simply because the doer could not control his impulse to do it. When a man is charged with murder, and it appears that he knew what he was doing, but that he could not resist it, then his assertion 'I couldn't help myself' is no defence in itself: see *A.-G. for South Australia* v. *Brown*:[5] though it may go towards a defence of diminished responsibility, in places where that defence is available, see *R.* v. *Byrne*;[6] but it does not render his act involuntary so as to entitle him to an unqualified acquittal. Nor is an act to be regarded as an involuntary act simply because it is unintentional or its consequences are unforeseen. When a man is charged with dangerous driving,

---

[1] (1889), 23 Q.B.D. 168, at p. 187.
[2] [1958] 1 Q.B. 277; [1958] 1 All E.R. 193.
[3] 1946 J.C. 37.
[4] [1960] 1 Q.B. 325; [1959] 3 All E.R. 418.
[5] [1960] A.C. 432; [1960] 1 All E.R. 734; p. 82, *supra.*
[6] [1960] 2 Q.B. 396; [1960] 3 All E.R. 1; p. 86, *supra.*

it is no defence for him to say, however truly, 'I did not mean to drive dangerously'. There is said to be an absolute prohibition against that offence, whether he had a guilty mind or not (see *Hill* v. *Baxter*[1] *per* Lord Goddard, C.J.) but even though it is absolutely prohibited, nevertheless he has a defence if he can show that it was an involuntary act in the sense that he was unconscious at the time and did not know what he was doing (see *H.M. Advocate* v. *Ritchie*,[2] *R.* v. *Minor*[3] and *Cooper* v. *McKenna, Ex parte Cooper*[4]).

Another thing to be observed is that it is not every involuntary act which leads to a complete acquittal. Take first an involuntrary act which proceeds from a state of drunkenness. If the drunken man is so drunk that he does not know what he is doing, he has a defence to any charge, such as murder or wounding with intent, in which a specific intent is essential, but he is still liable to be convicted of manslaughter or unlawful wounding for which no specific intent is necessary; see *Beard's* case.[5] Again, if the involuntary act proceeds from a disease of the mind, it gives rise to a defence of insanity, but not to a defence of automatism. Suppose a crime is committed by a man in a state of automatism or clouded consciousness due to a recurrent disease of the mind. Such an act is no doubt involuntary, but it does not give rise to an unqualified acquittal, for that would mean that he would be let at large to do it again. The only proper verdict is one which ensures that the person who suffers from the disease is kept secure in a hospital so as not to be a danger to himself or others. That is, a verdict of guilty but insane ...

. . . The major mental diseases, which the doctors call psychoses, such as schizophrenia, are clearly diseases of the mind. But in *R.* v. *Charlson*,[6] Barry, J., seems to have assumed that other diseases such as epilepsy or cerebral tumour are not diseases of the mind, even when they are such as to manifest themselves in violence. I do not agree with this. It seems to me that any mental disorder which has manifested itself in violence and is prone to recur is a disease of the mind.

---

[1] [1958] 1 Q.B. 277, at p. 282; [1958] 1 All E.R. 193, at p. 195. It is now established that the offence of dangerous driving is not absolute, see *Gosney*, p. 57, *supra*.

[2] 1926 J.C. 45.

[3] (1955), 15 W.W.R. (N.S.) 433.

[4] [1960] Qd. R. 406.

[5] *Director of Public Prosecutions* v. *Beard*, [1920] A.C. 479, at pp. 494, 498, 504; [1920] All E.R. Rep. 21, at pp. 25, 27, 30; p. 101, *infra*.

[6] [1955] 1 All E.R. 859.

At any rate it is the sort of disease for which a person should be detained in hospital rather than be given an unqualified acquittal.[1]

It is to be noticed that in *R.* v. *Charlson* and *R.* v. *Kemp*[2] the defence raised only automatism, not insanity.

In the present case the defence raised both automatism and insanity. And herein lies the difficulty because of the burden of proof. If the accused says he did not know what he was doing, then, so far as the defence of automatism is concerned, the Crown must prove that the act was a voluntary act; see *Woolmington's* case.[3] But so far as the defence of insanity is concerned, the defence must prove that the act was an involuntary act due to disease of the mind; see *M'Naghten's* case.[4] This apparent incongruity was noticed by Sir Owen Dixon, Chief Justice of the High Court of Australia, in an address which is to be found in 31 *Australian Law Journal* 255 and it needs to be resolved. The defence here say: Even though we have not proved that the act was involuntary, yet the Crown have not proved that it was a voluntary act: and that point at least should have been put to the jury.

My Lords, I think that the difficulty is to be resolved by remembering that, whilst the *ultimate* burden rests on the Crown of proving every element essential in the crime, nevertheless in order to prove that the act was a voluntary act, the Crown is entitled to rely on the *presumption* that every man has sufficient mental capacity to be responsible for his crimes: and that if the defence wish to displace that presumption they must give some evidence from which the contrary may reasonably be inferred. . . .

All the doctors agreed that psychomotor epilepsy, if it exists, is a defect of reason due to disease of the mind: and the judge accepted this view. No other cause was canvassed.

In those circumstances, I am clearly of opinion that, if the act of the appellant was an involuntary act, as the defence suggested, the evidence attributed it solely to a disease of the mind and the only defence open was the defence of insanity. There was no evidence of automatism apart from insanity. There was, therefore, no need for the judge to put it to the jury. And when the jury rejected the defence of

---

[1] But see *Quick and Paddison*, p. 95, *infra*.
[2] [1957] 1 Q.B. 399; [1956] 3 All E.R. 249.
[3] [1935] A.C. 462, at p. 482; [1935] All E.R. Rep. 1, at p. 8; p. 16, *supra*.
[4] (1843), 10 Cl. & Fin. 200, at p. 210; p. 74, *supra*.

insanity, they rejected the only defence disclosed by the evidence."

APPEAL DISMISSED.

R. v. QUICK AND PADDISON
[1973] 3 All E.R. 347

An overdose of insulin leading to hypoglycaemia is not a malfunctioning of the mind due to disease and the accused in such a case is entitled to have his defence of non-insane automatism left to the jury: but the defence of non-insane automatism will not succeed if his automatic state was foreseen, or, perhaps, reasonably foreseeable, by the accused and could have been avoided by him.

Quick was a nurse at a mental hospital. He assaulted a patient and was charged with assault occasioning actual bodily harm. At his trial Quick pleaded not guilty and adduced medical evidence that he was a diabetic and that at the time in question he was suffering from hypoglycaemia, i.e. an abnormally low amount of sugar in his blood, and was unaware of what he was doing. Bridge, J., ruled that the defence raised was one of insanity not automatism. In the light of that ruling Quick pleaded guilty. Another nurse, Paddison, was convicted by the jury of assault occasioning actual bodily harm on the basis that he had aided and abetted Quick. Quick appealed successfully against conviction, and in consequence the Court of Appeal allowed Paddison's appeal also.

Extracts from the Judgment of the Court of Appeal

Lawton, L.J.—

"In its broadest aspects these appeals raise the question what is meant by the phrase 'a defect of reason from disease of the mind' within the meaning of the M'Naghten Rules.[1] More particularly the question is whether a person who commits a criminal act whilst under the influence of hypoglycaemia can raise a defence of automatism, as the appellants submitted was possible, or whether such a person must

---

[1] (1843), 10 Cl. & Fin. 200; p. 74, *supra*.

rely on a defence of insanity if he wishes to relieve himself of responsibility for his acts, as Bridge, J., ruled.

Our examination of such authorities as there are must start with *Bratty* v. *A.-G. for Northern Ireland.*[1] . . . All their Lordships based their speeches on the basis that such medical evidence as there was pointed to Bratty suffering from a 'defect of reason from disease of the mind' and nothing else. Lord Denning discussed in general terms what constituted a disease of the mind, when he said:[2]

> 'The major mental diseases, which the doctors call psychoses, such as schizophrenia, are clearly diseases of the mind. But in *R.* v. *Charlson*[3], Barry, J., seems to have assumed that other diseases such as epilepsy or cerebral tumour are not diseases of the mind, even when they are such as to manifest themselves in violence. I do not agree with this. It seems to me that any mental disorder which has manifested itself in violence and is prone to recur is a disease of the mind. At any rate it is the sort of disease for which a person should be detained in hospital rather than be given an unqualified acquittal.'

If this opinion is right and there are no restricting qualifications which ought to be applied to it, Quick was setting up a defence of insanity. He may have been at the material time in a condition of mental disorder manifesting itself in violence. Such manifestations had occurred before and might recur. The difficulty arises as soon as the question is asked whether he should be detained in a mental hospital? No mental hospital would admit a diabetic merely because he had a low blood sugar reaction; and common sense is affronted by the prospect of a diabetic being sent to such a hospital when in most cases the disordered mental condition can be rectified quickly by pushing a lump of sugar or a teaspoonful of glucose into the patient's mouth.

The 'affront to common sense' argument, however, has its own inherent weakness, as counsel for the Crown pointed out. If an accused is shown to have done a criminal act whilst suffering from a 'defect of reason from disease of the mind', it matters not 'whether the disease is curable or incurable . . . temporary or permanent' (see *R.* v. *Kemp*[4], per Devlin, J.). If the condition is temporary, the Secretary

---

[1] [1963] A.C. 386; [1961] 3 All E.R. 523; p. 91, *supra*.
[2] [1963] A.C., at p. 412; [1961] 3 All E.R., at p. 534.
[3] [1955] 1 All E.R. 859.
[4] [1957] 1 Q.B. 399, at p. 407; [1956] 3 All E.R. 249, at p. 253.

of State may have a difficult problem of disposal; but what happens to those found not guilty by reason of insanity is not a matter for the courts.

In *R.* v. *Kemp*[1], where the violent act was alleged to have been done during a period of unconsciousness arising from arteriosclerosis, counsel for the accused submitted that his client had done what he had during a period of mental confusion arising from a physical, not a mental, disease. Devlin, J., rejected this argument saying[2]:

'It does not matter, for the purposes of the law, whether the defect of reasoning is due to a degeneration of the brain or to some other form of mental derangement. That may be a matter of importance medically, but it is of no importance to the law, which merely has to consider the state of mind in which the accused is, not how he got there.'

Applied without qualification of any kind, Devlin, J's, statement of the law would have some surprising consequences. Take the not uncommon case of the rugby player who gets a kick on the head early in the game and plays on to the end in a state of automatism. If, whilst he was in that state, he assaulted the referee it is difficult to envisage any court adjudging that he was not guilty by reason of insanity.

In *Hill* v. *Baxter*[3] . . . Lord Goddard, C.J., referred to some observations of Humphreys, J., in *Kay* v. *Butterworth*[4] which seemed to indicate that a man who became unconscious whilst driving due to the onset of a sudden illness should not be made liable at criminal law and went on as follows[5]:

'I agree that there may be cases when the circumstances are such that the accused could not really be said to be driving at all. Suppose he had a stroke or an epileptic fit, both instances of what may properly be called Acts of God; he might well be in the driver's seat even with his hands on the wheel but in such a state of unconsciousness that he could not be said to be driving . . .'

Lord Goddard, C.J., did not equate unconsciousness due to a sudden illness, which must entail the malfunctioning of

---

[1] [1957] 1 Q.B. 399; [1956] 3 All E.R. 249; p. 78, *supra*.
[2] [1957] 1 Q.B., at p. 407; [1956] 3 All E.R., at p. 253.
[3] [1958] 1 Q.B. 277; [1958] 1 All E.R. 193.
[4] (1945), 173 L.T. 191.
[5] [1958] 1 Q.B., at p. 282; [1958] 1 All E.R., at p. 195.

the mental processes of the sufferer, with disease of the mind and in our judgment no one outside a court of law would. Devlin, J., in his judgment accepted that some temporary loss of consciousness arising *accidentally* (the italics are ours) did not call for a verdict based on insanity. It is not clear what he meant by 'accidentally'. The context suggests that he may have meant 'unexpectedly' as can happen with some kinds of virus infections. He went on as follows:[1]

> 'If, however, disease is present the same thing may happen again and therefore since 1800 the law has provided that persons acquitted on this ground should be subject to restraint.'

If this be right anyone suffering from a tooth abscess who knows from past experience that he reacts violently to anaesthetics because of some constitutional bodily disorder which can be attributed to disease might have to go on suffering or take the risk of being found insane unless he could find a dentist who would be prepared to take the risk of being kicked by a recovering patient. It seems to us that the law should not give the words 'defect of reason from disease of the mind' a meaning which would be regarded with incredulity outside a court.

The last of the English authorities is *Watmore v. Jenkins.* . . .[2] In the course of the argument in that case counsel for the accused is reported[3] as having submitted, on the basis of how Lord Murray had directed the jury in *H.M. Advocate v. Ritchie*:[4]

> 'Automatism is a defence to a charge of dangerous driving provided that a person takes reasonable steps to prevent himself from acting involuntarily in a manner dangerous to the public. It must be caused by some factor which he could not reasonably foresee and not by a self-induced incapacity. . . .'

Subject to the problem of whether the conduct said to have been done in a state of automatism was caused by a disease of the mind, we agree with this submission. . . .

The first of the Commonwealth cases in date was *R. v. Cottle*[5] which was a decision of the New Zealand Court of

---

[1] [1958] 1 Q.B., at p. 285;   [1958] 1 All E.R., at p. 197.
[2] [1962] 2 Q.B. 572; [1962] 2 All E.R. 868.
[3] [1962] 2 Q.B., at p. 580.
[4] 1926 J.C. 45.
[5] [1958] N.Z.L.R. 999.

Appeal. . . . The importance of this case is that all the
members of the court seem to have accepted that not all
malfunctioning of the mind should be considered to arise
from a disease of the mind. Gresson, P., said[1]:

'Automatism, that is action without conscious volition,
may or may not be due to or associated with "disease of
the mind"—a term which defies precise definition and
which can comprehend mental derangement in the widest
sense whether due to some condition of the brain itself and
so to have its origin within the brain, or whether due to
the effect upon the brain of something outside the brain,
e.g. arterio sclerosis. The adverse effect upon the mind
of some happening, e.g. a blow, hypnotism, absorption of
a narcotic, or extreme intoxication all producing an effect
more or less transitory cannot fairly be regarded as amounting to or as producing "disease of the mind".'

Cleary, J., said much the same. North, J., accepted
that a sleepwalker who committed a criminal act could not
be said to have done so whilst insane. In expressing this
view he adopted the opinion which Stephen, J., gave in *R. v.
Tolson.* . . .[2]

There has, however, been a decision in Victoria about
the criminal responsibility of a woman alleged to have been
suffering from concussion when she did the criminal acts
alleged against her. . .: see *R. v. Carter*[3]. . . . Sholl, J., . . .
stated that he was not satisfied that the mental condition
associated with concussion did amount to a defect of reason
and that even if it did, it could not be said to have arisen
from a disease of the mind. He said:[4]

'The term "disease" in the *M'Naghten* (sic) formula
is not used, I think, with reference to a temporarily
inefficient working of the mind due only to such outside
agencies as alcohol or drugs or applied violence producing
trauma, . . .'

In this quagmire of law seldom entered nowadays save
by those in desperate need of some kind of a defence,
Bratty v. A.-G. for Northern Ireland[5] provides the only firm
ground. Is there any discernible path? We think there is—
judges should follow in a common sense way their sense of

[1] *Ibid.*, at p. 1011.
[2] (1889) 23 Q.B.D. 168, at p. 187; [1886–90] All E.R. Rep. 26, at p. 37.
[3] [1959] V.R. 105.
[4] *Ibid.*, at p. 110.
[5] [1963] A.C. 386; [1961] 3 All E.R. 523.

fairness. This seems to have been the approach of the New Zealand Court of Appeal in *R. v. Cottle*[1] and of Sholl, J., in *R. v. Carter*[2]. In our judgment no help can be obtained by speculating (because that is what we would have to do) as to what the judges who answered the House of Lords' questions in 1843[3] meant by disease of the mind. . . . Our task has been to decide what the law means now by the words 'disease of the mind'. In our judgment the fundamental concept is of a malfunctioning of the mind caused by disease. A malfunctioning of the mind of transitory effect caused by the application to the body of some external factor such as violence, drugs, including anaesthetics, alcohol and hypnotic influences cannot fairly be said to be due to disease. Such malfunctioning, unlike that caused by a defect of reason from disease of the mind, will not always relieve an accused from criminal responsibility. A self-induced incapacity will not excuse (see *R. v. Lipman*[4]) nor will one which could have been reasonably foreseen as a result of either doing, or omitting to do something, as, for example taking alcohol against medical advice after using certain prescribed drugs, or failing to have regular meals whilst taking insulin. From time to time difficult borderline cases are likely to arise. When they do, the test suggested by the New Zealand Court of Appeal in *R. v. Cottle*[5] is likely to give the correct result, viz. can this mental condition be fairly regarded as amounting to or producing a defect of reason from disease of the mind?

In this case Quick's alleged mental condition, if it ever existed, was not caused by his diabetes but by his use of the insulin prescribed by his doctor. Such malfunctioning of his mind as there was, was caused by an external factor and not by a bodily disorder in the nature of a disease which disturbed the working of his mind. It follows in our judgment that Quick was entitled to have his defence of automatism left to the jury and that Bridge, J's, ruling as to the effect of the medical evidence called by him was wrong. Had the defence of automatism been left to the jury, a number of questions of fact would have had to be answered. If he was in a confused mental condition, was it due to a hypoglycaemic episode or to too much alcohol? If the former, to what extent had he

---

[1] [1958] N.Z.L.R. 999.
[2] [1959] V.R. 105.
[3] *M'Naghten's Case* (1843), 10 Cl. E Fin. 200.
[4] [1970] 1 Q.B. 152; [1969] 3 All E.R. 410; p. 105, *infra*.
[5] [1958] N.Z.L.R. 999.

brought about his condition by not following his doctor's instructions about taking regular meals? Did he know that he was getting into a hypoglycaemic episode? If Yes, why did he not use the antidote of eating a lump of sugar as he had been advised to do? On the evidence which was before the jury Quick might have had difficulty in answering these questions in a manner which would have relieved him from responsibility for his acts. We cannot say, however, with the requisite degree of confidence, that the jury would have convicted him. It follows that his conviction must be quashed on the ground that the verdict was unsatisfactory."

APPEAL ALLOWED.

Intoxication

DIRECTOR OF PUBLIC PROSECUTIONS v. BEARD

[1920] A.C. 479

It is no defence that, through self-induced intoxication, the accused more readily gave way to some violent passion or did not know that he was doing wrong, but (a) where a disease of the mind within the meaning of the M'Naghten rules has been produced by alcoholic excess, and the other elements of the defence of insanity are proved, an accused has the defence of insanity to a criminal charge; and (b) the accused has a defence if, through self-induced intoxication, he lacked the specific intent[1] essential to constitute the offence charged.

Beard was charged with the murder of a girl of thirteen. He ravished her, and, in furtherance of the rape, he placed his hand over her mouth and his thumb upon her throat, in consequence of which she was suffocated. His defence was that he was drunk.

At the trial before Bailhache, J., the jury were directed, *inter alia*, that they must consider whether the accused knew that he was doing wrong. Beard was convicted of murder, and appealed to the Court of Criminal Appeal.

The Court of Criminal Appeal substituted a verdict of manslaughter on the ground that, on the authority of *R. v.*

---

[1] The meaning of "specific intent" in this context is discussed at p. 115–117, *infra*.

Meade,[1] the jury should have been asked whether the accused knew that what he did was dangerous.

The prosecution appealed to the House of Lords who allowed the appeal on the ground that since Beard had killed the girl in the course or furtherance of the rape, a felony of violence, he was guilty of murder on the basis of constructive malice aforethought (a doctrine which was subsequently abolished by s. 1 of the Homicide Act 1957),[2] there being no doubt that Beard had the intent to commit that felony.

Extracts from the Speeches of the House of Lords

Lord Birkenhead, L.C.—

"Under the law of England as it prevailed until early in the nineteenth century voluntary drunkenness was never an excuse for criminal misconduct; and indeed the classic authorities broadly assert that voluntary drunkenness must be considered rather an aggravation than a defence. . . .

Judicial decisions extending over a period of nearly one hundred years make it plain that the rigidity of this rule was gradually relaxed in the nineteenth century, though this mitigation cannot for a long time be affiliated upon a single or very intelligible principle. . . .

The conclusions to be drawn from these cases may be stated under three heads:—

1. That insanity, whether produced by drunkenness or otherwise, is a defence to the crime charged. The distinction between the defence of insanity in the true sense caused by excessive drinking, and the defence of drunkenness which produces a condition such that the drunken man's mind becomes incapable of forming a specific intention, has been preserved throughout the cases. The insane person cannot be convicted of a crime: *Felstead* v. *R.;*[3] but, upon a verdict of insanity, is ordered to be detained during His Majesty's pleasure. The law takes no note of the cause of the insanity. If actual insanity in fact supervenes, as the result of alcoholic excess, it furnishes as complete an answer to a criminal charge as insanity induced by any other cause. . . .

2. That evidence of drunkenness which renders the accused incapable of forming the specific intent essential to constitute the crime should be taken into consideration with

---

[1] [1909] 1 K.B. 895.
[2] See p. 189, *infra.*
[3] [1914] A.C. 534.

the other facts proved in order to determine whether or not he had this intent.[1]

3. That evidence of drunkenness falling short of a proved incapacity in the accused to form the intent necessary to constitute the crime, and merely establishing that his mind was affected by drink so that he more readily gave way to some violent passion, does not rebut the presumption that a man intends the natural consequences of his acts. . . .[2]

I do not think that the proposition of law deduced from these earlier cases is an exceptional rule applicable only to cases in which it is necessary to prove a specific intent in order to constitute the graver crime—e.g., wounding with intent to do grievous bodily harm. . . . It is true that in such cases the specific intent must be proved to constitute the particular crime, but this is, on ultimate analysis, only in accordance with the ordinary law applicable to crime, for, speaking generally (and apart from certain special offences), a person cannot be convicted of a crime unless the *mens* was *rea*. Drunkenness rendering a person incapable of the intent would be an answer, as it is for example in a charge of attempted suicide. In *R. v. Moore*[3] drunkenness was held to negative the intent in such a case, and Jervis, C.J., said: 'If the prisoner was so drunk as not to know what she was about, how can you say that she intended to destroy herself?'

My Lords, drunkenness in this case could be no defence unless it could be established that Beard at the time of committing the rape was so drunk that he was incapable of forming the intent to commit it, which was not in fact, and manifestly, having regard to the evidence, could not be contended. For in the present case the death resulted from two acts or from a succession of acts, the rape and the act of violence causing suffocation. These acts cannot be regarded separately and independently of each other. The capacity of the mind of the prisoner to form the felonious intent which murder involves is in other words to be explored in relation to the ravishment; and not in relation merely to the violent acts which gave effect to the ravishment. . . .

---

[1] See the comment at the end of this case.

[2] Lord Birkenhead's reference to a "proved incapacity to form the intent" must be read in the light of the subsequent decision in *Woolmington's* case, p. 16, *supra*. The accused does not have the burden of proving the defence of intoxication under the second of the three heads mentioned by Lord Birkenhead in *Beard's* case (*Broadhurst*, [1964] A.C. 441; [1964] 1 All E.R. 111, P.C.), although he must adduce evidence of his intoxication at the relevant time.

[3] (1852), 3 Car. & Kir. 319.

Neither should the learned judge in my opinion have introduced the question whether 'the prisoner knew that he was doing wrong' in a defence of drunkenness, where insanity was not pleaded. It is a dangerous and confusing question to put to a jury, for a drunken man's judgment upon such a question is very likely to be impaired, and it might well be perplexing to a jury to determine whether, if he knew what he was doing, he knew also that he was doing wrong. The general proposition that drunkenness is no excuse for crime may be seriously affected in its operation if such a question is to be a test by which the jury may determine whether the verdict should be murder or manslaughter. It is noteworthy that, notwithstanding that the judges ever since *M'Naghten's Case*[1] in 1843 have had these questions in mind as the test of insanity, there is no single case, known to me, where drunkenness has been the defence, in which the judge has directed the jury to consider whether the prisoner knew that he was doing wrong. Whenever this question has been put the defence has been that there existed insanity caused by drink. I look upon the direction of Bailhache, J., as an innovation which is not supported by authority and which should not be repeated or imitated. But while I think that the summing up was in some respects unhappily conceived, I am not prepared, reading it as a whole, to hold in this case that it amounted to, or should be treated as, a misdirection. The defence which is founded upon insanity is one one thing. The defence which is founded upon drunkenness is another. The relevant considerations are not identical. It is inconvenient to use the same language in charging juries in relation to different defences. But the portions of the summing up which I have criticised were in fact unduly favourable to the prisoner. He cannot complain of them unless they so confused the jury as to prevent them from properly appreciating the true issue, and I am not prepared to lay it down—though I have felt some doubt upon the point—that the actual direction given to the jury by Bailhache, J., disabled them from reaching a true conclusion upon the matters which required decision. . . ."

APPEAL ALLOWED.

Comment on Director of Public Prosecutions v. Beard

Lord Birkenhead's second proposition in *Beard's* case, that evidence of drunkenness which renders the accused incapable of

---

[1] (1843), 10 Cl. & Fin. 200; p. 74, *supra*.

forming the specific intent essential to constitute the offence
charged should be taken into account along with all the other
facts "proved" in order to determine whether he had that intent,
has been amended to some extent by s. 8 of the Criminal Justice
Act 1967.[1] Under that section a person is not to be presumed to
intend the natural and probable consequences of his act; instead
the question whether the accused had the necessary intent is to
be decided by the jury or magistrates on all the evidence. Thus,
a jury in deciding whether an accused, who pleads intoxication as
a defence to an offence requiring a specific intent, had the necessary intent must take into account all the evidence. The strongest
evidence, of course, is that the accused was too intoxicated to be
capable of forming the specific intent, but it is enough if, on all
the evidence, the jury find that while the accused's intoxication
was not such as to make him incapable of forming the specific
intent, i.e. he could have intended, he did not in fact have that
intent. One authority for this amendment is *Pordage*[2], where the
accused pleaded drunkenness on a charge of wounding with intent
to do grievous bodily harm. The trial judge directed the jury to
consider the accused's capacity to form the necessary specific
intent. The Court of Appeal held that this was wrong; the judge
should have told the jury to take the evidence of drunkenness
into account in deciding whether the accused did have the specific
intent to do grievous bodily harm.

As will be seen, in *Director of Public Prosecutions* v. *Majewski*
(p. 115–118, *infra*) the House of Lords rejected the contention that
s. 8 of the Criminal Justice Act had had an even more fundamental
effect on the defence of intoxication.

R. v. LIPMAN
[1970] 1 Q.B. 152

(1) *For the purposes of criminal responsibility there is no
distinction between the effect of drink voluntarily taken and of
drugs voluntarily consumed.* (2) *The fact that the accused was
unaware of what he was doing owing to the influence of drugs
voluntarily consumed is no defence to a charge of involuntary
manslaughter by means of an unlawful act.*

Lipman was charged with the murder of a girl. It was
not disputed that he had gone with her to her room, and that

---

[1] P. 19, *supra*.
[2] [1975] Crim. L.R. 575.

she had met her death in consequence of severe blows over the head and of asphyxia due to having had about eight inches of sheet thrust into her mouth. Lipman's defence was that he and the girl had gone together on a 'trip' involving the consumption of LSD and that, in the course of that trip, he had the illusion that he had got to the centre of the earth where he was attacked by snakes.

As to manslaughter, the trial judge directed the jury to consider whether (1) the accused must have realised, before he took the LSD, that the acts subsequently performed by him were dangerous; (2) the accused was aware that the consumption of the LSD involved the risk of harm to others; and (3) the accused was grossly negligent and reckless in taking the LSD. The jury returned a verdict of manslaughter under heads (1) and (3).

Lipman unsuccessfully appealed to the Court of Appeal.

Extracts from the Judgment of the Court of Appeal

Widgery, L.J.—

"For the purposes of criminal responsibility we see no reason to distinguish between the effect of drugs voluntarily taken and drunkenness voluntarily induced. As to the latter there is a great deal of authority. . . .

We can dispose of the present application by reiterating that when the killing results from an unlawful act of the prisoner no specific intent has to be proved to convict of manslaughter, and self-induced intoxication is accordingly no defence. Since in the present case the acts complained of were obviously likely to cause harm to the victim (and did, in fact, kill her) no acquittal was possible and the verdict of manslaughter, at the least, was inevitable. . . .

APPEAL DISMISSED.

DIRECTOR OF PUBLIC PROSECUTIONS v. MAJEWSKI
[1976] 2 All E.R. 142

It is a rule of substantive law that unless the offence charged requires proof of a specific intent it is no defence that, through self-induced intoxication, the accused lacked the mens rea normally required for that offence or was in a state of automatism at the material time. This rule of substantive law has not been abrogated by s. 8 of the Criminal Justice Act 1967.

A disturbance occurred in a public house and Majewski was ordered to leave by the landlord. He refused and butted the landlord in the face and punched a customer. Majewski was ejected from the bar but re-entered. He punched the landlord and started swinging a piece of broken glass at the landlord and a customer, cutting the landlord's arm. The landlord managed to restrain Majewski until the police arrived whereupon a fierce struggle took place to get him into a police car, during which Majewski kicked three police officers. Later he struck a police inspector who entered his police cell.

Majewski was charged on four counts of assault occasioning actual bodily harm and three counts of assaulting a police constable in the execution of his duty. His case was that at the material time he was acting under the influence of a combination of drugs (not medically prescribed) and alcohol, to such an extent that he did not know what he was doing. After medical evidence had been called by the defence as to the effect of the drugs and drink taken by Majewski, the judge ruled that he would direct the jury that on a charge of assault the question of whether Majewski had taken drugs or drink was immaterial. The jury, having been directed that self-induced intoxication was no defence to an offence not requiring a specific intent, such as the assaults in issue, convicted Majewski on six of the seven counts.

The Court of Appeal dismissed Majewski's appeal but granted him leave to appeal to the House of Lords, certifying that the following point of law of general public importance was involved: "Whether a defendant may properly be convicted of assault notwithstanding that, by reason of his self-induced intoxication, he did not intend to do the act alleged to constitute the assault".

Extracts from the Speeches of the House of Lords

Lord Elwyn-Jones, L.C.—

". . . [T]he crux of the case for the Crown was that, illogical as the outcome may be said to be, the judges have evolved for the purpose of protecting the community a substantive rule of law that, in crimes of basic intent as distinct from crimes of specific intent, self-induced intoxication provides no defence and is irrelevant to offences of basic intent, such as assault.

The case of counsel for the appellant was that there was no such substantive rule of law and that if there was, it did violence to logic and ethics and to fundamental principles of the criminal law which had been evolved to determine when and where criminal responsibility should arise. His main propositions were as follows: (i) No man is guilty of a crime (save in relation to offences of strict liability) unless he has a guilty mind. (ii) A man who, though not insane, commits what would in ordinary circumstances be a crime when he is in such a mental state (whether it is called 'automatism' or 'pathological intoxication' or anything else) that he does not know what he is doing, lacks a guilty mind and is not criminally culpable for his actions. (iii) This is so whether the charge involves a specific (or 'ulterior') intent or one involving only a general (or 'basic') intent. (iv) The same principle applies whether the automatism was the result of causes beyond the control of the accused or was self-induced by the voluntary taking of drugs or drink. (v) Assaults being crimes involving a guilty mind, a man who in a state of automatism unlawfully assaults another must be regarded as free from blame and be entitled to acquittal. (vi) It is logically and ethically indefensible to convict such a man of assault; it also contravenes s. 8 of the Criminal Justice Act 1967. (vii) There was accordingly a fatal misdirection.

A great deal of the argument in the hearing of the appeal turned on the application to the established facts of what Cave, J., in *R. v. Tolson*[1] called 'the somewhat uncouth maxim *"actus non facit reum, nisi mens sit rea"*'. The judgment of Stephen, J., in that case has long been accepted as authoritative. . . . Stephen, J., concluded[2]:

'The principle involved appears to me, when fully considered, to amount to no more than this. The full definition of every crime contains expressly or by implication a proposition as to a state of mind. Therefore, if the mental element of any conduct alleged to be a crime is proved to have been absent in any given case, the crime so defined

---

[1] (1889), 23 Q.B.D. 168, at p. 181; [1886–90] All E.R. Rep. 26, at p. 34; p. 32, *supra*.
[2] (1889), 23 Q.B.D., at p. 187; [1886–90] All E.R. Rep., at p. 37; p. 34, *supra*.

is not committed; or, again, if a crime is fully defined nothing amounts to that crime which does not satisfy that definition.'

What then is the mental element required in our law to be established in assault? This question has been most helpfully answered in the speech of Lord Simon of Glaisdale in *Director of Public Prosecution* v. *Morgan*[1]:

'By "crimes of basic intent" I mean those crimes whose definition expresses (or, more often, implies) a *mens rea* which does not go beyond the *actus reus*. The *actus reus* generally consists of an act and some consequence. The consequence may be very closely connected with the act or more remotely connected with it; but with a crime of basic intent the *mens rea* does not extend beyond the act and its consequence, however remote, as defined in the *actus reus*. I take assault as an example of a crime of basic intent where the consequence is very closely connected with the act. The *actus reus* of assault is an act which causes another person to apprehend immediate and unlawful violence. The *mens rea* corresponds exactly. The prosecution must prove that the accused foresaw that his act would probably cause another person to have apprehension of immediate and unlawful violence or would possibly have that consequence, such being the purpose of his act, or that he was reckless whether or not his act caused such apprehension. This foresight (the term of art is "intention") or recklessness is the *mens rea* in assault. For an example of a crime of basic intent where the consequence of the act involved in the *actus reus* is less immediate, I take the crime of unlawful wounding. The act is, say, the squeezing of a trigger. A number of consequences (mechnical, chemical, ballistic and physiological) intervene before the final consequence involved in the defined *actus reus*—namely, the wounding of another person in circumstances unjustified by law. But again here the *mens rea* corresponds closely to the *actus reus*. The prosecution must prove that the accused foresaw that some physical harm would ensue to another person in circumstances unjustified by law as a probable (or possible and desired) consequence of his act, or that he was reckless whether or not such consequence ensued.'

---

[1] [1975] 2 All E.R. 347, at pp. 363, 364.

How does the factor of self-induced intoxication fit into that analysis? If a man consciously and deliberately takes alcohol and drugs not on medical prescription, but in order to escape from reality, to go 'on a trip', to become hallucinated, whatever the description may be, and thereby disables himself from taking the care he might otherwise take and as a result by his subsequent actions causes injury to another—does our criminal law enable him to say that because he did not know what he was doing he lacked both intention and recklessness and is accordingly entitled to an acquittal? . . .

There are . . . decisions of eminent judges in a number of Commonwealth cases in Australia and New Zealand (but generally not in Canada nor in the United States), as well as impressive academic comment in this country, to which we have been referred, supporting the view that it is illogical and inconsistent with legal principle to treat a person who of his own choice and volition has taken drugs and drink, even though he thereby creates a state in which he is not conscious of what he is doing, any differently from a person suffering from the various mental conditions like epilepsy or diabetic coma and who is regarded by the law as free from fault. However, our courts have for a very long time regarded in quite another light the state of self-induced intoxication. The authority which for the last half century has been relied on in this context has been the speech of Lord Birkenhead, L.C., in *Director of Public Prosecutions* v. *Beard*[1] . . . Lord Birkenhead, L.C.,[2] concluded that (except in cases where insanity was pleaded) the decisions he cited—

> 'establish that where a specific intent is an essential element in the offence, evidence of a state of drunkenness rendering the accused incapable of forming such an intent should be taken into consideration in order to determine whether he had in fact formed the intent necessary to constitute the particular crime. If he was so drunk that he was incapable of forming the intent required he could not be convicted of a crime which was committed only if the intent was proved . . . .'

From this it seemed clear—and this is the interpretation which the judges have placed on the decision during the ensuing half-century—that it is only in the limited class of

---

[1] [1920] A.C. 479; [1920] All E.R. Rep. 21; p. 101, *supra*.
[2] [1920] A.C., at pp. 499, 500; [1920] All E.R. Rep., at pp. 27, 28.

cases requiring proof of specific intent that drunkenness can exculpate. Otherwise in no case can it exempt completely from criminal liability.

Unhappily what Lord Birkenhead, L.C.,[1] described as 'plain beyond question' [i.e. the above proposition] becomes less plain in the later passage in his speech[2] on which counsel for the appellant not unnaturally placed great emphasis. It reads:

'I do not think that the proposition of law deduced from these earlier cases is an exceptional rule applicable only only to cases in which it is necessary to prove a specific intent in order to constitute the graver crime—e.g. wounding with intent to do grievous bodily harm. . . . It is true that in such cases the specific intent must be proved to constitute the particular crime, but this is, on ultimate analysis, only in accordance with the ordinary law applicable to crime, for, speaking generally (and apart from certain special offences), a person cannot be convicted of a crime unless the mens was rea. Drunkenness, rendering a person incapable of the intent, would be an answer, as it is for example in a charge of attempted suicide.'

. . . In my view these passages are not easy to reconcile, but I do not dissent from the reconciliation suggested by my noble and learned friend Lord Russell of Killowen. Commenting on the passage[3] in 1920 shortly after it was delivered, however, Stroud wrote[4]:

'The whole of these observations . . . suggest an extension of the defence of drunkenness far beyond the limits which have hitherto been assigned to it. The suggestion, put shortly, is that drunkenness may be available as a defence, upon any criminal charge, whenever it can be shown to have affected *mens rea*. Not only is there no authority for the suggestion; there is abundant authority, both ancient and modern, to the contrary.'

It has to be said that it is on the latter footing that the judges have applied the law before and since *Beard's* case and have taken the view that self-induced intoxication, however gross and even if it has produced a condition akin to automatism, cannot excuse crimes of basic intent such as the charges of assault which have given rise to the present appeal.

---

[1] [1920] A.C., at p. 500; [1920] All E.R. Rep., at p. 28.
[2] [1920] A.C., at p. 504; [1920] All E.R. Rep., at p. 30.
[3] *Ibid.*
[4] (1920) 36 L.Q.R., at p. 270.

In *A.-G. for Northern Ireland* v. *Gallagher*[1] Lord Denning spoke of—

'the general principle of English law that, subject to very limited exceptions, drunkenness is no defence to a criminal charge nor is a defect of reason produced by drunkennes....'

Gallagher's case was followed by *Bratty* v. *A.-G. forNorthern Ireland*[2], Lord Denning[3] said:

'... Another thing to be observed is that it is not every involuntary act which leads to a complete acquittal. Take first an involuntary act which proceeds from a state of drunkenness. If the drunken man is so drunk that he does not know what he is doing, he has a defence to any charge, such as murder or wounding with intent, in which a specific intent is essential, but he is still liable to be convicted of manslaughter or unlawful wounding for which no specific intent is necessary, see *Beard's* case.'

The seal of approval is clearly set on the passage of the *Beard*[4] decision. In no case has the general principle of English law as described by Lord Denning in *Gallagher's* case and exposed again in *Bratty's* case been overruled in this House and the question now to be determined is whether it should be.

I do not for my part regard that general principle as either unethical or contrary to the principles of natural justice. If a man of his own volition takes a substance which causes him to cast off the restraints of reason and conscience, no wrong is done to him by holding him answerable criminally for any injury he may do while in that condition. His course of conduct in reducing himself by drugs and drink to that condition in my view supplies the evidence of mens rea, of guilty mind certainly sufficient for crimes of basic intent. It is a reckless course of conduct and recklessness is enough to constitute the necessary mens rea in assault cases: see *R.* v. *Venna*[5] per James, L.J. The drunkenness is itself an intrinsic, and integral part of the crime, the other part being the evidence of the unlawful use of force against the victim. Together they add up to criminal recklessness. ...

---

[1] [1963] A.C. 349, at p. 380; [1961] 3 All E.R. 299, at p. 313; p. 119, *infra*.
[2] [1963] A.C. 386; [1961] 3 All E.R. 523; p. 93, *supra*.
[3] [1963] A.C., at p. 410; [1961] 3 All E.R., at p. 533.
[4] [1920] A.C., at p. 499; [1920] All E.R. Rep., at p. 27.
[5] [1975] 3 All E.R. 788, at p. 793; p. 140, *infra*.

Acceptance generally of intoxication as a defence (as distinct from the exceptional cases where some additional mental element above that of ordinary mens rea has to be proved) would in my view undermine the criminal law and I do not think that it is enough to say, as did counsel for the appellant, that we can rely on the good sense of the jury or of magistrates to ensure that the guilty are convicted. It may well be that Parliament will at some future time consider, as I think it should, the recommendation in the Butler Committee Report on Mentally Abnormal Offenders[1] that a new offence of 'dangerous intoxication' should be created. But in the meantime it would be irresponsible to abandon the common law rule. . . . which the courts have followed for a century and a half.

The final question that arises is whether s. 8 of the Criminal Justice Act 1967[2] has had the result of abrogating or qualifying the common law rule. That section emanated from the consideration the Law Commission gave to the decision of the House in *Director of Public Prosecutions* v. *Smith*[3]. Its purpose and effect was to alter the law of evidence about the presumption of intention to produce the reasonable and probable consequences of one's acts. It was not intended to change the common law rule. In referring to 'all the evidence' it meant all the *relevant* evidence. But if there is a substantive rule of law that in crimes of basic intent, the factor of intoxication is irrelevant (and such I hold to be the substantive law), evidence with regard to it is quite irrelevant. Section 8 does not abrogate the substantive rule and it cannot properly be said that the continued application of that rule contravenes the section. For these reasons, my conclusion is that the certified question should be answered Yes, that there was no misdirection in this case and that the appeal should be dismissed.

My noble and learned friends and I think it may be helpful if we give the following indication of the general lines on which in our view the jury should be directed as to the effect on the criminal responsibility of the accused of drink or drugs or both, whenever death or physical injury to another person results from something done by the accused for which there is no legal justification and the offence with which the accused is charged is manslaughter or assault at common law or the statutory offence of unlawful wounding

[1] Cmnd. 6244 (1975).
[2] P. 19, *supra*.
[3] [1961] A.C. 290; [1960] 3 All E.R. 161; p. 207, *infra*.

under s. 20, or of assault occasioning actual bodily harm under s. 47 of the Offences against the Person Act 1861.

In the case of these offences it is no excuse in law that, because of drink or drugs which the accused himself had taken knowingly and willingly, he had deprived himself of the ability to exercise self-control, to realise the possible consequences of what he was doing or even to be conscious that he was doing it. As in the instant case, the jury may be properly instructed that they 'can ignore the subject of drink or drugs as being in any way a defence to' charges of this character."

Lord Russell of Killowen.—

". . . I entirely agree that the answer to the question posed is in the affirmative. . . .

There are two aspects of *Beard's* case which have given rise to misunderstanding as to what was there said. One misunderstanding is that a passage in the speech of Lord Birkenhead, L.C., is inconsistent with and indeed contradictory of the main tenor thereof. The other is that it lays down or assumes that rape is a crime of specific intent.

The first aspect to which I have referred is related to the following passage[1] of the report:

'I do not think that the proposition of law deduced from these earlier cases is an exceptional rule applicable only to cases in which it is necessary to prove a specific intent in order to constitute the graver crime—e.g. wounding with intent to do grievous bodily harm. . . . It is true that in such cases the specific intent must be proved to constitute the particular crime, but this is, on ultimate analysis, only in accordance with the ordinary law applicable to crime, for, speaking generally (and apart from certain special offences), a person cannot be convicted of a crime unless the mens was rea. Drunkenness, rendering a person incapable of the intent, would be an answer, as it is for example in a charge of attempted suicide. . . .'

The clue to the cited passage appears to me to be in the words 'in order to constitute the graver crime'. In my opinion the passage cited does no more than to say that special intent cases are not restricted to those crimes in which the absence of a special intent leaves available a lesser crime embodying no special intent, but embrace all cases of special intent even though no alternative lesser criminal charge is available. . . ."

APPEAL DISMISSED.

---

[1] [1920] A.C., at p. 504; [1920] All E.R. Rep., at p. 30.

Comment on Director of Public Prosecutions v. Majewski

The decision in *Majewski's* case affirms the proposition in *Beard's* case that evidence of self-induced intoxication negativing *mens rea* is a defence to a charge of an offence requiring proof of a "specific intent" but not to a charge of any other offence. Where he is charged with an offence not requiring a "specific intent" an accused who was suffering from self-induced intoxication at the time of committing the offence can be convicted even though he did not have the *mens rea* normally required for that offence, and even though he was then in a state of automatism.[1]

In *Majewski's* case the House of Lords recognised as a substantive rule of law that where self-induced intoxication is relied on by a person charged with an offence not requiring "specific intent", the prosecution need not prove any intention or other state of mind normally required for that offence. It follows, as the House stated, that s. 8 of the Criminal Justice Act 1967 has no application since it merely provides a rule of evidence as to how intention or foresight is to be proved; not when it must be proved. This substantive rule of law has to be read into the definition of every offence. Of course, substantive rules, such as those relating to insanity, duress and self-defence, are invariably implied into the definitions of offences, but the implication of the present rule is unusual in that it is adverse to the accused.

While the definition of "specific intent" is obscure, it is possible in the light of various judicial decisions to list offences which do, or do not, require "specific intent" *in the present context*. The following offences have been held to require a "specific intent": murder;[2] wounding or causing grievous bodily harm with intent to do grievous bodily harm, contrary to s. 18 of the Offences against the Person Act 1861;[3] theft;[4] attempt;[5] handling stolen goods.[6] On the other hand the following offences have been held not to require a "specific intent" in the present

---

[1] This confirms the statement by Lord Denning in *Bratty's* case, p. 93, *supra*, and the decision in *Lipman*, p. 105, *supra*.

[2] *Director of Public Prosecutions*, v. *Beard*, p. 101, *supra*.

[3] *Director of Public Prosecutions* v. *Majewski, passim; Bratty* v. *A.-G. for Northern Ireland, per* Lord Denning; *Pordage*, [1975] Crim. L.R. 575.

[4] *Ruse* v. *Read*, [1949] 1 K.B. 377; [1949] 1 All E.R. 398; *Director of Public Prosecutions* v. *Majewski, per* Lord Simon.

[5] *Director of Public Prosecution* v. *Majewski, per* Lord Salmon.

[6] *Durante*, [1972] 3 All E.R. 962.

context: manslaughter;[1] assault, battery and aggravated assaults;[2] wounding or inflicting grievous bodily harm, contrary to s. 20 of the Offences against the Person Act 1861;[3] rape;[4] taking a conveyance without lawful authority.[5]

These lists do not assist in defining "specific intent" in the present context. One of the problems of definition is that the term has been used in different senses in different contexts. Sometimes, it has been used in the sense of "direct intention" (or aim) as in *Mohan*.[6] While there is some support for this meaning in the present context in Lord Simon's speech in *Majewski's* case, "specific intent" cannot bear this meaning here because murder, at least, which is in the list of offences requiring proof of a specific intent in the context of the defence of intoxication, can be committed without proof of a direct intention, an oblique intention sufficing in murder.[7] Sometimes, "specific intent" has been used in the sense of the intent which has to be stated in the indictment, but no such intent is stated in the indictment of several of the offences listed as requiring a "specific intent" in the context of the defence of intoxication, e.g. murder and theft.

Instead of removing or reducing the difficulties of definition of "specific intent", the House of Lords in *Majewski's* case has added to the confusion. Lord Elwyn-Jones, L.C., (with whom Lords Diplock and Kilbrandon concurred), Lord Simon and Lord Edmund-Davies distinguished "crimes of specific intent" from "crimes of basic intent". Lord Elwyn-Jones approved (at p. 109, *supra*) a passage from the speech of Lord Simon in *Director of Public Prosecutions* v. *Morgan*[8] which states that "crimes of basic intent" are those "whose definition expresses (or more often, implies) a *mens rea* which does not go beyond the *actus reus* . . .".

---

[1] *Director of Public Prosecutions* v. *Beard*, p. 101, *supra; Lipman*, p. 105, *supra*.

[2] *Director of Public Prosecutions* v. *Majewski*. See also the cases cited in Cross and Jones, *Introduction to Criminal Law*, 8th ed., para. 5.33.

[3] *Bratty* v. *A.-G. for Northern Ireland*, p. 91, *supra, per* Lord Denning; *Director of Public Prosecutions* v. *Majewski, per* Lords Simon and Salmon.

[4] *Director of Public Prosecutions* v. *Majewski, per* Lord Russell, p. 114, *supra*. In Lord Russell's opinion the statement in *Beard*, p. 103, *supra*, that Beard would have had a defence if his drunkenness prevented him intending to commit rape did not indicate that rape is an offence of specific intent. All that was meant was that the intent to rape supplied the felonious intent necessary to commit constructive murder and, murder being an offence which always required a specific intent, an intent to rape was a specific intent in the context of that offence but not in the context of the offence of rape itself.

[5] *MacPherson*, [1973] R.T.R. 157.

[6] P. 5, *supra*. Also see Steane, p. 9, *supra*.

[7] *Hyam* v. *Director of Public Prosecutions*, p. 194, *infra*.

[8] [1975] 2 All E.R. 347, at p. 363.

Unfortunately, he omitted to note that Lord Simon's view was rejected by the majority of the House of Lords in *Morgan's* case. Moreover, acceptance of Lord Simon's view does not provide us with a valid definition of "specific intent" in the context of the defence of intoxication. Lord Simon said that an *actus reus* for the purpose of his view included a "consequence, however remote, as defined in the *actus reus*". Thus, on Lord Simon's view a "basic intent" exists in crimes where the necessary *mens rea* does not extend beyond the act and its required consequences, however remote, whereas a "specific intent" refers to an intent relating to matters ulterior to the act and necessary consequence of the *actus reus*, i.e. to a "further (or ulterior) intent".[1] An examination of the list of offences which require a "specific intent" in the context of the defence of intoxication reveals that a number of them, e.g. murder and causing grievous bodily harm with intent, do not require a further intent and are "crimes of basic intent" on Lord Simon's view. Nevertheless, Lord Simon and the other Law Lords recognised that the above two offences are ones of "specific intent". Consequently, the above distinction between "crimes of basic intent" and "crimes of specific intent" cannot be regarded as valid.

Another theory, to be found in the speeches of Lords Elwyn-Jones, Edmund-Davies and Russell is that the intoxicated person is convicted because he was reckless and recklessness was *mens rea* for the offence in question. From this one can imply that offences requiring intention as opposed to recklessness are offences of "specific intent". However, wilful blindness, which is a species of recklessness in its subjective sense, suffices for handling stolen goods, and some would say that the type of foresight which is sufficient for murder is better described as recklessness in its subjective sense than intention, yet these are offences of "specific intent" in the present context. In addition to this, it is difficult to accept this theory as justifying Majewski's conviction. First, the recklessness required for the offences in question in that case must be of the subjective type,[2] but Lord Elwyn-Jones, at least, appears to be talking in terms of recklessness in its objective sense. Moreover, even if "recklessness" was being used in its subjective sense, *mens rea* is a question for the jury. It is clear from the *ratio decidendi* of the case, stated by Lord Elwyn-Jones on behalf of all their Lordships (at p. 113, *supra*), which does not mention a requirement of recklessness, that the accused whose intoxication was self-induced is responsible for his acts as a matter

---

[1] P. 9, *supra*.
[2] See *Venna*, p. 140, *infra*.

of law. If this means that he is to be conclusively presumed to have been reckless in becoming intoxicated, the jury not being asked to reach a finding on this, the result is a direct conflict with s.8 of the Criminal Justice Act 1967.

The substantive rule of law confirmed in *Majewski's* case is clearly based on public policy, in particular the protection of the public. While it is permissible for extreme intoxication to provide a defence to murder or wounding with intent, acquittals also of offences such as manslaughter and serious assaults might outrage public opinion. Some people may think it would be better to adopt the proposal of the Butler Committee on Mentally Abnormal Offenders[1] that there should be an offence of dangerous voluntary intoxication. Lord Elwyn-Jones (at p. 113, *supra*) and two other members of the House of Lords accorded a degree of approval to this proposal in *Majewski's* case.

ATTORNEY-GENERAL FOR NORTHERN IRELAND v. GALLAGHER
[1961] 3 All E.R. 299

If a person, while sane and sober, forms an intention to kill, and then gets himself intoxicated so as to give himself Dutch courage to do the killing, and while drunk carries out his intention, he cannot rely on this self-induced drunkenness as a defence to a charge of murder.

Gallagher was charged with the murder of his wife. He was probably a psychopath, suffering from a disease of the mind which was liable to be exaggerated by drink. Gallagher formed the intention of killing his wife and, in furtherance of that intention, bought a knife and a bottle of whisky. On the same day he killed his wife with the knife and consumed a considerable quantity of the whisky. He pleaded insanity and drunkenness of such a degree that he was incapable of forming the intent necessary for murder. The summing-up contained a suggestion that, in considering the defence of insanity, the jury should pay attention to the accused's state of mind before he consumed the whisky and Gallagher was convicted. He successfully appealed to the

---

[1] Cmnd. 6244 (1975).

Northern Irish Court of Criminal Appeal. The court took the view that the summing-up was wrong in so far as it suggested that, in considering the applicability of the M'Naghten rules, regard might be had to any period of time before the homicidal act. The Attorney-General for Northern Ireland successfully appealed to the House of Lords.

Extracts from the Speeches of the House of Lords

Lord Denning.—

"My Lords, this case differs from all others in the books in that the respondent, whilst sane and sober, before he took to the drink, had already made up his mind to kill his wife. This seems to me to be far worse—and far more deserving of condemnation—than the case of a man who, before getting drunk, has no intention to kill, but afterwards in his cups, whilst drunk, kills another by an act which he would not dream of doing when sober. Yet, by the law of England, in this latter case his drunkenness is no defence even though it has distorted his reason and his will-power. So why should it be a defence in the present case? And is it made any better by saying that the man is a psychopath? The answer to the question is, I think, that the case falls to be decided by the general principle of English law that, subject to very limited exceptions, drunkenness is no defence to a criminal charge nor is a defect of reason produced by drunkenness. . . .

The general principle which I have enunciated is subject to two exceptions: (i) If a man is charged with an offence in which a specific intention is essential (as in murder, though not in manslaughter), then evidence of drunkenness, which renders him incapable of forming that intent, is an answer; see *Beard's* case. . . .[1] (ii) If a man by drinking brings on a distinct disease of the mind such as delirium tremens, so that he is temporarily insane within the M'Naghten rules,[2] that is to say, he does not at the time know what he is doing or that it is wrong, then he has a defence on the ground of insanity; see *R. v. Davis*[3] and *Beard's* case.[4]

Does the present case come within the general principle or the exceptions to it? It certainly does not come within the first exception. The respondent was not incapable of forming an intent to kill. Quite the contrary. He knew full

---

[1] [1920], A.C. 479, at pp. 501, 504; [1920] All E.R. Rep. 21, at pp. 28, 30.
[2] (1843), 10 Cl. & Fin. 200.
[3] (1881), 14 Cox C.C. 563.
[4] [1920], A.C. 479, at pp. 500, 501; [1920] All E.R. Rep. 21, at pp. 28, 29.

well what he was doing. He formed an intent to kill, he carried out his intention and he remembered afterwards what he had done. And the jury, properly directed on the point, have found as much, for they found him guilty of murder. Then does the case come within the second exception? It does not to my mind; for the simple reason that he was not suffering from a disease of the mind brought on by drink. He was suffering from a different disease altogether. . . .

My Lords, I think the law on this point should take a clear stand. If a man, whilst sane and sober, forms an intention to kill and makes preparation for it, knowing it is a wrong thing to do, and then gets himself drunk so as to give himself Dutch courage to do the killing, and whilst drunk carries out his intention, he cannot rely on this self-induced drunkenness as a defence to a charge of murder, nor even as reducing it to manslaughter. He cannot say that he got himself into such a stupid state that he was incapable of an intent to kill. So, also, when he is a psychopath, he cannot by drinking rely on his self-induced defect of reason as a defence of insanity. The wickedness of his mind before he got drunk is enough to condemn him, coupled with the act which he intended to do and did do. A psychopath who goes out intending to kill, knowing it is wrong, and does kill, cannot escape the consequences by making himself drunk before doing it. That is, I believe, the direction which the Lord Chief Justice gave to the jury and which the Court of Criminal Appeal found to be wrong. I think that it was right, and for this reason I would allow the appeal."

APPEAL ALLOWED.[1]

---

[1] The approach of the other Lords of Appeal was slightly different from that of Lord Denning for they appear to have considered that the summing-up as a whole directed the jury to consider whether the accused knew the nature and quality of his act at the time he did it. The reference to the position before the whisky was opened may have been designed to direct the jury to examine the question whether the accused could be said to have been suffering, at the time of the homicide, from a disease of the mind induced by drink in which case the M'Naghten Rules could have been applied.

Section 6 of the Criminal Justice Act (Northern Ireland), 1966 provides that the insane person whose mental abnormality was of a temporary nature and attributable solely to his own voluntary conduct in taking intoxicating liquor or drugs shall on a charge of murder be convicted of manslaughter unless, immediately before he took the intoxicating liquor or drugs, he had formed the intention to kill or cause serious bodily harm, in which case his crime will continue to be murder.

Corporations[1]

Note

A corporation, a legal person, can, of course, be criminally vicariously liable for the acts of its employees or agents to the same extent as any other employer or principal. Cases on vicarious liability appear on pp. 442–447, *infra*. As will be seen, the doctrine of vicarious liability is limited essentially to statutory offences of the regulatory type and even here it does not extend to charges of attempting or abetting the commission of such offences. However, starting in 1944 at the latest, a doctrine of personal corporate liability has developed whereby a corporation can be held criminally liable for virtually any offence committed by certain superior employees within the scope of their authority on the basis that their acts and state of mind are the acts and state of mind of the corporation.

R. v. I.C.R. HAULAGE, LTD.
[1944] K.B. 551

Through the acts and state of mind of a superior employee who can be identified with it a corporation can commit an offence, but some offences by their nature or the nature of their punishment cannot be committed by a corporation.

The appellant company and nine individuals were charged at the Kent Assizes with conspiring to defraud the purchaser of hard core by overcharging him, one of the other conspirators being the managing director of the appellant company.

Counsel for the appellant company moved to quash the indictment and the motion was refused by the Commissioner of Assize. The company was convicted together with some of the accused individuals, and the company unsuccessfully appealed to the Court of Criminal Appeal. The case is only reported on the question whether the Commissioner was right in rejecting the motion to quash the indictment.

---

[1] Corporate liability is considered in the Law Commission's Working Paper No. 44, published in 1972.

Extracts from the Judgment of the Court of Criminal Appeal

Stable, J.—

". . . Counsel for the company contended that the true principle was that an indictment against a limited company for any offence involving as an essential ingredient *mens rea* in the restricted sense of a dishonest or criminal mind must be bad for the reason that a company, not being a natural person, cannot have a mind honest or otherwise, and that, consequently, though under certain circumstances it is civilly liable for the fraud of its officers, agents or servants, it is immune from criminal process. Counsel for the Crown contended that a limited company, like any other entity recognised by the law, can as a general rule be indicted for its criminal acts which from the very necessity of the case must be performed by human agency and which in given circumstances become the acts of the company, and that for this purpose there was no distinction between an intention or other function of the mind and any other form of activity.

The offences for which a limited company cannot be indicted are, it was argued, exceptions to the general rule arising from the limitations which must inevitably attach to an artificial entity, such as a company. Included in these exceptions are the cases in which, from its very nature, the offence cannot be committed by a corporation, as, for example, perjury,[1] an offence which cannot be vicariously committed, or bigamy, an offence which a limited company, not being a natural person, cannot commit vicariously or otherwise. A further exception, but for a different reason, comprises offences of which murder is an example, where the only punishment the court can impose is corporal, the basis on which this exception rests being that the court will not stultify itself by embarking on a trial in which, if a verdict of guilty is returned, no effective order by way of sentence can be made. In our judgment these contentions of the Crown are substantially sound, and the existence of these exceptions, and it may be that there are others, is by no means inconsistent with the general rule. . . .

The latest authority is the *Director of Public Prosecutions* v. *Kent and Sussex Contractors, Ltd.*[2] A limited company

---

[1] It has been suggested that a company which authorises the swearing of a false affidavit may be guilty of perjury; Stephen's *Digest of Criminal Law*, 9th Edn. Illustration 3, pp. 4–5.

[2] [1944] K.B. 146, at p. 157.

was charged with offences under a Defence of the Realm regulation which involved an intent to deceive. The justices dismissed the informations on the ground that a body corporate could not be guilty of the offences charged, inasmuch as an act of will or state of mind which could not be imputed to a corporation was implicit in the commission of these offences. On a case stated to a Divisional Court this conclusion of law on the part of the justices was held to be erroneous, and the case was remitted to them to hear and determine. It is clear that the state of mind involved was a dishonest state of mind, namely, an intention to deceive and that the state of mind was an essential element in the offence. There is a distinction between that case and the present, in that there the offences were charged under a regulation having the effect of a statute, whereas here the offence is a common law misdemeanour; but, in our judgment, the distinction has no material bearing on the question we have to decide. Lord Caldecote, C.J., said:[1]

'The real point we have to decide . . . is whether a company is capable of an act of will or of a state of mind, so as to be able to form an intention to deceive or to have knowledge of the truth or falsity of a statement.'

and, after dealing with a number of authorities, he proceeds:[2]

'The offences created by the regulations are those of doing something with intent to deceive or of making a statement known to be false in a material particular. There was ample evidence, on the facts as stated in the special case, that the the company, by the only people who could act or speak or think for it, had done both these things, and I can see nothing in any of the authoririties to which we have been referred which requires us to say that a company is incapable of being found guilty of the offences with which the respondent company was charged.'

In his judgment in the same case Macnaghten, J., says as follows:

'It is true that a corporation can only have knowledge and form an intention through its human agents, but circumstances may be such that the knowledge and intention of the agent must be imputed to the body corporate. . . . If the responsible agent of a company, acting within the scope of his authority, puts forward on its behalf a document which

---

[1] *Ibid.*, at p. 151.
[2] *Ibid.*, at p. 155.

124   CAPACITY

he knows to be false and by which he intends to deceive,
I apprehend that, according to the authorities that my
Lord has cited, his knowledge and intention must be
imputed to the company.'

With both the decision in that case and the reasoning on
which it rests, we agree.

   In our judgment, both on principle and in accordance
with the balance of authority, the present indictment was
properly laid against the company, and the learned commissioner rightly refused to quash. We are not deciding that in
every case where an agent of a limited company acting in its
business commits a crime the company is automatically to
be held criminally responsible. Our decision only goes to the
invalidity of the indictment on the face of it, an objection
which is taken before any evidence is led and irrespective of
the facts of the particular case. Where in any particular case
there is evidence to go to a jury that the criminal act of an
agent, including his state of mind, intention, knowledge or
belief is the act of the company, and, in cases where the
presiding judge so rules, whether the jury are satisfied that
it has been proved, must depend on the nature of the charge,
the relative position of the officer or agent, and the other
relevant facts and circumstances of the case. It was because
we were satisfied on the hearing of this appeal that the facts
proved were amply sufficient to justify a finding that the
acts of the managing director were the acts of the company
and the fraud of that person was the fraud of the company,
that we upheld the conviction against the company. . . ."

APPEAL DISMISSED.

JOHN HENSHALL (QUARRIES), LTD. v. HARVEY
[1965] 1 All E.R. 725

*An employee who is not part of the "brains" of a corpora-
tion cannot be identified with it. While a corporation can be
convicted of aiding and abetting the commission of an offence,
this is only possible if one of its employees constituting the
"brains" of the corporation was aware of the facts constituting
the offence.*

The appellants were convicted of aiding and abetting
one H to drive a lorry with an excessive load on a road. By

an oversight, the appellants' weighbridge attendant, Burrell, allowed H to drive away from the appellants' premises with a lorry containing a load in excess of that permitted. The appellants successfully appealed against conviction to the Divisional Court.

Extracts from the Judgment of the Divisional Court

Lord Parker, C.J.—

"In my judgment, while sympathising with the justices in this rather difficult area of the law, they were wrong in convicting the appellants. Quite shortly, my reasons are as follows: there is absolutely no doubt that in the case of absolute offences as they are sometimes called, a master, whether an individual or a company, is criminally liable for the acts of any servant acting within the scope of his authority. That has been held in many cases; I need only mention two, *Mousell Brothers, Ltd.* v. *London and North Western Rly. Co.*[1] and *Police Commissioners* v. *Cartman.*[2] It is, however, quite clear that when one is dealing with aiding and abetting, as has been often said, the master must know of the facts out of which the offence arises, albeit he does not know that an offence is committed. In the case of *National Coal Board* v. *Gamble,*[3] Lord Goddard, C.J., quoting from *Ackroyds Air Travel, Ltd.* v. *Director of Public Prosecutions*[4] said: 'I stated the law with regard to aiding and abetting in this way: ". . . a person could only be convicted . . . as an aider and abettor if he knew all the circumstances which constituted the offence. Whether he realised that those circumstances constituted an offence was immaterial. If he knew all the circumstances and those circumstances constituted the offence . . . that was enough to convict him of being an aider and abettor." ' Accordingly, in the case of a master who is an individual, he must have actual knowledge of the circumstances which constitute the offence. The same position arises in the many offences of permitting somebody to do something unlawful, or indeed when any knowledge is necessary. In *Vane* v. *Yiannopoullos*[5] the House of Lords recently held, and in so holding followed a long line of

---

[1] [1917] 2 K.B. 836.
[2] [1896] 1 Q.B. 655.
[3] [1959] 1 Q.B. 11; [1958] 3 All E.R. 203.
[4] [1950] 1 All E.R. 933.
[5] [1965] A.C. 486; [1964] 3 All E.R. 820; p. 443, *infra*.

authority, that as an individual master does not know what is in the mind of his servant he must, for the purpose of knowingly committing an offence, be shown to have actual knowledge of it. There is possibly one exception to that, where he shuts his eyes and is regardless of whether a servant does perform his duty or not. It seems perfectly clear, without going through the authorities, that if in this case the appellants had been an individual master they would not have been fixed with knowledge of the actions of Mr. Burrell. It is quite clear however that Mr. Price, the appellant's manager, did not actually know, and from the findings in the case it is clear that they in no way shut their eyes to, what Mr. Burrell was doing, but took particular care to see that he performed his duty properly. In this case by an oversight he failed to do so.

. . . there is fundamentally no difference between a master who is an individual and a master who is a limited company, save that in the case of a limited company their knowledge must be the knowledge of those whom, in the case of *H. L. Bolton (Engineering) Co., Ltd.* v. *T. J. Graham & Sons, Ltd.*,[1] Denning, L.J., referred to as the brains of the company. There is no doubt that there are many cases where somebody who is in the position of the brains—maybe a director, the managing director, the secretary or a responsible officer of the company—has knowledge, his knowledge has been held to be the knowledge of the company. It seems to me that that is a long way away from saying that a company is fixed with the knowledge of any servant. Again, to adopt the simile of Denning, L.J., the knowledge of the hands as opposed to the brain, is not imputed to the company merely because it is the servant's duty to perform that particular task.

For those reasons, which I have endeavoured to state shortly, I think that the justices came to a wrong conclusion in law. I should have added this, that as is shown by *Vane's* case in the House of Lords, there can be cases in which a master is fixed with the knowledge of his servant, where there has been what is referred to as true delegation. If a master completely hands over the effective management of a business to somebody else, then as it is often said he cannot get out of his responsibility by such delegation."

APPEAL ALLOWED.

---

[1] [1957] 1 Q.B. 159; [1956] 3 All E.R. 624.

TESCO SUPERMARKETS, LTD. v. NATTRASS
[1971] 2 All E.R. 127

A shop manager employed by a company was held not to be identifiable with it and thus, despite his default, the company could rely on a statutory defence that it had taken all reasonable precautions and exercised due diligence and that the commission of the offence was due to the default of another person.

Tesco Supermarkets, Ltd. were charged with giving an indication that goods were offered for sale at a price less than that at which they were in fact offered contrary to s. 11 (2) of the Trade Descriptions Act 1968.[1] A poster in one of the company's shops managed by a Mr. Clement stated that Radiant Washing Powder was being sold at 2s. 11d. a packet instead of the normal 3s. 11d. It was the practice in the shop to remove all stock priced at the normal price while the reduced offer was operative. On the occasion in question, however, there being no stock marked with the reduced price, a Miss Rogers, a shop girl, put out stock marked with the normal price. Had Mr. Clement known of the facts, he would either have withdrawn the poster, or else sold the goods at the reduced price. The company relied on s. 24 (1) of the Act which reads as follows:

> "In any proceedings for an offence under this Act it shall, subject to subsection (2) of this section, be a defence for the person charged to prove (a) that the commission of the offence was due to a mistake or to reliance on information supplied to him or to the act or default of another person, an accident or some other cause beyond his control; and (b) that he took all reasonable precautions and exercised all due diligence to avoid the commission of such an offence by himself or any person under his control."

Extracts from the Speeches of the House of Lords

Lord Reid.—

"In order to avoid conviction the appellants had to

---

[1] "If any person offering to supply any goods gives, by whatever means, any indication likely to be taken as an indication that the goods are being offered at a price less than that at which they are in fact being offered he shall, subject to the provisions of this Act, be guilty of an offence."

prove facts sufficient to satisfy both parts of s. 24 (1) of the
1968 Act. The justices held that they:

> 'had exercised all due diligence in devising a proper system
> for the operation of the said store and by securing so far as
> was reasonably practicable that it was fully implemented
> and thus had fulfilled the requirements of s. 24 (1) (b)'.

But they convicted the appellants because in their view the
requirements of s. 24 (1) (a) had not been fulfilled; they held
that Mr. Clement was not 'another person' within the meaning of that provision. The Divisional Court held that the
justices were wrong in holding that Mr. Clement was not
'another person'. The respondent did not challenge this
finding of the Divisional Court so I need say no more about it
than that I think that on this matter the Divisional Court
was plainly right. But that court sustained the conviction
on the ground that the justices had applied the wrong test in
deciding the requirements of s. 24 (1) (b) had been fulfilled.
In effect that court held that the words 'he took all reasonable precautions . . . .' do not mean what they say; 'he' does
not mean the accused, it means the accused and all his
servants who were acting in a supervisory or managerial
capacity. . . .

Over a century ago the courts invented the idea of an
absolute offence. The accepted doctrines of the common law
put them in a difficulty. There was a presumption that when
Parliament makes the commission of certain acts an offence
it intends that *mens rea* shall be a constituent of that offence
whether or not there is any reference to the knowledge or
state of mind of the accused. And it was and is held to be an
invariable rule that where *mens rea* is a constituent of any
offence the burden of proving *mens rea* is on the prosecution.
Some day this House may have to re-examine that rule, but
that is another matter. For the protection of purchasers or
consumers Parliament in many cases made it an offence for
a trader to do certain things. Normally those things were done
on his behalf by his servants and cases arose where the doing
of the forbidden thing was solely the fault of a servant, the
master having done all he could to prevent it and being
entirely ignorant of its having been done. The just course
would have been to hold that, once the facts constituting the
offence had been proved, *mens rea* would be presumed unless
the accused proved that he was blameless. The courts could
not, or thought they could not, take that course. But they
could and did hold in many such cases on a construction of

the statutory provision that Parliament must be deemed to have intended to depart from the general rule and to make the offence absolute in the sense that *mens rea* was not to be a constituent of the offence.

This has led to great difficulties. If the offence is not held to be absolute the requirement that the prosecutor must prove *mens rea* makes it impossible to enforce the enactment in very many cases. If the offence is held to be absolute that leads to the conviction of persons who are entirely blameless: an injustice which brings the law into dispute. So Parliament has found it necessary to devise a method of avoiding this difficulty. But instead of passing a general enactment that it shall always be a defence for the accused to prove that he was no party to the offence and has done all he could to prevent it, Parliament has chosen to deal with the problem piecemeal and has in an increasing number of cases enacted in various forms with regard to particular offences that it shall be a defence to prove various exculpatory circumstances. In my judgment the main object of these provisions must have been to distinguish between those who are in some degree blameworthy and those who are not, and to enable the latter to escape from conviction if they can show they were in no way to blame. I find it almost impossible to suppose that Parliament . . . would as a matter of policy think it right to make employers criminally liable for the acts of some of their servants but not for those of others and I find it incredible that a draftsman, aware of that intention, would fail to insert any words to express it. But in several cases the courts, for reasons which it is not easy to discover, have given a restricted meaning to such provisions. It has been held that such provisions afford a defence if the master proves that the servant at fault was the person who himself did the prohibited act, but that they afford no defence if the servant at fault was one who failed in his duty of supervision to see that his subordinates did not commit the prohibited act. Why Parliament should be thought to have intended this distinction or how as a matter of construction these provisions can reasonably be held to have that meaning is not apparent.

In some of these cases the employer charged with the offence was a limited company. But in others the employer was an individual and still it was held that he, though personally blameless, could not rely on these provisions if the fault which led to the commission of the offence was the fault of a servant in failing to carry out his duty to instruct or supervise his subordinates. Where a limited company is the employer difficult questions do arise in a wide variety of circumstances in deciding which of its officers or servants is to be identified with the company so that his guilt is the guilt of the company.

I must start by considering the nature of the personality which by a fiction the law attributes to a corporation. A living person has a mind which can have knowledge or intention or be negligent and he has hands to carry out his intentions. A corporation has none of these; it must act through living persons, though not always one or the same person. Then the person who acts is not speaking or acting for the company. He is acting as the company and his mind which directs his acts is the mind of the company. There is no question of the company being vicariously liable. He is not acting as a servant, representative, agent or delegate. He is an embodiment of the company or, one could say, he hears and speaks through the persona of the company, within his appropriate sphere, and his mind is the mind of the company. If it is a guilty mind then that guilt is the guilt of the company. It must be a question of law whether, once the facts have been ascertained, a person in doing particular things is to be regarded as the company or merely as the company's servant or agent. In that case any liability of the company can only be a statutory or vicarious liability. . . .

In some cases the phrase alter ego has been used. I think it is misleading. When dealing with a company the word alter is I think misleading. The person who speaks and acts as the company is not alter. He is identified with the company. And when dealing with an individual no other individual can be his alter ego. The other individual can be a servant, agent, delegate or representative but I know of neither principle nor authority which warrants the confusion (in the literal or original sense) of two separate individuals. . . .

I think that the true view is that the judge must direct the jury that if they find certain facts proved then as a matter of law they must find that the criminal act of the officer, servant or agent including his state of mind, intention, knowledge or belief is the act of the company. I have already dealt with the considerations to be applied in deciding when such a person can and when he cannot be identified with the company. I do not see how the nature of the charge can make any difference. If the guilty man was in law identifiable with the company then whether his offence was serious or venial his act was the act of the company but if he was not so identifiable then no act of his, serious or otherwise, was the act of the company itself. . . .

It is sometimes argued—it was argued in the present case —that making an employer criminally responsible, even when he has done all that he could to prevent an offence, affords some additional protection to the public because this will induce him to do more. But if he has done all he can how can he do more?

. . . I have said that a board of directors can delegate part of their functions of management so as to make their delegate an embodiment of the company within the sphere of the delegation. But here the board never delegated any part of their functions. They set up a chain of command through regional and district supervisors, but they remained in control. The shop managers had to obey their general directions and also to take orders from their superiors. The acts or omissions of shop managers were not the acts of the company itself.

In my judgment the appellants established the statutory defence."

APPEAL ALLOWED.

CHAPTER 3

NON-FATAL OFFENCES AGAINST THE PERSON

Consent

R. v. DONOVAN
[1934] 2 K.B. 498

(1) *Where the use of force by one person against another is only criminal if done without the consent of such other person, the onus of proving its absence rests upon the prosecution.* (2) *Generally, consent is no defence to a charge of doing an act which is likely or intended to do bodily harm.*[1]

Donovan was charged and convicted of an indecent assault upon a girl of seventeen for the purposes of sexual gratification. His defence was that the girl had consented to being caned, and he appealed to the Court of Criminal Appeal on the ground that the jury had been misdirected on the question of consent.

The Court of Criminal Appeal quashed his conviction on this ground, holding that the onus of proving the absence of consent rested upon the prosecution, but the Court was also of opinion that, before any question of consent was put to them, the jury should have been asked whether the blows were likely or intended to cause an unlawful degree of bodily harm.

Extracts from the Judgment of the Court of Criminal Appeal

Swift, J.—

". . . First, it was of importance that the jury should be left in no doubt as to the incidence of the burden of proof in relation to consent. In *R. v. May*[2] the principle

---

[1] Also see *Coney*, p. 137. *infra.*
[2] [1912] 3 K.B. 572, at p. 575.

applicable to cases of this kind was laid down by this Court in these words: 'The Court is of opinion that if the facts proved in evidence are such that the jury can reasonably find consent, there ought to be a direction by the judge on that question, both as to the onus of negativing consent being on the prosecution and as to the evidence in the particular case bearing on the question.'

We have no doubt that the facts proved in the present case were such that the jury might reasonably have found consent; it is, indeed, difficult to reconcile some of the admitted facts with absence of consent. It was therefore of importance (if consent was in issue) that there should be no possibility of doubt in the minds of the jury upon the question whether it was for the Crown to negative consent, or for the defence to prove it. A second observation which may fairly be made is that consent, being a state of mind, is to be proved or negatived only after a full and careful review of the behaviour of the person who is alleged to have consented. Unless a jury is satisfied beyond reasonable doubt that the conduct of the person has been such that, viewed as a whole, it shows that she did not consent, then the prisoner is entitled to be acquitted. . . .

. . . the learned counsel for the Crown relied in this Court upon the submission which he had unsuccessfully made at the trial, and argued that, this being a case in which it was unnecessary for the Crown to prove absence of consent, this Court ought not to quash the conviction.

We have given careful consideration to the question of law which this submission raises. The learned counsel on both sides referred us to passages in the judgments in the case of *R. v. Coney*.[1] The subject-matter of that case was very different from that of the present case, but the judgments undoubtedly contain statements of the law which are of great value for the present purpose. Much reliance was placed, on behalf of the Crown, upon the following passage from the judgement of Cave, J.: 'The true view is, I think, that a blow struck in anger, or which is likely or intended to do corporal hurt, is an assault, but that a blow struck in sport, and not likely, nor intended to cause bodily harm, is not an assault, and that, an assault being a breach of the peace and unlawful, the consent of the person struck is immaterial.' We have considered the authorities upon which

[1] (1882), 8 Q.B.D. 534, at p. 539; p. 137. *infra.*

this view of the learned judge was founded, and we think it of importance that we should state our opinion as to the law applicable in this case. If an act is unlawful in the sense of being in itself a criminal act, it is plain that it cannot be rendered lawful because the person to whose detriment it is done consents to it. No person can license another to commit a crime. So far as the criminal law is concerned, therefore, where the act charged is in itself unlawful, it can never be necessary to prove absence of consent on the part of the person wronged in order to obtain the conviction of the wrongdoer. There are, however, many acts in themselves harmless and lawful which become unlawful only if they are done without the consent of the person affected. What is, in one case, an innocent act of familiarity or affection, may, in another, be an assault, for no other reason than that, in the one case there is consent, and in the other consent is absent. As a general rule, although it is a rule to which there are well established exceptions, it is an unlawful act to beat another person with such a degree of violence that the infliction of bodily harm is a probable consequence, and when such an act is proved, consent is immaterial. We are aware that the existence of this rule has not always been clearly recognised. In his *Digest of the Criminal Law* (6th edition), Art. 227, Sir James FitzJames Stephen enunciates the proposition that 'every one has a right to consent to the infliction upon himself of bodily harm not amounting to a maim.' This may have been true in early times when the law of this country showed remarkable leniency towards crimes of personal violence, but it is a statement which now needs considerable qualification. It is to be observed, indeed, that in Art. 230 of his Digest, the learned author says: 'It is uncertain to what extent any person has a right to consent to his being put in danger of death or bodily harm by the act of another.'

In early works of authority, such as Foster's *Crown Law* and East's *Pleas of the Crown*, much learning upon the distinction between lawful and unlawful acts is to be found in the chapters dealing with homicide. At p. 259 of the former work (third edition), Sir Michael Foster gives his reason for the proposition that a man who beats another 'in anger or from preconceived malice' is responsible if fatal consequences ensue, in the following words: 'What he did was *malum in se*, and he must be answerable for the consequence of it. He certainly beat him with an intention of doing him some bodily harm, he had no other intent, he could have no other;

he is therefore answerable for all the harm he did.' If an act is *malum in se* in the sense in which Sir Michael Foster used the words, that is to say, is, in itself, unlawful, we take it to be plain that consent cannot convert it into an innocent act.

There are, as we have said, well established exceptions to the general rule that an act likely or intended to cause bodily harm is an unlawful act. One of them is dealt with by Sir Michael Foster in the chapter just cited, where he refers to the case of persons who in perfect friendship engage by mutual consent in contests, such as 'cudgels, foils, or wrestling,' which are capable of causing bodily harm. The learned author emphasizes two points about such contests: (1) that bodily harm is not the motive on either side, and (2) that they are 'manly diversions, they intend to give strength, skill and activity, and may fit people for defence, public as well as personal, in time of need.' For these reasons, he says that he cannot call these exercises unlawful.

Another exception to the general rule, or, rather, another branch of the same class of exceptions, is to be found in cases of rough and undisciplined sport or play, where there is no anger and no intention to cause bodily harm. An example of this kind may be found in *R.* v. *Bruce.*[1] In such cases the act is not in itself unlawful, and it becomes unlawful only if the person affected by it is not a consenting party. It is not necessary to deal in this judgment with other exceptions to the rule which are wholly remote from the present case, such as the reasonable chastisement of a child by a parent or by a person *in loco parentis.* In the present case it was not in dispute that the motive of the appellant was to gratify his own perverted desires. If, in the course of so doing, he acted so as to cause bodily harm, he cannot plead his corrupt motive as an excuse, and it may truly be said of him in Sir Michael Foster's words that 'he certainly beat him with an intention of doing him some bodily harm, he had no other intent,' and that what he did was *malum in se.* Nothing could be more absurd or more repellent to the ordinary intelligence than to regard his conduct as comparable with that of a participant in one of those 'manly diversions' of which Sir Michael Foster wrote. Nor is his act to be compared with the rough but innocent horse-play in *R.* v. *Bruce*[1].

---

[1] (1847), 2 Cox C.C. 262, at p. 263.

Always supposing, therefore, that the blows which he struck were likely or intended to do bodily harm, we are of opinion that he was doing an unlawful act, no evidence having been given of facts which would bring the case within any of the exceptions to the general rule. In our view, on the evidence given at the trial, the jury should have been directed that, if they were satisfied that the blows struck by the prisoner were likely or intended to do bodily harm to the prosecutrix, they ought to convict him, and that it was only if they were not so satisfied, that it became necessary to consider the further question whether the prosecution had negatived consent. For this purpose we think that 'bodily harm' has its ordinary meaning and includes any hurt or injury calculated to interfere with the health or comfort of the prosecutor.[1] Such hurt or injury need not be permanent, but must, no doubt, be more than merely transient and trifling.

This being our view of the law, we considered the question whether, in all the circumstances, it would be right to quash the conviction. The whole case was conducted, in so far as it was conducted in the presence of the jury, upon the footing that the issue of consent was the 'vital question in the case'. It is not too much to say that, in all probability, the only question which the jury felt called upon to decide, as the case was left to them, was the question whether in fact the prosecutrix was shown to have consented. We may summarize the position by saying that, of the two questions which should have been left to the jury, the first was not left at all, while the second was left to them with an inadequate and misleading direction. It may well be that, if the first question had been left to the jury, they would have answered it by saying that the appellant intended to cause and inflicted blows likely to cause bodily harm to the prosecutrix, so that the second question would not have arisen. But, although we think it probable that this would have been the jury's view, it is, in our opinion, impossible to say that they must inevitably have so found. There are many gradations between a slight tap and a severe blow, and the question whether particular blows were likely or intended to cause bodily harm is one eminently fitted for

---

[1] This definition may require reconsideration in the light of the new definition of "grievous bodily harm" as "really serious bodily harm" in *Director of Public Prosecutions* v. *Smith*, p. 191, *infra*. The reference to comfort may be superfluous.

the decision of a jury upon evidence which they have heard.
We may have little doubt what that decision would have
been in this case, but we cannot, consistently with the practice of this Court, substitute ourselves for the jury and decide
a question of fact which was never left to them. . . ."

CONVICTION QUASHED.

R. v. CONEY
(1882), 8 Q.B.D. 534

*Consent to personal injury is no defence to the person who
inflicts the injury if the injury is of such a nature, or is inflicted
in such circumstances, that its infliction is injurious to the
public, as well as to the person injured.*

The facts of this case are set out at p. 426, *infra.*

Extracts from the Judgments of the Court for Crown Cases Reserved

Stephen, J.—
". . . The principle as to consent seems to me to be this:
when one person is indicted for inflicting personal injury
upon another, the consent of the person who sustains the
injury is no defence to the person who inflicts the injury,
if the injury is of such a nature, or is inflicted under such
circumstances, that its infliction is injurious to the public
as well as to the person injured. But the injuries given and
received in prize-fights are injurious to the public, both
because it is against the public interest that the lives and the
health of the combatants should be endangered by blows, and
because prize-fights are disorderly exhibitions, mischievous
on many obvious grounds. Therefore the consent of the
parties to the blows which they mutually receive does not
prevent those blows from being assaults. . . .

In all cases the question whether consent does or does
not take from the application of force to another its illegal
character, is a question of degree depending upon circumstances. . . ."

CONVICTION QUASHED.

R. v. CLARENCE
(1888), 22 Q.B.D. 23

Fraud only vitiates consent to physical contact if it is as to the nature of the act itself or the identity of the party who does the act.

See p. 163, *infra*.

Assault and Battery

Note

Assault and battery are separate common law misdemeanours,[1] although they are both commonly described as assault or common assault. While an assault often involves a battery, and *vice versa*, this need not be so.

There are also a number of statutory offences of aggravated assault (which term includes battery), such as assault occasioning actual bodily harm,[2] assault with intent to rob[3] and assaulting a constable in the execution of his duty.[4]

FAGAN v. METROPOLITAN POLICE COMMISSIONER
[1968] 3 All E.R. 442

It is an assault for someone who has driven his car inadvertently or negligently on to another's foot deliberately to allow the car to remain there.

Fagan was reversing his car on to a pedestrian crossing when he was asked by a constable to pull into the side of the road to produce some documents. He drove his car on to the constable's foot, but the magistrates were not satisfied that

---

[1] The punishment for common assault is provided by the Offences against the Person Act 1861, ss. 42, 43 and 47.

[2] Offences against the Person Act 1861, s. 47. "Actual bodily harm" means any hurt or injury (whether physical or mental) calculated to interfere with the health or comfort of the victim: *Miller*, [1954] 2 Q.B. 282; [1954] 2 All E.R. 529. Such harm must, of course, be a result of the accused's assault; see *Roberts* (1971), 56 Cr. App. Rep. 95.

[3] Theft Act 1968, s. 8; p. 273, *infra*.

[4] Police Act 1964, s. 51; p. 146, *infra*.

he did so deliberately. When asked by the constable to remove his car, Fagan refused to do so for some little time and the constable's foot was slightly injured. Fagan was charged with assaulting the constable in the execution of his duty, and the magistrates convicted him. He unsuccessfully appealed to Quarter Sessions who stated a case for the opinion of a Divisional Court which affirmed the conviction by a majority.

Extracts from the Judgments of the Divisional Court

James, J.—

"In our judgment, the question arising, which has been argued on general principles, falls to be decided on the facts of the particular case. An assault is any act which intentionally—or possibly recklessly[1]—causes another person to apprehend immediate and unlawful personal violence. Although 'assault' is an independent crime and is to be treated as such, for practical purposes today 'assault' is generally synonymous with the term 'battery', and is a term used to mean the actual intended use of unlawful force to another person without his consent. On the facts of the present case, the 'assault' alleged involved a 'battery'. Where an assault involved a battery, it matters not, in our judgment, whether the battery is inflicted directly by the body of the offender or through the medium of some weapon or instrument controlled by the action of the offender. An assault may be committed by the laying of a hand on another, and the action does not cease to be an assault if it is a stick held in the hand and not the hand itself which is laid on the person of the victim. So, for our part, we see no difference in principle between the action of stepping on to a person's toe and maintaining that position and the action of driving a car on to a person's foot and sitting in the car while its position on the foot is maintained. . . .

For our part, we think that the crucial question is whether, in this case, the act of the appellant can be said to be complete and spent at the moment of time when the car wheel came to rest on the foot, or whether his act is to be regarded as a continuing act operating until the wheel was removed. In our judgment, a distinction is to be drawn between acts which are complete—though results may

---

[1] The Court of Appeal has now held that recklessness suffices, see *Venna*, p. 140, *infra*.

continue to flow—and those acts which are continuing. Once the act is complete, it cannot thereafter be said to be a threat to inflict unlawful force on the victim. If the act, as distinct from the results thereof, is a continuing act, there is a continuing threat to inflict unlawful force. If the assault involves a battery and that battery continues, there is a continuing act of assault. For an assault to be committed, both the elements of *actus reus* and *mens rea* must be present at the same time. The '*actus reus*' is the action causing the effect on the victim's mind: see the observations of Parke, B., in *R.* v. *St. George*.[1] The '*mens rea*' is the intention to cause that effect. It is not necessary that *mens rea* should be present at the inception of the *actus reus*; it can be super-imposed on an existing act. On the other hand, the subse-quent inception of *mens rea* cannot convert an act which has been completed without *mens rea* into an assault."

Bridge, J. (dissenting)—

". . . I have been unable to find any way of regarding the facts which satisfied me that they amounted to the crime of assault. This has not been for want of trying; but at every attempt I have encountered the inescapable question: after the wheel of the appellant's car had accidentally come to rest on the constable's foot, what was it that the appellant *did* which constituted the act of assault? However the question is approached, the answer which I feel obliged to give is: precisely nothing."

APPEAL DISMISSED.

R. v. VENNA
[1975] 3 All E.R. 788

Recklessness in its subjective sense is sufficient mens rea for assault and for battery.

Venna was involved in a struggle with police officers who were trying to arrest him. He fell to the ground and proceeded to lash out with his legs. In doing so he kicked the hand of one of the officers, fracturing a bone. Venna was charged, *inter alia*, with assault occasioning actual bodily harm, contrary to s. 47 of the Offences against the Person

---

[1] (1840), 9 C. & P. 483, at pp. 490, 493; p. 143, *infra*.

Act 1861. The jury were directed that they could find Venna guilty if they found that he had deliberately brought his foot down on the officer's hand or had lashed out with his feet, "reckless as to who was there, not caring one iota as to whether he kicked somebody". Venna was convicted and appealed.

Extracts from the Judgment of the Court of Appeal

James, L.J.—

"In *Fagan* v. *Metropolitan Police Comr*,[1] it was said: 'An assault is any act which intentionally or possibly recklessly causes another person to apprehend immediate and unlawful personal violence.' In *Fagan* it was not necessary to decide the question whether proof of recklessness is sufficient to establish the mens rea ingredient of assault. That question falls for decision in the present case. . . .

On the evidence of the appellant himself, one would have thought that the inescapable inference was that the appellant intended to make physical contact with whoever might try to restrain him. Be that as it may, in the light of the direction given, the verdict may have been arrived at on the basis of 'recklessness'. Counsel for the appellant cited *Ackroyd* v. *Barrett*[2] in support of his argument that recklessness, which falls short of intention, is not enough to support a charge of battery, and argued that, there being no authority to the contrary, it is now too late to extend the law by a decision of the courts and that any extension must be by the decision of Parliament.

Counsel for the appellant sought support from the distinction between the offences which are assaults and offences which by statute include the element contained in the word 'maliciously', e.g. unlawful and malicious wounding contrary to s. 20 of the Offences against the Person Act 1861, in which recklessness will suffice to support the charge: see *R.* v. *Cunningham*.[3] In so far as the editors of textbooks commit themselves to an opinion on this branch of the law, they are favourable to the view that recklessness is or should logically be sufficient to support the charge of assault or battery. . . .

---

[1] [1969] 1 Q.B. 439, at p. 440; [1968] 3 All E.R. 442, at p. 442; p. 138, *supra*.

[2] (1894), 11 T.L.R. 115.

[3] [1957] 2 Q.B. 396; [1957] 2 All E.R. 412; p. 166, *infra*.

We think that the decision in *Ackroyd* v. *Barrett* is explicable on the basis that the facts of the case did not support a finding of recklessness. The case was not argued for both sides. *R.* v. *Bradshaw*[1] can be read as supporting the view that unlawful physical force applied recklessly constitutes a criminal assault. In our view the element of mens rea in the offence of battery is satisfied by proof that the defendant intentionally or recklessly applied force to the person of another. If it were otherwise, the strange consequence would be that an offence of unlawful wounding contrary to s. 20 of the Offences against the Person Act 1861 could be established by proof that the defendant wounded the victim either intentionally or recklessly, but if the victim's skin was not broken and the offence was therefore laid as an assault occasioning bodily harm contrary to s. 47 of the 1861 Act, it would be necessary to prove that the physical force was intentionally applied. . . .

We see no reason in logic or in law why a person who recklessly applies physical force to the person of another should be outside the criminal law of assault. In many cases the dividing line between intention and recklessness is barely distinguishable. This is such a case. In our judgment the direction was right in law. . . ."

APPEAL DISMISSED.

Note

As is implied in *Venna*, the *mens rea* for the offence of assault occasioning actual bodily harm is merely that for assault or battery: the prosecution does not have to prove that the accused foresaw actual bodily harm to his victim, see *Roberts* (1971), 56 Cr. App. Rep. 95.

STEPHENS v. MYERS
(1830), 4 C. & P. 349

A person may be guilty of an assault although he is prevented from touching his victim.

This was a civil action in which the plaintiff claimed damages for assault from the defendant. The plaintiff was chairman at a meeting where he sat at the same table as

---

[1] (1878), 14 Cox C.C. 83.

the defendant, but was separated from him by six or seven other people. The plaintiff ordered the defendant to leave the meeting on account of his disorderly behaviour, whereupon the defendant advanced toward the plaintiff with his fists clenched saying that he would remove him from the chair. Other people intervened before he was near enough to the plaintiff to have hit him.

Extract from the Summing-up to the Jury

Tindall, C.J.—

"It is not every threat, when there is no actual personal violence, that constitutes an assault, there must, in all cases, be the means of carrying the threat into effect.[1] The question I shall leave to you will be, whether the defendant was advancing at the time, in a threatening attitude, to strike the chairman, so that his blow would almost immediately have reached the chairman, if he had not been stopped; then though he was not near enough at the time to have struck him, yet if he was advancing with that intent, I think it amounts to an assault in law. If he was so advancing, that, within a second or two of time, he would have reached the plaintiff, it seems to me it is an assault in law. If you think he was not advancing to strike the plaintiff, then only can you find your verdict for the defendant; otherwise you must find it for the plaintiff, and give him such damages as you think the nature of the case requires."

VERDICT FOR THE PLAINTIFF.

R. v. ST. GEORGE[2]
(1840), 9 C. & P. 483

Since an assault is any act which, intentionally or recklessly, causes another to apprehend the immediate application of unlawful force, pointing an unloaded gun at another person who is unaware that it is unloaded may amount to an assault.

St. George was charged under a statute which has since been repealed with feloniously attempting to discharge loaded firearms by drawing the trigger. The evidence was

---

[1] *Sed quaere*; see next case.
[2] For a discussion of this case in relation to that of *James* (1844), 1 Car. & Kir. 530, see *Modern Approach to Criminal Law*, pp. 352–355.

that he had pointed a gun at the prosecutor, and the jury found that it was loaded. He was restrained from drawing the trigger. The judge expressed the view that a person could only be convicted of an assault under the particular section of the statute in question if the assault was connected with the presentation of loaded firearms, but he also expressed the view that the pointing of an unloaded gun at a person might amount to a common assault.

Extract from the Observations

PARKE, B.—

". . . My idea is, that the prisoner can only be found guilty under this Act of Parliament for that assault which was involved in, and connected with, the presentation of a loaded pistol. Suppose there was a common assault committed in the course of a dispute between the prisoner and the prosecutor, I do not think that the prisoner could be found guilty of that assault on an indictment charging him with felony. . . .

My idea is, that it is an assault to present a pistol at all, whether loaded or not. If you threw the powder out of the pan, or took the percussion cap off, and said to the party, 'this is an empty pistol,' then that would be no assault; for there the party must see that it was not possible that he should be injured; but if a person presents a pistol which has the appearance of being loaded, and puts the party into fear and alarm, that is what it is the object of the law to prevent. I think that if, in this case, it should be proved that the prisoner presented a pistol purporting to be a loaded pistol, and the jury are satisfied that it was so near as to produce danger to life if the pistol had gone off, that that would be an assault in point of law, and that the prisoner might be convicted of that assault upon this indictment."

VERDICT, GUILTY.

FAIRCLOUGH v. WHIPP
[1951] 2 All E.R. 834

The requirement that the accused's act must cause another to apprehend the immediate application of unlawful force means that an invitation to touch the invitor cannot amount to an

*assault on the person invited. Thus, the accused is not guilty
of an indecent assault if he invites a young girl to touch him in
circumstances amounting to gross indecency.*

The accused was charged with an indecent assault upon
a girl of nine. While making water on the bank of a river he
said to the girl as she was passing "touch it" and she did so.
The accused was acquitted, and the magistrates stated a
case for the opinion of the Divisional Court who were of
opinion that the accused was not guilty of the offence
charged.

Extract from the Judgments of the Divisional Court

Lord Goddard, C.J.—

"An assault can be constituted, without there being
battery, for instance, by a threatening gesture or a threat
to use violence against a person, but I do not know any
authority which says that where one person invites another
person to touch him that can be said to be an assault. The
question of consent or non-consent only arises if there is
something which can be called an assault and, without
consent, would be an assault. If that which was done to
this child was of an indecent nature and would have been
an assault if done against her will, it would also be an assault
if it was done with her consent because she could not consent
to an indecent assault[1]. Before we decide whether there has
been an indecent assault we must decide whether there has
been an assault, and I cannot hold that an invitation to
somebody to touch the invitor can amount to an assault on
the invitee."

APPEAL DISMISSED.

Comment on Fairclough v. Whipp

(1) Although it is still the case that conduct such as that of
the accused in *Fairclough* v. *Whipp* does not constitute an assault,
such conduct would now amount to a crime under the Indecency
with Children Act 1960, for s.1 punishes the committing or
inciting of gross indecency with a child of either sex under 14
with a maximum of two years' imprisonment.

(2) It is commonly said that mere words can never constitute
an assault, but the authority for this proposition is very slight,

---

[1] A person under 16 cannot give a valid consent to an indecent assault.
This is now provided by the Sexual Offences Act 1956, ss. 14 (2) and 15 (2).

and there is now a dictum of Lord Goddard in *Fairclough's* case which supports the contrary view, for it is clear that he considered that a threat to use violence may constitute an assault. For further discussion see Cross and Jones, *Introduction to Criminal Law*, 8th ed., para. 7.4.

R. v. DRISCOLL

(1841), Car. & M. 214

If one person assaults or threatens another, such other is only entitled to give such blows as may be reasonably necessary in self-defence.

Driscoll was charged with unlawfully and maliciously wounding the prosecutor. The evidence was that he had become involved in a dispute with the prosecutor in the course of which the prosecutor had advanced towards him with clenched fists. Driscoll's wife thereupon pushed the prosecutor down and Driscoll inflicted the injuries in respect of which he was charged.

Extract from the Summing-up to the Jury

Coleridge, J.—

"If one man strikes another a blow, that other has a right to defend himself, and to strike a blow in his defence, but he has no right to revenge himself: and if, when all the danger is past, he strikes a blow not necessary for his defence, he commits an assault and a battery. It is a common error to suppose, that one person has a right to strike another who has struck him, in order to revenge himself, and it very often influences people's minds; and I have, therefore, thought it right to state what the law upon the subject really is."

VERDICT, GUILTY.

Assaulting, Resisting or Obstructing a Constable

POLICE ACT 1964

"*Section 51*

(1) Any person who assaults a constable in the execution of his duty, or a person assisting a constable in the execution of his duty, shall be guilty of an offence and liable—

(*a*) on summary conviction to imprisonment for a term not exceeding six months or in the case of a second or

subsequent offence nine months, or to a fine not
exceeding £100, or to both;

(b) on conviction on indictment to imprisonment for a
term not exceeding two years or to a fine or to both.[1] ...

(3) Any person who resists or wilfully obstructs a constable in the execution of his duty, or a person assisting a
constable in the execution of his duty, shall be guilty of an
offence and liable on summary conviction to imprisonment
for a term not exceeding one month or to a fine not exceeding
£20 or to both."

KENLIN v. GARDINER
[1966] 3 All E.R. 931

*The use of reasonable force is permitted in self-defence
against an assault by a police officer, however technical the
assault may be, and, though the accused's ignorance that the
person assulted by him was a police officer is no defence to a
charge of assaulting a police officer in the execution of his duty
contrary to s. 51 of the Police Act 1964, a reasonable belief that
the officer was a thug is material on the issue of self-defence.*

The accused, two schoolboys, were observed going from
house to house by police officers. The boys were checking
up on members of their rugby team, but the officers thought
that they were engaged on some criminal purpose. When
the officers approached the boys, the boys thought that they
were thugs, and ran away. In capturing them the officers
technically committed assaults on the boys because they
were seeking to interrogate, not to arrest them. The boys
then committed what, subject to the question of self-defence,
would be an assault upon the officers. The magistrates convicted the boys of offences under s. 51 of the Police Act 1964,
but stated a case for the opinion of the Divisional Court.

The questions stated for the opinion of the Divisional
Court were as follows. (1) Whether the defence of "self-
defence" was open to a defendant in answer to a charge laid
under s. 51 (1) of the Act of 1964? (2) Whether *mens rea* was

---

[1] The Criminal Law Bill (p. 360, *infra*) makes the offence under s. 51(1)
triable only summarily and alters the penalties under s. 51(1) and (3).

an element required in proving an assault within the meaning of s. 51 (1)? (3) Whether a genuine mistake of fact, alone or considered together with the defence of self-defence, amounted to a defence to a charge laid under s. 51 (1)?

Extracts from the Judgments of the Divisional Court

Winn, L.J.—

"In the case of a charge of assault under s. 51 of the Police Act 1964, as in the case of any charge of assault, the justification of self-defence is available just as it is in the case of any other assault. I prefer calling it a justification, to calling it a defence, because it is for the prosecution to exclude justification and not for the defendant to establish it. That is subject to this, that if the self-defence, in this case self-defence by the appellants against a prior assault such as had been committed, in a technical sense, by the respondents taking hold of an arm of each of the appellants, was self-defence against an assault which was justified in law, as, for instance, a lawful arrest, then in law self-defence cannot afford justification for assault in resistance to justified assault by a police officer. So one comes back to the question in the end, in the ultimate analysis: was the respondent entitled in law to take hold of the first appellant by the arm, was he justified in committing that technical assault by the exercise of any power which he as a police constable possessed in the precise circumstances prevailing at that exact moment? The same question arises in regard to the other respondent and the second appellant a little later on. I regret that I feel myself compelled to answer that question in the negative. . . .

The justices have asked certain questions, as Lord Parker, C.J., said, rather in the nature of an examination paper. It is not necessary to give any detailed answers to them, but I will give the answers in case they themselves want to know them, as they have consulted the court. The answer to question (1) is—yes as to any assault unless the assault resisted was itself justifiable. The answer to questions (2) and (3) is that knowledge that the man attacked is a police officer is unnecessary, but a genuine mistake of fact as to the character of the person concerned, e.g., genuine and reasonable belief that he was a thug and not a police officer, would be highly material in judging the scope of reasonableness and the degree of force falling within the liberty or justification of self-defence."

APPEAL ALLOWED.

R. v. FENNELL
[1970] 3 All E.R. 215

A father's mistaken belief that a police officer was unlaw-fully detaining his son is no defence to a charge of assaulting the officer in the execution of his duty.

Fennell's son was involved in a fight and arrested by the prosecutor, a police officer. Fennell pressed the officer to release his son and he struck the officer who was on the point of taking his son to the police station. Fennell was convicted after the trial judge had directed the jury that, if the officer was acting in the execution of his duty as he was, the accused's mistaken belief that the officer had arrested his son unlaw-fully was no defence. Fennell unsuccessfully appealed to the Court of Appeal.

Extract from the Judgment of the Court of Appeal

Widgery, L.J.—
"The law jealously scrutinises all claims to justify the use of force and will not readily recognise new ones. Where a person honestly and reasonably believes that he or his child is in imminent danger of injury, it would be unjust if he were deprived of the right to use reasonable force by way of defence merely because he had made some genuine mistake of fact. On the other hand, if the child is in police custody and not in imminent danger of injury, there is no urgency of the kind which requires an immediate decision, and a father who forcibly releases the child does so at his peril. If in fact the arrest proves to be lawful, the father's use of force cannot be justified."

APPEAL DISMISSED.

R. v. WATERFIELD AND LYNN
[1963] 3 All E.R. 659

In determining whether a constable was acting in the execution of his duty at the material time it is normally pre-ferable to consider whether his conduct was prima facie an unlawful interference with a person's liberty or property. If so, it is then relevant to consider whether (a) his conduct fell within the general scope of any duty imposed by law and (b) whether such conduct, albeit within the scope of such a duty, was in excess of his powers.

The police were anxious to examine a car driven by Lynn, which had collided with a wall, in order to obtain evidence of its collision. Accordingly, two police officers, Willis and Brown, were stationed at the place where the car was parked. Lynn arrived and got into the driving seat of the car. He was told by P.C. Brown that a police sergeant wished to examine the car and that it had to remain where it was. Lynn asked who was going to stop him if he wished to go and P.C. Brown replied that he was. Waterfield then arrived and, having said that the police could not impound the car, told Lynn to drive it away. Lynn started the engine, whereupon P.C. Willis went to the front of the car and P.C. Brown to the back. P.C. Willis signalled Lynn to stop. Lynn put the car into reverse and came into slight contact with P.C. Brown. Lynn then drove the car forward after Waterfield had said: "Drive at him, he will get out of the way". P.C. Willis was forced to jump to one side as the car was driven away.

Inter alia, Lynn was charged with assaulting P.C. Willis in the execution of his duty and Waterfield with aiding and abetting this. Both were convicted and appealed to the Court of Criminal Appeal.

Extracts from the Judgment of the Court of Criminal Appeal

Ashworth, J.—

"The first issue raised in this appeal is whether on the facts as summarised above the police constables, and in particular, Willis, were acting in the due execution of their duty . . . ; the question is, whether they were entitled to [prevent the removal of the car] at any rate without making a charge or an arrest. It is convenient to emphasise at this point that the alleged offences were committed in King's Lynn and that special powers, for example those conferred on the Metropolitan Police under s. 66 of the Metropolitan Police Act 1839, or powers conferred under a special local Act, cannot be relied on as authorising the action of the two police constables.

In the judgment of this court it would be difficult, and in the present case it is unnecessary, to reduce within specific limits the general terms in which the duties of police constables have been expressed. In most cases it is probably more convenient to consider what the police constable was actually doing and in particular whether such conduct was prima facie an unlawful interference with a person's liberty or property. If so, it is then relevant to consider whether (a) such conduct falls within the general scope of any duty imposed by statute or recognised at common law and (b) whether such conduct, albeit within the general scope of such a duty, involved an unjustifiable use of powers associated with the duty. Thus, while it is no doubt right to say in general terms that police constables have a duty to prevent crime and a duty, when crime is committed, to bring the offender to justice, it is also clear from the decided cases that when the execution of these general duties involves interference with the person or property of a private person, the powers of constables are not unlimited. . . .

In the present case it is plain that the constables . . . were preventing Lynn and Waterfield taking the car away and were thereby interfering with them and with the car. It is to be noted that neither of the appellants had been charged or was under arrest and, accordingly, the decision in *Dillon* v. *O'Brien and Davis*[1] does not assist the prosecution. It was contended that the two police constables were acting in the execution of a duty to preserve for use in court evidence of crime, and in a sense they were, but the execution of that duty did not in the view of this court authorise them to prevent the removal of the car in the circumstances. . . . [I]n the view of this court the two police constables were not acting in the due execution of their duty at common law when they detained the car.

Apart however from the position at common law, it was contended that P.C. Willis was acting in the execution of a duty arising under s. 223 of the Road Traffic Act 1960.[2] That section, so far as material, provided that

'a person driving a motor vehicle on a road . . . shall stop the same on being so required by a police constable in uniform.'

That argument, however, assuming that the car park is a road, involves considerable difficulties. In the first place

----

[1] (1887), 16 Cox C.C. 245.
[2] Subsequently re-enacted by the Road Traffic Act 1972, s. 159.

its validity depends on a construction of the section which would enable the constable not merely to require a moving vehicle to stop but to require a stationary vehicle not to move. The court finds it unnecessary to reach a conclusion on that because, in the second place, it is to be observed that the section is merely giving a power as opposed to laying down a duty. It seems to this court that it would be an invalid exercise of the power given by the section if, as here, the object of its exercise was to do something, namely to detain a vehicle, which as already stated the constable had in the circumstances no right to do."

APPEALS AGAINST CONVICTIONS FOR ASSAULTING A CONSTABLE IN THE EXECUTION OF HIS DUTY ALLOWED.

Comment on R. v. Waterfield and Lynn

The decision in *Waterfield* that the police had no power to detain a car which they wished to examine in connection with inquiries in relation to an alleged offence was doubted by Lord Denning, M.R., in *Ghani* v. *Jones*[1]. Lord Denning apparently would be prepared to hold that a common law power of detention existed if certain conditions were satisfied. Of course, Lord Denning's views on this matter do not affect the validity of the general formula stated in *Waterfield* for determining whether a constable is acting in the execution of his duty.

For a rather extreme case where a constable was held to be acting in the execution of his duty, see *Johnson* v. *Phillips*.[2]

DUNCAN v. JONES
[1936] 1 K.B. 218

It is the duty of the police to prevent breaches of the peace and in the discharge of that duty they may forbid the holding of a meeting if they reasonably apprehend a breach of the peace although there may be nothing unlawful in the object of the meeting. A person who nevertheless proceeds with the holding of the meeting is guilty of obstructing the police in the execution of their duty.

About thirty people, including Mrs. Duncan, collected near an unemployed training centre with a view to holding

[1] [1970] 1 Q. 693; [1969] 3 All E. R. 1700.
[2] [1975] 3 All E.R. 682.

a meeting which had been advertised. About two months previously a similar meeting addressed by Mrs. Duncan had been held in the same place and had been followed by a disturbance inside the training centre. It was found as a fact that the police reasonably apprehended a breach of the peace and they forbade Mrs. Duncan to hold the meeting. She said "I'm going to hold it," stepped on to the box and started to address the people, whereupon she was arrested. She was convicted of obstructing P.C. Jones in the execution of his duty; she unsuccessfully appealed to Quarter Sessions and thence by way of case stated to the Divisional Court.

Extracts from the Judgments of the Divisional Court

Lord Hewart, C.J.—

". . . The right of assembly, as Professor Dicey puts it,[1] is nothing more than a view taken by the Court of the individual liberty of the subject. If I thought that the present case raised a question which has been held in suspense by more than one writer on constitutional law—namely, whether an assembly can properly be held to be unlawful merely because the holding of it is expected to give rise to a breach of the peace on the part of persons opposed to those who are holding the meeting—I should wish to hear much more argument before I expressed an opinion. This case, however, does not even touch that important question. . . .

The case stated which we have before us indicates clearly a causal connection between the meeting of May, 1933, and the disturbance which occurred after it—that the disturbance was not only post the meeting but was also propter the meeting. In my view, the deputy-chairman was entitled to come to the conclusion to which he came on the facts which he found and to hold that the conviction of the appellant for wilfully obstructing the respondent when in the execution of his duty was right. This appeal should, therefore be dismissed."

Humphreys, J.—

"I agree. I regard this as a plain case. It has nothing to do with the law of unlawful assembly. No charge of that sort was even suggested against the appellant. The sole question raised by the case is whether the respondent, who

---

[1] Dicey's *Law of the Constitution*, 8th ed., p. 499.

was admittedly obstructed, was so obstructed when in the execution of his duty.

It does not require authority to emphasize the statement that it is the duty of a police officer to prevent apprehended breaches of the peace. Here it is found as a fact that the respondent reasonably apprehended a breach of the peace. It then, as is rightly expressed in the case, became his duty to prevent anything which in his view would cause that breach of the peace. While he was taking steps so to do he was wilfully obstructed by the appellant. I can conceive no clearer case within the statutes than that."

APPEAL DISMISSED.

THOMAS v. SAWKINS
[1935] 2 K.B. 249

A police officer is entitled to attend and remain at a public meeting held on private premises if he reasonably apprehends that a breach of the peace is likely to occur.

The respondent, a police officer, was prosecuted before the justices for a common assault under s. 42 of the Offences against the Person Act 1861. The appellant, the prosecutor, was the convener of a meeting to protest against the Incitement to Disaffection Bill which was then before Parliament, and to advocate the removal of the chief of the County Constabulary. The meeting was held on private premises, and the public were invited to attend without charge. The respondent attended with another police officer, and they both refused to leave on being requested to do so by the appellant who laid his hand on the other police officer. The respondent removed the appellant's hand, saying that he would not have his superior officer molested. Both officers remained at the meeting where no breach of the peace was committed. The magistrates acquitted the respondent, but stated a case for the Divisional Court who were of opinion that the decision of the magistrates was correct.

Extract from the Judgment of the Divisional Court

Lord Hewart, C.J.—

". . . It is said . . . in the books no case is to be found which goes the length of deciding, that, where an offence is expected to be committed, as distinct from the case of an offence being or having been committed, there is any right in the police to enter on private premises and to remain there against the will of those who, as hirers or otherwise, are for the time being in possession of the premises. When, however, I look at the passages which have been cited from Blackstone's *Commentaries*, vol. 1, p. 356, and from the judgments in *Humphries* v. *Connor*[1] and *O'Kelly* v. *Harvey*[2] and certain observations of Avory, J. in *Lansbury* v. *Riley*,[3] I think that there is quite sufficient ground for the proposition that it is part of the preventive power, and, therefore, part of the preventive duty, of the police, in cases where there are such reasonable grounds of apprehension as the Justices have found here, to enter and remain on private premises. It goes without saying that the powers and duties of the police are directed, not to the interests of the police, but to the protection and welfare of the public.

It was urged in one part of the argument of Sir Stafford Cripps (counsel for the appellant) that what the police did here amounted to a trespass. It seems somewhat remarkable to speak of trespass when members of the public who happen to be police officers attend, after a public invitation, a public meeting which is to discuss as one part of its business the dismissal of the chief constable of the county. It is elementary that a good defence to an action for trespass is to show that the act complained of was done by authority of law, or by leave and licence.

I am not at all prepared to accept the doctrine that it is only where an offence has been, or is being committed, that the police are entitled to enter and remain on private premises. On the contrary, it seems to me that a police officer has *ex virtute officii* full right so to act when he has reasonable ground for believing that an offence is imminent or is likely to be committed."

APPEAL DISMISSED.

---

[1] (1864), 17 Ir. C.L.R. 1.
[2] (1883), 14 L.R. Ir. 105.
[3] [1914] 3 K.B. 229, at p. 236–7.

HINCHCLIFFE v. SHELDON
[1955] 3 All E.R. 406

A person is guilty of obstructing a constable in the execution of his duty if he makes it more difficult for him to carry out his duty.

The accused, the son of the licensee of a public house, found the police outside the house after hours. As the police were about to enter, the appellant shouted to his parents that the police were there with the result that the police were not admitted to the house for some little time. When the police entered the house they found no evidence that people had been drinking after hours, but suspected that this had been the case. The accused was convicted of obstructing the police in the course of their duty and the magistrates stated a case for the opinion of the Divisional Court. That court was of opinion the conviction was correct.

Extracts from the Judgment of the Divisional Court

Lord Goddard, C.J.—

". . . The appellant relies principally on *Bastable* v. *Little*,[1] a case in the early days of motoring, where it was held that it was not an offence for a person to say to motorists: 'Look out, you are just entering a police trap', or words to that effect, because there was no evidence in that case that the motorists were committing an offence, and there was no reason to say, as a matter of definite conclusion, that by the time they got to the police trap they would be committing an offence. That case, however, was followed three years later by *Betts* v. *Stevens*,[2] in which it was decided that directly it was shown that an offence was being committed by a motorist in that he was travelling more than twenty miles an hour when an Automobile Association scout gave him warning, then the scout was interfering with the police. The appellant, accordingly, submitted that he could not be convicted unless it was shown that an offence was being committed, but that is to overlook s. 151 (1) of the Licensing Act 1953. There is no such provision as that in the Road Traffic Acts. Section 151 (1) gives the police the right to enter licensed premises, whether an offence has been commit-

---

[1] [1907] 1 K.B. 59.
[2] [1910] 1 K.B. 1.

ted or not. They can go in to see whether it is likely that an offence will be committed. If they are detained from going in, that does obstruct them in the execution of their duty, because it gives the licensee, if he is committing an offence, the opportunity to get everything out of the way.

. . . 'Obstructing' means, for this purpose, making it more difficult for the police to carry out their duties. It is quite obvious that the appellant was detaining the police while giving a warning; he was making it more difficult for the police to get certain entry into the premises . . ."

APPEAL DISMISSED.

RICE v. CONNOLLY
[1966] 2 All E.R. 649

There is in general no legal duty to answer questions by the police, and failure to do so does not constitute wilful obstruction of a police officer in the execution of his duty.

A police officer observed Rice in suspicious circumstances in the early hours of the morning in a neighbourhood in which there had been a number of breaking offences during the night. Rice refused to answer questions or to accompany the police officer to the police station for identification. He said: "If you want me you had better arrest me." He was arrested, but it was not suggested that he was connected with any of the breakings, and he was released.

Rice was charged with obstructing the police officer in the execution of his duty and convicted by the magistrates. He unsuccessfully appealed to Quarter Sessions, and then appealed successfully by way of case stated to the Divisional Court.

Extract from the Judgment of the Divisional Court

Lord Parker, C.J.—

"What the prosecution have to prove is that there was an obstructing of a constable, that the constable was at the time acting in the execution of his duty, and that the person obstructing did so wilfully. To carry the matter a little further, it is in my view clear that to 'obstruct' in s. 51(3) is to do any act which makes it more difficult for the police to carry out their duty. That description of obstructing

I take from the case of *Hinchcliffe* v. *Sheldon*.[1] It is also in my judgment clear that it is part of the obligations and duties of a police constable to take all steps which appear to him necessary for keeping the peace, for preventing crime or for protecting property from criminal injury. There is no exhaustive definition of the powers and obligations of the police, but they are at least those, and they would further include the duty to detect crime and to bring an offender to justice.

It is quite clear that the appellant was making it more difficult for the police to carry out their duties, and that the police at the time and throughout were acting in accordance with their duties. The only remaining element of the alleged offence, and the one on which in my judgment this case depends, is whether the obstructing of which the appellant was guilty was a wilful obstruction. "Wilful" in this context in my judgment means not only 'intentional' but also connotes something which is done without lawful excuse, and that indeed is conceded by counsel who appears for the prosecution in this case. Accordingly, the sole question here is whether the appellant had a lawful excuse for refusing to answer the questions put to him. In my judgment he had. It seems to me quite clear that though every citizen has a moral duty or, if you like, a social duty to assist the police, there is no legal duty to that effect, and indeed the whole basis of the common law is that right of the individual to refuse to answer questions put to him by persons in authority, and a refusal to accompany those in authority to any particular place, short of course, of arrest. Counsel for the respondent has pointed out that it is undoubtedly an obstruction, and has been so held, for a person questioned by the police to tell a 'cock-and-bull' story, to put the police off by giving them false information, and I think he would say well, what is the real distinction, it is very little away from giving false information to giving no information at all: if that does in fact make it more difficult for the police to carry out their duties then there is a wilful obstruction. In my judgment there is all the difference in the world between deliberately telling a false story, something which on no view a citizen has a right to do, and preserving silence or refusing to answer, something which he has every right to do."

APPEAL ALLOWED.

---

[1] [1955] 3 All E.R. 406, at p. 408; p. 156, *supra*.

INGLETON v. DIBBLE
[1972] 1 All E.R. 275

Where a positive act is alleged to constitute a wilful obstruction of the police contrary to s. 51 (3) of the Police Act 1964, it need not be an act which is unlawful independently of its tendency to obstruct the police.

Dibble was charged with and convicted by the magistrates of obstructing Police Constable Tully in the execution of his duty. P.C. Tully had stopped Dibble who was driving a car without lights at night. On smelling alcohol, P.C. Tully requested Dibble to take a breath test under the Road Safety Act 1967. Dibble said that only five minutes had elapsed since he had had his last drink. It was accordingly agreed that a further quarter of an hour had to elapse before the test could be administered. During this time Dibble, when walking with P.C. Tully towards his brother's house, encountered a man who had been a passenger in his car and who was carrying a bottle of whisky. Dibble took the bottle and drank some of the whisky with the intention of rendering a valid breath test impossible.

Dibble appealed to Quarter Sessions where the recorder held that there was no case for him to answer. The prosecutor successfully appealed to the Divisional Court.

Extract from the Judgments of the Divisional Court

Bridge, J.—
"For my part I would draw a clear distinction between a refusal to act, on the one hand, and the doing of some positive act on the other. In a case, as in *Rice* v. *Connolly*[1], where the obstruction alleged consists of a refusal by the defendant to do the act which the police constable has asked him to do—to give information, it might be, or to give assistance to the police constable—one can see readily the soundness of the principle, if I may say so with respect, applied in *Rice* v. *Connolly*, that such a refusal to act cannot amount to a wilful obstruction under s. 51 unless the law imposes on the person concerned some obligation in the circumstances to act in the manner requested by the police officer.

---

[1] [1966] 2 Q.B. 414; [1966] 2 All E.R. 649; p. 157, *supra*.

On the other hand, I can see no basis in principle or in any authority which has been cited for saying that where the obstruction consists of a positive act, it must be unlawful independently of its operation as an obstruction of the police constable under s. 51 (3) of the Police Act 1964. If the act relied on as an obstruction had to be shown to be an offence independently of its effect as an obstruction, it is difficult to see what use there would be in the provisions of s. 51(3) of the 1964 Act.

In my judgment the act of the respondent in drinking the whisky when he did with the object and effect of frustrating the procedure under sections 2 and 3 of the Road Safety Act 1967, clearly was a wilful obstruction of P.C. Tully."

APPEAL ALLOWED.[1]

WILLMOTT v. ATACK
[1976] 3 All E.R. 794

On a charge of wilfully obstructing a constable in the execution of his duty the prosecution must prove that the accused's deliberate act which resulted in the obstruction was done with the intention of obstructing the constable.

A police officer, acting in the execution of his duty, arrested a motorist who began to struggle. Willmott, who knew the motorist, intervened between the motorist and the officer twice with the intention of assisting the officer by persuading the motorist not to resist but thereby making it more difficult for the officer to carry out his duties. Willmott was convicted by the magistrates of wilfully obstructing a constable in the execution of his duty, contrary to s. 51 (3) of the Police Act 1964, and appealed unsuccessfully to the Crown Court. Willmott then appealed to the Divisional Court.

Extract from the Judgments of the Divisional Court

Croom-Johnson, J.—

"The question is then: is it necessary for there to have

---

[1] The decision in *Ingleton* v. *Dibble* was extended in *Neal* v. *Evans*, [1976] R.T.R. 333, to a case where a driver, who had been involved in an accident and who suspected that he might be "breathalysed", consumed alcohol before the police arrived to request a specimen of breath.

been an intention for the acts of the appellant to have been to make it more difficult for the police to carry out their duties rather than, as appears to have been found by the Crown Court here, an intention on his part to make it more easy for the police to carry out their duties? If there was no hostility so far as the intervention by the appellant was concerned, and indeed there appears to be a clear finding of fact as to what the intention of the appellant was on each of the occasions when he did interfere, what is the answer to the question, 'Should there be an intention not merely to do the act but also that the act should be one of hindering the police rather than helping them?' One turns at this point to *Betts* v. *Stevens*[1] which was a case arising out of the warnings given once upon a time by A.A. patrolmen to those who were exceeding the speed limit of the existence of a nearby police trap. Darling, J., dealing with the question of intention said:

> 'The gist of the offence to my mind lies in the intention with which the thing is done. In my judgment in *Bastable* v. *Little*[2] I used these words: "In my opinion it is quite easy to distinguish the cases where a warning is given with the object of preventing the commission of a crime from the cases in which the crime is being committed and the warning is given in order that the commission of the crime may be suspended while there is danger of detection." I desire to repeat those words. Here I think it is perfectly plain upon the facts found by the magistrates in this case that the object of Betts' intervention was that the offence which was being committed should be suspended or desisted from merely whilst there was danger of the police detecting it and taking evidence of it, and that therefore he was obstructing the police in their duty to collect evidence of an offence which had been committed and was being committed. [Then comes an important passage:] He did that wilfully in order to obstruct them in their duty, and not in order to assist them in the performance of their duty nor in order to prevent a motorist upon the road from committing an offence.'

The point is clearly taken by Darling, J., in that case.

It is suggested that if any other construction than the one which the appellant is urging were placed on the words

---

[1] [1910] 1 K.B. 1; [1908–10] All E.R. Rep. Ext. 1245.
[2] [1907] 1 K.B. 59, at p. 63; cf. [1904–7] All E.R. Rep. Ext. 1147, at p. 1151.

'wilfully obstructs' in the subsection, the result would be that any well-meaning bystander who saw the police, for example, having difficulty making an arrest and went to try and help them, would find, if he should unfortunately be the unwitting cause of the criminal escaping through his intervention, that he had himself committed a criminal offence. When one looks at the whole context of s. 51, dealing as it does with assaults on constables in sub-s. (1) and concluding in sub-s. (3) with resistance and wilful obstruction in the execution of the duty, I am of the view that the interpretation of this subsection for which the appellant contends is the right one. It fits the words 'wilfully obstructs' in the context of the subsection, and in my view there must be something in the nature of a criminal intent of the kind which means that it is done with the idea of some form of hostility to the police with the intention of seeing that what is done is to obstruct, and that it is not enough merely to show that he intended to do what he did and that it did, in fact, have the result of the police being obstructed."

APPEAL ALLOWED.

Wounding and Grievous Bodily Harm

OFFENCES AGAINST THE PERSON ACT 1861

"Section 18

Whosoever shall unlawfully and maliciously by any means whatsoever wound[1] or cause any grievous bodily harm[2] to any person with intent to do some grievous bodily harm to any person, or with intent to resist or prevent the lawful apprehension or detainer of any person, shall be guilty of an offence, and being convicted thereof shall be liable to imprisonment for life."

"Section 20

Whosoever shall unlawfully and maliciously wound[1] or inflict any grievous bodily harm[2] upon any other person, either with or without any weapon or instrument, shall be guilty of an offence, and being convicted thereof shall be liable to imprisonment for not more than five years."

---

[1] To constitute a wound, the inner and outer skin must actually be broken, *Moriarty* v. *Brooks* (1834), 6 C. & P. 684; *McLoughlin* (1838), 8 C. & P. 635.

[2] Grievous bodily harm means really serious harm: *Director of Public Prosecutions* v. *Smith*, [1961] A.C. 290; [1960] 3 All E.R. 161; p. 191, *infra·*

R. v. CLARENCE
(1888), 22 Q.B.D. 23

It is neither an infliction of grievous bodily harm nor an assault for a man to infect his wife with gonorrhoea by having sexual intercourse with her, even though he was aware of his condition and she ignorant of it, and even though she would not have had intercourse with him had she known of his condition.

The accused was charged with unlawfully and maliciously causing grievous bodily harm to his wife contrary to s. 20 of the Offences against the Person Act 1861, and with an assault causing her actual bodily harm contrary to s. 47. He had had intercourse with his wife when he knew that he was suffering from gonorrhoea. His wife was unaware of his condition and would not have consented to intercourse had she known of it. The accused was convicted on both counts, but a case was reserved for the opinion of the Court for Crown Cases Reserved and that court was of opinion by a majority of nine to four that the convictions should be quashed.

Extracts from the Judgments of the Court for Crown Cases Reserved

Stephen, J.—

"Indeed though the word assault is not used in the section,[1] I think the words imply an assault and battery of which a wound or grievous bodily harm is the manifest immediate and obvious result. This is supported by *R. v. Taylor*[2] in 1869, in which it was held that a prisoner could upon an indictment under that section be convicted of a common assault, because each offence 'wounding' and 'grievous bodily harm' 'necessarily includes an assault', though the word does not occur in the section. . . .

Infection by the application of an animal poison appears to me to be of a different character from an assault. The administration of poison is dealt with by s. 24, which would be superfluous if poisoning were an 'infliction of grievous bodily harm either with or without a weapon or instrument'. The one act differs from the other in the

---

[1] P. 162, *supra*.
[2] (1869), L.R. 1 C.C.R. 194.

immediate and necessary connection between a cut or a blow and the wound or harm inflicted, and the uncertain and delayed operation of the act by which infection is communicated. If a man by a grasp of the hand infects another with small-pox, it is impossible to trace out in detail the connection between the act and the disease, and it would, I think, be an unnatural use of language to say that a man by such an act 'inflicted' small-pox on another. . . .

In *R.* v. *Hanson*,[1] in 1849, Vaughan Williams, J., after consulting Cresswell, J., held that the administration of cantharides was neither a common assault nor a common law misdemeanour; and *R.* v. *Walkden*[2] was a decision to the same effect by Parke, B. Upon these grounds I am of opinion that s. 20 does not apply to the case.

Is the case, then, within s. 47, as 'an assault occasioning actual bodily harm'? The question here is whether there is an assault. It is said there is none, because the woman consented, and to this it is replied that fraud vitiates consent, and that the prisoner's silence was a fraud. Apart altogether from this question, I think that the act of infection is not an assault at all, for the reasons already given. Infection is a kind of poisoning. It is the application of an animal poison, and poisoning, as already shewn, is not an assault. Apart, however, from this, is the man's concealment of the fact that he was infected such a fraud as vitiated the wife's consent to his exercise of marital rights, and converted the act of connection into an assault? It seems to me that the proposition that fraud vitiates consent in criminal matters is not true if takeu to apply in the fullest sense of the word, and without qualification. It is too short to be true, as a mathematical formula is true. If we apply it in that sense to the present case, it is difficult to say that the prisoner was not guilty of rape, for the definition of rape is having connection with a woman without her consent; and if fraud vitiates consent, every case in which a man infects a woman or commits bigamy, the second wife being ignorant of the first marriage, is also a case of rape. Many seductions would be rapes, and so might acts of prostitution procured by fraud, as for instance by promises not intended to be fulfilled. These illustrations appear to shew clearly that the maxim that fraud vitiates consent is too general to be applied to these matters as if it were absolutely true. I do not at all deny that in

---

[1] (1849), 2 Car. & Kir. 912.
[2] (1845), 6 L.T.O.S. 194.

some cases it applies, though it is often used with reference to cases which do not fall within it. For instance, it has nothing to do with such cases as assaults on young children. A young child who submits to an indecent act no more consents to it than a sleeping or unconscious woman. The child merely submits without consenting. The only cases in which fraud indisputably vitiates consent in these matters are cases of fraud as to the nature of the act done. As to fraud as to the identity of the person by whom it is done, the law is not quite clear. In *R*. v. *Flattery*,[1] in which consent was obtained by representing the act as a surgical operation, the prisoner was held to be guilty of rape. In the case where consent was obtained by the personation of a husband, there was before the passing of the Criminal Law Amendment Act of 1885 a conflict of authority. The last decision in England, *R*. v. *Barrow*,[2] decided that the act was not rape, and *R*. v. *Dee*,[3] decided in Ireland in 1884, decided that it was. The Criminal Law Amendment Act of 1885 'declared and enacted' that thenceforth it should be deemed to be rape, thus favouring the view taken in *R*. v. *Dee*.[3] I do not propose to examine in detail the controversies connected with these cases. The judgments in the case of *R*. v. *Dee*[3] examine all of them minutely, and I think they justify the observation that the only sorts of fraud which so far destroy the effect of a woman's consent as to convert a connection consented to in fact into a rape are frauds as to the nature of the act itself, or as to the identity of the person who does the act."

CONVICTIONS QUASHED.

Comment on R. v. Clarence

Although *Clarence* is authority that grievous bodily harm can only be "inflicted", for the purposes of s. 20 of the Offences against the Person Act, if it results from an assault or battery, the cases of *Lewis*[4] and *Cartledge* v. *Allen*[5] indicate that if A causes B reasonably to apprehend violence, but not immediate violence, and B suffers grievous bodily harm in trying to escape A will have inflicted grievous bodily harm on B for the purposes of s. 20, even though he has not committed an assault or battery on B.

---

[1] (1877), 2 Q.B.D. 410.
[2] (1868), L.R. 1 C.C.R. 156.
[3] (1884), 14 L.R. Ir. 468.
[4] [1970] Crim. L.R. 647.
[5] [1973] Crim. L.R. 530.

R. v. CUNNINGHAM
[1957] 2 Q.B. 396

For the purpose of a statutory offence malice connotes foresight of the prohibited consequence.

Cunningham was charged with larceny and with unlawfully and maliciously causing W. to take coal gas so as thereby to endanger her life contrary to s. 23 of the Offences against the Person Act 1861. He had torn a gas meter away from the wall and taken its contents. The effect of his conduct was to cause a quantity of gas to escape into the adjoining house in which W. was sleeping and thereby to cause her bodily harm. Cunningham pleaded guilty to larceny and, so far as the other charge was concerned, the trial judge directed the jury that the accused was acting maliciously if he was doing something which he knew he had no business to do. The accused was convicted and successfully appealed to the Court of Criminal Appeal on the ground that the jury had been misdirected with regard to the meaning of the word "maliciously".

Extracts from the Judgment of the Court of Criminal Appeal

Byrne, J.—

"Section 23 provides: 'Whosoever shall unlawfully and maliciously administer to or cause to be administered to or taken by any other person any poison or other destructive or noxious thing, so as thereby to endanger the life of such person, or so as thereby to inflict upon such person any grievous bodily harm, shall be guilty of felony. . .

Mr. Brodie cited the following cases: *R. v. Pembliton*,[1] *R. v. Latimer*[2] and *R. v. Faulkner*.[3] In reply, Mr. Snowden, on behalf of the Crown, cited *R. v. Martin*.[4]

We have considered those cases, and we have also considered, in the light of those cases, the following principle which was propounded by the late Professor C. S. Kenny

---

[1] (1874), L.R. 2 C.C.R. 119.
[2] (1886), 17 Q.B.D. 359; p. 12, *supra*.
[3] (1877), I.R. 11 C.L. 8.
[4] (1881), 8 Q.B.D. 54.

in the first edition of his *Outlines of Criminal Law* published in 1902 and repeated at p. 186 of the 16th edition edited by Mr. J. W. Cecil Turner and published in 1952: '. . . in any statutory definition of a crime, "malice" must be taken not in the old vague sense of "wickedness" in general but as requiring either (1) an actual intention to do the particular *kind* of harm that in fact was done; or (2) recklessness as to whether such harm should occur or not (*i.e.*, the accused has foreseen that the particular kind of harm might be done and yet has gone on to take the risk of it). It is neither limited to, nor does it indeed require, any ill will towards the person injured.'

We think that this is an accurate statement of the law. It derives some support from the judgments of Lord Coleridge, C.J., and Blackburn, J., in *Pembliton's* case.[1] In our opinion the word 'maliciously' in a statutory crime postulates foresight of consequence."

APPEAL ALLOWED ON THE COUNT UNDER S. 23 OF THE OFFENCES AGAINST THE PERSON ACT.

R. v. MOWATT
[1967] 3 All E.R. 47

Where, on a charge under s. 20 of the Offences against the Person Act 1861, the only issue is whether the accused did the acts complained of or whether he was acting in self-defence, it is unnecessary to direct the jury on the meaning of "maliciously". When a direction on the meaning of that word is necessary, the jury should be directed that the accused was acting maliciously if he foresaw any kind of physical harm to the person he attacked.

Mowatt was charged with wounding with intent contrary to s. 18 of the Offences against the Person Act 1861. He alleged that he was acting in self-defence when he assaulted the prosecutor. The jury returned a verdict of guilty under s. 20 of the Act, and Mowatt unsuccessfully appealed to the Court of Appeal on the ground that the judge had failed to direct the jury on the meaning of "maliciously" in s. 20.

---

[1] (1874), L.R. 2 C.C.R. 119, at p. 122.

Extracts from the Judgment of the Court of Appeal

Diplock, L.J.—

" 'Unlawfully and maliciously' was a fashionable phrase of parliamentary draftsmen in 1861. It runs as a theme with minor variations throughout the Malicious Damage Act 1861, and the Offences against the Person Act 1861.

R. v. *Cunningham*[1] was a case under s. 23 of the Offences against the Person Act 1861, . . .

In the words of the court ' "maliciously" in a statutory crime postulates foresight of consequence', and on this proposition we do not wish to cast any doubt. But the court in that case also expressed approval obiter of a more general statement by Professor C. Kenny, which runs as follows:[2]

'. . . In any statutory definition of a crime, "malice" must be taken not in the old vague sense of "wickedness" in general but as requiring either (i) an actual intention to do the particular kind of harm that in fact was done, or (ii) recklessness as to whether such harm should occur or not (i.e., the accused has foreseen that the particular kind of harm might be done, and yet has gone on to take the risk of it). It is neither limited to, nor does it indeed require, any ill-will towards the person injured.'

This generalisation is not, in our view, appropriate to the specific alternative statutory offences described in s. 18 and s. 20 of the Offences against the Person Act 1861, and s. 5 of the Prevention of Offences Act 1851, and if used in that form in the summing-up is liable to bemuse the jury. In s. 18 the word 'maliciously' adds nothing. The intent expressly required by that section is more specific than such element of foresight of consequences as is implicit in the word 'maliciously' and in directing a jury about an offence under this section the word 'maliciously' is best ignored[3]. In

---

[1] [1957] 2 Q.B. 396; [1957] 2 All E.R. 412; p. 166, *supra*.

[2] See Kenny's *Outlines of Criminal Law* (1st edn., 1902); the passage is repeated in the 18th edn. of that work in 1962 by J. W. Cecil Turner (see para. 158a). The passage in the 16th edn. was cited in *Cunningham*: see [1957] 2 All E.R., at p. 414.

[3] This is clearly correct in the case of wounding or causing grievous bodily harm with intent to do grievous bodily harm. However, it is doubtful whether "maliciously" in s. 18 should be ignored where the intent in question is to resist or prevent lawful apprehension, otherwise a person who causes unforeseen serious injury to another in trying to prevent arrest would be guilty of this serious offence.

the offence under s. 20 and in the alternative verdict which may be given on a charge under s. 18—for neither of which is any specific intent required—the word 'maliciously' does does import on the part of the person who unlawfully inflicts the wound or other grievous bodily harm an awareness that his act may have the consequence of causing some physical harm to some other person. That is what is meant by 'the particular kind of harm' in the citation from Professor Kenny's *Outlines of Criminal Law*. It is quite unneccessary that the accused should have foreseen that his unlawful act might cause physical harm of the gravity described in the section, i.e., a wound or serious physical injury. It is enough that he should have foreseen that some physical harm to some person, albeit of a minor character, might result.

In many cases in instructing the jury on a charge under s. 20 of the Act of 1861, or on the alternative verdict which may be given under that section when the accused is charged under s. 18 it may be unnecessary to refer specifically to the word 'maliciously.' The function of a summing-up is not to give the jury a general dissertation on some aspect of the criminal law, but to tell them what are the issues of fact on which they must make up their minds in order to determine whether the accused is guilty of a particular offence. There may, of course, be cases where the accused's awareness of the possible consequences of his act is genuinely in issue. *R.* v. *Cunningham* is a good example. But where the evidence for the prosecution, if accepted, shows that the physical act of the accused which caused the injury to another person was a direct assault which any ordinary person would be bound to realise was likely to cause some physical harm to the other person (as, for instance, an assault with a weapon or the boot or violence with the hands) and the defence put forward on behalf of the accused is not that the assault was accidental or that he did not realise that it might cause some physical harm to the victim, but is some other defence such as that he did not do the alleged act or that he did it in self-defence, it is unnecessary to deal specifically in the summing-up with what is meant by the word 'maliciously' in the section. It can only confuse the jury to invite them in the summing-up to consider an improbability not previously put forward and to which no evidence has been directed, to wit—that the accused did not realise what any ordinary person would have realised was a likely consequence of his act, and to tell the jury that the onus lies, not on the accused to establish, but on the prosecution to negative, that improbability, and to go on to talk about presumptions. To a jury who are not jurisprudents that sounds like jargon. In the absence of any evidence that the accused did not realise that it was a possible consequence of his act that some physical harm might be caused to the victim, the prosecution satisfy the relevant onus by proving the commission by the accused of an act which any ordinary person would realise was likely to have that consequence."

APPEAL DISMISSED.

Comment on R. v. Mowatt

The ruling that a person acts "maliciously" within the meaning of s. 20 of the Offences against the Person Act 1861 if he foresees that his act may have the consequence of causing some physical harm to some person, although he does not foresee the possibility of harm of the gravity prohibited by the statute (a wound or grievous bodily harm) is theoretically objectionable. However, it is not of great practical importance because an accused who, foreseeing only minimal physical harm, in fact causes considerable physical harm will be liable to the same maximum penalty of five years imprisonment as that for an offence under s. 20 on the ground that he is guilty of an assault causing actual bodily harm contrary to s. 47.

R. v. BELFON
[1976] 3 All E.R. 46

Foresight that really serious injury is likely to result from a deliberate act does not constitute the intent to do grievous bodily harm specified in s. 18 of the Offences against the Person Act 1861.

Belfon and another man attacked a group of people who had come out of a public house and had gone to protect a girl who was pushed to the ground by Belfon. During the attack Belfon slashed a man with an open razor, causing severe injuries to his forehead and wounds to his chin and lower chest. He was convicted, *inter alia*, of wounding with intent to do grievous bodily harm contrary to s. 18 of the Offences against the Person Act 1861, and appealed to the Court of Appeal.

Extracts from the Judgment of the Court of Appeal

Wien, J.—

"In the instant case the judge directed the jury in the following terms:

'The law about intent is this. . . . A person intends the consequences of his voluntary act in each of two quite separate cases; first when he desires those consequences and secondly when he foresees that they are likely to follow from his act but he commits the act recklessly irrespective of appreciating that those results will follow.'

This appeal raises the question whether that direction with yet a further elaboration was correct. . . .

Counsel for the Crown submitted that the direction was correct in that foreseeability of the consequences that are likely to follow from a voluntary act is of general application in considering the mens rea required to establish an offence. He conceded that recklessness by itself was insufficient but argued (a) that being reckless was equivalent to a disregard of the consequences, which it unquestionably is, and (b) that 'recklessly' in the context of the direction was an additional element to foreseeability. . . .

Counsel for the appellant submitted that the direction was plainly wrong. 'Recklessness' will not suffice to establish the specific intent required to cause grievous bodily harm though it might be sufficient to establish malice aforethought in a case of murder. . . .

We agree that recklessness cannot amount to the specific intent required by the section, for the reasons shortly to be stated. Counsel for the appellant further submitted that whilst foreseeability of serious physical injury that will probably flow from a deliberate act is a relevant factor in cases of murder, it has no application to a case of wounding with intent because the nature of the particular intent is defined in s. 18 and no further definition is permissible, let alone desirable.

Prior to *Hyam* v. *Director of Public Prosecutions*[1] one ventures to think that it would never have occurred to a judge to explain what 'intent' meant when directing a jury in a case of wounding with intent. He would have told the jury that what has to be proved is (1) a wounding of a person concerned, (2) that the wounding was deliberate and without

---

[1] [1975] A.C. 55; [1974] 2 All E.R. 41; p. 194, *infra*.

justification, that is that it was not by way of accident or self-defence, (3) that the wounding was committed with intent to do really serious bodily harm and (4) that the necessary intent must have been in the mind of the accused, that is the intent of a reasonable or sensible man is irrelevant, for the test is a subjective one and not objective. Nothing more than this was ever called for except in certain cases where an explanation of 'wounding' was desirable. . . .

[Having discussed the differing statements by the members of the House of Lords in *Hyam's* case[1] on the meaning of intention, Wien, J., continued:] Counsel for the Crown, in the instant case, derives support for his contention (though he does not seek it) from what was said by Lord Simon of Glaisdale in *Director of Public Prosecutions* v. *Lynch*[2] which concerned a defence of duress on a charge of murder by a person accused as a principal in the second degree. In reference to the second certified question, which in part dealt with willingness to participate in the crime of murder, he said:[3]

'An example is wounding with intent to do grievous bodily harm. The *actus reus* is the wounding; and the prosecution must start by proving a corresponding *mens rea*— namely, that the accused foresaw the wounding as a likely consequence of his act. But this crime is defined in such a way that its *mens rea* goes beyond foresight of the *actus reus*; so that the prosecution must in addition prove that the accused foresaw that the victim would, as a result of the act, probably be wounded in such a way as to result in serious physical injury to him.'

. . . This court attaches considerable weight to the opinion of Lord Simon. Nevertheless his remarks were obiter. They were expressed in a dissenting speech and so far as one can tell no argument was addressed to him, for it was not necessary to do so, whether one was entitled to enlarge on the intent necessary in the offence of wounding with intent to do grievous bodily harm. At any rate we do not find in that speech or in any of the speeches of their Lordships in *Hyam* v. *Director of Public Prosecutions*[4] anything which obliges us to hold that 'intent' in wounding with intent is proved by foresight that serious injury is likely to result from

---

[1] [1975] A.C. 55; [1974] 2 All E.R. 41; p. 194, *infra*.
[2] [1975] A.C. 653; [1975] 1 All E.R. 913; p. 435, *infra*.
[3] [1975] A.C., at p. 698; [1975] 1 All E.R., at p. 941.
[4] [1975] A.C. 55; [1974] 2 All E.R. 41; p. 194, *infra*.

a deliberate act. There is certainly no authority that recklessness can constitute an intent to do grievous bodily harm.
Adding the concept of recklessness to foresight not only does
not assist but will inevitably confuse a jury. Foresight and
recklessness are evidence from which intent may be inferred
but they cannot be equated either separately or in conjunction with intent to do grievous bodily harm.

We consider that the directions given by the judge in
this case were wrong in law. . . . It is unnecessary in such a
case as this to do anything different from what has been
done for many years."

APPEAL ALLOWED. CONVICTION FOR UNLAWFUL
WOUNDING, CONTRARY TO S. 20 OF THE OFFENCES AGAINST
THE PERSON ACT 1861, SUBSTITUTED.

Note on the reform of non-fatal offences against the person

In the Criminal Law Revision Committee's Working Paper
on Offences against the Person, published in August, 1976, a
number of provisional conclusions are reached[1] concerning the
reform of the offences mentioned in this chapter.

The Committee proposes that the offence of common
assault (assault and battery) should be retained but should be a
purely summary offence, the maximum penalty on summary
conviction being increased to six months' imprisonment or a fine
of £400 or both.[2] It also proposes that a number of statutory
assaults on particular types of people or in particular circumstances should be abolished, but it is uncertain whether the offence
of assaulting a constable under s. 51 (1) of the Police Act 1964
needs to be retained in the light of its various proposals.

The Committee proposes that ss. 18, 20 and 47 of the Offences
against the Person Act 1861 should be replaced by four new
offences. The substance of these would be:

(a) causing serious injury with intent to cause serious injury,
    punishable with a maximum of life imprisonment. This
    would cover most cases at present falling within s. 18 of
    the 1861 Act. As in the case of the next proposed offence
    the distinction between wounding and grievous bodily
    harm would disappear;

---

[1] Paras. 100–126.

[2] The repeal of ss. 42–45 of the Offences against the Person Act 1861
(discussed in Cross and Jones, *Introduction to Criminal Law*, 8th ed.,
paras. 1.5 and 7.8) is also proposed.

(b) causing serious injury recklessly, punishable with a maximum of ten years' imprisonment. This would replace s. 20 of the 1861 Act, but the mental element would be stricter since the accused would have to be aware that he is taking the risk of causing *serious* injury and persist in taking it.[1] This justifies an increase in the maximum penalty from five years' (under s. 20) to ten years' imprisonment;

(c) causing injury with intent to cause injury, punishable with a maximum of five years' imprisonment; and

(d) causing injury recklessly, punishable with a maximum of two years' imprisonment. Offences (c) and (d) would replace s. 47 of the 1861 Act (assault occasioning actual bodily harm). The Committee considers that "injury" should mean, at least, substantial hurt, including unconsciousness and "an hysterical and nervous condition", but leaves open whether it should not have a wider meaning.

The Committee has distinguished offences of intentional injury from those of reckless injury on the ground that the former are more culpable. In formulating the above four offences it has adopted the distinction between intention and recklessness proposed in Law Commission Working Paper No. 31, *The Mental Element in Crime*.[2] Pursuant to this, references in offences (a) and (c) to intention mean in effect that the accused's purpose is to cause serious injury (or injury) or that the accused has no substantial doubt that serious injury (or injury) will result from his conduct. References to recklessness in offences (b) and (d) mean in effect that the accused, knowing that there is a risk that serious injury (or injury) may result from his conduct, takes that risk and that it is unreasonable for him to take it having regard to the degree and nature of the risk he knows to be present.

---

[1] Cf. *Mowatt*, p. 167, *supra*.
[2] See further pp. 211, *infra*.

CHAPTER 4
HOMICIDE

Homicide Generally

R. v. SWINDALL AND OSBORNE
(1846), 2 Car. & Kir. 230

(1) *The contributory negligence of the deceased is no defence.* (2) *If two drivers encourage each other to drive their respective vehicles at a furious speed and one of them kills a third person, they may each be convicted of manslaughter although it is not clear which vehicle ran the deceased down.*

The accused were charged on an indictment containing several counts alleging that they had aided each other to commit manslaughter. They were each driving furiously along a road and encouraging each other to do so. The vehicle of one of them ran down and killed the deceased. The accused were convicted on all counts.

Extract from the Summing-up to the Jury

Pollock, C.B.—

"The prisoners are charged with contributing to the death of the deceased, by their negligence and improper conduct, and, if they did so, it matters not whether he was deaf, or drunk, or negligent, or in part contributed to his own death; for in this consists a great distinction between civil and criminal proceedings. If two coaches run against each other, and the drivers of both are to blame, neither of them has any remedy against the other for damages[1]. So, in order that one ship-owner may recover against another for any damage done, he must be free from blame: he cannot recover from the other if he has contributed to his own injury, however slight the contribution may be.[1] But, in the case of loss of life, the law takes a totally different view—the converse of that proposition is true; for there each party is responsible for any blame that may ensue, however large

---

[1] This statement of the law is not correct today.

175

the share may be; and so highly does the law value human life, that it admits of no justification wherever life has been lost, and the carelessness or negligence of any one person has contributed to the death of another person. Generally, it may be laid down, that, where one by his negligence has contributed to the death of another, he is responsible; therefore, you are to say, by your verdict, whether you are of opinion that the deceased came to his death in consequence of the negligence of one or both of the prisoners. A distinction has been taken between the prisoners: it is said that the one who went first is responsible, but that the second is not. If it is necessary that both should have run over the deceased, the case is not without evidence that both did so. But it appears to me that the law, as stated by Mr. Greaves, is perfectly correct. Where two coaches, totally independent of each other, are proceeding in the ordinary way along a road, one after the other, and the driver of the first is guilty of negligence, the driver of the second, who had not the same means of pulling up, may not be responsible. But when two persons are driving together, encouraging each other to drive at a dangerous pace, then whether the injury is done by the one driving the first or the second carriage, I am of opinion that in point of law the other shares the guilt."

VERDICT, GUILTY.

R. v. SMITH
[1959] 2 Q.B. 35

A wound may be a substantial cause of death although the deceased might not have died had he received proper medical treatment.

The accused, a British soldier serving abroad, was charged before a Court Martial with the murder of a fellow soldier whom he had stabbed in a barrack room fight. The deceased had been dropped twice when being carried to a reception station. He had been wounded in the lung and there was evidence that he might well have survived had he not been given artificial respiration. The accused was convicted and unsuccessfully appealed to the Courts Martial Appeal Court on the ground, *inter alia*, that the jury had not been properly directed on the question of causation.

Extract from the Judgment of the Courts Martial Appeal Court

Lord Parker, C.J.—

"It seems to the court that if at the time of death the original wound is still an operating cause and a substantial cause, then the death can properly be said to be the result of the wound, albeit that some other cause of death is also operating. Only if it can be said that the original wounding is merely the setting in which another cause operates can it be said that the death does not result from the wound. Putting it in another way, only if the second cause is so overwhelming as to make the original wound merely part of the history can it be said that the death does not flow from the wound.

There are a number of cases in the law of contract and tort on these matters of causation, and it is always difficult to find a form of words when directing a jury or, as here, a court which will convey in simple language the principle of causation. It seems to the court enough for this purpose to refer to one passage in the judgment of Lord Wright in *The Oropesa*, where he said:[1] 'To break the chain of causation it must be shown that there is something which I will call ultroneous, something unwarrantable, a new cause which disturbs the sequence of events, something which can be described as either unreasonable or extraneous or extrinsic.' To much the same effect was a judgment on the question of causation given by Denning, L.J., in *Minister of Pensions* v. *Chennell*.[2]

Mr. Bowen [counsel for the accused] placed great reliance on a case decided in this court of *R.* v. *Jordan*, and in particular on a passage in the headnote which says:[3] '. . . that death resulting from any normal treatment employed to deal with a felonious injury may be regarded as caused by the felonious injury, but that the same principle does not apply where the treatment employed is abnormal.' Reading those words into the present case, Mr. Bowen says that the treatment that this unfortunate man received from the moment that he was struck to the time of his death was abnormal. The court is satisfied that *Jordan's* case was a very particular case depending upon its exact facts. It incidentally arose in this court on the grant of an application to call

---

[1] [1943] P. 32, at p. 39.
[2] [1947] K.B. 250; [1946] 2 All E.R. 719.
[3] (1956), 40 Cr. App. Rep. 152.

further evidence, and leave having been obtained, two well-known medical experts gave evidence that in their opinion death had not been caused by the stabbing but by the introduction of terramycin after the deceased had shown that he was intolerant to it, and by the intravenous introduction of abnormal quantities of liquid. It also appears that at the time when that was done the stab wound which had penetrated the intestine in two places had mainly healed. In those circumstances the court felt bound to quash the conviction because they could not say that a reasonable jury properly directed would not have been able on that to say that there had been a break in the chain of causation; the court could only uphold the conviction in that case if they were satisfied that no reasonable jury could have come to that conclusion.

In the present case it is true that the judge-advocate did not in his summing-up go into the refinements of causation. Indeed, in the opinion of this court he was probably wise to refrain from doing so. He did leave the broad question to the court whether they were satisfied that the wound had caused the death in the sense that the death flowed from the wound, albeit that the treatment he received was in the light of after-knowledge a bad thing. In the opinion of this court that was on the facts of the case a perfectly adequate summing-up on causation; I say 'on the facts of the case' because, in the opinion of the court, they can only lead to one conclusion: a man is stabbed in the back, his lung is pierced and haemorrhage results; two hours later he dies of haemorrhage from that wound; in the interval there is no time for a careful examination, and the treatment given turns out in the light of subsequent knowledge to have been inappropriate and, indeed, harmful. In those circumstances no reasonable jury or court could, properly directed, in our view possibly come to any other conclusion than that the death resulted from the original wound. Accordingly, the court dismisses this appeal."

APPEAL DISMISSED.

R. v. BLAUE
[1975] 3 All E.R. 446

A refusal by the victim to have medical treatment which might have saved his life does not break the chain of causation.

Blaue attacked a girl with a knife, causing a serious stab wound which pierced her lung, necessitating surgery. The girl was a Jehovah's Witness and steadfastly refused to have a blood transfusion which was necessary before the operation could take place on the ground that it was contrary to her religious beliefs, despite being told that she would die other wise. She died the next day. Blaue was convicted of manslaughter on the ground of diminished responsibility after the judge had directed the jury that the question of causation was whether at the time of the girl's death the stab was still an operating, or substantial, cause of death. Blaue appealed to the Court of Appeal.

Extracts from the Judgment of the Court of Appeal

Lawton, L.J.—

"In *R. v. Holland*[1] the defendant, in the course of a violent assault, had injured one of his victim's fingers. A surgeon had advised amputation because of danger to life through complications developing. The advice was rejected. A fortnight later the victim died of lockjaw: '. . . the real question is', said Maule, J.,[2] 'whether in the end the wound inflicted by the prisoner was the cause of death?' That distinguished judge left the jury to decide that question as did the judge in this case. They had to decide it as juries always do, by pooling their experience of life and using their common sense. . . .

Maule, J's., direction to the jury reflected the common law's answer to the problem. He who inflicted an injury which resulted in death could not exuse himself by pleading that his victim could have avoided death by taking greater care of himself: see Hale[3]. . . .

There have been two cases in recent years which have some bearing on this topic: *R. v. Jordan*[4] and *R. v. Smith*.[5] . . . We share Lord Parker, C.J.'s, opinion[6] that *R. v. Jordan* should be regarded as a case decided on its own special facts and not as an authority relaxing the common law approach to causation. In *R. v. Smith* the man who had been stabbed would probably not have died but for a series of mishaps.

---

[1] (1841), 2 Mood. & R. 351.
[2] *Ibid.*, at p. 352.
[3] *Pleas of the Crown* (1800), pp. 427, 428.
[4] (1956), 40 Cr. App. Rep. 152. See pp. 177–178, *supra*.
[5] [1959] 2 Q.B. 35; [1959] 2 All E.R. 193; p. 176, *supra*.
[6] [1959] 2 Q.B., at p. 43; [1959] 2 All E.R., at p. 198.

These mishaps were said to have broken the cha... .. causation. Lord Parker, C.J., in the course of his judgment, commented as follows:[1]

> 'It seems to the court that if, at the time of death the original wound is still an operating cause and a substantial cause, then the death can properly be said to be the result of the wound, albeit that some other cause of death is also operating. Only if it can be said that the original wound is merely the setting in which another cause operates can it be said that the death does not result from the wound. Putting it another way, only if the second cause is so overwhelming as to make the original wound merely part of the history can it be said that the death does not flow from the wound.'

The physical cause of death in this case was the bleeding into the pleural cavity arising from the penetration of the lung. This had not been brought about by any decision made by the deceased girl but by the stab wound.

Counsel for the appellant tried to overcome this line of reasoning by submitting that the jury should have been directed that if they thought the girl's decision not to have a blood transfusion was an unreasonable one, then the chain of causation would have been broken. At once the question arises: reasonable by whose standards? Those of Jehovah's Witnesses? Humanists? Roman Catholics? Protestants of Anglo-Saxon descent? The man on the Clapham omnibus . . ?

As was pointed out to counsel for the appellant in the course of argument, two cases, each raising the same issue of reasonableness because of religious beliefs, could produce different verdicts, depending on where the cases were tried. A jury drawn from Preston, sometimes said to be the most Catholic town in England, might have different views about martyrdom to one drawn from the inner suburbs of London. Counsel for the apellant acceppted that this might be so; it was, he said, inherent in trial by jury. It is not inherent in the common law as expounded by Sir Matthew Hale and Maule, J. It has long been the policy of the law that those who use violence on other people must take their victims as they find them. This in our judgement means the whole man, not just the physical man. It does not lie in the mouth of the assailant to say that his victim's religious beliefs which inhibited him from accepting certain kinds of treatment were unreasonable. The question for decision is what caused

---

[1] [1959] 2 Q.B., at pp. 42, 43; [1959] 2 All E.R., at p. 198.

her death. The answer is the stab wound. The fact that the victim refused to stop this end coming about did not break the causal connection between the act and death. . . ."

APPEAL DISMISSED.

THABO MELI v. R.
[1954] 1 All E.R. 373

Where several people plan to kill the deceased and in fact kill him, the court will not necessarily divide the transaction into two parts in order to ascertain whether it was the act done with malice aforethought which in fact killed the deceased.

The accused were charged and convicted of murder before the High Court of Basutoland. They had planned to kill the deceased in a hut and throw his body over a cliff so as to make it appear that the death was accidental. The accused struck the deceased blows in the hut and threw him over a cliff. There was, however, some evidence that the deceased was not dead when thrown over the cliff but died in consequence of exposure. The accused unsuccessfully appealed to the Privy Council on the ground that the blows inflicted with malice aforethought were not the cause of the death of the deceased and that they lacked malice aforethought when they threw the deceased over the cliff because they believed him to be dead.

Extract from the Advice of the Privy Council

Lord Reid.—

"There is no doubt that the accused set out to do all these acts in order to achieve their plan, and as parts of their plan; and it is much too refined a ground of judgment to say that, because they were under a misapprehension at one stage and thought that their guilty purpose had been achieved before, in fact, it was achieved, therefore they are to escape the penalties of the law. Their Lordships do not think that this is a matter which is susceptible of elaboration. There appears to be no case, either in South Africa or England, or for that matter elsewhere, which resembles the present. Their Lordships can find no difference relevant to the present case between the law of South Africa and the law of England;

and they are of opinion that by both laws there can be no separation such as that for which the accused contend. Their crime is not reduced from murder to a lesser crime merely because the accused were under some misapprehension for a time during the completion of their criminal plot.

Their Lordships must, therefore, humbly advise Her Majesty that this appeal should be dismissed.''

APPEAL DISMISSED.

R. v. CHURCH
[1965] 2 All E.R. 72

Where the accused's acts can be treated as part of one transaction the fact that he believed his victim to be dead when he did the act which in fact killed her does not render him innocent of an offence of homicide.

See p. 228, *infra*.

R. v. ROSE
(1884), 15 Cox C.C. 540

Homicide is lawful if committed by one who reasonably believes that there is no other means of preventing the commission of a violent crime.

The accused was charged with murder. The evidence was that he was living with his mother and father, and that his father, a man of great physical strength, frequently quarrelled with his mother, whom he believed to have been unfaithful. The accused was a boy of 21, and there was no doubt that he would have been worsted in a fight with his father. In the night when the deceased met his death, the accused's mother called out "murder", and there was evidence of a violent quarrel between the accused's father and mother; the father forced the mother to the top of the stairs and threatened to knife her. The accused shot and killed his father, and there was no evidence of the presence of a knife.

Extract from Summing-up to the Jury

Lopes, J.—

"Homicide is excusable if a person takes away the life of another in defending himself, if the fatal blow which takes away life is necessary for his preservation. The law says not only in self-defence such as I have described may homicide be excusable, but also it may be excusable if the fatal blow inflicted was necessary for the preservation of life. In the case of parent and child, if the parent has reason to believe that the life of a child is in imminent danger by reason of an assault by another person, and that the only possible, fair, and reasonable means of saving the child's life is by doing something which will cause the death of that person, the law excuses that act. It is the same of a child with regard to a parent; it is the same in the case of a husband and wife. Therefore, I propose to lay the law before you in this form: If you think, having regard to the evidence, and drawing fair and proper inferences from it, that the prisoner at the bar acted without vindictive feeling towards his father when he fired the shot, if you think that at the time he fired that shot he honestly believed, and had reasonable grounds for the belief, that his mother's life was in imminent peril, and that the fatal shot which he fired was absolutely necessary for the preservation of her life, then he ought to be excused, and the law will excuse him, from the consequences of the homicide. If, however, on the other hand, you cannot come to that conclusion, if you think, and think without any reasonable doubt, that it is not a fair inference to be drawn from the evidence, but are clearly of opinion that he acted vindictively, and had not such a belief as I have described to you, or had not reasonable grounds for such a belief, then you must find him guilty of murder."

VERDICT, NOT GUILTY.

PALMER v. R.
[1971] 1 All E.R. 1077

There is no rule of law that, where self-defence is pleaded in answer to a charge of murder, the jury must be directed to convict of manslaughter if, though they think that the accused had reasonable grounds for believing that his life was in danger, he caused the death of the deceased by the use of unreasonable force.

Palmer was a member of a party thought to have stolen ganja from a house in Jamaica. The deceased was a member of a party which went in pursuit of Palmer's party. It was not disputed that the deceased was killed by a shot fired from a gun in the possession of one of Palmer's party, but Palmer's defence was that he had not got possession of the gun when the shot was fired. The trial judge took the view that, in addition to putting the defence raised by Palmer to the jury, it was proper to direct the jury with regard to the possibility of an acquittal on the ground of self-defence; but he did not tell the jury that they should return a verdict of manslaughter if of opinion that, though the case was one of self-defence, Palmer had used excessive force in further-ance of self-defence. Palmer was convicted of murder and unsuccessfully appealed to the Court of Criminal Appeal of Jamaica and then to the Privy Council.

Extracts from the Advice of the Privy Council

Lord Morris of Borth-y-Gest.—

"It was claimed that support for the contention of the appellant could be found in the judgments of the High Court of Australia in *R.* v. *Howe*[1]—judgments to which their Lordships pay the highest respect. . . .

On the assumption that an attack of a violent and felonious nature, or at least of an unlawful nature, was made or threatened so that a person under attack or threat of attack reasonably feared for his life or the safety of his person from injury, violation or indecent or insulting usage so that occasion had arisen entitling a person to resort to force to repel force or apprehended force, then Sir Owen Dixon, C.J., stated that the law was as follows:[2]

'Had he used no more force than was proportionate to the danger in which he stood, or reasonably supposed he stood, although he thereby caused the death of his assailant he would not have been guilty either of murder or man-slaughter. But assuming that he was not entitled to a complete defence to a charge of murder, for the reason only that the force of violence which he used against his assailant or apprehended assailant went beyond what was needed for his protection or what the circumstances could cause him

---

[1] (1958), 100 C.L.R. 448.
[2] (1958), 100 C.L.R., at pp. 460, 461.

reasonably to believe to be necessary for his protection, of what crime does he stand guilty? Is the consequence of the failure of his plea of self-defence on the ground that he is guilty of murder or does it operate to reduce the homicide to manslaughter? There is no clear and definite judicial decision providing an answer to this question but it seems reasonable in principle to regard such a homicide as reduced to man-slaughter, and that view has the support of not a few judicial statements to be found in the reports. . . .'

A wholly different line was taken in *De Freitas* v. *R.*,[1] which was an appeal from the Supreme Court of British Guiana to the Federal Supreme Court. After a review of many authorities the court preferred not to follow the development of the law propounded in *R.* v. *Howe.*[2] They sought to avoid the necessity of requiring a jury to go through a complicated and difficult process. An accused who has done no more than was in the opinion of the jury reasonably necessary in self-defence was entitled to be acquitted. If he has gone further then consideration as to provocation may reduce an offence so that the verdict should be one of manslaughter. . . .

But their Lordships consider in agreement with the approach in *De Freitas* v. *R.*[1] that if the prosecution have shown that what was done was not done in self-defence then that issue is eliminated from the case. If the jury consider that an accused acted in self-defence or if the jury are in doubt as to this then they will acquit. The defence of self-defence either succeeds so as to result in an acquittal or it is disproved in which case as a defence it is rejected. In a homicide case the circumstances may be such that it will become an issue whether there was provocation so that the verdict might be one of manslaughter. Any other possible issues will remain. If in any case the view is possible that the intent necessary to constitute the crime of murder was lacking then that matter would be left to the jury."

APPEAL DISMISSED.

---

[1] (1960), 2 W.I.R. 523.
[2] (1958), 100 C.L.R. 448.

R. v. McINNES
[1971] 3 All E.R. 295

(1) *There is no rule of law that, for a plea of self-defence to succeed in answer to a charge of murder or any lesser offence against the person, the accused must retreat as far as he can.* (2) *There is no rule of law that, on a charge of murder, the jury must be directed to return a verdict of manslaughter if they think that, though the occasion warranted action in self-defence, the accused used excessive force.*

McInnes was charged with murder by stabbing. His defence was that the deceased met his death by running against a knife which the accused was carrying. In addition to directing the jury with regard to accident, the trial judge also directed them on self-defence. The accused was convicted and unsuccessfully appealed to the Court of Appeal.

Extracts from the Judgment of the Court of Appeal

Edmund Davies, L.J.—

"The first criticism of the learned judge's treatment of self-defence is that he misdirected the jury in relation to the question of whether an attacked person must do all he reasonably can to retreat before he turns on his attacker. The direction given was in these terms:

"In our law if two men fight and one of them after a while endeavours to avoid any further struggle and retreats as far as he can, and then when he can go no further turns and kills his assailant to avoid being killed himself, that homicide is excusable, but notice that to show that homicide arising from a fight was committed in self-defence it must be shown that the party killing had reatreated as far as he could, or as far as the fierceness of the assault would permit him.'

One does not have to seek far for the source of this direction. It was clearly quoted from *Archbold*[1], which is in turn based on a passage in *Hale's Pleas of the Crown*.[2] In our judgment, the direction was expressed in too inflexible terms and might, in certain circumstances, be regarded as significantly

---

[1] *Archbold's Criminal Pleading, Evidence and Practice*, 1969. 37th edn., para. 2495.

[2] (1800), vol. I, pp. 481, 483.

misleading. We prefer the view expressed by the High Court of Australia[1] that a failure to retreat is only an element in the considerations on which the reasonableness of an accused's conduct is to be judged (see *Palmer* v. *R.*[2]), or, as it is put in *Smith and Hogan's Criminal Law.*[3]

> '. . . simply a factor to be taken into account in deciding whether it was necessary to use force, and whether the force used was reasonable.'

The modern law on the topic was, in our respectful view, accurately set out in *R.* v. *Julien*[4] by Widgery, L.J., in the following terms:

> 'It is not, as we understand it, the law that a person threatened must take to his heels and run in the dramatic way suggested by counsel for the appellant; but what is necessary is that he should demonstrate by his actions that he does not want to fight. He must demonstrate that he is prepared to temporise and disengage and perhaps to make some physical withdrawal; and to the extent that that is necessary as a feature of the justification of self-defence, it is true, in our opinion, whether the charge is a homicide charge or something less serious.'

In the light of the foregoing, how stands the direction given in the present case? Viewed in isolation, that is to say, without regard to the evidence adduced, it was expressed in too rigid terms. But the opportunity to retreat remains, as the trial judge said, 'an important consideration', and, when regard is had to the evidence as to the circumstances which prevailed, in our view it emerges with clarity that the appellant could have avoided this fatal incident with ease by simply walking or running away—as, indeed, he promptly did as soon as the deceased had been stabbed. . . .

The final criticism levelled against the summing-up is that the learned judge wrongly failed to direct the jury that, if death resulted from the use of excessive force by the appellant in defending himself against the aggressiveness of the deceased, the proper verdict was one not of guilty of murder but guilty of manslaughter. . . .

Section 3 (1) of the Criminal Law Act 1967 provides: 'A person may use such force as is reasonable in the circumstances in the prevention of crime . . .', and in our judgment

---

[1] In *R.* v. *Howe* (1958), 100 C.L.R. 448, at pp. 462, 464, 469.
[2] [1971] 1 All E.R. 1077, at p. 1085; [1971] 2 W.L.R. 831, at p. 840.
[3] (1969), 2nd Edn., p. 231.
[4] [1969] 2 All E.R. 856, at p. 858; [1969] 1 W.L.R. 839, at p. 843.

the degree of force permissible in self-defence is similarly limited. Deliberate stabbing was so totally unreasonable in the circumstances of this case, even on the appellant's version, that self-defence justifying a complete acquittal was not relied on before us, and rightly so. Despite the high esteem in which we hold our Australian brethren, we respectfully reject as far as this country is concerned the refinement sought to be introduced that, if the accused, in defending himself during a fisticuffs encounter, drew out against his opponent (who he had no reason to think was armed) the deadly weapon which he had earlier unsheathed and then 'let him have it', the jury should have been directed that, even on those facts, it was open to them to convict of manslaughter. They are, in our view, the facts of this case. It follows that in our judgment no such direction was called for.''

APPEAL DISMISSED.

Comment on R. v. Rose, Palmer v. R. and R. v. McInnes

According to the above three cases negligence may be a partial basis of liability in murder, for Rose would, according to Lopes, J., have been guilty of that offence if he had lacked reasonable grounds for believing that his mother's life was in danger, while Palmer and McInnes were held guilty of murder although they may have believed, albeit without reasonable grounds, that the force to which they resorted was necessary for their protection. It is true that each accused intended to kill or at least to cause grievous bodily harm, and it is proper for the law to require the utmost caution to be taken before effect is given to such intentions; but verdicts of manslaughter would appear to be more consonant with modern ideas.

The cases illustrate the "all or nothing" approach of the common law. The defences of prevention of crime or self-defence must either succeed or fail, there is no half-way house. A similar approach was adopted to the defence of necessity in *Dudley and Stephens*[1], and the difficulties occasioned in the civil law by the all or nothing approach to defences such as contributory negligence are notorious.

It is of some interest to recall that where the accused's mistake negatives the *mens rea* which the prosecution must prove in the first instance, his mistaken belief, however unreasonable, provides a defence: *Director of Public Prosecutions* v. *Morgan.*[2]

---

[1] (1884), 14 Q.B.D. 273; p. 401, *infra*.
[2] [1976] A.C. at p. 192; [1975] 2 All E.R. 347; p. 22, *supra*.

By way of comparison, the accused's mistake in a case such as *Rose* relates to a matter which he raises by way of defence and in such circumstances his belief must be reasonable to afford him a defence.

It is doubtful whether even the sanctity of human life justifies the rejection of the half-way house of a finding of manslaughter in cases such as the three set out above.

Murder

HOMICIDE ACT 1957

"*Section 1.—Abolition of 'constructive malice'*

(1) Where a person kills another in the course or furtherance of some other offence, the killing shall not amount to murder unless done with the same malice aforethought (express or implied) as is required for a killing to amount to murder when not done in the course or furtherance of another offence.

(2) For the purpose of the foregoing subsection, a killing done in the course or for the purpose of resisting an officer of justice, or of resisting or avoiding or preventing a lawful arrest, or of effecting or assisting an escape or rescue from legal custody, shall be treated as a killing in the course or furtherance of an offence."

R. v. VICKERS
[1957] 2 Q.B. 664

An intent to kill is express malice aforethought. An intention to do grievous bodily harm is implied malice aforethought, and implied malice aforethought has not been affected by s. 1 of the Homicide Act 1957.

Vickers was charged with capital murder in the course of theft. He had entered a shop with the intention of stealing from it. He had been detected by an old lady and he struck her several blows which killed her. There was no suggestion that Vickers intended to kill the deceased, but the trial judge directed the jury that the accused was guilty of murder if he intended to cause grievous bodily harm to the deceased. Vickers was convicted and unsuccessfully appealed to the Court of Criminal Appeal on the ground that causing grievous bodily harm with intent to do so was "another offence" within the meaning of s. 1 of the Homicide Act 1957 and that an intent to cause grievous bodily harm was no longer sufficient malice aforethought.

Extract from the Judgment of the Court of Criminal Appeal

Lord Goddard, C.J.—

"Murder is, of course, killing with malice aforethought, but 'malice aforethought' is a term of art. It has always been defined in English law as, either an express intention to kill, as could be inferred when a person, having uttered threats against another, produced a lethal weapon and used it on a victim, or implied, where, by a voluntary act, the accused intended to cause grievous bodily harm to the victim and the victim died as the result. If a person does an act which amounts to the infliction of grievous bodily harm he cannot say that he only intended to cause a certain degree of harm. It is called *malum in se* in the old cases and he must take the consequences. If he intends to inflict grievous bodily harm and that person dies, that has always been held in English law, and was at the time this Act was passed, sufficient to imply the malice aforethought which is a necessary constituent of murder.

It will be observed that the section preserves implied malice as well as express malice, and the words 'Where a person kills another in the course or furtherance of some other offence' cannot, in our opinion, be referred to the infliction of the grievous bodily harm if the case which is made against the accused is that he killed a person by having assaulted the person with intent to do grievous bodily harm, and from the bodily harm he inflicted that person dies. The 'furtherance of some other offence' must refer to the offence he was committing or endeavouring to commit other than the killing, otherwise there would be no sense in it. It was always the English law, as I have said, that if death was caused by a person in the course of committing a felony involving violence that was murder. Therefore, in the present case it is perfectly clear that the words 'Where a person kills another in the course or furtherance of some other offence' must be attributed to the burglary he was committing. The killing was in the course or furtherance of that burglary. He killed that person in the course of the burglary because he realised that the victim recognised him and he therefore inflicted girevous bodily harm on her, perhaps only intending to render her unconscious, but he did intend to inflict grievous bodily harm by the blows he inflicted upon her and by kicking her in the face, of which there was evidence. The section then goes on: 'the killing shall not amount to murder unless done with the same malice afore-thought (express or implied) as is required for a killing to amount to murder when not done in the course or furtherance of another offence.' It would seem clear, therefore, that the legislature is providing that where one has a killing committed in the course or furtherance of another offence, that other offence must be ignored. What have to be considered are the circumstances of the killing, and if the killing would amount to murder by reason of the express or implied malice, then that person is guilty of capital murder. It is not enough to say he killed in the course of the felony unless the killing is done in a manner which would amount to murder ignoring the commission of felony."

APPEAL DISMISSED.

DIRECTOR OF PUBLIC PROSECUTIONS v. SMITH
[1961] A.C. 290

(1) *"Grievous bodily harm" means really serious bodily harm both in the context of the law of murder and in that of s. 18 of the Offences against the Person Act* 1861.[1] (2) *Implied malice aforethought constituted by an intention to do grievous bodily harm has not been affected by s. 1 of the Homicide Act* 1957.

The facts of this case are set out at p. 208, *infra*.

Extract from the Speeches of the House of Lords
Viscount Kilmuir, L.C.—

"The last criticism of the summing-up which was raised before your Lordships was in regard to the meaning which the learned judge directed the jury was to be given to the words 'grievous bodily harm'. The passages of which complaint is made are the following: 'When one speaks of an intent to inflict grievous bodily harm upon a person, the expression grievous bodily harm does not mean for that

---

[1] P. 162, *supra*.

purpose some harm which is permanent or even dangerous. It simply means some harm which is sufficiently serious to interfere with the victim's health or comfort.'

'In murder the killer intends to kill, or to inflict some harm which will seriously interfere for a time with health or comfort.'

'If the accused intended to do the officer some harm which would seriously interfere at least for a time with his health and comfort, and thus perhaps enable the accused to make good his escape for the time being at least, but that unfortunately the officer died instead, that would be murder too.'

The direction in these passages was clearly based on the well known direction of Willes, J., in *R.* v. *Ashman*[1] and on the words used by Graham, B., in *R.* v. *Cox.*[2] Indeed, this is a direction which is commonly given by judges in trials for the statutory offence under section 18 of the Offences against the Person Act 1861 and has on occasions been given in murder trials: cf. *R.* v. *Vickers.*[3]

My Lords, I confess that whether one is considering the crime of murder or the statutory offence, I can find no warrant for giving the words 'grievous bodily harm' a meaning other than that which the words convey in their ordinary and natural meaning. 'Bodily harm' needs no explanation, and 'grievous' means no more and no less than 'really serious'. In this connection your Lordships were referred to the judgment of the Supreme Court of Victoria in the case of *R.* v. *Miller.*[4] In giving the judgment of the court, Martin, J., having expressed the view that the direction of Willes, J., could only be justified, if at all, in the case of the statutory offence, said: 'It is not a question of statutory construction but a question of the intent required at common law to constitute the crime of murder. And there does not appear to be any justification for treating the expression "grievous bodily harm" or the other similar expressions used in the authorities upon this common law question which are cited above as bearing any other than their ordinary and natural meaning.' In my opinion, the view of the law thus expressed by Martin, J., is correct, and I would only add that I can see no ground for giving the

---

[1] (1858), 1 F. & F. 88.
[2] (1818), Russ. & Ry. 362.
[3] [1957] 2 Q.B. 664; [1957] 2 All E.R. 741; p. 189, *supra* where such a direction was given.
[4] [1951] V.L.R. 346, at p. 357.

words a wider meaning when considering the statutory offence.

It was, however, contended before your Lordships on behalf of the respondent that the words ought to be given a more restricted meaning in considering the intent necessary to establish malice in a murder case. It was said that the intent must be to do an act 'obviously dangerous to life' or 'likely to kill'. It is true that in many of the cases the likelihood of death resulting has been incorporated into the definition of grievous bodily harm, but this was done, no doubt, merely to emphasize that the bodily harm must be really serious, and it is unnecessary, and I would add inadvisable, to add anything to the expression 'grievous bodily harm' in its ordinary and natural meaning.

To return to the summing-up in the present case, it is true that in the two passages cited the learned judge referred to 'grievous bodily harm' in the terms used by Willes, J., in *R.* v. *Ashman*,[1] but in no less than four further passages, and in particular in the vital direction given just before the jury retired, he referred to 'serious hurt' or 'serious harm'. Read as a whole, it is, I think, clear that there was no misdirection. Further, on the facts of this case it is quite impossible to say that the harm which the respondent must be taken to have contemplated could be anything but of a very serious nature coming well within the term 'grievous bodily harm'.

Before leaving this appeal I should refer to a further contention which was but faintly adumbrated, namely, that section 1 (1) of the Homicide Act 1957 had abolished malice constituted by a proved intention to do grievous bodily harm, and that, accordingly, *R.* v. *Vickers*,[2] which held the contrary, was wrongly decided. As to this it is sufficient to say that in my opinion the Act does not in any way abolish such malice. The words in parenthesis in section 1 (1) of the Act and a reference to section 5 (2) make this clear beyond doubt."

APPEAL ALLOWED.

---

[1] (1858), 1 F. & F. 88.
[2] [1957] 2 Q.B. 664; [1957] 2 All E.R. 741; p. 189, *supra*.

HYAM v. DIRECTOR OF PUBLIC PROSECUTIONS

[1974] 2 All E.R. 41

(1) *A direction to the jury that a person has malice aforethought if he foresees death or grievous bodily harm as the highly probable result of his act is correct.*

(2) *For this purpose "grievous bodily harm" means really serious harm and is not limited to harm of such a nature as to endanger life.*

Mrs. Hyam was the discarded mistress of Jones. She became suspicious of his relationship with a Mrs. Booth. One night she drove to the house where Mrs. Booth was living with her son and two daughters. She poured petrol through the letter box, pushed newspaper in and lit the paper which ignited the petrol. She then left without raising the alarm. Mrs. Booth and her son escaped but her two daughters were asphyxiated by the smoke generated by the fire.

Mrs. Hyam was charged with the murder of the two girls. She said that, although she realised that what she had done was dangerous, she had started the fire only with the intention of frightening Mrs. Booth and that she had not intended to cause death or grievous bodily harm. The trial judge directed the jury that the prosecution had to prove that Mrs. Hyam had intended to kill or do grievous bodily harm to Mrs. Booth. The jury were told that if they were satisfied that when Mrs. Hyam set fire to the house "she knew that it was highly probable that this would cause . . . serious bodily harm" the prosecution would have proved the necessary intent, and it was immaterial that her motive was merely to frighten Mrs. Booth. Mrs. Hyam was convicted of murder and appealed unsuccessfully to the Court of Appeal and to the House of Lords.

Extracts from the Speeches of the House of Lords

Lord Hailsham of St. Marylebone.—

"The Court of Appeal . . . , in giving leave to appeal to the House of Lords, certified that [the appeal] involved the following point of law of general public importance, namely, the question:

'Is malice aforethought in the crime of murder established by proof beyond reasonable doubt that when doing the act which led to the death of another the accused knew that it was highly probable that that act would result in death or serious bodily harm?' . . .

The abolition of the doctrine of constructive malice [by s. 1 of the Homicide Act 1957] laid the way open for the decision in *R. v. Vickers*[1] reargued before a particularly strong full Court of Criminal Appeal. Technically this decision only rejected the ingenious argument of some academic lawyers that, by enacting s. 1 of the Homicide Act 1957, Parliament, despite the express words of the section, had inadvertently got rid of the doctrine of implied malice as well as constructive malice. But, in giving the judgment of the court, Lord Goddard, C.J., took the opportunity to define the doctrine of implied malice so retained, and to give what has since become the classical definition of murder, repeatedly employed ever since, as killing 'with the intention [either] to kill or to do some grievous bodily harm'.[2] . . . It will be noticed that in this definition the reference is to intention and there is no reference to foresight of the consequences as such either as equivalent to intention in murder or as an alternative to the requisite intention, or to a 'high degree of probability' to describe the degree of certainty of what has to be foreseen, although both the foresight and the degree of probability must be at least material which the jury may and, on occasion, must use as the basis on which an adverse inference is drawn as to the intention of the killer. Not unnaturally counsel for the appellant in this case strongly stressed this circumstance in his argument before their Lordships. I have to remark that if at this stage we were to overthrow the decision in *R. v. Vickers* a very high proportion of those now in prison for convictions of murder must necessarily have their convictions set aside and verdicts of manslaughter substituted. This consideration ought not perhaps logically to affect our decision, but I am personally relieved to find that I find myself in agreement with the decision in *R. v. Vickers*.

. . . The question raised by Ackner, J's., charge to the jury is . . . (i) whether, on the assumption that the test is subjective, foresight of the probable consequences is an alternative species of malice aforethought to intention, or,

---

[1] [1957] 2 Q.B. 664; [1957] 2 All E.R. 741; p. 189, *supra*.
[2] [1957] 2 Q.B., at p. 672; [1957] 2 All E.R., at p. 744.

as Pearson, L.J., clearly suggests in *Hardy* v. *Motor Insurers'*
Bureau,[1] whether foresight of the probable consequences is
only another way of describing intention and (ii) on the
assumption that foresight can be used as an alternative or
equivalent of intention whether a high degree of probability
in that which is foreseen is enough. This seems to me the
point in this case, and I do not find it altogether easy to
decide. In order to equip myself to do so, I must embark on a
brief enquiry into the meaning of some ordinary words. It
has been pointed out more than once that 'motive' has two
distinct but related meanings. I do not claim to say which
sense is correct. Both are used but it is important to realise
that they are not the same. In the first sense 'motive' means
an emotion prompting an act. This is the sense in which I
used the term when I said that the admitted motive of the
appellant was jealously of Mrs. Booth. The motive for
murder in this sense may be jealousy, fear, hatred, desire for
money, perverted lust, or even, as in so called 'mercy killings',
compassion or love. In this sense motive is entirely distinct
from intention or purpose. It is the emotion which gives
rise to the intention and it is the latter and not the former
which converts an *actus reus* into a criminal act. . . . On the
other hand 'motive' can mean a 'kind of intention' (see
Glanville Williams[2]). In this sense, in his direction to the
jury, the judge has said: 'It matters not if her motive was . . .
to frighten Mrs. Booth.' . . . I agree with the Court of Appeal
that it is desirable, to avoid confusion, to use the word
'motive' in this context always in the first sense, and I have
attempted so to do.

It is, however, important to realise that in the second
sense too, motive, which in that sense is to be equated with
the ultimate 'end' of a course of action, often described as
its 'purpose' or 'object', although 'a kind of intention', is not
co-extensive with intention, which embraces, in addition to
the end, all the necessary consequence of an action including
the means to the end and any consequences intended along
with the end. In the present case the appellant's 'motive'—
in the second sense—may have been to frighten Mrs. Booth.
This does not exclude, and the jury must have affirmed, the
intention to expose the sleepers in the house to the high
probability of grievous bodly harm and in may cases it may
involve an actual intention to kill or cause grievous bodily
harm. . . .

---

[1] [1964] 2 Q.B., at p. 764; [1964] 2 All E.R., at p. 749.
[2] *Criminal Law* (2nd Edn.), p. 48.

I know of no better judicial interpretation of 'intention' or 'intent' than that given in a civil case by Asquith, L.J., (*Cunliffe* v. *Goodman*[1]) when he said:

'An "intention", to my mind, connotes a state of affairs which the party "intending"—I will call him X.—does more than merely contemplate. It connotes a state of affairs which, on the contrary, he decides, so far as in him lies, to bring about, and which, in point of possibility, he has a reasonable prospect of being able to bring about, by his own act of volition.'

If this be a good definition of 'intention' for the purposes of the criminal law of murder, and so long as it is held to include the means as well as the end and the inseparable consequences of the end as well as the means, I think it is clear that 'intention' is clearly to be distinguished alike from 'desire' and from foresight of the probable consequences. As the Law Commission pointed out in their disquisition[2] on *Director of Public Prosecutions* v. *Smith*[3], a man may desire to blow up an aircraft in flight in order to obtain insurance moneys. But if any passengers are killed he is guilty of murder, as their death will be a moral certainty if he carries out his intention. There is no difference between blowing up the aircraft and intending the death of some or all of the passengers. On the other hand, the surgeon in a heart transplant operation may intend to save his patient's life, but he may recognise that there is at least a high degree of probability that his action will kill the patient. In that case he intends his patient's life, but he foresees as a high degree of probability that he will cause his death, which he neither intends nor desires, since he regards the operation not as a means to killing his patient, but as the best, and possibly the only, means of ensuring his survival.

If this be the right view of the meaning of words, the question certified in this case must, strictly speaking, be asnwered in the negative. . . .

But this . . . does not dispose of the matter. Another way of putting the case for the Crown was that, even if it be conceded that foresight of the probable consequences is not the same thing as intention, it can, nevertheless, be an alternative type of malice aforethought, equally effective

---

[1] [1950] 2 K.B. 237, at p. 253; [1950] 1 All E.R. 720, at p. 724.
[2] Imputed Criminal Intent (*Director of Public Prosecutions* v. *Smith*), pp. 14, 15, para. 18 (12th December 1966).
[3] [1961] A.C. 290; [1960] 3 All E.R. 161; p. 207, *infra*.

as intention to convert an unlawful killing into murder. This view, which is inconsistent with the view that foresight of a high degree of probability is only another way of describing intention, derives some support from the way in which the proposition is put in Stephen's *Digest*[1] where it is said that malice aforethought for the purpose of the law of murder includes a state of mind in which there is—

> 'Knowledge that the act which causes death will probably cause the death of, or grievous bodily harm to, some person, whether such person is the person actually killed or not, although such knowledge is accompanied by indifference whether death or grievous bodily harm is caused or not, or by a wish that it may not be caused'.

If this be right, Ackner, J.'s, direction can be justified on the grounds that such knowledge is itself a separate species of malice aforethought, and not simply another way of describing intention. Apart from *Director of Public Prosecutions v. Smith* (if and insofar as it may be regarded as authority for this proposition) the dilegence of counsel was unable to discover an English case directly supporting this view, . . .

At this point counsel on both sides addressed a number of arguments to the House based on principle and public policy. . . .

Counsel for the defence argued that actual foresight of a high degree of probability was too indefinite a phrase to enable juries consistently to administer this important branch of the law. Reference was made to an observation of Lord Reid in a recent civil case (*Southern Portland Cement, Ltd. v. Cooper*[2]) with which I respectfully agree. Lord Reid said:

> 'Chance probability or likelihood is always a matter of degree. It is rarely capable of precise assessment. Many different expressions are in common use. It can be said that the occurrence of a future event is very likely, rather likely, more probable than not, not unlikely, quite likely, not improbable, more than a mere possibility, etc. It is neither practicable nor reasonable to draw a line at extreme probability.'

If I were to accept the direction of Ackner, J., as correct in the present case for all purposes, or to answer without qualification the question certified in the affirmative, I should, I think, be driven to draw the line in a criminal case

---

[1] *Digest of the Criminal Law* (1877), p. 144, art. 223.
[2] [1974] A.C. 623; [1974] 1 All E.R. 87.

of high importance at precisely the point at which it was said to be neither practicable nor reasonable to do so.

I must, however, qualify the negative answer I have proposed to the question certified as of general public importance. For the reasons I have given, I do not think that foresight of such a high degree of probability is at all the same thing as intention, and, in my view, it is not foresight but intention which constitutes the mental element in murder....

But what are we to say of the state of mind of a defendant who knows that a proposed course of conduct exposes a third party to a serious risk of death or grievous bodily harm, without actually intending those consequences, but nevertheless and without lawful excuse deliberately pursues that course of conduct regardless whether the consequences to his potential victim take place or not? In that case, if my analysis be correct, there is not merely actual foresight of the probable consequences, but actual intention to expose his victim to the risk of those consequences whether they in fact occur or not. Is that intention sufficient to reduce the crime to manslaughter notwithstanding a jury's finding that they are sure it was the intention with which the act was done? In my opinion, it is not . . . . The heart surgeon exposes his patient to the risk, but does everything he can to save his life, regarding his actions as the best or only means of securing the patient's survival. He is, therefore, not exposing his patient to the risk without lawful excuse or regardless of the consequences. The reckless motorist who is guilty of manslaughter, but not murder, is not at least ordinarily aiming his actions at anyone in the sense explained in *Director of Public Prosecutions* v. *Smith*. If he were, it is quite possible that, as in *Director of Public Prosecutions* v. *Smith*, he might be convicted of murder. In the field of guilty knowledge it has long been accepted both for the purposes of criminal and civil law that 'a man who deliberately shuts his eyes to the truth will not be heard to say that he did not know it'. (See *per* Lord Reid in *Southern Portland Cement, Ltd.* v. *Cooper*[1].) Cannot the same be said of the state of intention of a man who, with actual appreciation of the risks and without lawful excuse, wilfully decides to expose potential victims to the risk of death or really serious injury regardless of whether the consequences take place or not? This seems to me to be the truth underlying the statement of the law in Stephen's *Digest* . . . and of those phrases in *Director of Public Prosecutions* v. *Smith* in which it seems to me that a rational

[1] [1974] A.C., at p. 638; [1974] 1 All E.R., at p. 93.

man must be taken to intend the consequences of his acts. It is not a revival of the doctrine of constructive malice or the substitution of an objective for a subjective test of knowledge or intention. . . . It simply proclaims the moral truth that if a man, in full knowledge of the danger involved, and without lawful excuse, deliberately does that which exposes a victim to the risk of the probable grievous bodily harm (in the sense explained) or death, and the victim dies, the perpetrator of the crime is guilty of murder and not manslaughter to the same extent as if he had actually intended the consequence to follow, and irrespective of whether he wishes it. . . .

This is not very far from the situation in this case. . . . Once it is conceded that [Mrs. Hyam] was actually and subjectively aware of the danger to the sleeping occupants of the house in what she did, and that was the point which the judge brought to the jury's attention, it must surely follow naturally that she did what she did with the intention of exposing them to the danger of death or really serious injury regardless of whether such consequences actually ensued or not. Obviously in theory, a further logical step is involved after actual foresight of the probability of danger is established. But in practice and in the context of this case the step is not one which, given the facts, can be seriously debated. For this reason I do not think the summing-up can be faulted, since the judge drew the jury's attention to the only debatable question in the case, and gave them a correct direction in regard to it.

I therefore propose the following propositions in answer to the question of general public importance.

(1) Before an act can be murder it must be 'aimed at someone' as explained in *Director of Public Prosecutions* v. *Smith*, and must in addition be an act committed with one of the following intentions, the test of which is always subjective to the actual defendant: (i) The intention to cause death; (ii) The intention to cause grievous bodily harm in the sense of that term explained in *Director of Public Prosecutions* v. *Smith*, i.e. really serious injury; (iii) Where the defendant knows that there is a serious risk that death or grievous bodily harm will ensue from his acts, and commits those acts deliberately and without lawful excuse, the intention to expose a potential victim to that risk as the result of those acts. It does not matter in such circumstances whether the defendant desires those consequences to ensue or not and in none of these cases does it matter that the act and the

intention were aimed at a potential victim other than the one who succumbed.

(2) Without intention of one of these three types the mere fact that the defendant's conduct is done in the knowledge that grievous bodily harm is likely or highly likely to ensue from his conduct is not by itself enough to convert a homicide into the crime of murder. Nevertheless, for the reasons I have given in my opinion the appeal fails and should be dismissed.''

Viscount Dilhorne.—

"In this House counsel for the appellant contended that the question certified should be answered in the negative. He submitted that knowledge that a certain consequence was a highly probable consequence does not establish an intent to produce that result. 'All consequences that are foreseen are not', he said, 'necessarily intended'. . . .

With regard to [this] contention, so long ago as 1868 Cockburn, C.J., at the Central Criminal Court in the Fenian trials, *R.* v. *Desmond*[1], directed the jury that if a man did an act—

'not with the purpose of taking life, but with the knowledge or belief that life was likely to be sacrificed by it, that was not only murder by the law of England, but by the law of probably every other country.' . . .

Stephen in his *Digest*[2] treated . . . knowledge [that an act will probably cause the death of, or grievous bodily harm to, another] as a separate head of malice aforethought and distinct from those in which intent is necessary. The Royal Commission [on Capital Punishment][3] treated it as justifying a conviction for murder even if the accused did not intend to kill or to do grievous bodily harm. If this view is right, then Ackner, J., was wrong in telling the jury that proof of such knowledge established the necessary intent.

On the other hand, Lord Devlin in a lecture he gave in 1954[4] said that where a man has decided that certain consequences would probably happen, then—

'for the purposes of the law he intended them to happen, and it does not matter whether he wanted them to happen or not . . . it is criminal intent in the strict sense.'

---

[1] (1868), *Times*, 28th April.
[2] (1877), pp. 144, 145, art. 223.
[3] (1953), Cmd. 8932, p. 27, para. 74.
[4] *Criminal Responsibility and Punishment: Functions of Judge and Jury*, [1954] Crim. L.R. 661, at p. 667.

Pearson, L.J., appears to have been of the same opinion for in *Hardy* v. *Motor Insurer's Bureau*[1] he said:

'Then this is the syllogism. No reasonable man doing such an act could fail to foresee that it would in all probability injure the other person. The accused is a reasonable man. Therefore, he must have foreseen, when he did the act, that it would in all probability injure the other person. Therefore, he had the intent to injure the other person.'

Whether or not it be that the doing of the act with the knowledge that certain consequences are highly probable is to be treated as establishing the intent to bring about those consequences, I think it is clear that for at least 100 years such knowledge has been recognised as amounting to malice aforethought. In my opinion, it follows if the second contention advanced on behalf of the appellant is rejected, that the question certified should be answered in the affirmative.

While I do not think it is strictly necessary in this case to decide whether such knowledge establishes the necessary intent, for, if Ackner, J., was wrong about that, it is not such a misdirection as would warrant the quashing of the conviction as, even if it did not establish intent, it was correct in that such knowledge amounted to malice aforethought, I am inclined to the view that Ackner, J., was correct. A man may do an act with a number of intentions. If he does it deliberately and intentionally, knowing when he does it that it is highly probable that grievous bodily harm will result, I think most people would say and be justified in saying that whatever other intentions he may have had as well, he at least intended grievous bodily harm.

I think, too, that if Ackner, J., had left the question of intent in the way in which it is left in the vast majority of cases, namely, was it proved that the accused had intended to kill or do grievous bodily harm, no reasonable jury could on the facts of this case have come to any other conclusion than that she had intended to do grievous bodily harm, bearing in mind her knowledge and the fact that, before she set fire to the house, she took steps to make sure that Mr. Jones was not in as she did not want to harm him. If the normal direction had been given, much litigation would have been avoided.[2]

---

[1] [1964] 2 Q.B. 745, at pp. 763, 764; [1964] 2 All E.R. 742, at p. 748.
[2] This paragraph was referred to by the Court of Appeal in *Beer*, [1976] Crim. L.R. 690, where the court pointed out that it was undesirable to give a *"Hyam* direction" when the facts did not warrant it and that the occasions for a *"Hyam* direction" must be very few.

I now turn to the second contention advanced on behalf of the appellant. This has two facets; first, that the reference to the intent to cause grievous bodily harm has been based on the law that killing in the course or furtherance of a felony is murder, and that when the Homicide Act 1957 was enacted abolishing constructive malice it meant that it no longer sufficed to establish intent to do grievous bodily harm; and, secondly, that, if intent to do grievous bodily harm still made a killing murder, it must be intent to do grievous bodily harm of such a character that life was likely to be endangered.

Committing grievous bodily harm was for many, many years, and until all felonies were abolished, a felony. Consequently so long as the doctrine of constructive malice was part of the law of England, to secure a conviction for murder, it was only necessary to prove that the death resulted from an act committed in the course of or in furtherance of the commission of grievous bodily harm. But when one looks at the cases and the old textbooks, one does not find any indication that proof of intent to do grievous bodily harm was an ingredient of murder only on account of the doctrine of constructive malice. Indeed, one finds the contrary. . . .

Killing with intent to do grievous bodily harm has thus for many years been regarded as murder, quite apart from the doctrine of constructive malice. This was recognised by the Royal Commission on Capital Punishment. . . . The Royal Commission went on to recommend the abolition of constructive malice, and in para. 123 suggested a clause for inclusion in a Bill to bring that about.

Section 1 of the Homicide Act 1957 is in all material respects similar to the clause proposed. It would, indeed, be odd if the Royal Commission by recommending the abolition of constructive malice had in fact proposed the abolition of intent to do grievous bodily harm as an ingredient of murder when the Commission had not intended and did not recommend that. Parliament may, of course, do more by an Act than it intends but if, as in my opinion was the case, intent to do grievous bodily harm was entirely distinct from constructive malice, then the conclusion that Parliament did so by the Homicide Act 1957 must be rejected. In my opinion *R.* v. *Vickers*[1] was rightly decided and this House was right in saying that was so in *Director of Public Prosecutions* v. *Smith*[2].

---

[1] [1957] 2 Q.B. 664; [1957] 2 All E.R. 741; p. 189, *supra*.
[2] [1961] A.C. 290; [1960] 3 All E.R. 161; p. 191, *supra*.

I now turn to the second facet of the appellant's contention, namely, that the words 'grievous bodily harm' are to be interpreted as meaning harm of such a character as is likely to endanger life. In *R.* v. *Desmond*[1] Cockburn, C.J., said that 'knowledge or belief that life was likely to be sacrificed' made a death murder. This may have been unduly favourable to the accused. Stephen in his *Digest* did not limit grievous bodily harm to harm likely to endanger life, though, as counsel for the appellant pointed out, in his *History of the Criminal Law*[2] Stephen said that [the relevant passage] in his *Digest* and para. 174 of the draft Criminal Code produced by the Criminal Law Commission 1878–79 exactly corresponded. The draft Code did not use the words 'grievous bodily harm' but proposed that it would be murder if 'the offender means to cause the person killed any bodily injury which is known to the offender to be likely to cause death'. Therefore, counsel for the appellant contended, when Stephen referred to grievous bodily harm he meant harm likely to cause death. This inference was the sole foundation for this part of his argument.

In *R.* v. *Ashman*[3] Willes, J., said in a case where a man was charged with shooting with intent to do grievous bodily harm, that it was—

> 'not necessary that such harm should have been actually done, or that it should be either permanent or dangerous, if it be such as seriously to interfere with comfort or health, it is sufficient.'

Since then that interpretation has in a number of cases been placed on 'grievous bodily harm' in murder and other cases. . . So far from grievous bodily harm being limited to harm likely to endanger life, since *R.* v. *Ashman* its meaning has been extended. This extension was terminated by the decision in *Director of Public Prosecutions* v. *Smith*,[4] Viscount Kilmuir, L.C., saying that there was no warrant for giving the words a meaning other than that which the words convey in their ordinary and natural meaning. . . .

Our task is to say what, in our opinion, the law is, not what it should be. In the light of what I have said, in my opinion, the words 'grievous bodily harm' must, as Viscount Kilmuir, L.C., said, be given their ordinary and natural

---

[1] (1868), *Times*, 28th April.
[2] (1883), vol. 3, p. 80.
[3] (1858), 1 F. & F. 88, at p. 89.
[4] [1961] A.C. 290; [1960] 3 All E.R. 161; p. 191, *supra*.

meaning and not have the gloss put on them for which the appellant contends. . . .

To change the law to substitute 'bodily injury known to the offender to be likely to cause death' for 'grievous bodily harm' is a task that should, in my opinion, be left to Parliament if it thinks such a change expedient. If it is made, an accused will be able to say: true it is that I intended grievous bodily harm or that I knew such harm was likely to result but I never intended to kill the dead man or put his life in danger and I did not know that by doing him serious bodily injury I would put his life in danger. But I share the view of the majority of the Royal Commission [on Capital Punishment][1] that such a change would not lead to any great difference in the day to day administration of the law.

For these reasons in my opinion this appeal should be dismissed."

Lord Diplock (dissenting).—

"This appeal raises two separate questions. The first is common to all crimes of this class. It is: what is the attitude of mind of the accused towards the particular evil consequence of his physical act that must be proved in order to constitute the offence? The second is special to the crime of murder. It is: what is the relevant evil consequence of his physical act which causes death, towards which the attitude of mind of the accused must be determined on a charge of murder?

On the first question I do not desire to say more than that I agree with those of your Lordships who take the uncomplicated view that in crimes of this class no distinction is to be drawn in English law between the state of mind of one who does an act because he desires it to produce a particular evil consequence, and the state of mind of one who does the act knowing full well that it is likely to produce that consequence although it may not be the object he was seeking to achieve by doing the act. What is common to both these states of mind is willingness to produce the particular evil consequence: and this, in my view, is the *mens rea* needed to satisfy a requirement, whether imposed by statute or existing at common law, that in order to constitute the offence with which he is charged he must have acted with 'intent' to produce a particular evil consequence or, in the ancient phrase which still survives in crimes of homicide, with 'malice aforethought'.

---

[1] (1953), Cmd. 8932.

I turn then to the second question. . . .

For my part, I am satisfied that the decision of this House in *Director of Public Prosecutions* v. *Smith*[1] was wrong insofar as it rejected the submission that in order to amount to the crime of murder the offender, if he did not intend to kill, must have intended or foreseen as a likely consequence of his act that human life would be endangered. . . . I think the reason why this House fell into error was because it failed to appreciate that the concept of 'intention to do grievous bodily harm' only became relevant to the common law crime of murder as a result of the passing of Lord Ellenborough's Act in 1803 [which made it a felony to shoot at, stab or cut any other person with intent to do grievous bodily harm[2]] and the application to the new felony of the then current common law doctrine of constructive malice. This led this House to approach the problem as one of the proper construction of the word's 'grievous bodily harm' which because, though *only* because, of the doctrine of constructive malice had over the past 100 years become part of the standard definition of *mens rea* in murder, as well as part of the statutory definition of *mens rea* in the statutory offence of causing grievous bodily harm with intent to cause grievous bodily harm. I do not question that in the statutory offence 'grievous bodily harm' bears the meaning ascribed to it by this House in *Director of Public Prosecutions* v. *Smith* but the actual problem which confronted this House in *Director of Public Prosecutions* v. *Smith* and the Court of Criminal Appeal in *R.* v. *Vickers*[3] was a much more complex one. . . .

. . . Although Ackner, J.'s, direction to the jury was correct as respect the attitude of mind of the appellant towards the particular evil consequences of her physical act that must be proved in order to constitute the crime of murder, he followed the decision of this House in *Director of Public Prosecutions* v. *Smith* in his direction as to the nature of those particular evil consequences. So he stated them too broadly. . . .

For my part I would allow the appeal and substitute a

---

[1] [1961] A.C. 290; [1960] 3 All E.R. 161; p. 191, *supra*.

[2] This offence was subsequently amended and is now represented by that of wounding or causing grievous bodily harm with intent to do grievous bodily harm under s. 18 of the Offences against the Person Act 1861; p. 162, *supra*.

[3] [1957] 2 Q.B. 664; [1957] 2 All E.R. 741; p. 189, *supra*.

verdict of guilty of manslaughter for the verdict of guilty of murder."

APPEAL DISMISSED.

Comment on Hyam v. Director of Public Prosecutions

Lord Kilbrandon, agreeing with Lord Diplock that the appeal should be allowed, said:[1] "to kill with the intention of causing grievous bodily harm is murder only if grievous bodily harm means some injury which is likely to cause death: if murder is to be found proved in the absence of an intention to kill, the jury must be satisfied from the nature of the act itself or from other evidence that the accused knew that death was a likely consequence of the act and was indifferent whether that consequence followed or not."

The fifth member of the House, Lord Cross of Chelsea, joined with Lord Hailsham and Viscount Dilhorne in dismissing the appeal. However, he was not prepared to decide on the validity of *Vickers*[2] without having the fullest possible argument from counsel on both sides. He concluded:[3] "For my part, therefore, I shall content myself with saying that *on the footing that Vickers was rightly decided* the answer to the question put to us[4] should be 'Yes' and that this appeal should be dismissed."

The even split between those Lords who wished to uphold and to overrule *Vickers* means that the question of the correctness of that decision is still open in the House of Lords; the Court of Appeal is still bound by *Vickers* because the decision in *Hyam's* case, in which Lord Cross concurred, was on the basis that *Vickers* was correct.

DIRECTOR OF PUBLIC PROSECUTIONS v. SMITH

[1961] A.C. 290

An intention to do an unlawful act aimed at another person is malice aforethought provided the act was of such a kind that the ordinary responsible man would, in all the circumstances of the case, have contemplated death or grievous bodily harm as the natural and probable result.

---

[1] [1975] A.C., at p. 98; [1974] 2 All E.R., at p. 72.
[2] [1957] 2 Q.B. 664; [1957] 2 All E.R. 741; p. 189, *supra*.
[3] [1975] A.C., at p. 98; [1974] 2 All E.R., at p. 72.
[4] P. 195, *supra*.

Smith was charged with the capital murder of Police Constable Meehan who was acting in the course of his duties. A car driven by Smith and containing stolen goods had been stopped by an officer on point duty when Meehan questioned Smith about its contents and requested him to draw into the kerb. Instead of doing so, Smith drove away at an increasing speed and on an erratic course with Meehan clinging to the car. Meehan was thrown off Smith's car and killed by being run over by another car. It was not suggested that Smith intended to kill Meehan, but he was convicted of capital murder after a summing-up which contained the following passage: "If you are satisfied that . . . he must as a reasonable man have contemplated that grievous bodily harm was likely to result to that officer . . . and that such harm did happen and the officer died in consequence the accused is guilty of capital murder." Smith appealed to the Court of Criminal Appeal and that Court substituted a verdict of manslaughter on the ground that the basic question for the jury to determine was whether Smith personally contemplated grievous bodily harm to Meehan as the probable result of his conduct. The Prosecution successfully appealed.

Extracts from the Speeches of the House of Lords

Viscount Kilmuir, L.C.—

"Putting aside for a moment the distinction which the Court of Criminal Appeal were seeking to draw between results which were 'certain' and those which were 'likely', they were saying that it was for the jury to decide whether, having regard to the panic in which he said he was, the respondent in fact at the time contemplated that grievous bodily harm would result from his actions or, indeed, whether he contemplated anything at all. Unless the jury were satisfied that he in fact had such contemplation, the necessary intent to constitute malice would not, in their view, have been proved. This purely subjective approach involves this, that if an accused said that he did not in fact think of the consequences, and the jury considered that that might well be true, he would be entitled to be acquitted of murder.

My Lords, the proposition has only to be stated thus to make one realise what a departure it is from that upon which the courts have always acted. The jury must, of course, in such a case as the present make up their minds on the evidence whether the accused was unlawfully and voluntarily doing something to someone. The unlawful and voluntary act must cleary be aimed at someone in order to eliminate cases of negligence or of careless or dangerous driving. Once, however, the jury are satisfied as to that, it matters not what the accused in fact contemplated as the probable result or whether he ever contemplated at all, provided he was in law responsible and accountable for his actions, that is, was a man capable of forming an intent, not insane within the M'Naghten Rules and not suffering from diminished responsibility. On the assumption that he is so accountable for his actions, the sole question is whether the unlawful and voluntary act was of such a kind that grievous bodily harm was the natural and probable result. The only test available for this is what the ordinary responsible man would, in all the circumstances of the case, have contemplated as the natural and probable result. That, indeed, has always been the law. . . .

Strong reliance was, however, placed on the case of *R.* v. *Steane*,[1] in which Lord Goddard, C.J., said: 'No doubt, if the prosecution prove an act the natural consequence of which would be a certain result and no evidence or explanation is given, then a jury may, on a proper direction, find that the prisoner is guilty of doing the act with the intent alleged, but if on the totality of the evidence there is room for more than one view as to the intent of the prisoner, the jury should be directed that it is for the prosecution to prove the intent to the jury's satisfaction, and if, on a review of the whole evidence, they either think that the intent did not exist or they are left in doubt as to the intent, the prisoner is entitled to be acquitted.' That, however, was a very special case. The appellant had been charged and convicted of doing acts likely to assist the enemy, with intent to assist the enemy. His case was that while he might have done acts likely to assist the enemy he had only done so out of duress and in order to save his wife and children. Accordingly, this was a case where over and above the presumed intent there had to be proved an actual intent or, it might be said, a desire by the appellant to assist the enemy."

APPEAL ALLOWED.

---

[1] [1947]K.B. 997, at p. 1004; [1947] 1 All E.R. 813; p. 9, *supra.*

Comment on Director of Public Prosecutions v. Smith

It is only after much hesitation that the above extract was retained in this edition. It is arguable that the proposition stated in the headnote is no longer law, thanks to s. 8 of the Criminal Justice Act 1967. However, there is room for argument that that proposition does still represent the law, and so the above extract was retained.

Section 8 of the Criminal Justice Act 1967 reads as follows:

"A court or jury in determining whether a person has committed an offence (a) shall not be bound in law to infer that he intended or foresaw the result of his actions by reason only of its being a natural and probable consequence of those actions but (b) shall decide whether he did intend or foresee that result by reference to all the evidence drawing such inferences from the evidence as appear proper in the circumstances."

This was the first of three proposals by the Law Commission, and the Commission no doubt intended that it should be enacted simultaneously with the other two in which case there could have been no doubt that the doctrine of *Smith's* case had ceased to be applicable, even to murder; but it is just arguable that it retains its validity in the case of murder, although the doctrine has plainly ceased to be of general application. The doctrine retains its validity for murder, in strict theory, if it is one of substantive law but not, thanks to s. 8, if it is a proposition of the law of evidence.

The remaining proposals of the Law Commission which have not yet reached the statute book read as follows:

(1) "Where a person kills another, the killing shall not amount to murder unless done with an intent to kill." (2) "A person has an intent to kill if he means his actions to kill or if he is willing for his actions, though meant for another purpose, to kill in accomplishing that purpose."

The House of Lords in *Hyam* v. *Director of Public Prosecutions*[1] did not overrule the objective test of malice aforethought (the proposition in the headnote) adopted in *Smith's* case, although Lord Diplock thought that such a result had already been achieved by s. 8 of the Criminal Justice Act 1967. However, the subjective terms of the speeches in *Hyam's* case make it virtually certain that juries will be directed in all murder cases in subjective terms.

The proposition in the headnote would clearly cease to be applicable if the provisional proposals of the Criminal Law Revision Committee, which are contained in the next note, were enacted.

---

[1] [1975] A.C. 55; [1974] 2 All E.R. 41; p. 194, *supra*.

Note

In the Criminal Law Revision Committee's Working Paper on Offences against the Person, published in August 1976, a number of provisional conclusions are reached concerning the reform of the law of murder, which the Committee considers should remain an offence separate from manslaughter.

In reading the Committee's summary of their provisional view, which is set out shortly, it is essential to bear in mind the sense in which the Committee have used the word "intention" in their Working Paper. The Committee referred to Law Commission Working Paper No. 31, *The Mental Element in Crime*, where it is proposed that:

"A person intends an event not only
  (*a*) when his purpose is to cause that event but also

First (*b*) when he has no substantial doubt that that
  alternative event will result from his conduct.

Second (*b*) when he foresees that that event will
  alternative probably result from his conduct."

The Committee continued:

"Generally in this Working Paper when we refer to intention we mean intention in the more restricted sense as described in (*a*) and in the first alternative (*b*) of the Working Party's proposal.[1] If intention were given the meaning attributed to it in the second alternative (*b*) of the Working Party's proposal our discussion of the extent to which risk-taking [i.e. foresight or knowledge of the probability of killing or doing serious injury (but without an intent to kill or cause serious injury)] should be a sufficient mental element in murder would be otiose as this state of mind would, by reason of this definition, be included in any formula requiring intent to kill or intent to cause serious injury. In the interests of clarity, we discuss risk-taking in relation to murder under a separate head, although if risk-taking in some form were to be a sufficient mental element in murder, one way of achieving this would be to widen the meaning of intention."

The Committee summarised its provisional view on murder as follows:

---

[1] The first alternative represents the majority view of the Law Commission's Working Party and the second alternative represents the minority view of the Working Party.

"42. To sum up, our provisional view is that it should be murder if a person, with intent to kill, causes death. In addition, it should be murder for a person, with intent to cause serious injury, to cause death by an unlawful act such as to endanger life or, alternatively, for a person to cause death by an unlawful act intended to cause serious injury and known to the defendant to involve a risk of causing death. We invite comments on which of these alternatives is preferable.[1] We put forward for comment the proposition that it should also be murder to cause death by an unlawful act intended to cause fear (of death or serious injury) and known to the defendant to involve a risk of causing death. The concept of an intention to cause fear may be a novel one and we should welcome observations on whether this is thought to be a possible approach to the problem. We shall welcome comments also on the desirability, or otherwise, of including the most serious types of risk-taking cases (where there is no intent to kill or cause serious injury) within a definition of murder. Which of the alternative propositions restricting the intent to cause serious injury is chosen seems to us to depend to a large extent on whether any risk-taking cases (in the sense mentioned above) are to be included within a definition of murder (whether by adopting the proposal we considered of an act intended to cause fear and known to the defendant to involve a risk of causing death or by some other means).

43. As a consequence of our provisional view on a new definition of murder, we propose a new offence of causing death with intent to cause serious injury. This offence is necessary to cover those cases, at present amounting to murder, where a person, with intent to cause serious injury, causes the death of another but does not fall within either of the propositions discussed above which would limit the intent to cause serious injury in a definition of murder. We propose that the maximum penalty for this offence should be life imprisonment.

44. Although . . . the statement of the requisite intent is the most important element in any definition of murder, there are other elements in the common law definition which would have to be included in a new statutory definition. We mention here only the existing requirement that the death in question must occur within a year and a day from the time when the injury was inflicted. The reason for this rule,

---

[1] The Committee sought comments before 25th March 1977.

which applies to manslaughter as well, was apparently the difficulty of tracing causation where a long interval elapsed between the infliction of the injury and the death. An illustration of this can be found in the case of *Dyson*, [1908] 2 K.B. 454.[1] It is arguable that with the advance of medical science such a rule is no longer necessary. We think, however, that it would not be right for a person to remain almost indefinitely at risk of prosecution for murder; we therefore recommend that the new definition of murder should require that the death occurred within a year from the time when the injury was inflicted."

Mercy killing

In its Twelfth Report[2] the Criminal Law Revision Committee referred to certain tragic cases of murder in respect of which it is arguable that the mandatory imposition of life imprisonment is odious and indeed any sentence of imprisonment is inappropriate. An example of such a case is a deliberate killing done from motives of compassion, e.g. where a husband terminates the agonies of his dying wife. The Committee said, provisionally, that, while such conduct should remain murder, the judge should be able to make a hospital or probation order or grant a conditional discharge where he is satisfied that it would be contrary to the interests of justice for the convicted person to serve any sentence of imprisonment.

In its Working Paper on Offences against the Person, the Criminal Law Revision Committee, having referred to its earlier proposal, continued:

"80. . . . An alternative way is to try and treat such cases not as murder but as some other offence. We have not discussed the question of legalising mercy killing, because this is a matter on which opinion is deeply divided and we do not regard an exercise in law reform as a suitable occasion for the solution of this controversial issue. We have assumed, therefore, for our purposes, that mercy killing will continue to be against the law. In practice it appears that in a true case of mercy killing the defendant is unlikely to be convicted of murder and may be convicted of manslaughter by reason of diminished responsibility if there is

---

[1] In *Dyson* the defendant had inflicted injuries on a child in November 1906 and November 1907. The child died in March 1908. The jury were directed that they could find the defendant guilty if death was caused by the injuries inflicted in November 1906 but the Court of Criminal Appeal set aside the conviction on the ground that death must have occurred within a year and a day after the injury was inflicted.

[2] *Penalty for Murder*, Cmnd. 5184 (1973).

medical evidence of, for example, reactive depression. On a conviction of manslaughter in these circumstances, a probation order is likely to be made or a very light sentence imposed.

82. . . . We suggest that there should be a new offence which would apply to a person who, from compassion, unlawfully kills another person who is or is believed by him to be (1) permanently subject to great bodily pain or suffering, or (2) permanently helpless from bodily or mental incapacity, or (3) subject to rapid and incurable bodily or mental degeneration. We think that there should be a requirement that the defendant had reasonable cause for his belief that the victim was suffering from one of the conditions mentioned in (1), (2) or (3). This definition does not refer to the state of mind of the deceased. We can envisage circumstances in which a person would be within this offence although the deceased expressed a wish to live. In order to ensure that such a case does not fall within the definition of mercy killing put forward above, the definition would have to be amended to require that the killing was with the consent or without the dissent of the deceased.[1] We are conscious of the difficulties in any such requirement, for example in cases in which the deceased is unable to consent or not to dissent because he is unconscious or in the case of a young child. We shall welcome comments on this aspect of the definition.

83. We think that a maximum of 2 years' imprisonment would be an appropriate penalty although in practice it seems to us unlikely that imprisonment would be imposed in many cases.

84. There are advantages in having a separate offence as opposed to giving the judge a discretion in sentencing. If there were a separate offence it would mean that the prosecution would be able to charge the new offence rather than murder and the conviction would be of the new offence and not of murder. We think that the present law is objectionable in that there has to be a charge and conviction of murder in mercy killing cases, unless there is evidence of diminished responsibility, although the defendant may in fact serve a short prison sentence. We envisage that if there were a separate offence on these lines, the prosecution would have the choice of charging murder or the new offence. If

---

[1] Elsewhere in its report the Committee saw no reason for separating killing by consent generally from murder, see para. 73 of the Working Paper.

they charged murder, the defendant should be able to set up mercy killing as a defence. This approach would leave it to the jury to decide, as a question of fact, whether the case falls within the category of mercy killing. We think it is appropriate that the jury should determine whether the defendant killed out of compassion for the victim in the circumstances mentioned above rather than that it should be left to the judge to decide this for the purpose of sentence on a conviction of murder."

Manslaughter

Note

The extracts which follow immediately are concerned with the law of "voluntary manslaughter". This term is used to define cases where, although a person has killed with malice aforethought,[1] he did so pursuant to a suicide pact, while provoked or while suffering from diminished responsibility.[2] The existence of one of these circumstances reduces liability from murder to manslaughter.

HOMICIDE ACT 1957

"Section 4.—Suicide pacts

(1) It shall be manslaughter, and shall not be murder, for a person acting in pursuance of a suicide pact between him and another to kill the other or be a party to the other being killed by a third person.

(2) Where it is shown that a person charged with the murder of another killed the other or was a party to his being killed, it shall be for the defence to prove that the person charged was acting in pursuance of a suicide pact between him and the other.

(3) For the purposes of this section 'suicide pact' means a common agreement between two or more persons having for its object the death of all of them, whether or not each is to take his own life, but nothing done by a person who enters into a suicide pact shall be treated as done by him in pursuance of the pact unless it is done while he has the settled intention of dying in pursuance of the pact."[3]

---

[1] See, for instance, *Lee Chun-Chuen*, [1963] A.C. 220; [1963] 1 All E.R. 73.

[2] Pp. 86–90, *supra*.

[3] It is a statutory offence to aid and abet the suicide of another: Suicide Act 1961, s. 2.

HOMICIDE ACT 1957

"Section 3.—Provocation

Where on a charge of murder there is evidence on which the jury can find that the person charged was provoked (whether by things done or by things said or by both together) to lose his self-control, the question whether the provocation was enough to make a reasonable man do as he did shall be left to be determined by the jury; and in determining that question the jury shall take into account everything both done and said according to the effect which, in their opinion, it would have on a reasonable man."

MANCINI v. DIRECTOR OF PUBLIC PROSECUTIONS

[1942] A.C. 1

(1) *If a person who kills another with a deadly weapon in the course of a fight alleges that he acted in self-defence, it is not always necessary for the judge to direct the jury that they must return a verdict of manslaughter if they believe that the accused acted under provocation.*

(2) *The test to be applied in determining whether there is sufficient provocation to justify a verdict of manslaughter is the effect of the provocation on a reasonable man.*

Mancini was charged with the murder of one Distleman. The evidence which he gave at the trial was that he had been attacked by Distleman and one Fletcher in a club, and that Distleman had an open pocket-knife in his hand. Mancini stated that he struck out blindly with a dagger in self-defence, and that the dagger struck and killed Distleman.

Macnaghten, J., who was the trial judge, directed the jury fully on the question of self-defence, and he also told them that, if they were satisfied that Mancini struck the fatal blow in the heat of the fight without any premeditation, they might return a verdict of manslaughter. Apart from this, he did not allude to the question of provocation.

The jury found Mancini guilty of murder, and he unsuccessfully appealed to the Court of Criminal Appeal on the ground that the jury had not been adequately directed on the question of provocation. He unsuccessfully appealed to the House of Lords on the same ground.

Extracts from the Speeches of the House of Lords

Lord Simon, L.C.—

". . . The main case set up on behalf of the appellant at the trial was self-defence, and the learned judge devoted the first portion of a very careful summing-up to this question. The appellant's counsel found no fault with this part of the judge's charge at all. It was in fact, if anything, too favourable to the appellant, for Macnaghten, J., did not invite the jury to consider whether, even if it were true that the appellant was menaced with the penknife, that would justify the use of the appellant's terrible weapon so as to constitute a case of necessary self-defence, nor did the learned judge make any observations on the question whether the appellant could not have escaped from the threatened danger by retreating from the club. . . .

The fact that a defending counsel does not stress an alternative case before the jury (which he may well feel it difficult to do without prejudicing the main defence) does not relieve the judge from the duty of directing the jury to consider the alternative, if there is material before the jury which would justify a direction that they should consider it. Thus, in *R. v. Hopper*,[1] at a trial for murder the prisoner's counsel relied substantially on the defence that the killing was accidental, but Lord Reading, C.J., in delivering the judgment of the Court of Criminal Appeal, said[2]: 'We do not assent to the suggestion that as the defence throughout the trial was accident, the judge was justified in not putting the question as to manslaughter. Whatever the line of defence adopted by counsel at the trial of a prisoner, we are of opinion that it is for the judge to put such questions as appear to him properly to arise upon the evidence, even although counsel may not have raised some question himself. In this case it may be that the difficulty of presenting the alternative defences of accident and manslaughter may have actuated counsel in saying very little about manslaughter, but if we come to the conclusion, as we do, that there was some evidence—we say no more than that—upon which a question ought to have been left to the jury as to the crime

---

[1] [1915] 2 K.B. 431.
[2] *Ibid.*, at p. 435.

being manslaughter only, we think that this verdict of murder cannot stand.'

To avoid all possible misunderstanding, I would add that this is far from saying that in every trial for murder, where the accused pleads not guilty, the judge must include in his summing-up to the jury observatious on the subject of manslaughter. The possibility of a verdict of manslaughter instead of murder only arises when the evidence given before the jury is such as might satisfy them as the judges of fact that the elements were present which would reduce the crime to manslaughter, or, at any rate, might induce a reasonable doubt whether this was, or was not, the case. . . .

It is not all provocation that will reduce the crime of murder to manslaughter. Provocation, to have that result, must be such as temporarily deprives the person provoked of the power of self-control, as the result of which he commits the unlawful act which causes death. 'In deciding the question whether this was or was not the case, regard must be had to the nature of the act by which the offender causes death, to the time which elapsed between the provocation and the act which caused death, to the offender's conduct during that interval, and to all other circumtances tending to show the state of his mind': Stephen's *Digest of the Criminal Law*, Art. 317. The test to be applied is that of the effect of the provocation on a reasonable man, as was laid down by the Court of Criminal Appeal in *R. v. Lesbini*[1], so that an unusually excitable or pugnacious individual is not entitled to rely on provocation which would not have led an ordinary person to act as he did. In applying the test, it is of particular importance (a) to consider whether a sufficient interval has elapsed since the provocation to allow a reasonable man time to cool, and (b) to take into account the instrument with which the homicide was effected, for to retort, in the heat of passion induced by provocation, by a simple blow, is a very different thing from making use of a deadly instrument like a concealed dagger. In short, the mode of resentment must bear a reasonable relationship to the provocation if the offence is to be reduced to manslaughter. . . .

APPEAL DISMISSED.

---

[1] [1914] 3 K.B. 1116.

R. v. McCARTHY

[1954] 2 Q.B. 105

*In determining whether a plea of provocation should
succeed, the jury are not entitled to take account of the fact that
the accused was the worse for drink, the question always being
whether a reasonable man, in consequence of the provocation
received, could be driven through transport of passion and loss
of self-control, to the degree, method and continuance of the
violence which caused death.*

McCarthy was charged with murder and pleaded provocation. He had killed the deceased by knocking him down
and banging his head many times on the road. McCarthy's
evidence was that he had been drinking, that the deceased
had made indecent overtures to him, and that, in consequence of these overtures he lost control of himself and acted
as he did. The trial judge directed the jury to take no account
of the fact that the accused had been drinking, and McCarthy
was convicted of murder. He unsuccessfully appealed to the
Court of Criminal Appeal on the ground that the jury had
been misdirected.

Extract from the Judgment of the Court of Criminal Appeal

Lord Goddard, C.J.—

"We see no distinction between a person who by
temperament is unusually excitable or pugnacious and one
who is temporarily made excitable or pugnacious by self-
induced intoxication. It may be that an excitable pugnacious
or intoxicated person may be more easily provoked than a
man of quiet or phlegmatic disposition, but the former cannot
rely upon his excitable state of mind if the violence used is
beyond that which a reasonable, or as we may perhaps say,
an average person would use to repel an act which can in
law be regarded as provocation. No court has ever given, nor
do we think ever can give, a definition of what constitutes a
reasonable or an average man. That must be left to the
collective good sense of the jury, and what no doubt would
govern their opinion would be the nature of the retaliation
used by the provoked person. If a man who is provoked
retaliates with a blow from his fist on another grown man a

jury may well consider, and probably would, that there was nothing excessive in the retaliation even though the blow might cause the man to fall and fracture his skull, for the provocation might well merit a blow with the fist. It would be quite another thing, however, if the person provoked not only struck the man, but continued to rain blows upon him or to beat his head on the ground, as happened in the present case and as the accused apparently did in the case of *R. v. Thomas*[1] . . . . It is in our opinion now settled that apart from a man being in such a complete and absolute state of intoxication as to make him incapable of forming the intent charged, drunkenness which may lead a man to attack another in a manner which no reasonable sober man would do cannot be pleaded as an excuse reducing the crime to manslaughter if death results."

APPEAL DISMISSED.

BEDDER v. DIRECTOR OF PUBLIC PROSECUTIONS

[1954] 2 All E.R. 801

In determining whether provocation was sufficient to cause a reasonable man to do what the accused did, the jury are not entitled to take account of the physical peculiarities of the accused.

Bedder was charged with the murder of a prostitute by stabbing. He pleaded provocation. He was sexually impotent and had attempted to have intercourse with the deceased. His evidence was that she taunted him with his impotence and kicked him, thus causing him to lose control of himself and stab her twice with a knife he was carrying. In the course of his summing-up, the trial judge told the jury that an unusually excitable or pugnacious individual, a drunken one or a man who is sexually impotent is not entitled to rely on provocation which would not have led an ordinary person to act as the accused did. Bedder was convicted of murder and unsuccessfully appealed to the Court of Criminal Appeal and thence to the House of Lords.

---

[1] (1837), 7 Car. & P. 817.

Extract from the Speeches of the House of Lords

Lord Simonds, L.C.—

"My Lords, no other conclusion was open to the Court of Criminal Appeal, nor is any other conclusion open to your Lordships in view of the recent cases in this House of *Mancini*[1] and *Holmes*.[2] The relevant part of the former decision is accurately stated in the headnote in these words: 'The test to be applied is that of the effect of the provocation on a reasonable man, so that an unusually excitable or pugnacious person is not entitled to rely on provocation which would not have led an ordinary person to act as he did.' And Viscount Simon, L.C., in a speech in which all their Lordships concurred, referred ([1941] 3 All E.R. 272, at p. 277) with approval to the decision of the Court of Criminal Appeal in *R. v. Lesbini*.[3] It is worth recalling that, in that case, the court said ([1914] 3 K.B. 1116, at p. 1120): 'We agree with the judgment of Darling, J., in *R. v. Alexander*[4] and with the principles enunciated in *R. v. Welsh*,[5] where it is said that "there must exist such an amount of provocation as would be excited by the circumstances in the mind of a reasonable man, and so as to lead the jury to acribe the act to the influence of that passion" '.

Finally, in *Holmes'* case,[6] Viscount Simon, in a speech in which my noble and learned friend, Lord Porter and I, as well as Lord Macmillan and Lord du Parcq, concurred, after a prolonged hearing and an exhaustive examination of the relevant law used these words: 'If, on the other hand, the case is one in which the view might fairly be taken (a) that a reasonable person, in consequence of the provocation received, might be so rendered subject to passion or loss of control as to be led to use the violence with fatal results, and (b) that the accused was in fact acting under the stress of such provocation, then it is for the jury to determine whether on its view of the facts manslaughter or murder is the appropriate verdict.'

My Lords, in the face of this authority, I am at a loss to know what other direction than that which he gave could properly have been given by the learned judge to the jury

---

[1] [1942] A.C. 1; [1941] 3 All E.R. 272; p. 216, *supra*.
[2] *Holmes* v. *Director of Public Prosecutions*, [1946] A.C. 588; [1946] 2 All E.R. 124.
[3] [1914] 3 K.B. 1116.
[4] (1913), 109 L.T. 745.
[5] (1869), 11 Cox C.C. 336.
[6] [1946] A.C. 588; [1946] 2 All E.R. 124.

in this case. The argument, as I understood it, for the appellant was that the jury, in considering the reaction of the hypothetical reasonable man to the acts of provocation, must not only place him in the circumstances in which the accused was placed, but must also invest him with the personal physical peculiarities of the accused. Learned counsel, who argued the case for the appellant with great ability, did not, I think, venture to say that he should be invested with mental or temperamental qualities which distinguished him from the reasonable man: for this would have been directly in conflict with the passage from the recent decision of this House in *Mancini's* case[1] which I have cited. But he urged that the reasonable man should be invested with the peculiar physical qualities of the accused, as in the present case with the characteristic of impotence, and the question should be asked: what would be the reaction of the impotent reasonable man in the circumstances? For that proposition I know of no authority: nor can I see any reason in it. It would be plainly illogical not to recognise an unusually excitable or pugnacious temperament in the accused as a matter to be taken into account but yet to recognise for that purpose some unusual physical characteristic, be it impotence or another. Moreover, the proposed distinction appears to me to ignore the fundamental fact that the temper of a man which leads him to react in such and such a way to provocation, is, or may be, itself conditioned by some physical defect. It is too subtle a refinement for my mind or, I think, for that of a jury to grasp that the temper may be ignored but the physical defect taken into account.

It was urged on your Lordships that the hypothetical reasonable man must be confronted with all the same circumstances as the accused, and that this could not be fairly done unless he was also invested with the peculiar characteristics of the accused. But this makes nonsense of the test. Its purpose is to invite the jury to consider the act of the accused by reference to a certain standard or norm of conduct and with this object the 'reasonable' or the 'average' or the 'normal' man is invoked. If the reasonable man is then deprived in whole or in part of his reason, or the normal man endowed with abnormal characteristics, the test ceases to have any value. This is precisely the consideration which led this House in *Mancini's* case to say that an unusually excitable or pugnacious person is not

---

[1] [1942] A.C. 1; [1941] 3 All E.R. 272; p. 216, *supra*.

entitled to rely on provocation which would not have led an ordinary person to act as he did. In my opinion, then, the Court of Criminal Appeal was right in approving the direction given to the jury by the learned judge and this appeal must fail. . . ."

APPEAL DISMISSED.

PHILLIPS v. R.
[1969] 2 A.C. 130

The effect of s. 3 of the Homicide Act 1957 is that the jury has to consider two questions when provocation is pleaded in answer to a charge of murder: (1) was the accused in fact provoked? (2) would the provocation have made a reasonable man lose his self control and, having lost his self control, retaliate as the accused did?

Phillips was charged with the murder of his mistress. He alleged that she had provoked him by spitting at his mother and reduced him to a state of automatism by hitting him on the side of the head whereupon he killed her with a machete which he found in his mother's bag. Although the main defence was automatism, the Jamaican judge directed the jury with regard to provocation with reference to a Jamaican statute phrased in identical terms with those of s. 3 of the Homicide Act 1957. Phillips was convicted and unsuccessfully appealed to the Court of Appeal of Jamaica and to the Privy Council.

Extracts from the Advice of the Privy Council

Lord Diplock.—

"In their Lordships' view it is beyond question that at common law by which the matter was regulated both in Jamaica and in England until the legislation cited above, the relationship between the degree of retaliation and the nature of the provocation was a relevant factor in determining whether the offence proved was manslaughter and not murder. It is sufficient to refer to the words of Viscount Simon, L.C., in the House of Lords in *Mancini* v. *Director of Public Prosecutions*[1] with whose speech the rest of the House agreed. 'In short', he said at p. 9, 'the mode of resentment

---

[1] [1942] A.C. 1; [1941] 3 All E.R. 272; p. 216, *supra*.

must bear a reasonable relationship to the provocation if the offence is to be reduced to manslaughter.' This is an elliptic way of saying that the reaction of the defendant to the provocation must not exceed what would have been the reaction of a reasonable man.

In their Lordships' view the only changes in the common law doctrine of provocation which were effected by section 3c of the Offences against the Person (Amendment) Law (Jamaica), No. 43 of 1958 were (1) to abolish the common law rule that words unaccompanied by acts could not amount to provocation, and (2) to leave exclusively to the jury the function of deciding whether or not a reasonable man would have reacted to the provocation in the way in which the defendant did. These two changes are inter-related.

The test of provocation in the law of homicide is two-fold. The first, which has always been a question of fact for the jury assuming that there is any evidence upon which they can so find , is 'Was the defendant provoked into losing his self-control?' The second, which is one not of fact but of opinion, 'Would a reasonable man have reacted to the same provocation in the same way as the defendant did?'

In *Holmes* v. *Director of Public Prosecutions*,[1] the case which finally decided that even a sudden confession of adultery could not amount to provocation at common law, it was laid down that although the second question was also one for the jury it was nevertheless the function of the judge to make a preliminary ruling as to whether or not the provocation was such as *could* provoke a reasonable man to react to it in the way in which the defendant did. It was this decision, not that in *Mancini* v. *Director of Public Prosecutions*[1] which was reversed by the English legislation of 1957 and the Jamaican legislation of 1958.

In their Lordships' view section 3c of Law No. 43 of 1958, in referring to the question to be left to be determined by the jury as being 'whether the provocation was enough to make a reasonable man do as he [*sc.*, the person charged] did' explicitly recognises that what the jury have to consider, once they have reached the conclusion that the person charged was in fact provoked to lose his self-control is not merely whether in their opinion the provocation would have made a reasonable man lose his self-control but also whether, having lost his self-control, he would have retaliated in the same way as the person charged in fact did.

---

[1] [1946] A.C. 588; [1946] 2 All E.R. 124.
[2] [1942] A.C. 1; [1941] 3 All E.R. 272; p. 216, *supra*.

Before their Lordships, counsel for the appellant contended, not as a matter of construction but as one of logic,
that once a reasonable man had lost his self-control his
actions ceased to be those of a reasonable man and that
accordingly he was no longer fully responsible in law for them
whatever he did. This argument is based on the premise that
loss of self-control is not a matter of degree but is absolute;
there is no intermediate stage between icy detachment and
going berserk. This premise, unless the argument is purely
semantic, must be based upon human experience and is, in
their Lordships' view, false. The average man reacts to
provocation according to its degree with angry words, with
a blow of the hand, possibly if the provocation is gross and
there is a dangerous weapon to hand, with that weapon. . . .

Since the passing of the legislation it may be prudent to
avoid the use of the precise words of Viscount Simon in
Mancini v. *Director of Public Prosecutions*[1] 'the mode of
resentment must bear a reasonable relationship to the
provocation' unless they are used in a context which makes
it clear to the jury that this is not a rule of law which they
are bound to follow, but merely a consideration which may
or may not commend itself to them. But their Lordships
would repeat, it is the effect of the summing-up as a whole
that matters and not any stated verbal formula used in the
course of it."

APPEAL DISMISSED.

Comment on Phillips v. R.

This case has been followed by the Court of Appeal in
Brown,[2] the Court expressing the opinion that Parliament, when
using the simple and straight-forward language in s. 3 of the
Homicide Act 1957, was laying down a precise test which the jury
should apply. It followed that the proportionality of the mode of
retaliation to the provocation was simply a test to assist the jury
in determining whether the provocation was such as to cause a
reasonable man to do as the accused did.

In spite of the statement in *Phillips'* case that the only
changes made by s. 3 were (1) the abolition of the common law
rule that words unaccompanied by acts could not amount to
provocation, and (2) the introduction of the requirement that it is
exclusively for the jury to determine whether a reasonable man
would have reacted to the provocation as the accused did, a

---

[1] [1942] A.C. 1; [1941] 3 All E.R. 272; p. 216, *supra*.
[2] [1972] 2 Q.B. 229; [1972] 2 All E.R. 1328.

number of other restrictions which existed previously have been removed by that section: see Cross and Jones, *Introduction to Criminal Law*, 8th ed., paras. 8.22 and 8.23.

Note on the reform of the test of provocation

In its Working Paper on Offences against the Person the Criminal Law Revision Committee reaches the following provisional conclusions:

"54. We think that the test of provocation should be reformulated so that the accused is judged with due regard to any disability, physical or mental, from which he suffered. In our view, in place of the reasonable man test there should be a requirement that provocation is sufficient if, on the facts as they appeared to the accused, it constitutes a reasonable excuse for the loss of self-control on his part. Such a test would be more liberal than the present law. In particular it would enable any physical characteristics of the accused to be taken into account. In a case such as *Bedder*[1] the jury would be able to have regard to his sexual impotence in deciding whether he had a reasonable excuse for losing his self-control.

55. We discussed whether the test of reasonable excuse which we are proposing to replace the reasonable man test should apply not only to the loss of self-control on the part of the accused but also to what the accused did by way of reaction to the provocation. . . . It is arguable that it should not be necessary to show any relationship between the words or conduct relied upon as provocation and the method of killing used by the accused, since once the loss of self-control has been established, what the accused actually did was irrelevant. It is said that it is impossible to apply any test involving reasonableness to what a person does when he has lost his self-control because a person does not act reasonably in such circumstances. On the other hand it is arguable that there are degrees of self-control (the Privy Council rejected the view that loss of self-control is not a matter of degree in *Phillips* v. *R.*[2]) and that the words or conduct must be such as to constitute a reasonable excuse not only for the accused's loss of self-control but also for retaliating in the way that he did.

56. We find this point a very difficult one. Looking at the defence of provocation generally, we have borne in mind

---

[1] P. 220, *supra*.
[2] P. 223, *supra*.

the following points: First, it must be assumed that the accused had the mens rea which, apart from the defence of provocation, would put him in peril on a charge of murder. Second, the killing must have been done while the accused had lost his self-control to such an extent as to mitigate a killing. Third, in deciding whether he had so lost his self-control, the jury will be able to take into account the mode of killing, for example, whether the accused strangled his victim with his bare hands or whether he took time to load his revolver before shooting him. Taking into account these matters, the tentative view of the majority is, on balance, that the test we propose of reasonable excuse should apply only to the accused's loss of self-control and not to what the accused did by way of reaction to the provocation. Thus the existing requirement that one of the factors to be considered by the jury is the relationship between the provocation and the retaliation would cease to exist under our proposals, except to the extent that it is a factor to be considered in deciding whether the accused has in fact lost his self-control.

57. By way of restriction of the defence, we think that it should apply only to loss of self-control arising suddenly upon the provoking event, and not to cases where the accused's reaction is greatly delayed. This would restate the existing law. However, the jury could continue to take previous provocations into account where the present insult brought the accused to flashpoint."

Note

The extracts which follow are concerned with the law of "involuntary manslaughter". This term is used to define cases where the accused is not guilty of murder, because he lacked malice aforethought, but is guilty of manslaughter on the basis:

1. that he killed another by an unlawful and "dangerous" act (the doctrine of "constructive manslaughter"); or
2. that he killed another by "criminal negligence"; here, this term includes recklessness, in its subjective sense, as to bodily harm resulting, as well as recklessness in its objective sense, in which case gross inadvertent negligence as to the risk of death or, possibly, grievous bodily harm is required.[1]

---

[1] See pp. 11–16, *supra*. In *Stone and Dobinson*, [1977] 2 W.L.R. 169, which was reported too late for inclusion in this edition, the Court of Appeal may have taken the view that gross inadvertent negligence as to the risk of injury to health and welfare suffices for manslaughter.

ANDREWS v. DIRECTOR OF PUBLIC PROSECUTIONS
[1937] A.C. 576

An act which has become criminally unlawful simply because it was negligently performed is not an "unlawful act" for the purposes of constructive manslaughter, but it may result in liability for manslaughter on the basis of killing by criminal negligence.

See p. 246, *infra.*

R. v. CHURCH
[1965] 2 All E.R. 72

In order to support a conviction for manslaughter based on an intention to do an unlawful act, the act must be one which would, in the eyes of reasonable people, involve a risk of some bodily harm.

Church was charged with the murder of a woman. He admitted that he had had a fight with her and rendered her unconscious. He also admitted that he threw her unconscious body into a river but said that he believed that she was dead. The trial judge directed the jury that they could not convict of murder if they came to the conclusion that the accused believed the deceased to have been dead when he threw her into the river. He also directed them that such belief was irrelevant in the case of a charge of manslaughter. The jury convicted of manslaughter. Church unsuccessfully appealed to the Court of Criminal Appeal, that court being of opinion that, although the direction was defective with regard to manslaughter by an unlawful act, the case was a proper one for the application of the provisio to s. 4 (1) of the Criminal Appeal Act 1907.[1]

Extracts from the Judgment of the Court of Criminal Appeal

Edmund Davies, J.—

"The jury were thus told in plain terms that they could not convict of murder unless it had been proved that the

---

[1] See now the proviso to s. 2 (1) of the Criminal Appeal Act 1968.

appellant knew that Mrs. Nott was still alive when he threw her into the river or (at least) that he did not then believe that she was dead. We venture to express the view that such a direction was unduly benevolent to the appellant, and that the jury should have been told that it was still open to them to convict of murder, notwithstanding that the appellant may have thought his blows and attempt at strangulation had actually produced death when he threw the body in the river, if they regarded the appellant's behaviour from the moment he first struck her to the moment when he threw her into the river as a series of acts designed to cause death or grievous bodily harm: see *Thabo Meli* v. *R.*[1]

. . . Against the background of the basic direction regarding the nature of the Crown's burden of proof as to murder, it seems to this court that at least three possible bases of the manslaughter verdict call for consideration: (a) Criminal negligence. A grosser case of criminal negligence it would be difficult to imagine. . . . In the judgment of this court, the facts in the present case were such as to render an elaborate direction unnecessary. Utter recklessness was the standard which the jury were told had to be applied, and the evidence amply justified a verdict that it had been established. . . . (c)[2] An unlawful act causing death. Two passages in the summing-up are here material. They are these: (i)—

'If by an unlawful act of violence done deliberately to the person of another, that other is killed, the killing is manslaughter even though the accused never intended either death or grievous bodily harm to result. If (the deceased) was alive, as she was, when he threw her in the river, what he did was a deliberate act of throwing a living body into the river. That is an unlawful killing and it does not matter whether he believed she was dead, or not, and that is my direction to you,'

and (ii)—

'I would suggest to you, though, of course, it is for you to approach your task as you think fit, that a convenient way of approaching it would be to say: What do we think about this defence that he honestly believed the (deceased) to be dead? If you think that it is true, why then, as I have told you, your proper verdict would be one of manslaughter, not murder.'

---

[1] [1954] 1 All E.R. 373; p. 181, *supra*.
[2] Ground (b) was provocation of which there was only flimsy evidence.

Such a direction is not lacking in authority; see, for example, *Shoukatallie* v. *R.*,[1] in Lord Denning's opinion, and Dr. Glanville Williams' *Criminal Law* (2nd edn.) at p. 173. Nevertheless, in the judgment of this court it was a misdirection. It amounted to telling the jury that, whenever any unlawful act is committed in relation to a human being which resulted in death there must be, at least, a conviction for manslaughter. This might at one time have been regarded as good law: see, for example, *R.* v. *Fenton*.[2] It appears to this court, however, that the passage of years has achieved a transformation in this branch of the law and, even in relation to manslaughter, a degree of *mens rea* has become recognised as essential. To define it is a difficult task, and in *Andrews* v. *Director of Public Prosecutions*[3] Lord Atkin spoke of 'the element of "unlawfulness" which is the elusive factor'. Stressing that we are here leaving entirely out of account those ingredients of homicide which might justify a verdict of manslaughter on the grounds of (a) criminal negligence, or (b) provocation or (c) diminished responsibility, the conclusion of this court is that an unlawful act causing the death of another cannot, simply because it is an unlawful act, render a manslaughter verdict inevitable. For such a verdict inexorably to follow, the unlawful act must be such as all sober and reasonable people would inevitably recognise must subject the other person to, at least, the risk of some harm resulting therefrom, albeit not serious harm[4]. See, for example, *R.* v. *Franklin*,[5] *R.* v. *Senior*,[6] *R.* v. *Larkin*[7] in Humphrey, J.'s judgment, *R.* v. *Buck and Buck*[8] and *R.* v. *Hall*.[9]

If such be the test, as we adjudge it to be, then it follows that, in our view, it was a misdirection to tell the jury simpliciter that it mattered nothing for manslaughter whether or not the appellant believed Mrs. Nott to be dead when he

---

[1] [1962] A.C. 81; [1961] 3 All E.R. 996.
[2] (1830), 1 Lew. C.C. 179.
[3] [1937] A.C. 576, at p. 581; [1937] 2 All E.R. 552, at p. 555; p. 246, *infra*.
[4] Contrast recent Australian cases where it is said that the act must be one which anyone in the accused's situation would realise would expose the deceased "to an appreciable danger of some really serious injury" (*R.* v. *Haywood*, [1971] V.R. 755).
[5] (1883), 15 Cox C.C. 163.
[6] [1899] 1 Q.B. 283.
[7] [1943] 1 K.B. 174; [1943] 1 All E.R. 217.
[8] (1960), 44 Cr. App. Rep. 213, at p. 218; see p. 416, *infra*.
[9] (1961), 45 Cr. App. Rep. 366, at pp. 370, 373.

threw her in the river. Nevertheless, quite apart from our decision that the direction on criminal negligence was an adequate one in the circumstances, such a misdirection does not, in our judgment, involve that the conviction for manslaughter must, or should be, quashed. In the light of *Thabo Meli* v. *R.*[1], it is conceded on behalf of the appellant that, on a murder charge, the trial judge was perfectly entitled to direct the jury, as he did:

> 'Unless you find that something happened in the course of this evening between the infliction of the injuries and the decision to throw the body into the water, you may undoubtedly treat the whole course of conduct of the [appellant] as one.'

For some reason, however, which is not clear to this court, counsel for the appellant denies that such an approach is possible when one is considering a charge of manslaughter. We fail to see why. We adopt as sound Dr. Glanville Williams' view[2] . . . that,

> 'If a killing by the first act would have been manslaughter, a later destruction of the supposed corpse should also be manslaughter.'

Had Mrs. Nott died of her initial injuries, a manslaughter verdict might quite conceivably have been returned on the basis that the appellant inflicted them under the influence of provocation or that the jury were not convinced that they were inflicted with murderous intent. All that was lacking in the direction given in this case was that, when the judge turned to consider manslaughter, he did not again tell the jury that they were entitled (if they thought fit) to regard the conduct of the appellant in relation to Mrs. Nott as constituting throughout a series of acts which culminated in her death, and that, if that was how they regarded the appellant's behaviour, it mattered not whether he believed her to be alive or dead when he threw her in the river."

APPEAL DISMISSED.

---

[1] [1954] 1 All E.R. 373; p. 181, *supra.*
[2] *Criminal Law*, 2nd ed., p. 174.

R. v. LAMB
[1967] 2 All E.R. 1282

*All the elements of the unlawful act necessary to render a
person guilty of manslaughter on the ground that he intended
to do an unlawful act must be proved.*

Lamb was charged with manslaughter. He was inexperienced in the use of firearms. He had a revolver and,
acting in jest to the knowledge of his victim, he pointed it
at the deceased, his best friend. The accused pulled the
trigger and the deceased was shot and killed. The accused
knew that there were two bullets in the revolver, but he
did not know that pulling the trigger would cause the cylinder
to rotate with the result that one of the bullets would be
brought under the firing pin. The trial judge in effect
directed the jury that the accused had done an unlawful and
dangerous act, and his direction with regard to criminal
negligence contained no reference to the accused's belief that
the pulling of the trigger would have no effect on the position
of the bullets. Lamb was convicted of manslaughter, but
successfully appealed to the Court of Appeal.

Extracts from the Judgment of the Court of Appeal
Sachs, L.J.—
"The trial judge took the view that the pointing of the
revolver and the pulling of the trigger was something which
could of itself be unlawful, even if there were no attempt to
alarm or intent to injure. This view is exemplified in a passage
in his judgment which will be cited later. It was no doubt
on this basis that he had before commencing his summing-up
stated that he was not going to:

'involve the jury in any consideration of the niceties
of the question whether or not the (action of the appellant)
did constitute or did not constitute an assault';

and thus he did not refer to the defence of accident or the
need for the prosecution to disprove accident before coming
to a conclusion that the act was unlawful. Counsel for the
Crown, however, had at all times put forward the correct
view that for the act to be unlawful it must constitute at
least what he then termed 'a technical assault'. In this

court, moreover, he rightly conceded that there was no
evidence to go to the jury of any assault of any kind. Nor
did he feel able to submit that the acts of the appellant
were on any other ground unlawful in the criminal sense
of the word. Indeed no such submission could in law be
made: if, for instance, the pulling of the trigger had had
no effect because the striking mechanism or the ammunition
had been defective no offence would have been committed
by the appellant. Another way of putting it is that *mens
rea* being now an essential ingredient in manslaughter
(compare *Andrews* v. *Director of Public Prosecutions*[1] and
R. v. *Church*[2]) this could not in the present case be established
in relation to the first ground except by proving that
element of intent without which there can be no assault.
It is perhaps as well to mention that when using the phrase
'unlawful in the criminal sense of that word' the court has
in mind that it is long settled that it is not in point to
consider whether an act is unlawful merely from the angle of
civil liabilities. That was first made clear in *R.* v. *Franklin*.[3]
The relevant extracts from this and from later judgments
are collected in *Russell on Crime* (11th edn. 1958), pp.
651–658. The whole of that part of the summing-up which
concerned the first ground was thus vitiated by misdirections
based on an erroneous concept of the law; . . .

When the gravamen of a charge is criminal negligence
—often referred to as recklessness—of an accused, the jury
have to consider amongst other matters the state of his mind,
and that includes the question of whether or not he thought
that that which he was doing was safe. In the present case it
would, of course, have been fully open to a jury, if properly
directed, to find the accused guilty because they considered
his view as to there being no danger was formed in a criminally
negligent way. But he was entitled to a direction that the
jury should take into account the fact that he had indisputably formed this view and that there was expert evidence
as to this being an understandable view. Strong though the
evidence of criminal negligence was, the appellant was
entitled as of right to have his defence considered but he
was not accorded this right and the jury was left without a
direction on an essential matter."

APPEAL ALLOWED.

---

[1] [1937] 2 All E.R. 552, at pp. 555, 556; see p. 246, *infra*.
[2] [1965] 2 All E.R. 72, at p. 76; see p. 228, *supra*.
[3] (1883), 15 Cox C.C. 163.

DIRECTOR OF PUBLIC PROSECUTIONS v. NEWBURY AND JONES
[1976] 2 All E.R. 365

A person can be convicted of constructive manslaughter if it is proved that he intentionally did an unlawful and dangerous act and that that act killed another. In judging whether the act was dangerous the test is whether sober and reasonable people would recognise that it would subject the other person to, at least, the risk of some bodily harm resulting therefrom, albeit not serious harm. The test is not whether the accused realised that he might cause harm to someone by his act.

Just as a train approached a bridge over the track, part of a paving stone was pushed off the parapet of the bridge. The stone came through the window of the cab and killed the guard who was sitting next to the driver. Newbury and Jones were jointly concerned in pushing the stone off the parapet and were convicted of manslaughter. They appealed unsuccessfully to the Court of Appeal and to the House of Lords.

Extracts from the Speeches of the House of Lords

Lord Salmon.—

"... The point of law certified to be of general importance is:

'Can a defendant be properly convicted of manslaughter, when his mind is not affected by drink or drugs, if he did not foresee that his act might cause harm to another?'

The learned trial judge did not direct the jury that they should acquit the appellants unless they were satisfied beyond a reasonable doubt that the appellants had foreseen that they might cause harm to someone by pushing the piece of paving stone off the parapet into the path of the approaching train. In my view the learned trial judge was quite right not to give such a direction to the jury. The direction which he gave is completely in accordance with established law, which, possibly with one exception to which I shall presently refer, has never been challenged. In *R. v. Larkin*[1] Humphreys, J., said:

---

[1] [1943] 1 All E.R. 217, at p. 219.

'Where the act which a person is engaged in performing is unlawful, then if at the same time it is a dangerous act, that is, an act likely to injure another person, and quite inadvertently he causes the death of that other person by that act, then he is guilty of manslaughter.'

I agree entirely with Lawton, LJ., that that is an admirably clear statement of the law which has been applied many times. It makes it plain (a) that an accused is guilty of manslaughter if it is proved that he intentionally did an act which was unlawful and dangerous and that that act inadvertently caused death and (b) that it is unnecessary to prove that the accused knew that the act was unlawful or dangerous. This is one of the reasons why cases of manslaughter vary so infinitely in their gravity. They may amount to little more than pure inadvertence and sometimes to little less than murder.

I am sure that in *R.* v. *Church*[1] Edmund Davies, J., in giving the judgment of the court, did not intend to differ from or qualify anything which had been said in *R.* v. *Larkin*. Indeed he was restating the principle laid down in that case by illustrating the sense in which the word 'dangerous' should be understood. Edmund Davies, J., said:[2]

'For such a verdict [guilty of manslaughter] inexorably to follow, the unlawful act must be such as all sober and reasonable people would inevitably recognise must subject the other person to, at least, the risk of some harm resulting therefrom, albeit not serious harm.'

The test is still the objective test. In judging whether the act was dangerous, the test is not did the accused recognise that it was dangerous but would all sober and reasonable people recognise its danger.

Counsel for the appellants in his very able argument did not and indeed could not contend that the appellants' act which I have described was lawful, but he did maintain that the law as stated in *R.* v. *Larkin* had undergone a change as a result of a passge in the judgment of Lord Denning, M.R., in *Gray* v. *Barr*[3] which reads as follows:

'. . . in manslaughter of every kind there must be a guilty mind. Without it the accused must be acquitted: see *R.* v.

---

[1] [1966] 1 Q.B. 59; [1965] 2 All E.R. 72; p. 228, *supra*.
[2] [1966] 1 Q.B., at p. 70; [1965] 2 All E.R., at p. 76.
[3] [1971] 2 Q.B. 554, at p. 568; [1971] 2 All E.R. 949, at p. 956.

Lamb.[1] In the category of manslaughter relating to an unlawful act, the accused must do a dangerous act with the *intention* of frightening or harming someone or with the *realisation* that it is likely to frighten or harm someone, and nevertheless he goes on and does it, regardless of the consequences. If his act does thereafter, in unbroken sequence, cause the death of another, he is guilty of manslaughter.'

I do not think that Lord Denning, M.R., was attempting to revolutionise the law relating to manslaughter if his judgment is read in the context of the tragic circumstances of the case, which I must now shortly recite. James Gray and his wife had been married about eight years when they met and became very friendly with the Barrs, who lived close by. Both marriages were happy. Unfortunately Mr. Gray became infatuated with Mrs. Barr and she fell in love with him. . . . The association between Mr. Gray and Mrs. Barr continued. This was too much for Mrs. Gray, and her husband set her and their children up in a home. . . . Mrs. Barr left her home but did not go to live with Mr. Gray. . . . On 13th June 1967 Mr. Barr took his wife out to dinner. She promised to give up Mr. Gray. He drove her home but when he had put his car away, he discovered that his wife had run away and assumed that she had gone to spend the night with Mr. Gray. Mr. Barr was beside himself. He took his 12 bore shotgun, loaded both barrels, and set off for Mr. Gray's house, which he found in darkness. He entered the house and found Mr. Gray standing at the top of the stairs. Mr. Barr believed that his wife was in the bedroom. She was not; she was later found unconscious in a field where she had attempted to commit suicide. Mr. Barr started to mount the stairs holding his gun at the high port and threatening Mr. Gray with it to force him to get out of the way. Mr. Gray refused to move. Two shots were fired, one into the ceiling and the other killed Mr. Gray. According to Mr. Barr's account. . . . Mr. Gray grappled with him, the gun went off and fired one shot into the ceiling; Mr. Barr then slipped on the stairs and accidentally the gun fired another shot which killed Mr. Gray. There was much sympathy for Mr. Barr when he was tried at the Old Bailey for murder. The summing-up read like an invitation to acquit him of both murder and manslaughter—an invitation which the jury accepted, no doubt gratefully. Mrs. Gray then sued Mr. Barr

---

[1] [1967] 2 Q.B. 981; [1967] 2 All E.R. 1282.

for damages in respect of her husband's death to which in
reality he had no defence. Mr. Barr however, in the third
party proceedings which he had brought against the Prudential Assurance Co. Ltd., claimed an indemnity under a
'hearth and home' policy covering him against all sums he
became liable to pay as damages in respect of bodily injury
to any person caused by accident. The learned trial judge
gave judgment against Mr. Barr in Mrs. Gray's favour. . . .
He dismissed Mr. Barr's claim for an indemnity on grounds
of public policy having come to the conclusion that, in spite
of the jury's verdict, Mr. Barr was clearly guilty of manslaughter. Mr. Barr appealed, amongst other things, against
the judgment in favour of the Prudential. That appeal was
dismissed. Every member of the Court of Appeal, agreeing
with the learned trial judge, found that in spite of Mr. Barr's
acquittal at the Old Bailey he had been, on his own story,
undoubtedly guilty of manslaughter. They also agreed with
the learned trial judge that on grounds of public policy a
man is not entitled to be indemnified against damages for
which he became liable as a result of committing a crime of
violence.

I have taken a little time in dealing with the facts of
Barr's case to show that the Court of Appeal was in a very
different position from that of the Court of Appeal (Criminal
Division). It was not considering whether a conviction
could be upheld but whether an acquittal could be justified.
It was concerned to decide whether the facts established by
Mr. Barr's own evidence proved that he was guilty of
manslaughter which, of course, they did; but this does not
mean that nothing short of such facts can prove manslaughter
Lord Denning, M.R.'s, judgment is certainly capable of being
read in a contrary sense, and indeed has been so understood
by some judges, but I doubt whether he intended that it
should be. If he did, then I am afraid I cannot agree with
him. Neither of the other members of the court in *Gray* v. *Barr*
said anything in support of the proposition which some
believe that Lord Denning, M.R., intended to propound.
Indeed, the second member[1] of that court cited *R.* v. *Larkin*[2]
with approval.

R. v. *Lamb*[3] was referred to by Lord Denning, M.R.,[4] for

[1] [1971] 2 Q.B., at p. 576; [1971] 2 All E.R., at pp. 960, 961, *per*
Salmon, L.J.
[2] [1943] 1 K.B. 174; [1943] 1 All E.R. 217.
[3] [1967] 2 Q.B. 981; [1967] 2 All E.R. 1282; p. 232, *supra*.
[4] [1971] 2 Q.B., at p. 568; [1971] 2 All E.R., at p. 956.

the proposition that in manslaughter there must always be a guilty mind. This is true of every crime except those of absolute liability. The guilty mind usually depends on the intention of the accused. Some crimes require what is sometimes called a specific intention, for example murder, which is killing with intent to kill or inflict grievous bodily harm. Other crimes need only what is called a basic intention, which is an intention to do the acts which constitute the crime. Manslaughter is such a crime: see *R.* v. *Larkin*[1] and *R.* v. *Church*[2]. *R.* v. *Lamb* is certainly no authority to the contrary. . . .

My Lords, I would dismiss this appeal."

Lord Edmund-Davies.—

"My Lords, for the reasons developed in the speech of my noble and learned friend, Lord Salmon, I concur in holding that these appeals against conviction should be dismissed.

R. v. *Church*, which the learned trial judge adopted for the purpose of his direction to the jury, marked no new departure in relation to the offence of involuntary manslaughter. Insofar as the charge was based on the commission of an unlawful act causing death, the Court of Criminal Appeal was there concerned to demolish the old notion . . . that, whenever *any* unlawful act is committed in relation to a human being which causes his death, there must at least be a conviction for manslaughter. In delivering the judgment of the court, I therefore said:[3]

'Stressing that we are leaving entirely out of account those ingredients of homicide which might justify a verdict of manslaughter on the grounds of (a) criminal negligence, or (b) provocation, or (c) diminished responsibility, the conclusion of this court is that an unlawful act causing the death of another *cannot*, simply because it is an unlawful act, render a manslaughter verdict inevitable.'

The key sentence which followed has often been quoted. I would respectfully say that Lord Widgery, C.J. (who was a member of the court in *R.* v. *Church*) was perfectly correct in observing in *R.* v. *Lipman*:[4] 'The development recognized by *R.* v. *Church* relates to the *type* of act from which a

---

[1] [1943] 1 K.B. 174; [1943] 1 All E.R. 217.
[2] [1966] 1 Q.B. 59; [1965] 2 All E.R. 72; p. 228, *supra.*
[3] [1966] 1 Q.B., at p. 70; [1965] 2 All E.R., at p. 76.
[4] [1970] 1 Q.B., at p. 159; [1969] 3 All E.R., at p. 415.

charge of manslaughter may result, not in the intention (real or assumed) of the prisoner.'

But, in so far as *R.* v. *Church* has been regarded as laying down that for the proof of manslaughter in such circumstances what is required is no more than the *intentional* committing of an unlawful act of the designated type or nature, it followed a long line of authorities which the court there cited. Of these the best known is possibly *R.* v. *Larkin*, dealt with in detail in the speech of my noble and learned friend, Lord Salmon. Accordingly, if *R.* v. *Church* was wrong, so was its long ancestry.

I believe that *R.* v. *Church* accurately applied the law as it then existed. I believe, further, that, since it was decided, nothing has happened to change the law in relation to the constituents of involuntary manslaughter caused by an unlawful act. The Criminal Justice Act 1967 has certainly effected no such change, for, as I sought to show in *Director of Public Prosecutions* v. *Majewski*,[1] s. 8 thereof[2] has nothing to do with *when* intent or foresight or any other mental state has to be established, but simply *how* it is to be determined where such determination is called for."

APPEALS DISMISSED.

R. v. LOWE
[1973] 1 All E.R. 805

The unlawful act in constructive manslaughter must be an offence of commission and not omission. Thus, if death inadvertently results from an offence of omission there can only be a conviction for manslaughter if the accused's conduct resulting in death was criminally negligent.

Lowe and Miss Marshall had been living together for several years and had had four previous children, only one of whom had been taken into care. Miss Marshall's intelligence was subnormal and Lowe's low average. The child who was the subject of the indictment was born on 28th August 1971 and was not apparently ill until about ten days before its death on 4th November 1971. The child had last been seen

---

[1] [1976] 2 All E.R. 142, at p. 170.
[2] P. 19, *supra*.

by a social worker on 5th October when it was observed that
she was vomiting up her milk. According to Lowe, he was
not worried about the child's condition until 30th October,
when he suggested that Miss Marshall should take it to the
doctor. Later that day she lied to him that she had done so,
that the doctor had been out but that she had got some
medicine. Two days later, Lowe alleged, he had again urged
her to take the child to the doctor and again she subsequently
lied that she had done so. After the child had been found
dead suffering from dehydration and gross emaciation Miss
Marshall said she had been unwilling to risk disclosing its
state of health lest it should be removed from her and taken
into care.

Lowe was charged with manslaughter (count 1) and
cruelty by wilfully neglecting the child so as to cause her
unnecessary suffering or injury to health, contrary to s. 1 (1)
of the Children and Young Persons Act 1933 (count 2). Lowe
was convicted on both counts and appealed. The Court of
Appeal dismissed his appeal in relation to the second count
on the ground that the judge had been correct in directing
the jury that in order to constitute wilful neglect so as to
cause unnecessary suffering or injury it was not necessary
that Lowe should have foreseen the probable or possible
result of his failure to call a doctor: the sole question was
whether his failure to do so was deliberate and thereby
occasioned the results referred to in s. 1 of the Act of 1933[1].
However, the court did allow Lowe's appeal against conviction for manslaughter for reasons which appear below.

Extracts from the Judgment of the Court of Appeal

Phillimore, L.J.—
   "The trial judge . . . proceeded to deal with the count of
manslaughter. He left it to the jury to say whether they
thought that the appellant's conduct towards the child had
been reckless and whether its death had been caused thereby.
Quite separately, however, he directed the jury that if they
found the appellant guilty of the second count they must,
as a matter of law, find him guilty of the first, namely of
manslaughter. Having found him guilty of the second count

---

[1] For a critical appraisal of this part of the decision see [1973] Crim.
L.R. 240.

they also found him guilty of the first and made it clear that they did so solely as a result of the direction by the trial judge; in other words, they did *not* find the appellant guilty of reckless conduct resulting in the child's death.

Counsel for the Crown defends the direction given by the trial judge, namely that if they found the appellant guilty on the second count the jury must as a matter of law convict him of manslaughter on count 1, even though they acquitted him of conduct which was reckless. He based his argument on *R.* v. *Senior*[1], a case where a child had died following the failure of the father to call in a doctor in circumstances where it was contrary to his religious beliefs so to do. In that case the court held that there was evidence that the prisoner had wilfully neglected the child in a manner likely to cause injury to its health and having thereby caused or accelerated its death he was rightly convicted of manslaughter. It is to be observed that in a passage in his judgment in *R.* v. *Senior* Lord Russell of Killowen, C.J., interpreted the words 'wilful neglect' in the manner . . . which this court accepts.

Counsel for the appellant's answer is that the decision in *R.* v. *Senior* cannot be regarded as good law in the light of the unanimous decision of the House of Lords in *Andrews* v. *Director of Public Prosecutions*[2]. True, that case involved motor manslaughter as a result of neglect, but the speech of Lord Atkin is in the widest terms and is clearly intended to apply to every case of manslaughter by neglect. In the course of citing *R.* v. *Bateman*[3], Lord Atkin said,[4] quoting Lord Hewart, C.J.:

'In explaining to juries the test which they should apply to determine whether the negligence, in the particular case, amounted or did not amount to a crime, judges have used many epithets, such as "culpable", "criminal", "gross", "wicked", "clear", "complete". But, whatever epithet be used and whether an epithet be used or not, in order to establish criminal liability the facts must be such that, in the opinion of the jury, the negligence of the accused went beyond a mere matter of compensation between subjects and showed such disregard for the life and safety of others, as to amount to a crime against the State and conduct deserving punishment.'

---

[1] [1899] 1 Q.B. 283; [1895–99] All E.R. Rep. 511.
[2] [1937] A.C. 576; [1937] 2 All E.R. 552; p. 246, *infra*.
[3] (1925), 94 L.J.K.B. 791; [1925] All E.R. Rep. 45; p. 244, *infra*.
[4] [1937] A.C., at pp. 582, 583; [1937] 2 All E.R., at p. 555, 556; p. 248, *infra*.

Lord Atkin then went on to say:

'... the substance of the judgment is most valuable, and, in my opinion, is correct. .... The principle to be observed is that cases of manslaughter in driving motor cars are but instances of a general rule applicable to all charges of homicide by negligence. Simple lack of care such as will constitute civil liability is not enough. For purposes of the criminal law there are degrees of negligence, and a very high degree of negligence is required to be proved before the felony is established. Probably of all the epithets that can be applied "reckless" most nearly covers the case.'

Now in the present case the jury negatived recklessness. How then can mere neglect albeit wilful amount to man-slaughter?

This court feels there is something inherently unattractive in a theory of constructive manslaughter. It seems strange that an omission which is wilful solely in the sense that it is not inadvertent, the consequences of which are not in fact foreseen by the person who is neglectful should, if death results, automatically give rise to an indeterminate sentence instead of the maximum of two years which would otherwise be the limit imposed.

We think there is a clear distinction between an act of omission and an act of commission likely to cause harm. Whatever may be the position in regard to the latter it does not follow that the same is true of the former. In other words if I strike a child in a manner likely to cause harm it is right that if the child dies I may be charged with manslaughter. If, however, I omit to do something with the result that it suffers injury to health which results in its death, we think that a charge of manslaughter should not be an inevitable consequence, even if the omission is deliberate."

APPEAL ALLOWED IN PART.

R. v. FINNEY

(1874), 12 Cox C.C. 625

Negligence must be gross in order to render a person guilty of manslaughter on this basis.

The accused was an attendant at a lunatic asylum at which the deceased was a patient. After he had bathed the deceased, the accused told him to get out, and there was evidence that the deceased was capable of understanding and obeying such an instruction. While the accused's attention was diverted by a new attendant, the accused turned on the hot tap in the bath in which the deceased had been washed, and the deceased, who had not got out of the bath, was scalded to death. The accused said that he believed that the deceased had got out of the bath, and, in any event, he intended to turn on the cold tap.

Extracts from the Summing-up to the Jury

Lush, J.—

"To render a person liable for neglect of duty there must be such a degree of culpability as to amount to gross negligence on his part. . . . It is not every little trip or mistake that will make a man so liable. It was the duty of the attendant not to let water into the bath while the patient was therein. According to the prisoner's own account, he did not believe that he was letting the water in while the deceased remaind there. . . . If the prisoner, seeing that the man was in the bath, had knowingly turned on the tap and turned on the hot instead of the cold water, I should have said there was gross negligence, for he ought to have looked to see; but from his own account he had told the deceased to get out and thought he had got out. If you think that indicates gross carelessness, then you should find the prisoner guilty of manslaughter; but if you think it inadvertence not amounting to culpability, or what is properly termed an accident, then the prisoner is not liable."

VERDICT, NOT GUILTY.

R. v. JONES
(1874), 12 Cox C.C. 628

Pointing a gun at a person without looking to see whether it is loaded is negligence sufficient to found a conviction for manslaughter.

The accused was charged with manslaughter of a child. While the child was out of the room, he picked up a gun and held it pointed at the door. He did not examine the gun, and believed it to be unloaded. When the child came in through the door, the gun went off and killed him.

Extract from the Summing-up to the Jury

Lush, J.—

"No doubt the prisoner did not intend to discharge the gun at the child. What he did was either an accident or was negligence on his part. The charge is that he so carelessly handled the gun as to occasion the death of the deceased. If a person points a gun without examining whether it is loaded or not, and it happens to be loaded and death results, he is guilty of negligence and manslaughter. Can you come to any other conclusion than that the prisoner did either in joke or otherwise point the gun at the boy? If he held the gun pointed at the boy, and so held it until the child came out of the pantry, and it went off, what can that be but so improperly and carelessly handling the gun as to be negligence, and therefore manslaughter?"

VERDICT, GUILTY.

R. v. BATEMAN
(1925), 133 L.T. 730

In order that a person may be convicted of manslaughter by criminal negligence, the jury must be satisfied that he showed such a disregard for the life of others as to amount to a crime against the state.

Bateman was a doctor who was charged and convicted of manslaughter. The evidence was that he had attended the deceased upon her giving birth to a dead child. The accouchement was a difficult one, and the mother died some days after the birth. The prosecution gave evidence of negligence against the accused under three heads. Two of them depended on medical technique and the third was that he had not caused the deceased to be removed to hospital as soon as he should.

Bateman successfully appealed to the Court of Criminal Appeal on the ground that the trial judge had not adequately directed the jury on the difference between civil and criminal negligence.

Extracts from the Judgment of the Court of Criminal Appeal

Lord Hewart, C.J.—

". . . In expounding the law to juries on the trial of indictments for manslaughter by negligence the judges have often referred to the distinction between civil and criminal liability for death by negligence. The law of criminal liability for negligence is conveniently explained in that way. If A has caused the death of B by alleged negligence, then, in order to establish civil liability, the plaintiff must prove (in addition to pecuniary loss caused by the death) that A owed a duty to B to take care, that that duty was not discharged, and that such default caused the death of B. To convict A of manslaughter, the prosecution must prove the three things above mentioned and must satisfy the jury, in addition, that A's negligence amounted to a crime. In the civil action, if it is proved that A fell short of the standard of reasonable care required by law, it matters not how far he fell short of that standard. The extent of his liability depends not on the degree of negligence, but on the amount of damage done. In the criminal court, on the contrary, the amount and degree of negligence are the determining question. There must be *mens rea*. . . .

In explaining to juries the test which they should apply to determine whether the negligence, in the particular case, amounted or did not amount to a crime, the judges have used many epithets, such as 'culpable', 'criminal', 'gross', 'wicked', 'clear', 'complete'. But, whatever epithet be used and whether an epithet be used or not, in order to establish criminal liability the facts must be such that, in the opinion of the jury, the negligence of the accused went beyond a mere matter of compensation between subjects and showed such disregard for the life and safety of others as to amount to a crime against the State and conduct deserving punishment. . .

To support an indictment for manslaughter the prosecution must prove the matters necessary to establish civil liability (except pecuniary loss), and, in addition, must satisfy the jury that the negligence or incompetence of the accused went beyond a mere matter of compensation and showed such disregard for the life and safety of others as to amount to a crime against the State and conduct deserving punishment. . . .

It is, nevertheless, most desirable that in trials for manslaughter by negligence, it should be impressed on the

jury that the issue is not negligence or no negligence, but
felony or no felony. It is desirable that, as far as possible, the
explanation of criminal negligence to a jury should not be a
mere question of epithets. It is, in a sense, a question of
degree, and it is for the jury to draw the line, but there is a
difference in kind between the negligence which gives a right
to compensation and the negligence which is a crime."

APPEAL ALLOWED.

ANDREWS v. DIRECTOR OF PUBLIC PROSECUTIONS

[1937] A.C. 576

*A higher degree of negligence is required for manslaughter
than for dangerous driving.*

Andrews was charged and convicted of manslaughter by
running someone down while driving a car. He unsuccessfully
appealed to the Court of Criminal Appeal and thence to the
House of Lords on the ground of misdirection to the jury by
the trial judge.

He had also been charged with the offence of dangerous
driving under s. 11 of the Road Traffic Act 1930[1]. In the course
of his summing-up the trial judge told the jury that a person
was guilty of manslaughter if he caused death in the performance of an unlawful act. The House of Lords did not
regard this as a correct direction in such a case but they
were satisfied that, taking the summing-up as a whole, the
jury had been properly directed.

Extracts from the Speeches of the House of Lords

Lord Atkin.—

" . . . of all crimes manslaughter appears to afford
most difficulties of definition, for it concerns homicide in
so many and so varying conditions. From the early days
when any homicide involved penalty the law has gradually
evolved 'though successive differentiations and integrations'
until it recognises murder on the one hand, based mainly,
though not exclusively, on an intention to kill and manslaughter on the other hand, based mainly, though not
exclusively, on the absence of intention to kill, but with the

---

[1] Re-enacted by S. 2 of the Road Traffic Act 1972.

presence of an element of 'unlawfulness' which is the elusive factor. In the present case it is only necessary to consider manslaughter from the point of view of an unintentional killing caused by negligence, i.e., the omission of a duty to take care. I do not propose to discuss the development of this branch of the subject as treated in the successive treatises of Coke, Hale, Foster and East and in the judgments of the Courts to be found either in directions of juries by individual judges or in the more considered pronouncements of the body of judges which preceded the formal Court of Crown Cases Reserved. Expressions will be found which indicate that to cause death by any lack of due care will amount to manslaughter; but as manners softened and the law became more humane a narrower criterion appeared. After all, manslaughter is a felony, and was capital, and men shrank from attaching the serious consequences of a conviction for felony to results produced by mere inadvertence. The stricter view became apparent in prosecutions of medical men or men who professed medical or surgical skill for manslaughter by reason of negligence. . . .

The principle to be observed is that cases of manslaughter in driving motor-cars are but instances of a general rule applicable to all charges of homicide by negligence. Simple lack of care such as will constitute civil liability is not enough: for purposes of the criminal law there are degrees of negligence: and a very high degree of negligence is required to be proved before the felony is established. Probably of all the epithets that can be applied 'reckless' most nearly covers the case. It is difficult to visualise a case of death caused by reckless driving in the connotation of that term in ordinary speech[1] which would not justify a conviction for manslaughter: but it is probably not all-embracing, for 'reckless' suggests an indifference to risk whereas the accused may have appreciated the risk and intended to avoid it and yet shown such a high degree of negligence in the means adopted to avoid the risk as would justify a conviction. If the principle of *Bateman's* case[2] is observed it will appear that the law of manslaughter has not changed by the introduction of motor vehicles on the road. Death caused by their negligent driving, though unhappily much more frequent, is to be treated in law as death caused

---

[1] On the whole "recklessness" appears to be used in an objective sense in the law of manslaughter.

[2] (1925), 19 Cr. App. Rep. 8; p. 244, *supra.*

by any other form of negligence: and juries should be directed accordingly. . . .

I entertain no doubt that the statutory offence of dangerous driving may be committed, though the negligence is not of such a degree as would amount to manslaughter if death ensued. As an instance, in the course of argument it was suggested that a man might execute the dangerous manoeuvre of drawing out to pass a vehicle in front with another vehicle meeting him, and be able to show that he would have succeeded in his calculated intention but for some increase of speed in the vehicles in front: a case very doubtfully of manslaughter but very probably of dangerous driving. . . . It therefore would appear that in directing the jury in a case of manslaughter the judge should in the first instance charge them substantially in accordance with the general law, that is, requiring the high degree of negligence indicated in *Bateman's* case[1] and then explain that such degree of negligence is not necessarily the same as that which is required for the offence of dangerous driving, and then indicate to them the conditions under which they might acquit of manslaughter and convict of dangerous driving. A direction that all they had to consider was whether death was caused by dangerous driving within s. 11 of the Road Traffic Act 1930, and no more, would in my opinion be a misdirection.

In dealing with the summing-up in the present case I feel bound to say with every respect to the learned and very careful judge that there are passages which are open to criticism. In particular at the beginning of his charge to the jury he began with the statement that if a man kills another in the course of doing an unlawful act he is guilty of manslaughter, and then proceeded to ascertain what the unlawful act was by considering s. 11 of the Road Traffic Act 1930. If the summing-up rested there, there would have been misdirection. There is an obvious difference in the law of manslaughter between doing an unlawful act and doing a lawful act with a degree of carelessness which the Legislature makes criminal. If it were otherwise a man who killed another while driving without due care and attention would *ex necessitate* commit manslaughter. But as the summing-up proceeded the learned judge reverted to, and I think rested the case on, the principles which have been just stated. . . ."

APPEAL DISMISSED.

---

[1] (1925), 19 Cr. App. Rep. 8; p. 244, *supra*.

R. v. LAMB
[1967] 2 All E.R. 1282

In determining whether an accused was guilty of man-slaughter by criminal negligence, the jury must be told to take into account his beliefs with regard to material facts although, in some circumstances, such beliefs may have been formed in circumstances amounting to criminal negligence.

See p. 232, *supra*.

Note on the reform of involuntary manslaughter

In its Working Paper on Offences against the Person the Criminal Law Revision Committee reaches the following provisional conclusions:

"89. We do not favour the continuation of the doctrine of constructive manslaughter. . . . In our view, the mere fact that the defendant was engaged on an unlawful act and killed in consequence of it should not make him guilty of any homicide offence where he did not foresee the possibility of causing death or serious injury.

90. Nor do we propose the continuation of manslaughter by gross negligence, where the defendant does not foresee the possibility of causing death or serious injury. . . . To amount to a crime of such gravity as manslaughter there should be recklessness [in its subjective sense] on the part of the defendant. It seems that even under the present law prosecutions on account of negligence are rare, where there is no foresight of the possibility of causing death or injury (leaving aside cases of killing under the influence of drink or drugs. . .). . . .

91. We think that there should be a new offence of causing death recklessly (the name of manslaughter no longer being used in this connection), punishable with a maximum penalty of 14 years' imprisonment. The offence should require that the offender was reckless whether death or serious injury (and not some lesser degree of injury) resulted from his actions. By 'reckless' in this context we mean reckless in the sense described by the Working Party of the Law Commission in their Working Paper No. 31 on the Mental Element in Crime, namely, that:

'A person is reckless if,
(a) Knowing that there is a risk that an event may result from his conduct . . . he takes that risk, and

(b) It is unreasonable for him to take it having regard to the degree and nature of the risk which he knows to be present.'

92. The offence we are proposing would cover most cases of killing by gross negligence which are at present prosecuted as manslaughter since in practice this mental element is usually present. It would cover also some of those cases which at present amount to constructive manslaughter (cases of killing in the course of an unlawful act) where recklessness can be proved."

Infanticide

INFANTICIDE ACT 1938

"Section 1.—Offence of infanticide

(1) Where a woman by any wilful act or omission causes the death of her child being a child under the age of twelve months, but at the time of the act or omission the balance of her mind was disturbed by reason of her not having fully recovered from the effect of giving birth to the child or by reason of the effect of lactation consequent on the birth of the child, then, notwithstanding that the circumstances were such that but for this Act the offence would have amounted to murder, she shall be guilty of an offence, to wit of infanticide, and may for such offence be dealt with and punished as if she had been guilty of the offence of manslaughter of the child."

Note

By s. 1 (2) of the Infanticide Act 1938, where a woman is tried for the murder of a child under the age of 12 months, it is open to the jury to return a verdict of not guilty of murder but guilty of infanticide. Thus, infanticide can either be charged in the first instance or serve as a defence on a murder charge.

The Butler Committee on Mentally Abnormal Offenders has recommended that the above provisions should be repealed since their purpose is now sufficiently covered by the defence of diminished responsibility.[1] No practical differences would result from this proposal if the Committee's proposals concerning the defence of diminished responsibility[2] were implemented.

---

[1] Cmnd. 6244, paras. 19.22–19.27. For a further consideration of infanticide, see the Criminal Law Revision Committee's Working Paper on Offences against the Person, paras. 66–71.

[2] Pp. 86–90, *supra.*

CHAPTER 5

OFFENCES AGAINST THE THEFT ACT 1968

Theft

THEFT ACT 1968

"Section 1.—Basic definition of theft

(1) A person is guilty of theft if he dishonestly appropriates property belonging to another with the intention of permanently depriving the other of it; and 'thief' and 'steal' shall be construed accordingly.

(2) It is immaterial whether the appropriation is made with a view to gain, or is made for the thief's own benefit.

(3) The five following sections of this Act shall have effect as regards the interpretation and operation of this section (and, except as otherwise provided by this Act, shall apply only for purposes of this section).

Section 2.—'Dishonestly'

(1) A person's appropriation of property belonging to another is not to be regarded as dishonest—

(*a*) if he appropriates the property in the belief that he has in law the right to deprive the other of it, on behalf of himself or of a third person; or

(*b*) if he appropriates the property in the belief that he would have the other's consent if the other knew of the appropriation and the circumstances of it; or

(c) (except where the property came to him as trustee or personal representative) if he appropriates the property in the belief that the person to whom the property belongs cannot be discovered by taking reasonable steps.

(2) A person's appropriation of property belonging to another may be dishonest notwithstanding that he is willing to pay for the property.

Section 3.—'Appropriates'

(1) Any assumption by a person of the rights of an owner amounts to an appropriation, and this includes, where

he has come by the property (innocently or not) without stealing it, any later assumption of a right to it by keeping or dealing with it as owner.

(2) Where property or a right or interest in property is or purports to be transferred for value to a person acting in good faith, no later assumption by him of rights which he believed himself to be acquiring shall, by reason of any defect in the transferor's title, amount to theft of the property.

Section 4.—'Property'

(1) 'Property' includes money and all other property, real or personal, including things in action and other intangible property.

(2) A person cannot steal land, or things forming part of land and severed from it by him or by his directions, except in the following cases, that is to say—

(*a*) when he is a trustee or personal representative, or is authorised by power of attorney, or as liquidator of a company, or otherwise, to sell or dispose of land belonging to another, and he appropriates the land or anything forming part of it by dealing with it in breach of the confidence reposed in him; or

(*b*) when he is not in possession of the land and appropriates anything forming part of the land by severing it or causing it to be severed, or after it has been severed; or

(*c*) when, being in possession of the land under a tenancy, he appropriates the whole or part of any fixture or structure let to be used with the land.

For purposes of this subsection 'land' does not include incorporeal hereditaments; 'tenancy' means a tenancy for years or any less period and includes an agreement for such a tenancy, but a person who after the end of a tenancy remains in possession as statutory tenant or otherwise is to be treated as having possession under the tenancy, and 'let' shall be construed accordingly.

(3) A person who picks mushrooms growing wild on any land, or who picks flowers, fruit or foliage from a plant growing wild on any land, does not (although not in possession of the land) steal what he picks, unless he does it for reward or for sale or other commercial purpose.

For purposes of this subsection "mushroom" includes any fungus and "plant" includes any shrub or tree.

(4) Wild creatures, tamed or untamed, shall be regarded as property; but a person cannot steal a wild creature not tamed nor ordinarily kept in captivity, or the carcase of any

such creature, unless either it has been reduced into possession
by or on behalf of another person and possession of it has
not since been lost or abandoned, or another person is in
course of reducing it into possession.

Section 5.—'Belonging to another'

(1) Property shall be regarded as belonging to any
person having possession or control of it, or having in it any
proprietary right or interest (not being an equitable interest
arising only from an agreement to transfer or grant an
interest).

(2) Where property is subject to a trust, the persons to
whom it belongs shall be regarded as including any person
having a right to enforce the trust, and an intention to defeat
the trust shall be regarded accordingly as an intention to
deprive of the property any person having that right.

(3) Where a person receives property from or on account
of another, and is under an obligation to the other to retain
and deal with that property or its proceeds in a particular
way, the property or proceeds shall be regarded (as against
him) as belonging to the other.

(4) Where a person gets property by another's mistake,
and is under an obligation to make restoration (in whole or
in part) of the property or its proceeds or of the value thereof,
then to the extent of that obligation the property or proceeds
shall be regarded (as against him) as belonging to the person
entitled to restoration, and an intention not to make
restoration shall be regarded accordingly as an intention
to deprive that person of the property or proceeds.

(5) Property of a corporation sole shall be regarded as
belonging to the corporation notwithstanding a vacancy
in the corporation.

*Section 6.—'With the intention of permanently depriving the
other of it'*

(1) A person appropriating property belonging to
another without meaning the other permanently to lose the
thing itself is nevertheless to be regarded as having the
intention of permanently depriving the other of it if his
intention is to treat the thing as his own to dispose of regardless of the other's rights; and a borrowing or lending of it
may amount to so treating it if, but only if, the borrowing or
lending is for a period and in circumstances making it
equivalent to an outright taking or disposal.

(2) Without prejudice to the generality of subsection (1)
above, where a person, having possession or control (lawfully

or not) of property belonging to another, parts with the property under a condition as to its return which he may not be able to perform, this (if done for purposes of his own and without the other's authority) amounts to treating the property as his own to dispose of regardless of the other's rights.

Section 7.—Theft
A person guilty of theft shall on conviction on indictment be liable to imprisonment for a term not exceeding ten years."

LAWRENCE v. METROPOLITAN POLICE COMMISSIONER
[1971] 2 All E.R. 1253

The words "without the consent of the owner" should not be read into s. 1 of the Theft Act 1968.

Lawrence was a taxi driver charged with theft of £6. The prosecution case was that, on being approached at Victoria Station by Mr. Occhi, a newly arrived Italian with little knowledge of English who requested to be driven to Ladbroke Grove, he said that the journey would be an expensive one. The lawful fare was in the region of 10s. 6d. Mr. Occhi handed Lawrence a pound together with his open wallet and Lawrence was alleged to have removed six further pounds before driving Occhi to Ladbroke Grove. Lawrence was convicted and appealed unsuccessfully to the Court of Appeal and House of Lords.

Extracts from the Speeches of the House of Lords
Viscount Dilhorne.—
"Prior to the passage of the Theft Act 1968, which made radical changes in and greatly simplified the law relating to theft and some other offences, it was necessary to prove that the property alleged to have been stolen was taken 'without the consent of the owner' (Larceny Act 1916, s. 1(1)).
These words are not included in s. 1(1) of the Theft Act 1968, but the appellant contended that the subsection should be construed as if they were, as if they appeared after the word 'appropriates'. Section 1(1) provides:

'A person is guilty of theft if he dishonestly appropriates property belonging to another with the intention of permanently depriving the other of it; and "thief" and "steal" shall be construed accordingly.'

I see no ground for concluding that the omission of the words 'without the consent of the owner' was inadvertent and not deliberate, and to read the subsection as if they were included is, in my opinion, wholly unwarranted. Parliament by the omission of these words has relieved the prosecution of the burden of establishing that the taking was without the owner's consent. That is no longer an ingredient of the offence.

Megaw, L.J., delivering the judgment of the Court of Appeal,[1] said that the offence created by s. 1(1) involved four elements: '(i) a dishonest (ii) appropriation (iii) of property belonging to another (iv) with the intention of permanently depriving the owner of it.' I agree. That there was appropriation in this case is clear. Section 3(1) states that any assumption by a person of the rights of an owner amounts to an appropriation. Here there was clearly such an assumption. That an appropriation was dishonest may be proved in a number of ways. In this case it was not contended that the appellant had not acted dishonestly. Section 2(1) provides, *inter alia*, that a person's appropriation of property belonging to another is not to be regarded as dishonest if he appropriates the property in the belief that he would have the other's consent if the other knew of the appropriation and the circumstances of it. *A fortiori*, a person is not to be regarded as acting dishonestly if he appropriates another's property believing that with full knowledge of the circumstances that other person has in fact agreed to the appropriation. The appellant, if he believed that Mr. Occhi, knowing that £7 was far in excess of the legal fare, had nevertheless agreed to pay him that sum, could not be said to have acted dishonestly in taking it. When Megaw, L.J., said that if there was true consent, the essential element of dishonesty was not established, I understand him to have meant this. Belief or the absence of belief that the owner had with such knowledge consented to the appropriation is relevant to the issue of dishonesty, not to the question whether or not there has been an appropriation. That may occur even though the owner has permitted or consented to the property

---

being taken. So proof that Mr. Occhi had consented to the appropriation of £6 from his wallet without agreeing to paying a sum in excess of the legal fare does not suffice to show that there was not dishonesty in this case. There was ample evidence that there was.

I now turn to the third element 'property belonging to another'. Counsel for the appellant contended that if Mr. Occhi consented to the appellant taking the £6, he consented to the property in the money passing from him to the appellant and that the appellant had not, therefore, appropriated property belonging to another. He argued that the old distinction between the offence of false pretences and larceny had been preserved. I am unable to agree with this. The new offence of obtaining property by deception created by s. 15(1) of the Theft Act 1968 also contains the words 'belonging to another'. ' A person who by any deception dishonestly obtains property belonging to another with the intention of permanently depriving the other of it . . .' commits that offence. 'Belonging to another' in s. 1(1) and in s. 15(1) in my view signifies no more than that, at the time of the appropriation or the obtaining, the property belonged to another with the words 'belonging to another' having the extended meaning given by s. 5. . . .

The first question posed in the certificate was:

> 'Whether section 1(1) of the Theft Act 1968 is to be construed as though it contained the words "without having the consent of the owner" or words to that effect.'

In my opinion, the answer is clearly No.
The second question was:

> 'Whether the provisions of section 15(1) and of section 1(1) of the Theft Act 1968 are mutually exclusive in the sense that if the facts proved would justify a conviction under section 15(1) there cannot lawfully be a conviction under section 1(1) on those facts.'

Again, in my opinion, the answer is No. There is nothing in the Act to suggest that they should be regarded as mutually exclusive and it is by no means uncommon for conduct on the part of an accused to render him liable to conviction for more than one offence. Not infrequently there is some overlapping of offences. In some cases the facts may justify a charge under s. 1(1) and also a charge under s. 15(1). On the other hand, there are cases which only come within s. 1(1) and some which are only within s. 15(1). If in this case the appellant had been

charged under s. 15(1), he would, I expect, have contended
that there was no deception, that he had simply appropriated
the money and that he ought to have been charged under
s. 1(1). In my view, he was rightly charged under that
section."

APPEAL DISMISSED.

R. v. WOODMAN
[1974] 2 All E.R. 955

*Property can belong to another for the purposes of theft even
though that person is unaware of its existence if he is in control
of the place where the property is.*

English China Clays owned a disused factory, whose site
contained a great deal of scrap metal. They sold the metal
to the Bird Group who removed the bulk of it. A certain
quantity of metal was too inaccessible to be removed in such
a way as to be attractive to the Bird Group so that it was
left on the site. When the site had been cleared by the Bird
Group a barbed wire fence was erected round its perimeter
by English China Clays who also put up a number of notices
such as "Private Property. Keep Out" and "Trespassers will
be prosecuted". English China Clays were not aware that
any scrap metal remained on the site after the Bird Group
had done its work. Subsequently, Woodman took a van to the
site and removed a quantity of the scrap metal which
remained.

Woodman was charged with theft, the indictment
alleging that the scrap metal belonged to English China
Clays, and convicted. He appealed to the Court of Appeal,
contending that the scrap was not property "belonging to
another" within ss. 1(1) and 5(1) of the Theft Act 1968
since English China Clays, having sold it, had no proprietary
right or interest in it and, being ignorant of its presence on
the site, had neither possession nor control of it.

Extracts from the Judgment of the Court of Appeal

Lord Widgery, C.J.—
"The recorder took the view that the contract of sale
between English China Clays and the Bird Group had

divested English China Clays of any proprietary right to any scrap on the site. It is unnecessary to express a firm view on that point, but the court are not disposed to disagree with that conclusion that the proprietary interest in the scrap had passed.

The recorder also took the view on the relevant facts that it was not possible to say that English China Clays were in possession of the residue of the scrap. It is not quite clear why he took that view. It may have been because he took the view that difficulties arose by reason of the fact that English China Clays had no knowledge of the existence of this particular scrap at any particular time. But the recorder did take the view that so far as control was concerned there was a case to go to the jury on whether or not this scrap was in the control of English China Clays, because if it was, then it was to be regarded as their property for the purposes of a larceny charge even if they were not entitled to any proprietary interest. . . .

We have formed the view without difficulty . . . that there was ample evidence that English China Clays were in control of the site and had taken considerable steps to exclude trespassers as demonstrating the fact that they were in control of the site, and we think that in ordinary and straightforward cases if it is once established that a particular person is in control of a site such as this, then prima facie he is in control of articles which are on the site.

The point was well put in an article written by no less a person than Oliver Wendell Holmes Jnr. in his book *The Common Law*, dealing with possession. Considering the very point we have to consider here, he said:

'There can be no *animus domini* unless the thing is known of; but an intent to exclude others from it it may be contained in the larger intent to exclude others from the place where it is, without any knowledge of the object's existence. . . . In a criminal case,[1] the property in iron taken from the bottom of a canal by a stranger was held well laid in the canal company, although it does not appear that the company knew of it, or had any lien upon it. The only intent concerning the thing discoverable in such instances is the general intent which the occupant of land has to exclude the public from the land, and thus, as a consequence, to exclude them from what is upon it.'

---

[1] *R.* v. *Rowe* (1859), 8 Cox C.C. 139.

So far as this case is concerned, arising as it does under the Theft Act 1968, we are content to say that there was evidence of English China Clays being in control of the site and prima facie in control of articles on the site as well. The fact that it could not be shown that they were conscious of the existence of this or any particular scrap iron does not destroy the general principle that control of a site by excluding others from it is prima facie control of articles on the site as well.

There has been some mention in argument of what would happen if, in a case like the present, a third party had come and placed some article within the barbed wire fence and thus on the site. The article might be an article of some serious criminal consequence such as explosives or drugs. It may well be that in that type of case the fact that the article has been introduced at a late stage in circumstances in which the occupier of the site had no means of knowledge would produce a different result from that which arises under the general presumption to which we have referred, but in the present case there was in our view ample evidence to go the jury on the question of whether English China Clays were in control of the scrap at the relevant time."

APPEAL DISMISSED.

R. v. TURNER (No. 2)
[1971] 2 All E.R. 441

The owner of a chattel may be guilty of stealing it by dishonestly taking it out of the possession of another and the question whether he was acting dishonestly depends on whether he believed that he was entitled to act as he did.

Turner had his car repaired by a garage. He told Mr. Brown, the proprietor of the garage, that he would come and pay for the repairs on the following day. In the meantime Mr. Brown retained possession of the car which he left outside his garage. Turner took the car away without paying for the repairs. He was convicted of theft of the car and unsuccessfully appealed to the Court of Appeal.

Extracts from the Judgment of the Court of Appeal

Lord Parker, C.J.—

"It is argued from that, in default of proof of a lien—
and the judge in his summing-up directed the jury that they
were not concerned with the question of whether there was a
lien—that Mr. Brown was merely a bailee at will and accordingly that he had no sufficient possession.

The words 'belonging to another' are specifically
defined in s. 5 of the Act. Section 5(1) provides:

'Property shall be regarded as belonging to any
person having possession or control of it, or having in it
any proprietary right or interest . . .'

As I have said, the judge directed the jury that they were no,
concerned in any way with lien and the sole question wat
whether Mr. Brown had possession or control. This court is
quite satisfied that there is no ground whatever for qualifyins
the words 'possession or control' in any way. It is sufficieng
if it is found that the person from whom the property is takent
or to use the words of the Act, appropriated, was at the time
in fact in possession or control . . . .

The second point that is taken relates to the necessity
for proving dishonesty. Section 2(1) provides:

'A person's appropriation of property belonging to another
is not to be regarded as dishonest—(a) if he appropriates
the property in the belief that he has in law the right to
deprive the other of it, on behalf of himself or of a third
person . . .'

. . . [Counsel for the appellant says] that if in fact one
disregards lien entirely as the jury were told to do, then
Mr. Brown was a bailee at will, and the car could have been
taken back by the appellant perfectly lawfully at any time
whether any money was due in regard to repairs or whether
it was not. He says, as the court understands it, first that if
there was that right, then there cannot be theft at all, and
secondly, that if and insofar as the mental element is relevant, namely belief, the jury should have been told that he
had this right and be left to judge, in the light of the existence
of that right, whether they thought he may have believed,
as he said, that he did have a right.

This court, however, is quite satisfied that there is
nothing in this point whatever. The whole test of dishonesty
is the mental element of belief. No doubt, although the
appellant may for certain purposes be presumed to know

the law, he would not at the time have the vaguest idea
whether he did have in law a right to take the car back again,
and accordingly when one looks at his mental state, one
looks at it in the light of what he believed. The jury were
properly told that if he believed that he had a right, albeit
there was none, he would nevertheless fall to be acquitted."

APPEAL DISMISSED.

R. v. HALL
[1972] 2 All E.R. 1009

*A travel agent who receives payments for advance bookings
of flights and pays the money received into his firm's general
account is not, in the absence of some further arrangement,
under an obligation to deal with the money in a particular way
so as to bring the case within s. 5(3) of the Theft Act 1968.*[1]

Hall, a travel agent, received payments for flights to be
made by seven clients. He paid the money into his firm's
general account. None of the flights materialised, and none
of the money was repaid. He was charged and convicted of
theft of the money but successfully appealed to the Court of
Appeal.

Extracts from the Judgment of the Court of Appeal

Edmund Davies, L.J.—

"Two points were presented and persuasively developed
by the appellant's counsel: (1) that, while the appellant has
testified that all monies received had been used for business
purposes, even had he been completely profligate in its
expenditure he could not in any of the seven cases be
convicted of 'theft' as defined by the Theft Act 1968; . . . (2)
that s. 1(1) of the Theft Act 1968 dealing with a person who
'dishonestly appropriates', it is essential that the Crown
establish that the appellant was acting dishonestly at the
time he appropriated. . . . We dispose of point (2) by simply
saying that, although the summing-up could with advantage
have made the legal position clearer, we have come to the
conclusion that it dealt adequately with this aspect of the
offence charged, and had there been no other ground of
criticism we should have been constrained to dismiss the
appeal . . . .

---

[1] P. 253, *supra.*

Point (1) turns on the application of s. 5(3) of the Theft Act 1968 . . . Counsel for the appellant . . . referred us to a passage in the Eighth Report of the Criminal Law Revision Committee[1] which reads as follows:

'Subsection (3) [of cl. 5 "belonging to another"] provides for the special case where property is transferred to a person to retain and deal with for a particular purpose and he misapplies it or its proceeds. An example would be the treasurer of a holiday fund. The person in question is in law the owner of the property; but the subsection treats the property, as against him, as belonging to the person to whom he owes the duty to retain and deal with the property as agreed. He will therefore be guilty of stealing from them if he misapplies the property . . .'

But, in our judgment, what was not here established was that these clients expected [Hall] "to retain and deal with that property or its proceeds in a particular way" and that an "obligation to do so was undertaken by the appellant." We must make clear, however, that each case turns on its own facts. Cases could, we suppose, conceivably arise where by some special arrangement (preferably evidenced by documents), the client could impose on the travel agent an "obligation" falling within s. 5(3). But no such special arrangement was made in any of the seven cases here being considered."

APPEAL ALLOWED.

R. v. MEECH

[1973] 3 All E.R. 939

If A gives B a cheque to cash for him, the proceeds belong to A, as against B, under s. 5(3) of the Theft Act 1968.

McCord obtained a cheque for £1,450 by fraud from a finance company. Meech, who was unaware of the fraud, agreed to cash the cheque for McCord. For that purpose Meech paid the cheque into his own bank account and subsequently withdrew £1,410 from it, the difference between the two sums being represented by a debt of £40 owed to Meech by McCord. By the time he withdrew the £1,410 Meech had become aware that McCord had obtained the original cheque dishonestly and he had arranged with two others to stage a fake robbery, with Meech as victim, so as

---

[1] Theft and Related Offences, Cmnd. 2977 (1966), p. 127.

to provide an explanation for his inability to hand over the money to McCord. The fake robbery took place and the money was shared by Meech and the other two men. All three were convicted of theft and appealed against conviction.

Extracts from the Judgment of the Court of Appeal

Roskill, L.J.—

"It is, we think, clear that none of them could have been charged with theft unless the Crown could successfully invoke s. 5(3) of the Theft Act 1968. On no view had any of the appellants stolen the hire purchase finance company's cheque from that company. Nor had they stolen that cheque from McCord since Meech had received it from McCord with McCord's full consent. But the Crown argued that Meech was at all material times under an 'obligation' to McCord from whom Meech had received the cheque, to deal with the proceeds of that cheque in a particular way, namely, by returning those proceeds (less £40) to McCord, that those proceeds were, therefore, 'as against' Meech to be regarded as belonging to McCord, and that Meech, instead of fulfilling that 'obligation' or being lawfully excused from its performance, had in concert with Parslow and Jolliffe dishonestly misappropriated the £1,410 in cash in the manner which we have already described. . . .

Starting from this premise—that 'obligation' means 'legal obligation'—it was argued that even at the time when Meech was ignorant of the dishonest origin of the cheque, as he was at the time when he agreed to cash the cheque and hand the proceeds less £40 to McCord, McCord could never have enforced that obligation because McCord had acquired the cheque illegally. In our view this submission is unsound in principle. The question has to be looked at from Meech's point of view not McCord's. Meech plainly assumed an 'obligation' to McCord which on the facts then known to him he remained obliged to fulfil and on the facts as found he must be taken at that time honestly to have intended to fulfil. The fact that on the true facts if known McCord might not and indeed would not subsequently have been permitted to enforce that obligation in a civil court does not prevent that 'obligation' on Meech having arisen. The argument confuses the creation of the obligation with the subsequent discharge of that obligation either by performance or otherwise. That the obligation might have become impossible of performance by Meech or of enforcement by McCord on grounds of illegality or for reasons of public policy is irrelevant. The opening words of s. 5(3) clearly look to the time of the creation of or the acceptance of the obligation by the bailee and not to the time of performance by him of the obligation so created and accepted by him. . . .

[I]t was said that the £1,410 obtained by Meech from his bank by cashing his own cheque were not 'the proceeds' of the original cheque but of Meech's own cheque. The answer to that contention is that it is clear that the money received by Meech when he cashed his own cheque plainly emanated from the original cheque and can properly be regarded on the facts of this case as the proceeds of the original cheque. . . .

We think that the learned judge's direction when he said that the time of the appropriation was the time of the fake robbery was right. A dishonest intention had been formed before the money was withdrawn but the misappropriation only took place when the three men divided up the money at the scene of the fake robbery. It was then that the performance of the obligation by Meech finally became impossible by the dishonest act of these three men acting in concert together.

APPEALS DISMISSED.

Comment on R. v. Meech

It is difficult to see how there was a legal obligation of the type specified by s. 5(3) of the Theft Act 1968 in this case. The Court of Appeal held that there was an initial obligation owed to McCord by Meech to retain and deal with the original cheque in a particular way and that this sufficed for the purposes of s. 5(3) even though that obligation became unenforceable by McCord on Meech's discovery of the fraud. The court based this initial obligation on the fact that on Meech's knowledge of the facts there was an obligation to McCord, but s. 5(3) does not talk in terms of an obligation believed by the accused to exist but of an actual obligation. Moreover, it appears to require the existence of such an obligation at the time of the appropriation (which was held to be the time of the fake robbery). It is certainly odd that, on the view taken by the Court of Appeal, an obligation which may never have existed and certainly did not exist at the time of the appropriation could be held to suffice for the purposes of s. 5(3).

It may be that the case merited a simpler solution since under the law of property McCord might have had a proprietary interest in the proceeds of the cheque for the purposes of s. 5(1) of the Theft Act 1968.

R. v. GILKS
[1972] 3 All E.R. 280

*A punter who is overpaid winnings in consequence of a
bookmaker's mistake of which he is aware is guilty of theft,
assuming that he acted dishonestly; but the case does not come
within s. 5(4) of the Theft Act 1968[1] because "obligation" in
that subsection means legal obligation.*

Gilks placed bets with a firm of bookmakers in a betting
shop. On the day in question his winnings amounted to £10.62
but the firm's acting manager mistakenly paid him a further
£106.63, apparently because he thought that a bet made by
Gilks on Fighting Scot, an unplaced horse in one of the day's
races, had been made on Fighting Taffy, the winner. Gilks
was aware of the overpayment at the time he received it,
but refused to repay the money on the ground that bookmakers are a race apart and it was "Ladbrokes' hard lines".
Gilks was charged with and convicted of theft of £106.63.
The trial judge held that the money belonged to the firm of
bookmakers under s. 5(1) of the Theft Act at the time Gilks
received it, but he also held that, if he was wrong, the case
was covered by s. 5(4). On the question of dishonesty, the
trial judge told the jury that the test was whether the
defendant believed that, when dealing with a bookmaker, "if
he makes a mistake you can take the money and keep it, and
there is nothing dishonest about it".
Gilks unsuccessfully appealed to the Court of Appeal.

Extracts from the Judgment of the Court of Appeal

Cairns, L.J.—
    "The subsection [s. 5(4)] introduced a new principle
into the law of theft but long before it was enacted it was held
in *R. v. Middleton*[2], that where a person was paid by mistake
(in that case by a post office clerk) a sum in excess of that
properly payable, the person who accepted the overpayment
with knowledge of the excess was guilty of theft. Counsel for
the appellant seeks to distinguish the present case from that
one on the basis that in R. v. *Middleton*[2] the depositor was

---

[1] P. 253, *supra.*
[2] (1873), L.R. 2 C.C.R. 38.

entitled to withdraw 10s from his Post Office Savings Bank account and the clerk made a mistake in thinking he was entitled to withdraw more than £8, whereas in the present case there was no mistake about the appellant's rights— whether his horse won or lost he had no legal right to payment. In our view this argument is fallacious. A bookmaker who pays out money in the belief that a certain horse has won, and who certainly would not have made the payment but for that belief, is paying by mistake just as much as the Post Office clerk in *R.* v. *Middleton*[1].

The gap in the law which s. 5(4) was designed to fill was, as the deputy chairman rightly held, that which is illustrated by the case of *Moynes* v. *Coopper*[2]. There a workman received a paypacket containing £7 more than was due to him but did not become aware of the overpayment till he opened the envelope some time later. He then kept the £7. This was was held not to be theft because there was no *animus furandi* at the moment of taking, and *R.* v. *Middleton*[1] was distinguished on that ground. It was observed[3] that the law as laid down in *R.* v. *Middleton*[1] was reproduced and enacted in s. 1(2)(i) of the Larceny Act 1916. It would be strange indeed if s. 5(4) of the 1968 Act, which was designed to bring within the net of theft a type of dishonest behaviour which escaped before, were to be held to have created a loophole for another type of dishonest behaviour which was always within the net.

An alternative ground on which the deputy chairman held that the money should be regarded as belonging to Ladbrokes was that 'obligation' in s. 5(4) meant an obligation whether a legal one or not. In the opinion of this court that was an incorrect ruling. In a criminal statute, where a person's criminal liability is made dependent on his having an obligation, it would be quite wrong to construe that word so as to cover a moral or social obligation as distinct from a legal one. . . .

On the face of it the appellant's conduct was dishonest; the only possible basis on which the jury could find that the prosecution had not established dishonesty would be if they thought it possible that the appellant did have the belief which he claimed to have . . . .

It is contended that the jury may have understood this direction to mean that the appellant would be acting dis-

---

[1] (1873), L.R. 2 C.C.R. 38.
[2] [1956] 1 Q.B. 439; [1956] 1 All E.R. 450.
[3] [1956] 1 Q.B., at p. 445; [1956] 1 All E.R., at p. 452.

honestly unless (a) he believed he had the right to take the
money and keep it and (b) he believed there was nothing
dishonest about that conduct. It is said that the jury may
have thought that the appellant's state of mind was 'I
believe that in law I am entitled to take from my bookmaker
anything he is foolish enough to pay me, though of course I
know that it would be dishonest to do so', and he pointed
that under s.1(1) this would entitle him to be acquitted
whereas the direction might be taken to mean that he would
be guilty.

In our opinion this is too refined an argument. We think
it is clear that in the context the word 'and' meant 'and
therefore' or 'and so' and the jury would understand it in that
way."

APPEAL DISMISSED.

Comment on R. v. Gilks

To constitute theft at common law and under the Larceny
Act 1916 it was essential that there should have been a taking of
possession by the accused without the consent of the owner. If
goods or money were delivered by A., the owner, to B., the
accused, with the intention that B. should become their owner,
B. was not guilty of theft (although he might have been guilty of
obtaining by false pretences); but, if A. were mistaken as to the
identity of B. (believing him to be C. for example), or as to the
identity of the thing transferred (believing peas to be beans for
example), it was held, rather artificially, that B.'s reception of the
goods amount to a constructive taking.

In *Middleton*[1] it was held in the majority judgment of
the Court for Crown Cases Reserved that the post office clerk
either made a mistake as to Middleton's identity (believing him to
be the depositor who had given notice of withdrawal of the larger
sum), or else made a mistake as to the identity of the debt which
he was discharging. In *Moynes* v. *Coopper*[2] on the other hand, the
wages clerk made no mistake as to identity; his mistake was that
a full week's wages was due to Coopper, being unaware of the fact
that Coopper had already received the greater part of this sum
as an advance payment. Coopper did not become aware of the
overpayment for some time after he received it, and the implication of Lord Goddard's judgment in the Divisional Court,
accepted by the Court of Appeal in *Gilks*, was that Coopper
would have been guilty of theft had he been aware of the clerk's

---

[1] (1873), L.R. 2 C.C.R. 38; cited in the above judgment.
[2] [1956] 1 All E.R. 450; cited in the above judgment.

mistake on receipt of the pay envelope. It is, however, by no means clear that this would have been so for, there being no mistake as to identity, it is arguable that both ownership and possession of the coins would have passed to Coopper as they certainly would have passed if the clerk's mistake with regard to the advance had been induced by Coopper's false pretence[1]. It is just arguable that the acting manager made a mistake as to the identity of the bet he was paying in Gilks's case, but the artificiality of the argument is such as to make it most unconvincing.

It is regrettable that the over subtle distinctions of the old law of theft should be called in aid in the construction of the Theft Act 1968. In this context the question is whether B. can be said to have appropriated goods or money belonging to A. when A. hands them to him with the intention that he should become their owner under a mistake as to the amount due, a mistake of which B. was aware at the time of the handing-over. Normally s. 5(4) will enable an affirmative answer to be given; but, even when, as in Gilks's case, this subsection is held to be inapplicable, an affirmative answer can be given provided a man can be said to assume the rights of an owner when he dishonestly allows ownership to be transferred to him.

A point about *Gilks* which is perhaps only surprising at first sight is that it is authority for the proposition that a person can act dishonestly although he does precisely what the law allows him to do, viz., accept and retain an overpayment on a wagering transaction.[2]

In the end, the true view may prove to be that *Morgan* v. *Ashcroft* was wrongly decided, in which event s. 5(4) of the Theft Act 1968 would clearly apply to the facts of *Gilks*.

In *Morgan* v. *Ashcroft* it was held that a bookmaker cannot sue civilly for money paid under a mistake of fact when he has overpaid one of his clients. The underlying principles that the court will not take account of wagering transactions and that, in order to support a claim for money paid under a mistake of fact, the mistake must be such that, had the facts been as supposed, there would have been a legal obligation to make the payment, are certainly ones which should some day be reviewed by the House of Lords.

---

[1] 72 Law Quarterly Review 181.
[2] *Morgan* v. *Ashcroft*, [1938] 1 K.B. 49; [1937] 3 All E.R. 92.

R. v. FEELY
[1973] 1 All E.R. 341

The question whether an appropriation is dishonest within the meaning of s. 1(1) of the Theft Act 1968[1] is a question of fact to be determined by a jury when there is one.

Feely was a branch manager of a firm of bookmakers who, like other employees of the firm, had received a circular from his employers forbidding him to borrow their money by taking it from the till. He took about £30 from a safe at his branch in order to give it to his father. When the deficiency was discovered, Feely gave an IOU to his successor as branch manager and said that he intended to repay the sum, taking it out of money due to him from his employers, who in fact owed him about twice that amount.

Feely was charged with theft and convicted after the judge had directed the jury that it is dishonest for an employee to do what he knows his employers are not prepared to tolerate, but had failed to make it plain to the jury that it was for them to decide whether the accused's conduct was in fact dishonest. Feely successfully appealed to the Court of Appeal who quashed his conviction on the ground that the question whether an appropriation was dishonest is one of fact.

Extracts from the Judgment of the Court of Appeal

Lawton, L.J.—

". . . In s. 1(1) of the Theft Act 1968 the word 'dishonestly' can only relate to the state of mind of the person who does the act which amounts to appropriation. Whether an accused person has a particular state of mind is a question of fact which has to be decided by the jury when there is a trial on indictment and by the justices when there are summary proceedings. The Crown did not dispute this proposition, but it was submitted that in some cases (and this, it was said, was such a one) it was necessary for the trial judge to define 'dishonestly' and when the facts fell within the definition he had a duty to tell the jury that if there had been an appropriation it must have been dishonestly done. We do not agree that judges should define what 'dishonestly' means.

---

[1] P. 251, *supra*.

This word is in common use whereas the word 'fraudulently' which was used in s. 1(1) of the Larceny Act 1916 had acquired as a result of case law a special meaning. Jurors, when deciding whether an appropriation was dishonest can be reasonably expected to, and should, apply the current standards of ordinary decent people. In their own lives they have to decide what is and what is not dishonest. We can see no reason why, when in a jury box, they should require the help of a judge to tell them what amounts to dishonesty. We are fortified in this opinion by a passage in the speech of Lord Reid in *Brutus* v. *Cozens*,[1] a case in which the words 'insulting behaviour' in s.5 of the Public Order Act, 1936 had to be construed. The Divisional Court[2] had adjudged that the meaning of the word 'insulting' in this statutory context was a matter of law. Lord Reid's comment was as follows:

'In my judgment that is not right. The meaning of an ordinary word of the English language is not a question of law. The proper construction of a statute is a question of law. If the context shows that a word is used in an unusual sense the court will determine in other words what that unusual sense is. But there is in my opinion no question of the word 'insulting' being used in any unusual sense. . . . It is for the tribunal which decides the case to consider, not as law but as fact, whether in the whole circumstances the words of the statute do or do not as a matter of ordinary usage of the English language cover or apply to the facts which have been proved.'

When this trenchant statement of principle is applied to the word 'dishonestly' in s. 1(1) of the Theft Act 1968 and to the facts of this case it is clear in our judgment that the jury should have been left to decide whether the appellant's alleged taking of the money had been dishonest. They were not, with the result that a verdict of guilty was returned without their having given thought to what was probably the most important issue in the case. . . .

It is possible to imagine a case of taking by an employee in breach of instructions to which no-one would, or could reasonably, attach moral obloquy; for example, that of a manager of a shop, who having been told that under no circumstances was he to take money from the till for his own purposes, took 40p from it, having no small change himself, to

---

[1] [1972] 2 All E.R. 1297.
[2] [1972] 2 All E.R. 1.

pay for a taxi hired by his wife who had arrived at the shop
saying that she only had a £5 note which the cabby could not
change. To hold that such a man was a thief and to say that
his intention to put the money back in the till when he
acquired some change was at the most a matter of mitigation
would tend to bring the law into contempt. In our judgment
a taking to which no moral obloquy can reasonably attach
is not within the concept of stealing either at common law or
under the Theft Act 1968. . . .

If the principle enunciated in *R. v. Cockburn*[1] was right
there would be a strange divergence between the position of a
man who obtains cash by passing a cheque on an account
which has no funds to meet it and one who takes money from
a till. The man who passes the cheque is deemed in law not to
act dishonestly if he genuinely believes on reasonable grounds
that when it is presented to the paying bank there will be
funds to meet it: see *Halstead* v. *Patel*[2], *per* Lord Widgery,
C.J. But, according to the decision in *R. v. Cockburn*,[3] the
man who takes money from a till intending to put it back and
genuinely believing on reasonable grounds that he will be
able to do so (see *per* Winn, L.J.) should be convicted of
theft. Lawyers may be able to appreciate why one man
should be adjudged to be a criminal and the other not; but
we doubt whether anyone else would. People who take money
from tills and the like without permission are usually thieves;
but if they do not admit that they are by pleading guilty, it
is for the jury, not the judge, to decide whether they have
acted dishonestly."

APPEAL ALLOWED.

Comment on R. v. Feely

The principle laid down in *Feely's* case also applies to
"dishonestly" in ss. 15 and 16 of the Theft Act 1968 (p. 000,
infra); see *Greenstein*[4] and *Lewis*.[5]

Despite what is said in the last paragraph of the extract, it
would be wrong to treat *Feely* as authority for the proposition
that, as a matter of law, a person must have reasonable grounds
for his belief that he would be able to pay or repay or, as in
Lewis (where dishonestly obtaining property by deception

---

[1] [1968] 1 All E.R. 466.
[2] [1972] 2 All E.R. 147, at 152.
[3] [1968] 1 All E.R. 466.
[4] [1976] 1 All E.R. 1.
[5] [1976] Crim. L.R. 383.

was involved), that when his cheque is presented to the bank
there will be funds to meet, in order to prevent an appropriation
or obtaining being dishonest. *Feely* decided that for the purposes
of the Theft Act 1968, dishonesty is a subjective concept having
nothing to do with reasonable belief: the question is did the
accused genuinely believe, not did the accused believe on reasonable grounds. Of course, the reasonableness of his belief is of the
utmost evidential importance when the issue of the genuineness
of his belief is under consideration. Cf. *Lewis*[1] and *Waterfall*.[2]

R. v. EASOM
[1971] 2 All E.R. 945

*A conditional intention to permanently deprive is not
sufficient to render an appropriator guilty of theft.*

A plain-clothes policewoman placed a handbag next to
her aisle seat in a cinema. Easom, who was sitting behind,
picked the bag up, opened it and examined its contents. He
then closed the bag and replaced it with its contents intact
on the floor of the cinema. He was apprehended and convicted of theft of the bag and its contents. He successfully
appealed to the Court of Appeal.

Extract from the Judgment of the Court of Appeal

Edmund Davies, L.J.—
   "In the respectful view of this court, the jury were
misdirected. In every case of theft the appropriation must be
accompanied by the intention of permanently depriving the
owner of his property. What may be loosely described as a
'conditional' appropriation will not do. If the appropriator
has it in mind merely to deprive the owner of such of his
property as, on examination, proves worth taking and then
finding that the booty is to him valueless, leaves it ready to
hand to be repossessed by the owner, he has not stolen. If a
dishonest postal sorter picks up a pile of letters, intending to
steal any which are registered, but, on finding that none of
them are, replaces them, he has stolen nothing, and this is so
notwithstanding the provisions of s. 6(1) of the Theft Act
1968. In the present case the jury were never invited to

---

[1] [1976] Crim. LR. 383.
[2] [1970] 1 Q.B. 148; [1969] 3 All E.R. 1048.

consider the possibility that such was the appellant's state of mind or the legal consequences flowing therefrom. Yet the facts are strongly indicative that this was exactly how his mind was working, for he left the handbag and its contents entirely intact and to hand once he had carried out his exploration. For this reason we hold that conviction of the full offence of theft cannot stand. . . ."

APPEAL ALLOWED.

Robbery
THEFT ACT 1968

"*Section 8.*—

(1) A person is guilty of robbery if he steals, and immediately before or at the time of doing so, and in order to do so, he uses force on any person or puts or seeks to put any person in fear of being then and there subjected to force.

(2) A person guilty of robbery, or of an assault with intent to rob, shall on conviction on indictment be liable to imprisonment for life."

Burglary
THEFT ACT 1968

"*Section 9.*—

(1) A person is guilty of burglary if—

    (*a*) he enters any building or part of a building as a trespasser and with intent to commit any such offence as is mentioned in sub-section (2) below; or

    (*b*) having entered any building or part of a building as a trespasser he steals or attempts to steal anything in the building or that part of it or inflicts or attempts to inflict on any person therein any grievous bodily harm.

(2) The offences referred to in subsection (1) (*a*) above are offences of stealing anything in the building or part of a building in question, of inflicting on any person therein any grievous bodily harm or raping any woman therein, and of doing unlawful damage to the building or anything therein.

(3) References in subsections (1) and (2) above to a building shall apply also to an inhabited vehicle or vessel,

and shall apply to any such vehicle or vessel at times when
the person having a habitation in it is not there as well as at
times when he is.

(4) A person guilty of burglary shall on conviction on
indictment be liable to imprisonment for a term not exceeding
fourteen years.''

R. v. COLLINS
[1972] 2 All E.R. 1105

*In order that a person may be convicted of burglary under
s. 9(1)(a) of the Theft Act 1968 he must have known that he
was entering the premises in question as a trespasser, or at least
have been reckless in that regard.*

Collins was charged with and convicted of burglary by
entering a girl's bedroom with intent to commit rape. He had
climbed up a stepladder and, observing that the girl in
question, with whom he had a slight acquaintance, was
sleeping naked near the window, he descended, undressed,
and then reascended, naked. On awaking and observing a
naked male form either just outside or just inside her bedroom window, the girl, mistakenly believing that it was her
boy friend with whom she frequently had intercourse,
beckoned Collins into bed with her. The parties then had
intercourse and, on discovering her mistake, the girl slapped
Collins and withdrew from the room. There was some evidence that Collins, on entering the bedroom, intended to have
intercourse with the girl, if necessary by force, but it was
not clear whether he had entered the room before the girl
signified her assent to his presence there.

Collins successfully appealed to the Court of Appeal on
the ground that the judge had not directed the jury that they
could only convict if satisfied that he did not believe that the
girl had assented to his presence when he entered her bedroom.

Extracts from the Judgment of the Court of Appeal
Edmund Davies, L.J.—
"Under s. 9 of the Theft Act 1968 which renders a
person guilty of burglary if he enters any building or part of a
building as a trespasser and with intent to commit rape, the

entry of the appellant into the building must first be proved. Well, there is no doubt about that, for it is common ground that he did enter this girl's bedroom. Secondly, it must be proved that he entered as a trespasser. We will develop that point a little later. Thirdly, it must be proved that he entered as a trespasser with intent at the time of entry to commit rape therein.

The second ingredient of the offence—the entry must be as a trespasser—is one which has not, to the best of our knowledge, been previously canvassed in the courts. . . . According to the learned editors of *Archbold*:

> 'Any intentional, negligent or reckless entry into a building will, it would appear, constitute a trespass if the building is in the possession of another person who does not consent to the entry. Nor will it make any difference if the entry was the result of a reasonable mistake on the part of the defendant, so far as trespass is concerned.'

If that be right, then it would be no defence for this man to say (and even were he believed in saying), "Well, I honestly thought that this girl was welcoming me into the room and I therefore entered, fully believing that I had her consent to go in." If *Archbold* is right, he would nevertheless be a trespasser, since the apparent consent of the girl was unreal, she being mistaken as to who was at her window. We disagree. We hold that, for the purpose of s. 9 of the Theft Act 1968, a person entering a building is not guilty of trespass if he enters without knowledge that he is trespassing or at least without acting recklessly as to whether or not he is unlawfully entering. . . .

Having so held, the pivotal point of this appeal is whether the Crown established that the appellant at the moment that he entered the bedroom knew perfectly well that he was not welcome there or, being reckless whether he was welcome or not, was nevertheless determined to enter. . . .

How did the learned judge deal with this matter? We have to say regretfully that there was a flaw in his treatment of it."

APPEAL ALLOWED.[1]

---

[1] The prime importance of this case is the point as to the requirement of *mens rea* with regard to the trespass in burglary; but the judgment of the Court of Appeal also makes the following further points: (1) a conditional intent suffices for this type of burglary, *e.g.* an intent to have intercourse and to do so without consent if necessary; (2) the doctrine of trespass *ab initio* under which an originally lawful entry may, (*continued overleaf*)

THEFT ACT 1968

"Section 10.—Aggravated Burglary

(1) A person is guilty of aggravated burglary if he commits any burglary and at the time has with him any firearm or imitation firearm, any weapon of offence, or any explosive; and for this purpose—

(*a*) 'firearm' includes an airgun or air pistol, and 'imitation firearm' means anything which has the appearance of being a firearm, whether capable of being discharged or not; and

(*b*) 'weapon of offence' means any article made or adapted for use for causing injury to or incapacitating a person, or intended by the person having it with him for such use; and

(*c*) 'explosive' means any article manufactured for the purpose of producing a practical effect by explosion, or intended by the person having it with him for that purpose.

(2) A person guilty of aggravated burglary shall on conviction on indictment be liable to imprisonment for life."

Temporary Deprivation

THEFT ACT 1968

"Section 11.—Removal of articles from places open to the public

(1) Subject to subsections (2) and (3) below, where the public have access to a building in order to view the building or part of it, or a collection or part of a collection housed in it, any person who without lawful authority removes from the building or its grounds the whole or part of any article displayed or kept for display to the public in the building or that part of it or in its grounds shall be guilty of an offence.

For this purpose 'collection' includes a collection got together for a temporary purpose, but references in this section to a collection do not apply to a collection made or exhibited for the purpose of effecting sales or other commercial dealings.

---

on the occurrence of an unlawful act on the premises sometimes be treated as trespassory for the purposes of the civil law, has no application to burglary; (3) for the purposes of the law of burglary, the consent of a licensee in the building will suffice. As to the third point, the girl was technically a licensee for the occupier of the house was her mother.

(2) It is immaterial for purposes of subsection (1) above, that the public's access to a building is limited to a particular period or particular occasion; but where anything removed from a building or its grounds is there otherwise than as forming part of, or being on loan for exhibition with, a collection intended for permanent exhibition to the public, the person removing it does not thereby commit an offence under this section unless he removes it on a day when the public have access to the building as mentioned in subsection (1) above.

(3) A person does not commit an offence under this section if he believes that he has lawful authority for the removal of the thing in question or that he would have it if the person entitled to give it knew of the removal and the circumstances of it.

(4) A person guilty of an offence under this section shall, on conviction on indictment, be liable to imprisonment for a a term not exceeding five years."

R. v. DURKIN
[1973] 2 All E.R. 872

"A collection intended for permanent exhibition to the public" in s. 11(2) of the Theft Act 1968 is simply a collection intended to be permanently available for exhibition to the public.

Teesside council owned two art galleries, one being in Middlesbrough. The entire permanent collection of pictures owned by the council was very seldom on view at one time in either gallery, only a part being exhibited at a given time. However, all the pictures in the permanent collection were shown at least once a year and sections of it were exhibited at various times throughout the twelve months.

At 1.30 a.m. on a day when it was not open to the public, Durkin broke into the Middlesbrough gallery and removed a painting by L. S. Lowry which was part of the permanent collection. Like the other pictures in that collection it was not on permanent exhibition in the Middlesbrough gallery but had been exhibited there for about three weeks before Durkin took it.

Durkin was convicted of taking the painting contrary to s. 11(1) of the Theft Act 1968. He appealed to the Court of Appeal, contending that the picture did not form part of "a collection intended for permanent exhibition to the public" within s.11(2), since each picture in the collection was only seldom exhibited, and therefore, by virtue of s.11(2), no offence had been committed since he had removed the picture on a day when the public did not have access to the gallery.

Extract from the Judgment of the Court of Appeal

Edmund Davies, L.J.—

"With the learned judge, we hold that 'a collection intended for permanent exhibition to the public' is simply one intended to be permanently *available* for exhibition to the public, and that such intention was sufficiently manifested in the present case by the local authority's settled practice of periodically displaying to the public in the Middlesborough art gallery the Lowry picture and the others in their Teesside permanent collection."

APPEAL DISMISSED.

THEFT ACT 1968

"*Section 12.—Taking motor vehicle or other conveyance without authority*

(1) Subject to subsections (5) and (6) below, a person shall be guilty of an offence if, without having the consent of the owner or other lawful authority, he takes any conveyance for his own or another's use or, knowing that any conveyance has been taken without such authority, drives it or allows himself to be carried in or on it.

(2) A person guilty of an offence under subsection (1) above shall on conviction on indictment be liable to imprisonment for a term not exceeding three years.

. . .

(4) If on the trial of an indictment for theft the jury are not satisfied that the accused committed theft, but it is proved that the accused committed an offence under subsection (1) above, the jury may find him guilty of the offence under subsection (1).

(5) Subsection (1) above shall not apply in relation to pedal cycles; but, subject to subsection (6) below, a person who, without having the consent of the owner or other lawful authority, takes a pedal cycle for his own or another's use,

or rides a pedal cycle knowing it to have been taken without such authority, shall on summary conviction be liable to a fine not exceeding fifty pounds.

(6) A person does not commit an offence under this section by anything done in the belief that he has lawful authority to do it or that he would have the owner's consent if the owner knew of his doing it and the circumstances of it.

(7) For purposes of this section—

(a) 'conveyance' means any conveyance constructed or adapted for the carriage of a person or persons whether by land, water or air, except that it does not include a conveyance constructed or adapted for use only under the control of a person not carried in or on it, and 'drive' shall be construed accordingly; and

(b) 'owner', in relation to a conveyance which is the subject of a hiring agreement or hire-purchase agreement, means the person in possession of the conveyance under that agreement.''

R. v. PEART
[1970] 2 All E.R. 823

A consent obtained by misrepresentations concerning the purpose for which a conveyance is required is a defence to taking the conveyance contrary to s. 12 (1) of the Theft Act 1968.

Peart induced Black to lend him his car by falsely representing that he had to go to Alnwick by 2.30 p.m. or else he would lose a contract. Peart was stopped later in the evening after the time at which he had promised to return the car while driving the car in Burnley. He was convicted of taking the car without the consent of the owner contrary to s. 12 of the Theft Act 1968. He successfully appealed to the Court of Appeal.

Extracts from the Judgment of the Court of Appeal

Sachs, L.J.—

"So far as any issue relevant to the present case is concerned, this court is of the clear opinion that there are no material differences between the currently operating subsection of the Theft Act 1968 and those of the Road Traffic Acts 1930 and 1960 which have just been mentioned. It is, of course, well known that s. 28 of the 1930 Act was introduced to provide a simple criminal remedy for the spate of occasions when cars were taken against the wishes of owners from the streets or from a garage without permanently intending to deprive the owner of that vehicle. It was intended in its very nature to deal with takings made without any reference to the owner. Forty years have gone by since the 1930 Act was passed, and this is, so far as this court is aware, the first time that it has been suggested that it should be applied to occasions when consent was obtained by false pretences . . . .

Whether fraudulent representations vitiate consent was the subject of considerable discussion in the days when there was a distinction between larceny by a trick and obtaining goods by false pretences. That discussion and the resulting decisions must have been known to those who framed and passed the 1930 Act. The principles applicable to consent in relation to obtaining property—and I use the word 'property' in its technical sense—thus seem to this court to be in general applicable to consent to obtaining possession with licence to take and drive. An example of a fraudulent representation which did not vitiate the consent is to be found in *London Jewellers, Ltd*. v. *Attenborough*,[1] decided after the passing of the 1930 Act. There have been other decisions since, but it is not necessary to cite them. In substance these decisions can be said to establish that there may well be a distinction between fraudulent representations of facts that are regarded as fundamental and of facts that are not; those regarded as fundamental fall within a somewhat narrow category, *e.g.* fraudulent representations as to identity or as to the nature of a transaction. These distinctions are of a kind which it would be unfortunate to introduce into the particular provisions under consideration, which were clearly intended to apply to offences of quite a simple type.

Whilst, however, reserving the point whether, in regard to s. 12(1) of the Theft Act 1968, a fundamental misrepresentation can vitiate consent, this court has today to deal with a false pretence of the most usual category, no different in principle to the false pretences which come before the courts on a very great variety of occasions. If this court acceded to the submission put forward by the Crown, it would have some far reaching consequences which can hardly have been within the intention of the legislature.''

APPEAL ALLOWED.

---

[1] [1934] 2 K.B. 206; [1934] All E.R. Rep. 270.

R. v. PHIPPS AND R. v. McGILL
(1970), 54 Cr. App. Rep. 300

An offence under s. 12 of the Theft Act 1968, is committed if a car is borrowed for a particular purpose and used for some other purpose.

McGill was charged and convicted of taking a car without the consent of the owner contrary to s. 12 of the Theft Act 1968, and Phipps was charged with permitting himself to be carried in a car which had been so taken. McGill had borrowed a car from Larking for the purpose of taking Mrs. McGill to Victoria station, but he continued to drive the car with Phipps as a passenger for another purpose instead of returning it to its owner. Phipps and McGill unsuccessfully appealed to the Court of Appeal.

Extracts from the Judgment of the Court of Appeal

Fenton Atkinson, L.J.—

"The point that Miss Pearlman takes on their behalf is that so long as the original taking and driving away was with the consent of the owner, it really does not matter for how long they kept it thereafter, or what they did with it short of actually stealing it, and that if they decided the next day to drive off or to take it to the Continent on a holiday, they could not have been taking and driving away without authority, even though they knew perfectly well that the owner would object strongly to what they were doing.

In our view, that is an impossible submission with respect to Miss Pearlman, who has said everything possible in support of this appeal.

The learned Common Serjeant put it to the jury in this way: 'The allegation against him is that having lawfully borrowed the car with Mr. Larking's consent for a particular purpose and for a particular purpose only, he'—referring here, of course, to McGill—'thereafter did not return the car, and if that is the position, then as from the time he decided not to return the car and drove it off on his own business after having taken his wife to Victoria Station, or rather brought her back again because she had missed the train, as from then, as a matter of law, and common sense, if he did not have Mr. Larking's permission, he took it and drove it away, and it is that subsequent taking and driving that the Crown allege constitutes the offence in this matter . . .'

In our view, the way in which the matter was put by the learned Common Serjeant was perfectly accurate."

APPEALS DISMISSED.

Comment on R. v. Peart and R. v. Phipps and McGill

Phipps and McGill can be reconciled with *Peart* on the basis that in the latter the issue before the Court of Appeal was whether the judge's direction as to the effect of the fraud on the initial consent was correct. As Sachs, L. J., pointed out in *Peart*, the issue had not been left to the jury whether there had been a fresh taking at some time after the van was originally driven away and Peart's conviction was quashed because of a misdirection on the only issue left to the jury, viz., whether there was an effective consent when the van was originally taken.

McKNIGHT v. DAVIES
[1974] R.T.R. 4

An employee who makes unauthorised use of his employer's vehicle may "take" it for the purposes of s. 12 of the Theft Act 1968.

McKnight was employed as a lorry driver. His duty was to make deliveries to shops and on completion of these to return the lorry to his employer's depot. One evening, having completed his deliveries, McKnight was driving back to the depot when the roof of the lorry struck a bridge. When he saw the damage to the lorry he was scared and drove it to a public house and had a drink. After that he drove three men to their homes on the outskirts of Cardiff, drove back to the centre of the city, had another drink and then drove home, parking the lorry nearby. Early the next morning he drove the lorry to his employer's depot. McKnight was convicted of taking a conveyance contrary to s. 12 of the Theft Act 1968, and appealed to the Divisional Court.

Extracts from the Judgments of the Divisional Court

Lord Widgery, C.J.—

"There can, I think, be little doubt that the lorry was being used, following the accident with the bridge, for the defendant's own use, and the argument centres on whether on the facts found he can be said to have 'taken' the conveyance at all.

... In *R. v. Phipps*[1] the Court of Appeal clearly rejected the argument that a lawful acquisition of possession or control of the vehicle meant that an unauthorised use by the driver could never amount to a taking for the purpose of section 12.

... It is, therefore, not in itself an answer in the present case for the defendant to say that he was lawfully put in control of the vehicle by his employers. The difficulty which I feel is in defining the kind of unauthorised activity on the part of the driver, whose original control is lawful, which will amount to an unlawful taking for the purpose of section 12. Not every brief, unauthorised diversion from his proper route by an employed driver in the course of his working day will necessarily involve a 'taking' of the vehicle for his own use. If, however, as in *R. v. Wibberley*[2] he returns to the vehicle after he has parked it for the night and drives it off on an unauthorised errand, he is clearly guilty of the offence. Similarly, if in the course of his working day, or otherwise while his authority to use the vehicle is unexpired, he appropriates it to his own use in a manner which repudiates the rights of the true owner, and shows that he has assumed control of the vehicle for his own purposes, he can properly be regarded as having taken the vehicle within section 12.

As Professor Smith puts it (in *Smith's Law of Theft*[3]) he has 'altered the character of his control over the vehicle, so that he no longer held as servant but assumed possession of it in the legal sense.' In the present case I think that the defendant took the vehicle when he left the first public house. At that point he assumed control for his own purposes in a manner which was inconsistent with his duty to his employer to finish his round and drive the vehicle to the depot. . . .''

APPEAL DISMISSED.

---

[1] (1970), 54 Cr. App. Rep. 300; p. 281, *supra*.
[2] [1966] 2 Q.B. 214; [1965] 3 All E.R. 718.
[3] 2nd ed., p. 113.

Deception
THEFT ACT 1968

"Section 15.—Obtaining property by deception

(1) A person who by any deception dishonestly obtains property belonging to another, with the intention of permanently depriving the other of it, shall on conviction on indictment be liable to imprisonment for a term not exceeding ten years.

(2) For purposes of this section a person is to be treated as obtaining property if he obtains ownership, possession or control of it, and 'obtain' includes obtaining for another or enabling another to obtain or to retain.

(3) Section 6 above[1] shall apply for purposes of this section, with the necessary adaptation of the reference to appropriating, as it applies for purposes of section 1.

(4) For purposes of this section 'deception' means any deception (whether deliberate or reckless) by words or conduct as to fact or as to law, including a deception as to the present intentions of the person using the deception or any other person.

Section 16.—Obtaining pecuniary advantage by deception

(1) A person who by any deception dishonestly obtains for himself or another any pecuniary advantage shall on conviction on indictment be liable to imprisonment for a term not exceeding five years.

(2) The cases in which a pecuniary advantage within the meaning of this section is to be regarded as obtained for a person are cases where—

(a) any debt or charge for which he makes himself liable or is or may become liable (including one not legally enforceable) is reduced or in whole or in part evaded or deferred; or

(b) he is allowed to borrow by way of overdraft, or to take out any policy of insurance or annuity contract, or obtains an improvement of the terms on which he is allowed to do so; or

(c) he is given the opportunity to earn remuneration or greater remuneration in an office or employment, or to win money by betting.

(3) For purposes of this section 'deception' has the same meaning as in section 15 of this Act."

---

[1] Pp. 253–254, *supra*.

[2] See the 13th Report of the Criminal Law Revision Committee, *S. 16 of the Theft Act* 1968, Cmnd. 6733 (1977).

LAWRENCE v. METROPOLITAN POLICE COMMISSIONER
[1971] 2 All E.R. 1253

The provisions of s. 1(1) and s. 15(1) of the Theft Act 1968 are not mutually exclusive.

See p. 254, *supra*.

METROPOLITAN POLICE COMMISSIONER v. CHARLES
[1976] 3 All E.R. 112

(1) *A person who draws a cheque impliedly represents that it will be honoured in the ordinary course of events, but a person who draws a cheque backed by a cheque card impliedly represents in addition that he has authority, as between himself and his bank, to use the card in order to oblige the bank to honour the cheque.* (2) *S.16 of the Theft Act 1968 does not require that the person deceived should suffer loss as a result.*

On 31st October 1972 Charles opened a bank account at a branch of the National Westminster Bank. On 23rd November 1972 he was allowed an overdraft with a limit of £100 for one month, a facility which was later extended for a further month. On 19th December 1972 he was given a cheque card. The card was in common form and contained an undertaking by the bank that any cheque not exceeding £30 would be honoured subject to certain conditions relating to the manner in which the cheque was drawn.

With the use of his cheque card Charles drew a number of cheques and his overdraft had risen to £248 to his knowledge by 2nd January 1973. That evening Charles went to the Golden Nugget club, a gaming club, and in the course of the night he used all the cheques in a new cheque book to purchase chips for gaming. Each cheque was for £30 made out to the manager of the club, Mr. Cersell, and he used his cheque card in relation to each cheque. The bank consequently had to honour all the cheques with the result that they paid out, and Charles' overdraft rose by, a further £750.

Charles was charged on a number of counts and convicted, *inter alia*, on two counts of dishonestly obtaining by deception a pecuniary advantage, namely increased borrowing by way of overdraft from his bank. Having appealed unsuccessfully to the Court of Appeal, Charles appealed to the House of Lords.

Extracts from the Speeches of the House of Lords

Lord Edmund-Davies.—

"Both in the Court of Appeal and before your Lordships there was considerable discussion as to what representation is to be implied by the simple act of drawing a cheque. Reference was made to *R.* v. *Page*[1] where the Court of Appeal, Criminal Division, adopted with apparent approval the following passage which (citing *R.* v. *Hazelton*[2]) has appeared in Kenny's *Outlines of Criminal Law*[3] ever since the first edition appeared in 1902:

'Similarly, the familiar act of drawing a cheque (a document which on the face of it is only a command of a future act) has been held to imply at least three statements about the present: (1) that the drawer has an account with that bank; (2) that he has authority to draw on it for that amount; (3) that the cheque, as drawn, is a valid order for the payment of that amount (i.e. that the present state of affairs is such that, in the ordinary course of events, the cheque will on its future presentment be duly honoured). It may be well to point out, however, that it does not imply any representation that the drawer now has money in this bank to the amount drawn for, inasmuch as he may well have authority to overdraw, or may intend to pay in (before the cheque can be presented) sufficient money to meet it.'

My noble and learned friend, Lord Fraser of Tullybelton, rightly pointed out that representations (1) and (2) were supererogatory in the light of representation (3), which embraced both of them. My noble and learned friend, Lord Diplock, also criticised representation (2) on the ground that the representation made by the simple act of drawing a cheque does not relate to or rest on 'authority' but is rather a representation that the drawer has contracted with his bank to honour his cheques. Notwithstanding the antiquity

---

[1] [1971] 2 Q.B. 330; [1971] 2 All E.R. 870.
[2] (1874), L.R. 2 C.C.R. 134.
[3] 19th ed., p. 359, para. 346.

of the quoted passage, it accordingly appears right to restrict
the representation made by the act of drawing and handing
over a cheque to that which has been conveniently labelled
'Page (3)'. The legal position created by such an act was even
more laconically described by Pollock, B., in *R.* v. *Hazelton*[1]
in this way:

> 'I think the real representation made is that the cheque
> will be paid. It may be said that that is a representation
> as to a future event. But that is not really so. It means
> that the existing state of facts is such that in ordinary course
> the cheque will be met.'

With understandable enthusiasm, counsel for the
accused submitted that this was correct and that such
representation was manifestly true when made, as was
demonstrated by the later honouring of all the accused's
cheques. But it has to be remembered that we are presently
concerned to enquire what was the *totality* of the representations; with whether they were true or false to the accused's
knowledge; whether they deceived; and whether they induced
the party to whom they were addressed to act in such a
manner as led to the accused obtaining 'increased borrowing
by way of overdraft'. What of the production and use of the
cheque card when each of the 25 cheques in the new cheque-
book was drawn on the night of 2nd–3rd January 1973? Is
counsel for the accused right in submitting that the only
representation made by its production was the perfectly
correct one that, 'This cheque, backed by this card, will be
honoured without question?' In my judgment, he is not.
The accused knew perfectly well that he would not be able
to get more chips at the club simply by drawing a cheque.
The cheque alone would not have been accepted; it had to
be backed by a cheque card. The card played a vital part,
for . . . in order to make the bank liable to the payee there
must be knowledge on the payee's part that the drawer
has the bank's authority to bind it, for in the absence of such
knowledge the all-important contract between payee and
bank is not created; and it is the representation by the
drawer's production of the card that he has that authority
that creates such contractual relationship and estops the
bank from refusing to honour the cheque. By drawing the
cheque the accused represented that it would be met, and by
producing the card so that the number thereon could be
indorsed on the cheque he in effect represented, 'I am

---

[1] (1874), L.R. 2 C.C.R., at p. 140.

authorised by the bank to show this to you and so create a direct contractual relationship between the bank and you that they will honour this cheque'. The production of the card was the badge of the accused's ostensible authority to make such a representation on the bank's behalf. And this emerges with clarity from the evidence of the club manager, Mr. Cersell, who repeatedly stressed during his lengthy testimony that the accused's cheque would not have been accepted unless accompanied by a cheque card the signature on which corresponded with that of the accused when making out the cheque. . . .

There remains to be considered the vitally important question of whether it was established that it was as a result of such dishonest deception that the club's staff were induced to give chips for cheques and so, in due course, caused the accused's bank account to become improperly overdrawn. This point exercised the Court of Appeal, though they were not troubled by the fact that, whereas the deception alleged was said to have induced the club servants to accept the cheques, the pecuniary advantage was obtained from and damnified only the bank. In that they were, in my judgment, right, for *R.* v. *Kovacs*[1] correctly decided (as, indeed, counsel for the accused accepted) that, in the words of Lawton, L.J.[2]:

'Section 16(1) does not provide either expressly or by implication that the person deceived must suffer any loss arising from the deception. What does have to be proved is that the accused by deception obtained for himself or another a pecuniary advantage. What there must be is a causal connection between the deception used and the pecuniary advantage obtained.'

. . . In my judgment, it . . . emerges clearly from the evidence of Mr. Cersell that [he was induced to act as he did by the deception]. He accepted that—

'with a cheque card so long as the conditions on the back are met the bank will honour that card irrespective of the state of the drawer's account or the authority or lack of it which he has in drawing on the account, [and that] . . . All those matters, in fact, once there is a cheque card, are totally irrelevant. . . .'

But in this context it has again to be borne in mind that the witness made clear that the accused's cheques were accepted *only* because he produced a cheque card, and he repeatedly

[1] [1974] 1 All E.R. 1236.
[2] *Ibid.*, at p. 1238.

stressed that, had he been aware that the accused was using his cheque book and cheque card 'in a way in which he was not allowed or entitled to use [them]' no cheque would have been accepted. The evidence of that witness, taken as a whole, points irresistibly to the conclusions (a) that by his dishonest conduct the accused deceived Mr. Cersell in the manner averred in the particulars of the charges and (b) that Mr. Cersell was thereby induced to accept the cheques because of his belief that the representations as to both cheques and card were true. . . .

For these reasons I would dismiss the appeal."

APPEAL DISMISSED.

DIRECTOR OF PUBLIC PROSECUTIONS v. RAY
[1973] 3 All E.R. 131

A person who makes a representation which is true at the time, but which subsequently becomes untrue, practices a deception if he fails to inform the representee of the change.

Ray ordered a meal in a restaurant, thereby impliedly representing that he would pay for it, which was then his true intention. Having eaten the meal, Ray decided not to pay for it and sat inactively at his table until the waiter left the room, when he made his escape. Ray was convicted by the magistrates of obtaining a pecuniary advantage contrary to s.16(1) of the Theft Act 1968, in that by deception he had evaded a debt for which he was liable. Ray appealed successfully to the Divisional Court but the Director of Public Prosecutions appealed to the House of Lords.

Extracts from the Speeches of the House of Lords

Lord MacDermott.—

"To prove the charge against the respondent the prosecution had to show that he (i) by a deception (ii) had dishonestly (iii) obtained for himself (iv) a pecuniary advantage. The last of these ingredients no longer raises on the facts of this appeal, the problems of interpretation which were recently considered by this House in *Director of Public Prosecutions* v. *Turner*.[1] By that decision a debt is

---

[1] [1974] A.C. 357; [1973] 3 All E.R. 124; p. 292, *infra*.

'evaded' even if the evasion falls short of being final or permanent and is only for the time being; and a pecuniary advantage has not to be proved in fact as it is enough if the case is brought within s. 16(2)(a) or (b) or (c).

On the facts here, this means that the respondent's debt for the meal he had eaten was evaded for the purposes of sub-s. (2)(a); and that in consequence he obtained a pecuniary advantage within the meaning of subs-s. (1). No issue therefore arises on the ingredients I have numbered (iii) and (iv). Nor is there any controversy about ingredient (ii). If the respondent obtained a pecuniary advantage as described he undoubtedly did so dishonestly. The case is thus narrowed to ingredient (i) and that leaves two questions for consideration. First, do the facts justify a finding that the respondent practised a deception? And secondly, if he did was his evasion of the debt obtained by that deception?

The first of these questions involves nothing in the way of words spoken or written. If there was a deception on the part of the respondent it was by his conduct in the course of an extremely common form of transaction which, because of its nature, leaves much to be implied from conduct. Another circumstance affecting the ambit of this question lies in the fact that, looking only to the period *after* the meal had been eaten and the respondent and his companions had decided to evade payment, there is nothing that I can find in the discernible conduct of the respondent which would suffice in itself to show that he was then practising a deception. . . .

There is, however, no sound reason that I can see for restricting the enquiry to this final phase. One cannot, so to speak, draw a line through the transaction at the point where the intention changed and search for evidence of deception only in what happened before that or only in what happened after that. In my opinion the transaction must for this purpose be regarded in its entirety, beginning with the respondent entering the restaurant and ordering his meal and ending with his running out without paying. The different stages of the transaction are all linked and it would be quite unrealistic to treat them in isolation.

Starting then at the beginning one finds in the conduct of the respondent in entering and ordering his meal evidence that he impliedly represented that he had the means and the intention of paying for it before he left. That the respondent did make such a representation was not in dispute and in the absence of evidence to the contrary it would be difficult to reach a different conclusion. If this representation had then been false and matters had proceeded thereafter as they did (but without any change of intention) a conviction for the offence charged would, in my view, have had ample material to support it. But as the representation when originally made in this case was not false there was therefore no deception at that point. Then the meal is served and eaten and the intention to evade the debt replaces the intention to pay. Did this change of mind produce a deception?

My Lords, in my opinion it did. I do not base this conclusion merely on the change of mind that occurred for that in itself was not manifest at the time and did not amount to 'conduct' on the part of the respondent. But it did falsify the representation which had already been made because that initial representation must, in my view, be regarded not as something then spent and past but as a continuing representation which remained alive and operative and had already resulted in the respondent and his defaulting companions being taken on trust and treated as ordinary, honest customers. It covered the whole transaction up to and including payment and must therefore, in my opinion, be considered as continuing and still active at the time of the change of mind. When that happened, with the respondent taking (as might be expected) no step to bring the change to notice, he practised to my way of thinking a deception just as real and just as dishonest as would have been the case if his intention all along had been to go out without paying.

Holding for these reasons that the respondent practised a deception, I turn to what I have referred to as the second question. Was the respondent's evasion of the debt obtained by that deception?

I think the material before the justices was enough to show that it was. The obvious effect of the deception was that the respondent and his associates were treated as they had been previously, that is to say as ordinary, honest customers whose conduct did not excite suspicion or call for precautions. In consequence the waiter was off his guard and vanished into the kitchen. That gave the respondent the opportunity of running out without hindrance and he took it. I would therefore answer this second question in the affirmative."

APPEAL ALLOWED. CONVICTION RESTORED.[1]

---

[1] Also see *Nordeng*, p. 295, *infra*.

DIRECTOR OF PUBLIC PROSECUTIONS v. TURNER

[1973] 3 All E.R. 124

(1) *If the case falls within s.* 16(2)(a), (b) *or* (c)[1] *of the Theft Act* 1968 *a pecuniary advantage is deemed to be obtained, so that it is irrelevant that no pecuniary advantage has in fact been obtained.* (2) *For the purposes of s.* 16(2)(a) *"debt" means an obligation to pay money.* (3) *Unlike the deferment or reduction of a debt, a debt can be evaded within the meaning of s.* 16(2)(a) *without the agreement of the creditor.*

Turner employed Black and his brother to do some work in a house. When Black went to collect their wages Turner told him that he did not have any ready cash and asked him to accept a cheque for the sum due. Black did so, but on the following Monday the cheque was dishonoured, as Turner knew it would be. Turner was convicted of obtaining by deception a pecuniary advantage, namely the evasion of a debt for which he was liable. He appealed successfully to the Court of Appeal but the Director of Public Prosecutions appealed to the House of Lords.

Extracts from the Speeches of the House of Lords

Lord Reid.—

"No question arises in the present case with regard to sub-s. (1). It is rightly admitted that Black was induced to take the cheque by dishonest deception on the part of the respondent. On the view which I take of sub-s. (2) we do not have to consider what is meant by pecuniary advantage.

But sub-s. (2) requires meticulous examination and analysis. I think we must proceed by examining each important word in it. The first part is drafted in an unusual way. Does it mean that in the cases set out in heads (a), (b) and (c) a pecuniary advantage is to be deemed to have been obtained, so that it is irrelevant to consider whether in fact any such advantage was obtained, and equally irrelevant to prove that nothing in the nature of pecuniary advantage was in fact obtained by the accused? I think that that must be its meaning though I am at a loss to understand why that was not clearly stated. 'Is to be regarded as obtained' must,

---

[1] P. 284, *supra.*

I think, mean is to be deemed to have been obtained even if in fact there was none.   I must therefore reject the first argument submitted for the respondent.   It was strenuously argued that a penniless man can obtain no advantage, pecuniary or other, by evading his debt or by getting it reduced or deferred because he could not have paid any of it in any case.   That might be a forceful argument if obtaining a pecuniary advantage in fact were a necessary element in the offence here charged.   But if in the circumstances of this case a pecuniary advantage is deemed to have been obtained, then it need not be proved and its absence in fact is no defence.

1 turn then to para. (a).   The first question is what is meant by the word 'debt'.   I get no assistance from its being linked with the word 'charge' because during the argument no one was able to suggest any case to which 'charge' could apply in this context.   Debt normally has one or other of two meanings: it can mean an obligation to pay money or it can mean a sum of money owed.   It cannot have the latter meaning here.   The paragraph deals with cases where a debt is 'reduced', 'evaded' or 'deferred'.   No doubt you can reduce a sum of money, but to speak of a sum of money being evaded or deferred is nonsense.   It is an elementary principle of construction that a word must be given the same meaning in different parts of the same provision. . . .

[I]f 'debt' is given its ordinary meaning of an obligation to pay money I find no difficulty in applying that meaning throughout the paragraph.   You can make yourself liable, you can be liable, or you may become liable for an obligation. An obligation may not be legally enforceable.   And in my opinion it is quite proper to speak of an obligation being reduced or being evaded or being deferred.

An obligation is reduced if the creditor agrees with the debtor that the amount owed shall be reduced.   An obligation is deferred if creditor and debtor agree that the date of performance shall be postponed.   An obligation is evaded if by some contrivance the debtor avoids or gets out of fulfilling or performing his obligation.   In the days when such things happened, a welshing bookmaker not only evaded his pursuers, he also evaded his obligations.   Evasion does not necessarily mean permanent escape.   If the bookmaker evaded his pursuers on Monday, the fact that he is caught and made to pay up on Tuesday does not alter the fact that he evaded his obligations on Monday.   Unlike reducing and deferring an obligation, evading an obligation is a unilateral operation.   It leaves the obligation untouched and does not connote any activity on the part of the creditor. When the evasion ceases he can seek to recover the debt in any way open to him.

Now I must apply the law to the facts of the present case. When Black went to collect the wages he was entitled to get cash. But the respondent induced him to take a cheque instead. It is I think clear that if nothing is said to the contrary, the law implies that the giver of a cheque represents that it will be honoured. The respondent knew that it would not. So there was ample material from which the jury could infer (1) dishonesty, (2) deception in that by giving the cheque the respondent induced Black to believe, contrary to the fact known to the respondent, that it would be honoured, and (3) that the deception caused Black to accept the cheque.

The respondent evaded his obligation to pay immediately in legal tender by giving a worthless cheque instead. It does not matter whether or not he could then have paid in cash because it does not matter whether or not in fact he obtained any pecuniary advantage by giving the cheque.

A good deal was said in argument about the effect in law of giving a cheque in payment of a debt instead of legal tender. There was no extensive citation of the law on this matter but I think I should state my view because it throws some light on the meaning of s. 16 (2)(a). Normally everyone who accepts a cheque in payment takes it in discharge of the debt. But in law, unless anything is said to the contrary, the discharge is presumed to be subject to a resolutive condition that if the cheque is dishonoured the discharge is void ab initio; the condition operates retrospectively so that the debt revives in its original form. I can illustrate the meaning of that by supposing that the debt carried interest. When the cheque for the principal sum and accrued interest is accepted, discharge of the obligation causes the interest to cease to accrue. But when the cheque is dishonoured and the debt for the principal sum revives, interest becomes payable for the period between the acceptance of the cheque and its dishonour so there is no question of the debt being deferred or suspended during the period between acceptance of the cheque and its presentation for payment. And as regards s. 16 there is no overlap between deferment and evasion."

APPEAL ALLOWED. CONVICTION RESTORED.

Comment on Director of Public Prosecutions v. Turner

The other members of the House of Lords agreed with Lord Reid on the questions of interpretation which were material to the appeal. However, Lord Pearson disagreed with Lord Reid's observations on whether there was an overlap between evasion and deferment of a debt. Lord Pearson took the view that since the general rule that acceptance of a cheque by a debtor constitutes a conditional discharge of the debt, the condition being that if the cheque is dishonoured the debt will revive, the acceptance of the worthless cheque by Black constituted a deferment, as well as an evasion, of the debt by Turner; the obligation to pay having been deferred until the cheque was dishonoured and the debt revived. Lord MacDermott inclined to the same view although he was "not quite sure" that there might be overlapping at times between the evasion and deferment of a debt. Lord Morris of Borth-y-Gest reserved the question of overlap for future consideration.

In *Nordeng, infra*, which was not a "cheque case", the Court of Appeal took the view that the same conduct on the part of a debtor might be both an evasion and a deferment of the debt.

R. v. NORDENG
(1976), 62 Cr. App. Rep. 123

A person who goes into a hotel and makes use of its facilities thereby makes himself liable to pay the cost of accommodation, refreshment and service provided. He evades that debt if he succeeds in getting the management to look to a third party for payment. Depending on the circumstances, the evasion of the debt may be whole or in part.

Nordeng stayed at four hotels, whose bills were not paid. In three of the hotels, the Holiday Inn, the Colonnade and the Royal Lancaster, he had stayed on the basis that the bills would be paid by a Norwegian company of which he was the sales director. Nordeng was convicted on four counts of obtaining a pecuniary advantage by deception, namely the evasion of a debt for which he made himself liable, by falsely pretending that the cost of his accommodation would be paid at the end of his stay, and also (in the case of the three hotels) that the bill would be paid by the company and he was authorised to incur the debt. Nordeng appealed to the Court of Appeal.

Extracts from the Judgment of the Court of Appeal

Stephenson, L.J.—

"We have to ask 'on the facts as the jury, properly directed on the evidence, could reasonably have found them, were debts for which the appellant made himself liable to these hotels in whole or in part evaded?' Only if they were, can a pecuniary advantage be regarded as obtained for the appellant, can any question of deception or dishonesty be considered, and can the appellant's conviction be upheld.

Counsel for the appellant submits three grounds for answering this question in the negative:

1. The appellant never made himself personally liable to any of the hotels except the Conway Court Hotel, and the judge misdirected himself in leaving counts 1, 3 and 4—this submission does not apply to count 2—to the jury and misdirected the jury in letting them think that if these three hotels looked to the company for payment . . ., but looked to it as a result of the appellant's fraud or deception, he would still be liable to pay these bills. . . .

Counsel for the appellant relied on the case of *Royle*[1] to support her contention that this was a misdirection. We do not think that that case is any authority for the proposition that if an hotel looks to a company for payment of a customer's bill, or even for a time looks only to a company for payment, there cannot be an offence against this section because there is no debt for which the customer makes himself liable. We would approach the question whether in such circumstances this offence had been committed not through the law of principal and agent, void and voidable contracts or 'the tangled undergrowth of quasi-contract' (see *Royle's* case[2]), but by giving the words of section 16(2) their ordinary meaning and the word 'debt' its ordinary meaning of an obligation to pay money: *D.P.P.* v. *Turner*.[3] 'An obligation is evaded if by some contrivance the debtor avoids or gets out of fulfilling or performing an obligation,' said Lord Reid, and he added that 'evasion does not necessarily mean permanent escape.'[4] These words, quoted by the judge to the jury, seem to us exactly to fit the present case.

When a person goes into an hotel and makes use of its facilities, he thereby makes himself liable to pay the bill which

---

[1] [1971] 3 All E.R. 1359.
[2] *Ibid.*, at p. 1366.
[3] P. 292, *supra*.
[4] P. 293, *supra*.

will ultimately be presented. The obligation to pay the cost of the accommodation, refreshment and service provided for him is a debt for which he makes himself liable. He evades this debt if he succeeds in getting the management to charge a third party. If he deceives the management into looking exclusively to the third party, then he evades it altogether. If he deceives the management into looking primarily to the third party and secondarily to him, then he evades it temporarily, but nevertheless evades it, or part of it. If this deceit is dishonest, as it generally must be, then the offence is committed. If there is no dishonesty or deception, it is not committed. But it is not a defence for the person accused of this offence to say: 'By my very deception I induced the hotel to enter into a contract which excluded me from liability.' That is a contrivance by which the debtor evades his obligation to pay the bill, and we think that what the judge was in effect telling the jury—correctly—was that the debtor cannot take advantage of his own deceitful and dishonest contrivance to turn his own obligation or liability into someone else's. . . .

2. The evidence in support of all four counts established not an evasion of the debts in question, but only a deferment of them. The judge misdirected himself in rejecting a defence submission to that effect.

The answer to this submission has already been given. *D.P.P* v. *Turner* (*supra*) establishes that evasion may be temporary and is unilateral. It does not 'connote any activity on the part of the creditor' (*per* Lord Reid[1]), but he may be deceived by the contrivance which evades the debtor's obligation into inactivity or acquiescence or attempts to obtain performance of the obligation from a third party. And the same conduct on the debtor's part may be both an evasion and a deferment, as Lord Pearson (dissenting on that point[2]) thought Turner's conduct was. Whether or not the appellant deferred his debts to these hotels, for the reasons which we have given we consider that he evaded them.

3. [The third submission made by counsel for the appellant related to the first count where it was possible that the appellant, when he checked in at the Holiday Inn, had believed that the company would pay the bill. The trial judge had directed the jury that if, during his stay, the

---

[1] Pp. 293–294, *supra*.
[2] P. 295, *supra*.

appellant had realised that there was no chance that the company would pay the bill which was being run up by him they could convict him.]

In our judgment these directions were corrrect. . . . There are . . . many courses of conduct which start honest but cannot be continued without dishonesty. What began with an honest belief or intention becomes by a change of mind or circumstances a deliberate or reckless deception. *Ray* v. *Sempers* [*Director of Public Prosecutions* v. *Ray*[1]] provides an apt illustration of a change of intention to pay for a meal turning an honest representation of present intention to pay into a false representation and so a deception contrary to section 16. Another illustration would be provided by the appellant's dealings with the Holiday Inn if the jury were willing to look at them with indulgence towards the appellant."

APPEAL DISMISSED.

Blackmail

THEFT ACT 1968

"*Section 21.—*

(1) A person is guilty of blackmail if, with a view to gain for himself or another or with intent to cause loss to another, he makes any unwarranted demand with menaces; and for this purpose a demand with menaces is unwarranted unless the person making it does so in the belief—

(a) that he has reasonable grounds for making the demand; and

(b) that the use of the menaces is a proper means of reinforcing the demand.

(2) The nature of the act or omission demanded is immaterial, and it is also immaterial whether the menaces relate to action to be taken by the person making the demand.

(3) A person guilty of blackmail shall on conviction on indictment be liable to imprisonment for a term not exceeding fourteen years.

Section 34.—

(2) For purposes of this Act—

(a) 'gain' and 'loss' are to be construed as extending only to gain or loss in money or other property, but as extending to any such gain or loss whether temporary or permanent; and—

---

[1] P. 289, *supra*.

(i) 'gain' includes a gain by keeping what one has, as well as a gain by getting what one has not; and

(ii) 'loss' includes a loss by not getting what one might get, as well as a loss by parting with what one has; . . ."

Handling Stolen Goods

THEFT ACT 1968

"Section 22.—

(1) A person handles stolen goods if (otherwise than in the course of the stealing) knowing or believing them to be stolen goods he dishonestly receives the goods, or dishonestly undertakes or assists in their retention, removal, disposal or realisation by or for the benefit of another person, or if he arranges to do so.

(2) A person guilty of handling stolen goods shall on conviction on indictment be liable to imprisonment for a term not exceeding fourteen years.

Section 24.—

(1) The provisions of this Act relating to goods which have been stolen shall apply whether the stealing occurred in England or Wales or elsewhere, and whether it occurred before or after the commencement of this Act, provided that the stealing (if not an offence under this Act) amounted to an offence where and at the time when the goods were stolen; and references to stolen goods shall be construed accordingly.

(2) For purposes of those provisions references to stolen goods shall include, in addition to the goods originally stolen and parts of them (whether in their original state or not),—

(*a*) any other goods which directly or indirectly represent or have at any time represented the stolen goods in the hands of the thief as being the proceeds of any disposal or realisation of the whole or part of the goods stolen or of goods so representing the stolen goods; and

(*b*) any other goods which directly or indirectly represent or have at any time represented the stolen goods in the hands of a handler of the stolen goods or any part of them as being the proceeds of any disposal or realisation of the whole or part of the stolen goods handled by him or of goods so representing them.

(3) But no goods shall be regarded as having continued to be stolen goods after they have been restored to the person

from whom they were stolen or to other lawful possession or custody, or after that person and any other person claiming through him have otherwise ceased as regards those goods to have any right to restitution in respect of the theft.

(4) For purposes of the provisions of this Act relating to goods which have been stolen (including subsections (1) to (3) above) goods obtained in England or Wales or elsewhere either by blackmail or in the circumstances described in section 15(1) of this Act shall be regarded as stolen; and 'steal', 'theft' and 'thief' shall be construed accordingly.

Section 34.—

(2) For purposes of this Act.—

(*b*) 'goods', except in so far as the context otherwise requires, includes money and every other description of property except land, and includes things severed from the land by stealing."

RE ATTORNEY-GENERAL'S REFERENCE
(No. 1 of 1974)
[1974] 2 All E.R. 899

For the purposes of s. 24(3) of the Theft Act 1968, stolen goods are "restored to other lawful possession or custody" if a police officer acting in the execution of his duty reduces them into his possession. Whether a police constable who comes across goods and, suspecting them to be stolen, examines and keeps observation on them with a view to tracing the thief or a handler thereby reduces them into his possession depends upon his intentions.

A police constable found an unlocked unattended car containing packages of new clothing, woollen goods, which he suspected, and which in fact subsequently proved to be, stolen. The constable removed the rotor arm from the vehicle to immobilise it, and kept observation. After about ten minutes, the accused appeared, got into the car and attempted to start the engine. He was arrested and charged with stealing the new clothing, and secondly and alternatively with handling the stolen goods, in that he had received them knowing them to be stolen. The trial judge ruled that there was no evidence to support the first charge, and that he would not leave that to the jury. In relation to the second charge, counsel for the accused submitted that there was no case to answer, relying on the following part of s. 24(3) of the Theft Act 1968:

". . . no goods shall be regarded as having continued to be stolen goods after they have been restored to the person from whom they were stolen or to other lawful possession or custody. . . ."

Counsel for the accused contended that the goods had been restored to other lawful possession or control, namely the constable's, before the accused returned to the car and that by virtue of s. 24(3) the goods had ceased to be stolen goods by that time, which was the time when the accused was alleged to have received them. The judge accepted the submission and directed the jury to acquit on the receiving charge.

This direction resulted in a reference by the Attorney-General to the Court of Appeal under s. 36 of the Criminal Justice Act 1972, whereby the Attorney-General may refer a point of law arising at a trial on indictment at which the accused has been acquitted. The opinion of the Court of Appeal does not affect the acquittal but provides authoritative guidance for the future.

Extracts from the Opinion of the Court of Appeal

Lord Widgery, C.J.—

"[The Attorney-General expresses the point of law referred] in this way:

'Whether stolen goods are restored to lawful custody within the meaning of Section 24(3) of the Theft Act 1968 when a Police Officer, suspecting them to be stolen, examines and keeps observation on them with a view to tracing the thief or a handler.'

One could put the question perhaps in a somewhat different way by asking whether on the facts set out in the reference the conclusion as a matter of law was clear to the effect that the goods had ceased to be stolen goods. In other words, the question which is really in issue in this reference is whether the trial judge acted correctly in law in saying that those facts disclosed a defence within s. 24(3) of the 1968 Act.

Section 24(3) is not perhaps entirely happily worded. It has been pointed out in the course of argument that in the sentence [quoted above] there is only one relevant verb, and that is 'restore'. The section contemplates that the stolen goods should be restored to the person from whom they were stolen or to other lawful possession or custody. It is pointed out that the word 'restore', although it is entirely appropriate when applied to restoration of the goods to the true owner, is not really an appropriate verb to employ if one is talking about a police officer stumbling on stolen goods and taking them into his own lawful custody or possession.

We are satisfied that despite the absence of another and perhaps more appropriate verb, the effect of s. 24(3) is to enable a defendant to plead that the goods had ceased to be stolen goods if the facts are that they were taken by a police officer in the course of his duty and reduced into possession by him.

Whether or not s. 24(3) is intended to be a codification of the common law or not, it certainly deals with a topic on which the common law provides a large number of authorities. I shall refer to some of them in a moment. . . . It is to be observed that in common law nothing short of a reduction into possession, either by the true owner or by a police officer acting in the execution of his duty, was regarded as sufficient to change the character of the goods from stolen goods into goods which were no longer to be so regarded.

[Having referred to a number of authorities, his Lordship continued:] Now to return to the present problem again with those authorities in the background: did the conduct of the police officer . . . amount to a taking of possession of the woollen goods in the back seat of the motor car? . . . In our judgment it depended primarily on the intentions of the police officer. If the police officer seeing these goods in the back of the car had made up his mind that he would take them into custody, that he would reduce them into his possession or control, take charge of them so that they could not be removed and so that he would have the disposal of them, then it would be a perfectly proper conclusion to say that he had taken possession of the goods. On the other hand, if the truth of the matter is that he was of an entirely open mind at that stage as to whether the goods were to be seized or not, . . . but merely stood by so that when the driver of the car appeared he could ask certain questions of that driver as to the nature of the goods and why they were there, then there is no reason whatever to suggest that he had taken the goods into his possession or control. It may be, of course, that he had both objects in mind. It is possible in a case like this that the police officer may have intended by removing the rotor arm both to prevent the car from being driven away and to enable him to assert control over the woollen goods as such. But if the jury came to the conclusion that the proper explanation of what had happened was that the police officer had not intended at that stage to reduce the goods into his possession or to assume the control of them, and at that stage was merely concerned to ensure that the driver, if he appeared, could not get away without answering questions, then in that case the proper conclusion of the jury would have been to the effect that the goods had not been reduced into the possession of the police and therefore a defence under s. 24(3) of the 1968 Act would not be of use to this particular defendant.

In the light of those considerations it has become quite obvious that the trial judge was wrong in withdrawing the issue from the jury. As a matter of law he was not entitled to conclude from the facts . . . that these goods were reduced into the possession of the police officer. What he should have done in our opinion would have been to have left that issue to the jury for decision, directing the jury [in accordance with principles outlined above]."

DETERMINATION ACCORDINGLY.

R. v. DEAKIN

[1972] 3 All E.R. 803

Like the seller of stolen goods, a person who buys them participates in their realisation for the benefit of another.

Deakin purchased some stolen spirits, knowing they had been stolen. He was charged with handling stolen goods contrary to s. 22(1) of the Theft Act 1968, the particulars of the indictment alleging that he had dishonestly undertaken the realisation of stolen goods by or for the benefit of one of the thieves and the man who had delivered the spirits. Deakin was convicted and appealed to the Court of Appeal, contending, *inter alia*, that, as the purchaser, he could not be said to have "undertaken the realisation" of the stolen goods for the benefit of anyone.

Extract from the Judgment of the Court of Appeal

Phillimore, L.J.—

"Can it be said that on the evidence adduced the appellant dishonestly undertook the realisation of the stolen goods? This court thinks that the matter is clear. Realisation merely involves the exchange of goods for money. It seems to the court that he who pays is just as much involved in the realisation as he who receives the payment and since the former pays the latter the realisation is clearly for the benefit of the latter, albeit it may also benefit the former."[1]

APPEAL DISMISSED.

R. v. PITCHLEY

(1972), 57 Cr. App. Rep. 30

Although a person who, having received stolen goods innocently, has permitted them to remain under his control after discovering the truth cannot be convicted of handling stolen goods on the basis of dishonestly receiving them, he can be convicted of that offence on the basis that he has dishonestly assisted in their retention for the benefit of another.

Pitchley's son stole £150 and gave it to Pitchley for safekeeping. The next day, Friday, November 6th, Pitchley paid the money into his Post Office savings account. According to him, it was only on Saturday, November 7th, that he learnt the money was stolen and he then took no action because he did not wish to report his son to the police and did not think of returning the money to its owner. Pitchley was convicted of dishonestly handling the stolen money, contrary to s. 22(1) of the Theft Act 1968, and appealed to the Court of Appeal.

Extracts from the Judgment of the Court of Appeal

Cairns, L.J.—

"The main point that has been taken by Mr. Kalisher, who is appearing for the appellant in this court, is that, assuming that the jury were not satisfied that the appellant

---

[1] It is probably more accurate to say that Deakin had assisted in the realisation of the stolen goods by or for the benefit of another rather than undertaken such realisation.

received the money knowing it to have been stolen, and that is an assumption which clearly it is right to make, then there was no evidence after that, that from the time when the money was put into the savings bank, that the appellant had done any act in relation to it. His evidence was, and there is no reason to suppose that the jury did not believe it, that at the time when he put the money into the savings bank he still did not know or believe that the money had been stolen —it was only at a later stage that he did. That was on the Saturday according to his evidence, and the position was that the money had simply remained in the savings bank from the Saturday, to the Wednesday when the police approached the appellant. . . .

Did the conduct of the appellant between the Saturday and the Wednesday amount to an assisting in the retention of this money for the benefit of his son Brian? The court has been referred to the case of *Brown*[1] which was a case where stolen property had been put into a wardrobe at the appellant's house and when police came to inquire about it the appellant said to them: 'Get lost.' The direction to the jury had been on the basis that it was for them to consider whether in saying: 'Get lost', instead of helping the police constable, he was dishonestly assisting in the retention of stolen goods. This court held that that was a misdirection but there are passages in the judgment in the case of *Brown* which, in the view of this court, are of great assistance in determining what is meant by 'retention' in this section. I read first of all from p. 528 setting out the main facts a little more fully: 'A witness named Holden was called by the prosecution. He gave evidence that he and others . . . had stolen the goods, and that he had brought them to the appellant's flat . . . and had hidden them there . . . in the wardrobe. Holden went on to say that later and before the police arrived he told the appellant where the cigarettes were; in other words, he said that the appellant well knew that the cigarettes were there and that they had been stolen.' There was no evidence that the appellant had done anything active in relation to the cigarettes up to the time when the police arrived. The Lord Chief Justice, Lord Parker, in the course of his judgment at p. 530 said this: 'It is urged here that the mere failure to reveal the presence of the cigarettes, with or without the addition of the spoken words "Get lost", was incapable itself of amounting to an assisting in the retention of the goods within the meaning of the subsection. The court has come to the conclusion that that is right. It does not seem to this court that the mere failure to tell the police, coupled if you like with the words "Get lost", amounts in itself to an assisting in their retention. On the other hand, those matters did afford strong evidence of what was the real basis of the charge here, namely, that knowing that they had been stolen, he permitted them to remain there or, as it has been put, provided accommodation for these stolen goods in order to assist Holden to retain them.' . . .

In this present case there was no question on the evidence of the appellant himself, that he was permitting the money[1] to remain under his control in his savings bank book, and it is clear that this court in the case of *Brown* regarded such permitting as sufficient to constitute retention within the meaning of retention.

In the course of the argument, Nield, J., cited the dictionary meaning of the word 'retain'—keep possession of, not lose, continue to have. In the view of this court, that is the meaning of the word 'retain' in this section. It was submitted by Mr. Kalisher that, at any rate, it was ultimately for the jury to decide whether there was retention or not and that even assuming that what the appellant did was of such a character that it could constitute retention, the jury ought to have been directed that it was for them to determine as a matter of fact, whether that was so or not. The court cannot agree with that submission. The meaning of the word 'retention' in the section is a matter of law in so far as the construction of the word is necessary.[2] It is hardly a difficult question of construction because it is an ordinary English word and in the view of this court, it was no more necessary for the Deputy Chairman to leave to the jury the question of whether or not what was done amounted to retention, than it would be necessary for a judge in a case where goods had been handed to a person who knew that they had been stolen to direct the jury it was for them to decide whether or not that constituted receiving."

APPEAL DISMISSED.

---

[1] When the stolen money was paid into Pitchley's account it ceased to be identifiable and was thereafter represented by the like amount credited to his account. The Post Office's debt to Pitchley in relation to this amount, a thing in action, was presumably held to be "goods" and to be goods which were the proceeds of the original stolen goods by virtue of s. 24(2)(*b*) of the Theft Act 1968.

[2] Cf. "dishonestly" in theft: *Feely*, p. 269, *supra*.

R. v. GRAINGE
[1974] 1 All E.R. 928

Wilful blindness as to whether goods are stolen is sufficient to constitute the knowledge or belief required for a conviction for handling stolen goods but constructive knowledge is insufficient.

Grainge, O'Connor and a third man entered an office equipment shop. During their visit O'Connor stole a pocket calculator. The salesman followed them into the street and saw one of them pass the calculator to Grainge. Grainge was charged with handling stolen goods, contrary to s. 22(1) of the Theft Act 1968, the particulars of the offence being that he had received the calculator knowing or believing it to be stolen. In evidence Grainge said: "I never gave it a second thought. He is a friend of mine. I have known him two or three years. He has never been dishonest. I never even asked him about it. I just put it in my pocket. I thought it was a radio." Grainge was convicted and appealed to the Court of Appeal.

Extracts from the Judgment of the Court of Appeal

Eveleigh, J.—

"The appeal against conviction is based on grounds which may be summarised as follows: (a) The recorder misdirected the jury to the effect that suspicion that the goods were stolen was an alternative to knowledge or belief as an essential mental element, and failed to direct them that the test thereof was subjective and not objective. (b) The recorder failed to direct the jury that knowledge or belief must be proved at the time when the goods were received. The recorder said:

'. . . you have got to decide whether there was any element of dishonesty about it [and that] he handled it dishonestly, that at that time he knew or believed or suspected that the article had been stolen. That is what is referred to as guilty knowledge.'

He then referred to the circumstances from which knowledge could be inferred and continued:

'So those are the three elements, the theft, the dishonest handling and the guilty knowledge, the knowledge or belief or suspicion that the property was stolen when it was handled.'

In our judgment this passage in its reference to suspicion was a misdirection. . . . Section 22 of the Theft Act 1968 . . . provides, *inter alia*, that if 'knowing or believing' goods to be stolen a person dishonestly receives them he is guilty of the offence of handling stolen goods. The section does not say that suspicion is enough. . . .

The various expressions used [subsequently] by the recorder went some way to eradicating the error introduced when he had spoken of suspicion as an actual ingredient of the offence. In all the circumstances, however, this court does not think that he completely succeeded. The summing-up as a whole could well have left the jury with the impression that suspicious circumstances, irrespective of whether the accused himself appreciated they were suspicious, imposed a duty as a matter of law to act and enquire and that a failure so to do was to be treated as knowledge or belief.

In *Atwal* v. *Massey*[1] the justices had asked—

'whether the fact that the Appellant ought to have known that the kettle was stolen is sufficient to render him guilty of an offence under Section 22 of the Theft Act 1968.'
In that case Lord Widgery, C.J., said:[1]

'If when the justices say that the appellant ought to have known that the kettle was stolen they mean that any reasonable man would have realised that it was stolen, then that is not the right test. It is not sufficient to establish an offence under s. 22 that the goods were received in circumstances which would have put a reasonable man on his enquiry. The question is a subjective one: was the appellant aware of the theft or did he believe the goods to be stolen or did he, suspecting the goods to be stolen, deliberately shut his eyes to the consequences. It may be that the justices meant the word "ought" to have the second meaning, namely that he suspected but closed his eyes, but we do not think that we ought to speculate on such a possibility, but rather that we ought to deal with this matter on the words used by the justices in the case.'

. . . No doubt the recorder was seeking to explain the position to the jury along the lines indicated by Lord Widgery, C.J. It is, however, impossible to be satisfied that the jury did interpret the words in a manner consistent with

---

[1] [1971] 3 All E.R. 881, at p. 882.

the definition of the offence as laid down by s. 22 of the Act. . . .

As to the second ground of appeal the recorder used the word 'handled' and not the word 'received' when he said it was 'at that time', i.e. when it was handled, the knowledge had to be proved. Counsel for the appellant submitted that the jury were not clearly directed that on an indictment . . . which charged a receiving guilty knowledge had to be shown to exist at the time of the receipt. We think there is substance in the point.

In the judgment of this court the recorder ought to have made plain that it was at that moment of receipt and not at any time during the handling thereafter that guilty knowledge had to be proved. For these reasons the appeal is allowed.''

APPEAL ALLOWED.

Going Equipped for Stealing, etc.

THEFT ACT 1968

"*Section 25.*—

(1) A person shall be guilty of an offence if, when not at his place of abode, he has with him any article for use in the course of or in connection with any burglary, theft or cheat.

(2) A person guilty of an offence under this section shall on conviction on indictment be liable to imprisonment for a term not exceeding three years.

(3) Where a person is charged with an offence under this section, proof that he had with him any article made or adapted for use in committing a burglary, theft or cheat shall be evidence that he had it with him for such use. . . .

(5) For purposes of this section an offence under section 12(1) of this Act of taking a conveyance shall be treated as theft, and 'cheat' means an offence under section 15 of this Act."

CHAPTER 6

OTHER OFFENCES AGAINST PROPERTY

Criminal Damage

CRIMINAL DAMAGE ACT 1971

"Section 1.—Destroying or damaging property

(1) A person who without lawful excuse destroys or damages any property belonging to another intending to destroy or damage any such property or being reckless[1] as to whether any such property would be destroyed or damaged shall be guilty of an offence.

(2) A person who without lawful excuse destroys or damages any property, whether belonging to himself or another—

- (a) intending to destroy or damage any property or being reckless[1] as to whether any property would be destroyed or damaged; and
- (b) intending by the destruction or damage to endanger the life of another or being reckless[1] as to whether the life of another would be thereby endangered;

shall be guilty of an offence.

(3) An offence committed under this section by destroying or damaging property by fire shall be charged as arson.

Section 2.—Threats to destroy or damage property

A person who without lawful excuse makes to another a threat, intending that that other would fear it would be carried out,—

- (a) to destroy or damage any property belonging to that other or a third person; or
- (b) to destroy or damage his own property in a way which he knows is likely to endanger the life of that other or a third person;

shall be guilty of an offence.

---

[1] For the meaning of recklessness in this context, see *Briggs*, [1977] 1 All E.R. 475; p. 11, *supra*, where the offence under s.1(1) of this Act was in issue.

Section 3.—Possessing anything with intent to destroy or damage property

A person who has anything in his custody or under his control intending without lawful excuse to use it or cause or permit another to use it—

(*a*) to destroy or damage any property belonging to some other person; or

(*b*) to destroy or damage his own or the user's property in a way which he knows is likely to endanger the life of some other person;

shall be guilty of an offence.

Section 4.—Punishment of Offences

(1) A person guilty of arson under section 1 above or of an offence under section 1(2) above (whether arson or not) shall on conviction on indictment be liable to imprisonment for life.

(2) A person guilty of any other offence under this Act shall on conviction on indictment be liable to imprisonment for a term not exceeding ten years.

Section 5.—'Without lawful excuse'

(1) This section applies to any offence under section 1(1) above and any offence under section 2 or 3 above other than one involving a threat by the person charged to destroy or damage property in a way which he knows is likely to endanger the life of another or involving an intent by the person charged to use or cause or permit the use of something in his custody or under his control so to destroy or damage property.

(2) A person charged with an offence to which this section applies shall, whether or not he would be treated for the purposes of this Act as having a lawful excuse apart from this subsection, be treated for those purposes as having a lawful excuse—

(*a*) if at the time of the act or acts alleged to constitute the offence he believed that the person or persons whom he believed to be entitled to consent to the destruction of or damage to the property in question had so consented, or would have so consented to it if he or they had known of the destruction or damage and its circumstances; or

(*b*) if he destroyed or damaged or threatened to destroy

or damage the property in question or, in the case of a charge of an offence under section 3 above, intended to use or cause or permit the use of something to destroy or damage it, in order to protect property belonging to himself or another or a right or interest in property which was or which he believed to be vested in himself or another, and at the time of the act or acts alleged to constitute the offence he believed—

(i) that the property, right or interest was in immediate need of protection; and

(ii) that the means of protection adopted or proposed to be adopted were or would be reasonable having regard to all the circumstances.

(3) For the purposes of this section it is immaterial whether a belief is justified or not if it is honestly held.

(4) For the purposes of subsection (2) above a right or interest in property includes any right or privilege in or over land, whether created by grant, licence or otherwise.

(5) This section shall not be construed as casting doubt on any defence recognised by law as a defence to criminal charges.

Section 10.—Interpretation

(1) In this Act 'property' means property of a tangible nature, whether real or personal, including money and—

(a) including wild creatures which have been tamed or are ordinarily kept in captivity, and any other wild creatures or their carcases if, but only if, they have been reduced into possession which has not been lost or abandoned or are in the course of being reduced into possession; but

(b) not including mushrooms growing wild on any land or flowers, fruit or foliage of a plant growing wild on any land.

For the purposes of this subsection 'mushroom' includes any fungus and 'plant' includes any shrub or tree.

(2) Property shall be treated for the purposes of this Act as belonging to any person—

(a) having the custody or control of it;

(b) having in it any proprietary right or interest (not being an equitable interest arising only from an agreement to transfer or grant an interest); or

(c) having a charge on it.

(3) Where property is subject to a trust, the persons to

whom it belongs shall be so treated as including any person having a right to enforce the trust.

(4) Property of a corporation sole shall be so treated as belonging to the corporation notwithstanding a vacancy in the corporation.''

R. v. SMITH (D.R.)
[1974] 1 All E.R. 632

No offence is committed under s.1(1) of the Criminal Damage Act 1971 by a person who destroys or damages property belonging to another if he does so in the honest belief, whether reasonable or not, that the property is his own, for the existence of that belief negatives the mens rea which the prosecution must prove in the first instance.

Smith became the tenant of a flat, which included a conservatory. In the conservatory Smith installed some electric wiring for use with stereo equipment. Also, with the landlord's permission, he put up roofing material and asbestos wall panels and laid floor boards. In law these became the property of the landlord. Subsequently, Smith gave notice to quit and later damaged the roofing, wall panels and floor boards he had installed in order, according to him, to remove the wiring. He was charged with criminal damage contrary to s.1(1) of the Criminal Damage Act 1971 and convicted after the judge had withdrawn from the jury Smith's defence that he honestly believed that the damage he did was to his own property, that he believed he was entitled to damage his own property and therefore had a lawful excuse for his actions causing the damage, on the basis that this could not constitute a lawful excuse. Smith appealed to the Court of Appeal.

Extracts from the Judgment of the Court of Appeal

James, L.J.—

"The offence created includes the elements of intention or recklessness and the absence of lawful excuse. There is in s. 5 of the Act a partial 'definition' of lawful excuse. Section 5 applies to offences under s.1(1) and, not relevant for present purposes, to offences under ss. 2 and 3 with certain exceptions.

It is argued for the appellant that an honest, albeit erroneous, belief that the act causing damage or destruction was done to his own property provides a defence to a charge brought under s.1(1). The argument is put . . . that the offence charged includes the act causing the damage or destruction and the element of *mens rea*. The element of *mens rea* relates to all the circumstances of the criminal act. The criminal act in the offence is causing damage to or destruction of 'property belonging to another' and the element of *mens rea*, therefore, must relate to 'property belonging to another'. Honest belief, whether justifiable or not, that the property is the defendant's own negatives the element of *mens rea*. . . .

It is conceded by counsel for the Crown that there is force in the argument that the element of *mens rea* extends to 'property belonging to another'. But, it is argued, the section creates a new statutory offence and that it is open to the construction that the mental element in the offence relates only to causing damage to or destroying property. That if in fact the property damaged or destroyed is shown to be another's property the offence is committed although the defendant did not intend or foresee damage to another person's property. . . .

It is not without interest to observe that under the law in force before the passing of the Criminal Damage Act 1971, it was clear that no offence was committed by a person who destroyed or damaged property belonging to another in the honest but mistaken belief that the property was his own or that he had a legal right to do the damage[1]. . . .

If the direction given by the deputy judge in the present case is correct, then the offence created by s. 1(1) of the 1971 Act involves a considerable extension of the law in a surprising direction. Whether or not this is so depends on the construction of the section. Construing the language of s. 1(1) we have no doubt that the *actus reus* is 'destroying or damaging property belonging to another'. It is not possible to exclude the words 'belonging to another' which describe the 'property'. Applying the ordinary principles of *mens rea*, the intention and recklessness and the absence of lawful excuse required to constitute the offence have reference to property belonging to another. It follows that in our judgment no offence is committed under this section if a person destroys or causes damage to property belonging to another

---

[1] *R.* v. *Twose* (1879), 14 Cox C.C. 327.

if he does so in the honest though mistaken belief that the property is his own, and provided that the belief is honestly held it is irrelevant to consider whether it is a justifiable belief."

APPEAL ALLOWED.

Forgery

FORGERY ACT 1913

"Section 1.—Definition of forgery
(1) For the purposes of this Act, forgery is the making of a false document in order that it may be used as genuine, and in the case of the seals and dies mentioned in this Act the counterfeiting of a seal or die, and forgery with intent to defraud or deceive, as the case may be, is punishable as in this Act provided.

(2) A document is false within the meaning of this Act if the whole or any material part thereof purports to be made by or on behalf or on account of a person who did not make it nor authorise its making; or if, though made by or on behalf or on account of the person by whom or by whose authority it purports to have been made, the time or place of making, where either is material, or in the case of a document identified by number or mark, the number or any distinguishing mark identifying the document, is falsely stated therein; and in particular a document is false:

(a) if any material alteration, whether by addition, insertion, obliteration, erasure, removal, or otherwise, has been made therein;

(b) if the whole or some material part of it purports to be made by or on behalf of a fictitious or deceased person;

(c) if, though made in the name of an existing person, it is made by him or by his authority with the intention that it should pass as having been made by some person, real or fictitious, other than the person who made or authorised it.[1]

---

[1] The definition of "false document" in subs. (2) was not intended to be an exclusive definition, but to remove doubts on this subject, it was provided by the Criminal Justice Act 1925, s. 35, that a document may be a false document for the purposes of the Forgery Act 1913 notwithstanding that it is not false in any such manner as is described in subs. (2).

(3) For the purposes of this Act—

(*a*) it is immaterial in what language a document is expressed or in what place within or without the King's dominions it is expressed to take effect;

(*b*) forgery of a document may be complete even if the document when forged is incomplete, or is not or does not purport to be such a document as would be binding or sufficient in law;

(*c*) the crossing on any cheque, draft on a banker, post-office money order, postal order, coupon or other document the crossing of which is authorised or recognised by law, shall be a material part of such cheque, draft, order, coupon, or document.

Section 4.—Forgery of other[1] documents with intent to defraud or to deceive a misdemeanour

(1) Forgery of any document, if committed with intent to defraud, shall be a misdemeanour and punishable with imprisonment for any term not exceeding two years.

(2) Forgery of any public document, if committed with intent to defraud or deceive, shall be a misdemeanour and punishable with imprisonment for any term not exceeding two years.

Section 6. —Uttering

(1) Every person who utters any forged document, seal, or die[2] shall be guilty of an offence and on conviction thereof shall be liable to the same punishment as if he himself had forged the document, seal, or die.

(2) A person utters a forged document, seal, or die, who, knowing the same to be forged, and with either of the intents necessary to constitute the offence of forging the said document, seal, or die, uses, offers, publishes, delivers, disposes of, tenders in payment or in exchange, exposes for sale or

---

[1] By s. 2 it is an offence to forge documents such as wills, deeds, bonds, banknotes, documents of title and insurance policies, provided this is done with intent to defraud. By s.3 it is an offence to forge certain public documents, such as a document bearing the stamp or impression of any royal seal, or a birth or death certificate, provided this is done with intent to defraud or deceive. The offences under these two sections carry a higher maximum sentence than an offence under s. 4.

[2] Forgery of seals and dies may only be committed in relation to those official seals or dies enumerated in s. 5 of the Act, under which there are a number of offences, each limited to particular types of such seals or dies and with different maximum sentences, of forging such seals or dies with intent to defraud or deceive.

exchange, exchanges, tenders in evidence, or puts off the said forged document, seal, or die.

(3) It is immaterial where the document, seal, or die was forged.

Section 7.—Demanding property on forged documents, etc.

Every person shall be guilty of felony and on conviction thereof shall be liable to imprisonment for any term not exceeding fourteen years, who, with intent to defraud, demands, receives, or obtains, or causes or procures to be delivered, paid or transferred to any person, or endeavours to receive or obtain or to cause or procure to be delivered, paid or transferred to any person any money, security for money or other property, real or personal:—

(a) under, upon, or by virtue of any forged instrument whatsoever, knowing the same to be forged; or

(b) under, upon, or by virtue of any probate or letters of administration, knowing the will, testament, codicil, or testamentary writing on which such probate or letters of administration shall have been obtained to have been forged, or knowing such probate or letters of administration to have been obtained by any false oath, affirmation, or affidavit."

R. v. CLOSS
(1857), Dears. & B. 460

Signing the name of another on a picture does not make it a document within the law of forgery.

The evidence was that the accused obtained a sum of money from the prosecutor as the purchase price of a picture upon which the accused, a picture dealer, had written the name of John Linnell, a contemporary artist of some repute who had not painted the picture in question. The indictment contained three counts. The first alleged an obtaining of money by false pretences, and on this the accused was acquitted. The second count alleged cheating, and the third forgery. The accused was convicted on these two counts but a case was reserved for the opinion of the Court for Crown Cases Reserved as to whether or not the second and third counts, or either, sufficiently disclosed an offence.

Extract from the Judgments of the Court for Crown Cases Reserved

Cockburn, C.J.—

". . . As to the third count we are all of opinion that there was no forgery. A forgery must be of some document or writing; and this was merely in the nature of a mark put upon the painting with a view of identifying it, and was no more than if the painter put any other arbitrary mark as a recognition of the picture being his. . . ."

CONVICTION QUASHED.[1]

R. v. SMITH
(1858), Dears. & B. 566

A facsimile of another's wrapper is not a document, or not a false document, within the meaning of the law as to forgery.

Smith was charged with forging documents, and uttering them knowing them to be forged. He sold baking powder, and the evidence was that he had caused ten thousand wrappers which the jury found to be almost identical with those used by Messrs. Borwick for their baking powder to be printed.

He was convicted, but a case was stated for the Court for Crown Cases Reserved who were of opinion that the wrappers were not "documents", or not "false documents", within the meaning of the law as to forgery.

Extracts from the Judgments of the Court for Crown Cases Reserved

Pollock, C.B.—

"We are all of opinion that this conviction is bad. The defendant may have been guilty of obtaining money by false pretences; of that there can be no doubt; but the real offence here was the inclosing the false powder in the false wrapper. The issuing of this wrapper without the stuff within it would be no offence. In the printing of these wrappers there is no forgery, nor could the man who printed them be indicted. The real offence is the issuing them with the

---

[1] The conviction on the second count was also quashed. The Theft Act 1968, s. 32 abolished the common law offence of cheating, except as regards offences relating to the public revenue.

fraudulent matter in them. I waited in vain to hear Mr. Huddleston shew that these wrappers came within the principle of documents which might be the subject of forgery at common law. Speaking for myself, I doubt very much whether these papers are within that principle. They are merely wrappers, and in their present shape I doubt whether they are anything like a document or instrument which is the subject of forgery at common law. To say that they belong to that class of instruments seems to me to be confounding things together as alike which are essentially different. It might as well be said, that if one tradesman used brown paper for his wrappers, and another tradesman had his brown paper wrappers made in the same way, he could be accused of forging the brown paper."

Bramwell, B.—

"I think that this was not a forgery. Forgery supposes the possibility of a genuine document, and that the false document is not so good as the genuine document, and that the one is not so efficacious for all purposes as the other. In the present case one of these documents is as good as the other—the one asserts what the other does—the one is as true as the other, but one gets improperly used. . . ."

CONVICTION QUASHED.

R. v. GAMBLING
[1974] 3 All E.R. 479

To be a forgery a document must not only tell a lie, it must tell a material lie about itself.

Gambling opened five separate National Savings Bank accounts at different Post Offices in different names and filled in five declarations which were false in that he did not give his correct name. He was charged on five counts of endeavouring to obtain a security for money by virtue of a forged instrument contrary to s. 7 of the Forgery Act 1913. He was convicted and appealed to the Court of Appeal.

Extracts from the Judgment of the Court of Appeal
May, J.—

"Section 7 of the Forgery Act 1913 makes it an offence if a person, with intent to defraud, endeavours to obtain a security for money by virtue of a forged instrument. There was no dispute that the appellant did try to obtain a security for money; nor that he did so by means of the particular application form referred to in each count, which it was accepted was an 'instrument'. The issues which did arise, however, were: (1) Were the instruments 'forged'? (2) if so, were they used with intent to defraud? Now s. 1(1) of the Act provides that 'forgery is the making of a false document in order that it may be used as genuine'. This definition involves two considerations: first, that the relevant document should be false; and secondly, that it was made in order that it might be used as genuine. . . .

Given . . . that each application form was 'false', was it made 'in order that it may be used as genuine'? Indeed what do these words involve in the context of the present case? Clearly they require proof of an intent on the part of the maker of the false document that it shall in fact be used as genuine. We think that they also involve that the untrue statement in the document must be the reason or one of the reasons which results in the document being accepted as genuine when it is thereafter used by the maker. It is this concept which we think is sought to be expressed in the aphorism—as to the usefulness of which views may differ strongly—that the document must not only tell a lie, it must tell a lie about itself: cf. *R.* v. *Dodge*.[1] If this is correct, then it seems to us to follow that in cases such as the present in which the falsity of a document arises from the use of a fictitious name or signature, or both, then that document is a forgery only if, as counsel for the appellant contended, having regard to all the circumstances of the transaction, the identity of the maker of the document is a material factor: cf. *R.* v. *Hassard*.[2]

In many cases the materiality of the identity of the maker would be so obvious that evidence would be unnecessary; for example, when the document is a cheque or bill of exchange and the purported signature of the drawer, or endorser, or the acceptor has been written by someone other than the person whose signature it purports to be. In other cases, such as the present, evidence would be required, and the materiality or otherwise of the identity of the maker of the document must be a matter for the jury.

There was in this case evidence on which the jury, properly directed, could have concluded, and very probably would have done so, that if the Post Office had known for

[1] [1972] 1 Q.B. 416; [1971] 2 All E.R. 1523.
[2] [1970] 2 All E.R. 647.

example that the appellant, signing one of the forms in the name of Mr. Davos, was not Mr. Davos, they would have refused to open the account. The identity of the maker of the false document would thus, in our opinion, have been a material factor. The trial judge was therefore right to reject the submission that there was no case to go to the jury. However, this question was ultimately a matter for them and they should have been directed in the sense we have sought to outline. Unfortunately no such direction was given."

APPEAL ALLOWED.

R. v. MARTIN
(1879), 5 Q.B.D. 34

While ordinarily the name signed on a cheque is material, it may be immaterial in exceptional circumstances, as where a person in the presence of another who knows him well signs a cheque with a false forename and gives it as his own to the other. In such a case there is no material falsity since the recipient will not be misled as to the identity of the drawer of the cheque.

Robert Martin met the prosecutor who knew him well, and purchased a pony and carriage from him. He gave a cheque in payment of the purchase price which he signed in the name of William Martin. He had an account at the bank upon which the cheque was drawn, but it was closed, and the cheque was dishonoured.

Martin was convicted of forgery, but a case was stated for the opinion of the Court for Crown Cases Reserved who were of opinion that the conviction was wrong.

Extract from the Judgments of the Court for Crown Cases Reserved

Cockburn, C.J.—

"The case is concluded by authority. In *Dunn's* case[1] it was agreed by the judges that 'in all forgeries the instrument supposed to be forged must be a false instrument in itself; and that if a person give a note entirely as his own, his subscribing it by a fictitious name will not make it a forgery, the credit there being wholly given to himself, without any regard to the name, or any relation to a third

---

[1] (1765), 1 Leach 57.

person.' Upon authority, as well as upon principle, it is clear that this conviction should be quashed."

CONVICTION QUASHED.

R. v. RITSON
(1869), L.R. 1 C.C.R. 200

The false dating of a document is a forgery if the date of the document is material.

W. Ritson was the owner of land upon the security of which he obtained an advance from the prosecutor. He subsequently executed a deed of assignment for the benefit of his creditors, and, as the amount due to the prosecutor exceeded the value of the land, it was conveyed to the prosecutor by W. Ritson with the consent of the trustee of the deed of assignment. W. Ritson then executed a deed conveying the land in question to his son S. Ritson, but the deed was dated prior to that of the deed of assignment and the conveyance to the prosecutor. S. Ritson claimed the land from the prosecutor.

W. Riston and S. Ritson were charged with, and convicted of, forging the conveyance to S. Ritson with intent to defraud the prosecutor. A case was stated for the opinion of the Court for Crown Cases Reserved, and this Court was of opinion that the conviction was correct.

Extract from the Judgments of the Court for Crown Cases Reserved

Blackburn, J.—

". . . By 24 and 25 Vict. c. 98, s. 20,[1] it is felony to 'forge' any deed with intent to defraud. The material word in this section is 'forge.' There is no definition of 'forge' in the statute, and we must therefore inquire what is the meaning of the word. The definition in Comyns (*Digest*, tit. Forgery, A.I.) is 'forgery is where a man fraudulently writes or publishes a false deed or writing to the prejudice of the right of another'—not making an instrument containing that which is false, which, I agree with Mr. Torr, would not be forgery, but making an instrument which

---

[1] Re-enacted by s. 2(1)(b) of the Forgery Act 1913.

purports to be that which it is not. Bacon's *Abridgement.*, (tit. Forgery, A.), which, it is well known, was compiled from the MS. of Chief Baron Gilbert, explains forgery thus: 'The notion of forgery doth not so much consist in the counterfeiting of a man's hand and seal . . . but in the endeavouring to give an appearance of truth to a mere deceit and falsity, and either to impose that upon the world as the solemn act of another which he is in no way privy to, or at least to make a man's own act appear to have been done at a time when it was not done, and by force of such a falsity to give it an operation which in truth and justice it ought not to have.' The material words, as applicable to the facts of the present case, are, 'to make a man's own act appear to have been done at a time when it was not done.' When an instrument professes to be executed at a date different from that at which it really was executed, and the false date is material to the operation of the deed, if the false date is inserted knowingly and with a fraudulent intent, it is a forgery at common law.

Ordinarily the date of a deed is not material, but it is here shown by extrinsic evidence that the date of the deed was material. Unless the deed had been executed before the 5th day of May [the date of the conveyance to the prosecutor], it could not have conveyed any estate in the land in question. The date was of the essence of the deed, and as a false date was inserted with a fraudulent intent, the deed was a false deed, within the definition in Bacon's *Abridgement*. . . ."

CONVICTION AFFIRMED.

R. v. RILEY
[1896] 1 Q.B. 309[1]

The falsification of the time of despatch of a telegram may amount to forgery, and a telegram is an instrument within what is now s. 7 of the Forgery Act 1913.

Riley was convicted of feloniously obtaining money from Messrs. Crompton and Radcliffe, a firm of bookmakers, by means of a forged instrument. He had obtained permission from one Barber to place bets with this firm in his

---

[1] This decision has been followed since the coming into force of the Forgery Act 1913, in *Cade*, [1914] 2 K.B. 209.

name. Riley was a clerk at the head post office, and he despatched a telegram placing a bet on the winner of a race which had already been run. He falsely indicated that it had been handed in at a branch office prior to the running of the race.

A case was stated for the opinion of the Court for Crown Cases Reserved who were of opinion that the conviction was correct.

Extracts from the Judgments of the Court for Crown Cases Reserved

Hawkins, J.—

". . . By the 24 and 25 Vict. c. 98, s. 38,[1] 'Whosoever with intent to defraud shall demand, receive, or obtain, or cause or procure to be delivered or paid to any person, or endeavour to receive or obtain, or to cause or procure to be delivered or paid to any person, any chattel, money, security for money, or other property whatsoever under, upon, or by virtue of *any forged or altered instrument whatsoever*, knowing the same to be forged or altered,' shall be guilty of felony. . . .

I proceed to discuss the question reserved for our consideration: whether the telegram described in the case constitutes a forged instrument in law; and whether it is such an instrument as is contemplated by s. 38.

My answer to both these questions is in the affirmative.

In 4 Blackstone's *Commentaries*, 247, forgery at common law is defined as 'the fraudulent making or alteration of a *writing* to the prejudice of another man's right.' I seek for no other definition for the purposes of the present discussion. That a postal telegram is a writing is to my mind clear. It originates in a written message addressed and signed by the sender, and delivered by him into the post office of despatch for the express purpose that it shall, in the very words in which it is penned, be transmitted by means of an electric wire to another post office, which I will call the arrival office, and that it shall there again on its arrival be committed to writing *verbatim et literatim*, and that such last-mentioned writing shall be handed to the person to whom it is addressed. The writing delivered in at the office of despatch is the authority of the postmaster to transmit the message, and of the postmaster at the arrival

---

[1] Re-enacted by s. 7 of the Forgery Act 1913; p. 317, *supra*.

office to commit it to writing and to deliver it to the addressee as the sender's written message to him. This message sent out from the arrival office is, in my opinion, as binding upon the sender as though he had written it with his own hand. . . .

Assuming the telegram to be such a writing as I have stated, a bare reading of the contents of it, coupled with the admission of its falsity and of the purpose for which it was made, are overwhelming to establish that it was fraudulently made to the prejudice of another man's right, and thus a forgery at common law. For this I need only cite the judgment of Blackburn, J., in *R.* v. *Ritson*[1]. . . .

In this case, unless the telegram was dated and despatched before the race was run, it would have been inoperative. The time of despatch was therefore material: falsely to write the telegram so as to make it appear that it was sent in for despatch before the race was run, when it was not sent in till afterwards, was to make it appear on the face of it to be that which it was not. . . .

In my view of the case, the telegram in question is an *instrument of contract*; it is the instrument which completed the wager offered by Crompton and Radcliffe to those who were able and disposed to accept it (see *Carlill* v. *Carbolic Smoke Ball Co., Ltd.*,[2] and the cases there cited), and thenceforth an obligation was imposed upon each party in honour to fulfil it according to the result of the race. I say *in honour*, because, though it was clearly not an illegal contract, it could not be enforced by any legal process. In virtue of it, and upon the assumption that the telegram was what it purported to be, Messrs. Crompton and Radcliffe paid the £9.

Assuming the document to be an 'instrument,' I come to the only remaining question, whether it is such within the meaning of s. 38 of the statute. Why should it not be so? It is contended that the section has reference only to such instruments as are mentioned in the earlier sections of the statute, and that s. 38 applies only to those forged instruments which are punishable as felonies.

Such a construction is, I think, erroneous. There is no definition of the word 'instrument' in the statute to fetter us in giving to it the ordinary and general interpretation. It was clearly the intention of the legislature by s. 38 to create a new offence. . . ."

CONVICTION AFFIRMED.

---

[1] (1869), L.R. 1 C.C.R. 200, at p. 204; p. 322, *supra*.
[2] [1892] 2 Q.B. 484; *affirmed*, [1893] 1 Q.B. 256.

R. v. GEACH
(1840), 9 C. & P. 499

A person has an intent to defraud for the purposes of the law of forgery although he intends to make good, and in fact makes good, any loss which may be incurred as a result of his action.

Geach forwarded a bill of exchange to his bank for discount by them. He had forged the acceptance thereon, and the bank discounted the bill. Geach subsequently paid off the bill, but, on his being charged with forgery, the jury were directed as a matter of law that this, or his intention to do so at the time the bank discounted the bill, was immaterial.

Extract from the Summing-up to the Jury
Parke, B.—

"Upon the questions, whether the acceptance is a forgery, and whether the prisoner knew it to be so, there can be no question, if you believe the evidence of Mr. Edward Williams; and with respect to the intent to defraud, I have no doubt that you will take the law from me, which is this, that a person is guilty of forgery, notwithstanding he may himself intend ultimately to take up the bill, and may suppose that the party whose name is forged will be no loser. If, in the present case, you are satisfied that the prisoner knew this acceptance to be forged, and uttered it as true and believed that the bankers would advance money on it, which they would not otherwise do, that is ample evidence of an intent to defraud, and evidence upon which a jury ought to act. It appears that this bill has since been paid by the prisoner; but that will make no difference, if the offence has been once completed at the time of the uttering."

VERDICT, GUILTY.

WELHAM v.
DIRECTOR OF PUBLIC PROSECUTIONS
[1961] A.C. 103

It is unnecessary to prove an intention to cause economic loss in order to establish an intent to defraud within the meaning of the Forgery Act 1913.

The accused was charged with uttering forged documents with intent to defraud contrary to s. 6 of the Forgery Act 1913. He had witnessed forged hire purchase agreements, the object of which was to enable finance companies to make advances in excess of the permitted amount and thus to evade the credit squeeze legislation. The accused was convicted after a direction which in effect told the jury that it was unnecessary for the prosecution to show that the accused intended to cause economic loss to anyone and that he intended to defraud if he intended to induce officials of the Inland Revenue to abstain from making inquiries about the advances. The accused unsuccessfully appealed to the Court of Criminal Appeal and thence to the House of Lords.

Extracts from the Speeches of the House of Lords

Lord Denning—

"At this point it becomes possible to point the contrast in the statute between an 'intent to deceive' and an 'intent to defraud'. 'To deceive' here conveys the element of deceit, which induces a state of mind, without the element of fraud, which induces a course of action or inaction. Take the case of a private document. For instance, where a man fabricates a letter so as to puff himself up in the opinion of others. Bramwell, B., put the instance: 'If I were to produce a letter purporting to be from the Duke of Wellington inviting me to dine, and say, "See what a respectable person I am" ': *R.* v. *Moah.*[1] There would then be an intent to deceive but it would not be punishable at common law or under the statute, because then it would not be done with intent to defraud. Take next the case of a public document. For instance, a parish register. If a man should falsify it so as to make himself appear to be descended of noble family, for the sake of his own glorification, he would not be guilty of an intent to defraud and would therefore not be punishable at common law (see *R.* v. *Hodgson*[2]), but he would have an intent to deceive and he would be punishable under the present statute, as indeed he was under its predecessors, such as the Forgery Act 1861, s. 36.

So much for the principal point under discussion. Mr. Gerald Gardiner did make a further point. He said that the intent must be to defraud the particular person to whom the

---

[1] (1858), 7 Cox C.C. 503, at p. 504.
[2] (1856), Dears. & B. 3, at p. 8.

document is first presented or his agent, and that it was insufficient if he intended to defraud somebody else. This is not correct. It has long been ruled that it is no answer to a charge of forgery, to say that there was no intent to defraud any particular person, because a general intent to defraud is sufficient to constitute the crime. So also it is no answer to say that there was no intent to defraud the recipient, if there was intent to defraud somebody else: see *R.* v. *Taylor*.[1]

In my judgment, section 4 (1) of the Forgery Act 1913 only restates the requirements of the common law of forgery. The 'intent to defraud' there mentioned is the same intent as was required by the common law. It is satisfactory to find that in the cases subsequent to the Act the courts have been giving it the same meaning as they did before (*R.* v. *Bassey*[2] is particularly in point), and I am glad to find this confirmed by what my noble and learned friend, Lord Tucker, said in *Board of Trade* v. *Owen*.[3]

Applying this meaning to the present case, it appears that Welham on his own evidence had an intent to defraud, because he uttered the hire-purchase documents for the purpose of fraud and deceit. He intended to practise a fraud on whomsoever might be called upon to investigate the loans made by the finance companies to the motor dealers. Such a person might be prejudiced in his investigation by the fraud. That is enough to show an intent to defraud."

APPEAL DISMISSED.[4]

Note

In Law Commission Report No. 55, *Forgery and Counterfeit Currency*, published in 1973, the Law Commission made a number of proposals for the reform of the law of forgery. These proposals are summarised in Cross and Jones, *Introduction to Criminal Law*, 8th ed., para. 12.14.

---

[1] (1779), 1 Leach 214.
[2] (1931), 47 T.L.R. 222.
[3] [1957] A.C. 602, at p. 622.
[4] The speeches in this case approve in general terms the well-known statement of Buckley, J., in *Re London and Globe Finance Corporation, Ltd.*, [1903] 1 Ch. 728 at p. 732; "To deceive is, I apprehend, to induce a man to believe that a thing is true which is false, and which the person practising the deceit knows or believes to be false. To defraud is to deprive by deceit; it is by deceit to induce a man to act his injury. More tersely it may be put, that to deceive is by falsehood to induce a state of mind; to defraud is by deceit to induce a course of conduct." Cf. the meaning of "defraud" in conspiracy to defraud, p. 345, *infra*.

CHAPTER 7

OFFENCES AGAINST PUBLIC ORDER

Unlawful Assembly

BEATTY v. GILLBANKS
(1882), 9 Q.B.D. 308

*An assembly formed for a lawful purpose does not con-
stitute an unlawful assembly merely because to the knowledge of
its organisers it will be opposed.*

The Salvation Army held regular processions through
the streets of Weston-super-Mare. Another body of persons
called the Skeleton Army was organised to impede its
passage. Clashes took place and breaches of the peace
occurred. Warning was given by the police and the magistrates to the leaders of the Salvation Army but they nevertheless held a procession and further breaches of the peace
occurred. The leaders were then summoned at petty sessions
for holding an unlawful assembly; they were ordered to be
bound over and appealed successfully by way of case stated
to the Queen's Bench Division.

Extracts from the Judgments of the Divisional Court

Field, J.—
"The appellants complain that in consequence of this
assembly they have been found guilty of a crime of which
there is no reasonable evidence that they have been guilty.
The charge against them is, that they unlawfully and
tumultuously assembled, with others, to the disturbance of
the public peace and against the peace of the Queen. Before
they can be convicted it must be shewn that this offence has
been committed. There is no doubt that they and with them
others assembled together in great numbers, but such an
assembly to be unlawful must be tumultuous and against the
peace. As far as these appellants are concerned there was
nothing in their conduct when they were assembled together
which was either tumultuous or against the peace. But it is

329

said, that the conduct pursued by them on this occasion was such, as on several previous occasions, had produced riots and disturbance of the peace and terror to the inhabitants, and that the appellants knowing when they assembled together that such consequences would again arise are liable to this charge.

Now I entirely concede that every one must be taken to intend the natural consequences of his own acts, and it is clear to me that if this disturbance of the peace was the natural consequence of acts of the appellants they would be liable, and the justices would have been right in binding them over. But the evidence set forth in the case does not support this contention; on the contrary, it shews that the disturbances were caused by other people antagonistic to the appellants, and that no acts of violence were committed by them. . . .

What has happened here is that an unlawful organization has assumed to itself the right to prevent the appellants and others from lawfully assembling together, and the finding of the justices amounts to this, that a man may be convicted for doing a lawful act if he knows that his doing it may cause another to do an unlawful act. There is no authority for such a proposition, and the question of the justices whether the facts stated in the case constituted the offence charged in the information must therefore be answered in the negative."

APPEAL ALLOWED.

WISE v. DUNNING
[1902] 1 K.B. 167

A breach of the peace is a natural consequence of inflammatory language and gestures.

The appellant was a Protestant lecturer who held meetings in Liverpool. At these meetings he used language and gestures which were insulting to Catholics, and some breaches of the peace occurred. It was the declared intention of the appellant to hold further meetings, and he was brought before the magistrate by the police and bound over to keep the peace. A local Act of Parliament prohibited the use of insulting words in the streets of Liverpool whereby a breach of the peace might be occasioned. The appellant had not broken the peace himself, nor had he incited anyone else to do so, and he appealed by way of case stated to the Divisional Court.

Extract from the Judgments of the Divisional Court

Darling, J.—

". . . Counsel for the appellant contended that the natural consequence must be taken to be the legal acts which are a consequence. I do not think so. The natural consequence of such conduct is illegality. I think that the natural consequence of this 'crusader's' eloquence has been to produce illegal acts, and that from his acts and conduct circumstances have arisen which justified the magistrate in binding him over to keep the peace and be of good behaviour. In the judgment of O'Brien, C.J. in R. v. *Justices of Londonderry*[1] there is this passage: 'Now I wish to make the ground of my judgment clear, and carefully to guard against being misunderstood. I am perfectly satisfied that the magistrates did not make the order which is impugned by reason of there having been, or there being likely to be, any obstruction of the highway, and that the true view of what took place is that the defendants were bound over in respect of an apprehended breach of the peace; and, in my opinion, there was no evidence to warrant that apprehension.' It is clear that, if there had been evidence to warrant that apprehension, the Chief Justice would have held the magistrates' decision in that case to be right. It is said that *Beatty* v. *Gillbanks*[2] is in conflict with that decision. I am not sure that it is. I am inclined to think that . . . the whole question is one of fact and evidence. But I do not hesitate to say that, if there be a conflict between these two cases, I prefer the law as it is laid down in R. v. *Justices of Londonderry*.[3] If that be a right statement of the law, as I think it is, the magistrate was perfectly justified in coming to the conclusion he did come to in this case, even without taking into consideration the question of the local Act of Parliament to which we were referred.

For these reasons I am of opinion that the magistrate's order was right."

APPEAL DISMISSED.

---

[1] (1891), 28 L.R. Ir. 440, at p. 447.
[2] (1882), 9 Q.B.D. 308; p. 329, *supra*.
[3] (1891), 28 L.R. Ir. 440.

Comment on Beatty v. Gillbanks and Wise v. Dunning

Although the appellant in *Wise* v. *Dunning* was not charged with the offence of unlawful assembly the case has been included here because it is very likely that such a charge would have been successful. In *Beatty* v. *Gillbanks* the Divisional Court held that the Salvation Army members were not guilty of unlawful assembly because the disturbances were caused by other persons, whom the Salvation Army did not incite, and had not been caused by the Salvation Army members because on the facts it was not the natural and probable consequence of their procession that the Skeleton Army should create the commotion. *Beatty* v. *Gillbanks* was distinguished in *Wise* v. *Dunning* on the ground that the disorder in the latter case was a natural and probable consequence of the appellant's insults.

Thus, the position seems to be as follows. If members of a lawful meeting or procession publicly insult opponents who are provoked, or are likely to be provoked, into committing a breach of the peace they can properly be convicted of unlawful assembly; but if they do not offer insults but provoke, as they know is likely, a breach of the peace by their meeting or procession they do not commit unlawful assembly.

While the specific point has not been decided, it may be that, as the members of the Salvation Army in *Beatty* v. *Gillbanks* had been forbidden by the police to hold their procession and persisted in doing so, they would now, since the decision in *Duncan* v. *Jones* (p. 152, *supra*), have been guilty of the offence of obstructing a constable in the execution of his duty.

KAMARA v. DIRECTOR OF PUBLIC PROSECUTIONS

[1973] 2 All E.R. 1242

(1) *An unlawful assembly need not occur in a public place.* (2) *Where an assembly has taken place in a building it is not necessary, in proving the crime of unlawfully assembling in such a manner as to disturb the public peace, to show that fear was engendered in persons beyond the bounds of the building.*

Kamara and the other appellants were students from Sierra Leone who held political opinions contrary to those of the party in power in that country. In order to gain publicity for their grievances they agreed to occupy the Sierra Leone High Commission in London. Pursuant to that agreement they went to the High Commission. The caretaker opened the door and they entered. Then they locked in a room the caretaker and about ten other members of the staff, some of whom were physically held or pushed but no blows were struck and there was no violence. One of the appellants was carrying an imitation firearm which he had used to threaten the caretaker after entering; other members of the staff who saw the imitation firearm also thought it was real.

The appellants were convicted of conspiracy to trespass (an offence which will be abolished if the Criminal Law Bill[1] becomes law) and of unlawful assembly.[2] Their appeals to the Court of Appeal were dismissed, as were their appeals to the House of Lords. The extracts which follow are concerned with the appeals against conviction for unlawful assembly, the question certified by the Court of Appeal being whether it was necessary in proving the offence of unlawfully assembling in such a manner as to disturb the public peace to show that fear was engendered in persons beyond the bounds of a building.

Extracts from the Speeches of the House of Lords

Lord Hailsham of St. Marylebone, L.C.—

"I share the view of the Court of Appeal[3] that the logic implicit in the decision in *Button* v. *Director of Public Prosecutions*[4] (a case of affray) requires that we should come to an analogous decision in the present case in a sense adverse to the appellants. I also agree with Lawton, L.J., that such a decision would also be correct even if the matter were *res integra*. . . . I agree with Lawton, L.J., when he said:[5]

'Both affray and unlawful assembly belong to the group of common law offences designed to uphold public order and to protect the public generally against lawlessness and

---

[1] P. 360 *et seq., infra.*
[2] Two of the appellants were also convicted of having an imitation firearm with intent to commit an indictable offence, contrary to s. 18 (1) of the Firearms Act 1968.
[3] [1972] 3 All E.R. 999.
[4] [1966] A.C. 591; [1965] 3 All E.R. 587; p. 339, *infra.*
[5] [1972] 3 All E.R., at p. 1007.

disorder and in our judgment the same concepts should apply to both offences. As with affray, the public peace can be endangered by a rowdy, disorderly meeting just as much as if it is held inside a building as outside. In this case there was ample evidence that a number of persons inside were scared as well they might have been. The fact that no one outside was is of no importance.'

The appellants sought to rely on a number of cases in which unlawful assembly was defined by judicial authority by use of some such phrase as 'terror and alarm in the neighbourhood' (cf. *R.* v. *Stephens,*[1] per Patteson, J.; *R.* v. *Vincent,*[2] per Alderson, B.). I agree with Lawton, L.J., that in those cases 'in the neighbourhood' must be read in the context as simply the equivalent of those nearby. I note that in the earliest definition at which I have looked, namely, that contained in the first edition of Hawkins,[3] the expression 'neighbourhood' is not used, but the expression is 'such circumstances of terror as cannot but endanger the public peace'. I consider that the public peace is in question when either an affray or a riot or unlawful assembly takes place in the presence of innocent third parties. . . . No doubt unlawful assembly differs from an affray, because, unlike affray, it implies a common purpose, and because, unlike affray, actual violence is unnecessary provided the public peace is endangered, but in my view it is analogous to affray in that (1) it need not be in a public place and (2) that the essential requisite in both is the presence or likely presence of innocent third parties, members of the public not participating in the illegal activities in question. It is their presence, or the likelihood of it, and the danger to their security in each case which constitutes the threat to public peace and the public element necessary to the commission of each offence. I therefore answer the second question certified by the Court of Appeal by saying that it is not necessary in proving the crime of unlawfully assembling in such a manner as to disturb the public peace to show that fear was engendered beyond the bounds of the building."

APPEALS DISMISSED.

---

[1] (1839), 3 State Tr. N.S. 1189, at p. 1234.
[2] (1839), 9 C. & P. 91, at p. 109.
[3] *Pleas of the Crown* (1716), vol. 1, c. 65, s. 9.

Riot

FIELD v. METROPOLITAN POLICE RECEIVER

[1907] 2 K.B. 853

A person whose property is damaged in a riot may sue for compensation out of police funds under the Riot (Damages) Act 1886. To constitute a riot five elements are necessary; 1, a number of persons not less than three; 2, a common purpose; 3, execution or inception of common purpose; 4, intent on the part of the persons engaged to assist each other by force, if necessary; 5, force or violence displayed so as to alarm at least one person of reasonable firmness and courage.

A number of youths exceeding three gathered together and behaved rowdily: some of them stood with their backs to a wall while others ran up against it with the result that part of the wall collapsed. The caretaker of the adjoining building came out and the youths dispersed. It was held on appeal from the County Court that there was no evidence of an intention to assist each other by force nor of force or violence displayed so as to alarm any person of reasonable firmness and courage and so there was no riot.

Extract from the Judgment of the Divisional Court

Phillimore, J.—

". . . Riot is a crime, a misdemeanour at common law. The writer who appears to require the fewest elements to constitute this crime, and who, therefore, is the strongest authority in favour of the plaintiffs, is Lord Coke. He says that riot is where three or more do any unlawful act, as to beat any man, or to hunt in his park, or take possession of another man's land, or cut or destroy his corn, etc. This would seem to imply that any assault or malicious injury to property done by three or more is a riot. It is to be observed, however, that if this is Lord Coke's meaning, he stands alone; also that the whole chapter, which embraces four or five kinds of crime, is short and sketchy, and that his definition of rout is an illogical one, derived, as we see by reference to Brooke, from the reading of Serjeant Marrow in the Inner Temple on the Statute of Peace, a reading very properly criticized by Brooke. Blackstone follows Coke in his definition of rout—a definition which has been since abandoned by text writers, and he nearly follows Coke in his definition of riot; but he makes it plain that there must always be force or violence to constitute a riot. Hawkins requires that the rioters should have an intent mutually to assist one another against anyone who should oppose them in the execution of their enterprise, and should actually execute the same in a violent and turbulent manner to the terror of the people (s. 1). A riot ought to be accompanied, he says, by some offer of violence either to the person of a man or to his possessions, as by beating him or forcing him to quit possession of his land or goods, etc. (s. 4); and there must be at least some such circumstances either of actual force or violence, or at least of an apparent tendency thereto, as are naturally apt to strike terror into the people (s. 5). Stephen says that an unlawful assembly must be (1) with intent to commit a crime by open force, or (2) with intent to carry out any common purpose in such a manner as to give firm and courageous persons reasonable ground to apprehend a breach of the peace, and a riot is an unlawful assembly which has actually begun to execute its purpose by a breach of the peace and to the terror of the public. In *R. v. Soley*[1] Lord Holt, C.J., says: 'If I am writing a letter and three or more come hallooing and jogging me, is this a riot? No; it ought to be *in terrorem populi*.' In *R. v. Langford*,[2] where five persons were indicted for riot for ejecting an old man out of a cottage which they claimed, and then demolishing it, the conviction was supported because such force was used as to terrify the old man. *Drake v. Footitt*[3] was the case of a violent election riot, where the only question was whether a felony had been committed. In *R. v. Cunninghame Graham*[4] Charles, J., largely relying upon the passages in Hawkins, instructed the jury that a 'riot is a disturbance of the peace by three persons at the least, who, with intent to help one another against any person who opposes them in the execution of some enterprise or other, actually execute that enterprise in a violent and turbulent manner to the alarm of the people.'

From these passages we deduce that there are five necessary elements of a riot (1) number of persons, three at least; (2) common purpose; (3) execution or inception of the

---

[1] (1707), 11 Mod. Rep. 100.
[2] (1842), Car. & M. 602.
[3] (1881), 7 Q.B.D. 201.
[4] (1888), 16 Cox C.C. 420.

common purpose; (4) an intent to help one another by force if necessary against any person who may oppose them in the execution of their common purpose; (5) force or violence not merely used in demolishing, but displayed in such a manner as to alarm at least one person of reasonable firmness and courage. In this case element No. 1 was present. As to elements Nos. 2 and 3, there was evidence upon which the learned Judge could have found their existence, though, as far as we can judge from the notes of the evidence and without seeing the witnesses, we think we should not have found the same way. But as to elements Nos. 4 and 5 there is no evidence. The youths ran away as soon as the single caretaker came forward; there is no reason to suppose that they would have resisted if he had come forward earlier and required them to desist. It is true that the caretaker's wife was frightened by the noise of the falling wall, but no one says that he was alarmed by the youths, though the witnesses may have been frightened by other youths on other occasions. Nor was the conduct of the youths such as would be calculated to alarm persons of reasonable firmness and courage. We cannot hold that there was a riot. The appeal must be allowed, and judgment must be entered for the defendant."

APPEAL ALLOWED.

FORD v. METROPOLITAN POLICE DISTRICT RECEIVER

[1921] 2 K.B. 344

Where there is evidence of at least one person being frightened and all the other elements of a riot as set out in Field's case[1] are present the court may find that there is a riot.

On Peace Night, 1919, rejoicings took place at Canning Town. A bonfire was lighted and to get fuel the crowd, which was in a good humour, broke into an empty house and stripped its woodwork. An action was brought for compensation under the Riot (Damages) Act 1886, and a next door neighbour gave evidence that he did not interfere because he feared he would be killed if he did so. It was held that the necessary elements of a riot were present.

---

[1] P. 335, *supra.*

Extract from the Judgment

Bailhache, J.—

The learned judge enumerated the first three elements of riot and continued:

". . . Fourthly, an intent on the part of the above persons to help one another, by force if necessary, against any person who may oppose them in the execution of the common purpose. I think again that that is satisfied. These people went there with crowbars and pickaxes, and I think there is no doubt that anybody who had interfered with them would have been subjected to rough usage. Fifthly, there must be force or violence, not merely used in and about the common purpose, but displayed in such a manner as to alarm at least one person of reasonable firmness and courage. The determination of this point has given me some trouble, and it is round this one of the elements necessary to constitute a riot that the discussion has most largely turned. The evidence is that of Mr. Whowell, who said that he saw the people coming and that he was afraid they would break into his premises, and that he went out and begged them not to do so. They did not do so, and I do not think they were ever minded to do so. Mr. Whowell said he did not like to interfere with these people injuring the plaintiff's house, because he thought he would have been killed if he had. This is probably an exaggeration, but at any rate, he was afraid. The question, to my mind, is whether that evidence is sufficient to establish the fifth element above mentioned. I have no reason to doubt that Mr. Whowell is a man of reasonable firmness and courage, and it seems to me that his evidence is sufficient. I do not think the fourth and fifth elements can be said to be absent because the people assembled go about the business in hand quietly if not interfered with. If that were so any number of persons might at any time assemble with the unlawful intent of demolishing another's house, and if nobody interfered with them it would be said that as they never threatened anybody what they did did not constitute a riot. That seems to me an impossible view to take, and it might be true of any riot that ever took place. . . ."

JUDGMENT FOR PLAINTIFF.

Comment on Field v. Metropolitan Police Receiver and Ford v. Metropolitan Police District Receiver

In *R. v. Sharp and Johnson*,[1] Lord Goddard, C.J., thought that the fifth element of riot enumerated above might require reconsideration at some future time. However, that element has been applied subsequently by the Northern Irish Court of Appeal in *Devlin* v. *Armstrong*.[2] In that case it was held that, while a conviction for riotous behaviour required proof that a person of reasonable firmness and courage has been put in fear, this might be done without necessarily calling a witness to state that he or some other person was in a state of alarm, if there was sufficient material from which the fact could be inferred.

Affray

BUTTON v. DIRECTOR OF PUBLIC PROSECUTIONS
[1965] 3 All E.R. 587

To constitute an affray it is not necessary that the fight should occur in a public place.

Button and others fought in a dance hall and were charged, *inter alia*, with affray. The trial judge directed the jury that an affray must occur in a public place but that they were entitled to treat the dance hall in question as a public place. The accused were convicted and appealed unsuccessfully to the Court of Criminal Appeal who were of opinion that an affray need not occur in a public place. The accused then appealed unsuccessfully to the House of Lords.

Extracts from the Speeches of the House of Lords

Lord Gardiner, L.C.—

"The essence of the offence is that two or more fight together to the terror of the Queen's subjects.[3] Nowhere in the earlier writings is it suggested that the place where the fight occurs is a decisive matter.

---

[1] [1957] 1 Q.B. 552; [1957] 1 All E.R. 577.
[2] [1971] N.I. 13; applied in *O'Brien* v. *Freil*, [1974] N.I. 29.
[3] But see further the next case.

Lambard's Eirenarcha (1610 edn.), c. 3, p. 125, under the side note 'Affray and assault' said:

> 'The words affray and assault be indifferently used of most men, and that also in some of our booke cases, but yet (in my opinion) there wanteth not a just difference between them. For affray is derived of the french effrayer which signifieth to terrifie, or bring feare.'

He described it (ibid.) as a 'common wrong'. It is true that assault and affray were sometimes spoken of loosely as if they were interchangeable. This is perhaps not surprising since in each case the wrongful act is the same yet the mischief of the act falls on the victim in the offence of assault but on the bystander in the offence of affray.

In 1583 *Fitzherbert's l'Office et Authority de Justices de Peace*, having dealt with affrays on a high street and affrays in the presence of the constable, referred to (1617 edn. at p. 147) 'an affray which has taken place in a house' and also said (*ibid.*) 'If two men are affraying in a house and the door of the house is shut even if no one is hurt before the entry into the house yet the constable may enter . . .'

. . . In 1769, however, *Blackstone* (vol. 4, p. 145) used words which led to subsequent error. Citing *Hawkins* he defined affray as 'the fighting of two or more persons in some public place, to the terror of His Majesty's subjects: for, if the fighting be in private, it is no affray but an assault'. There are two reasons which lead me to think that he cannot have been intending to depart from the views expressed by former writers. First he goes on to cite *Hawkins* as to the power of the constable to break open doors when an affray is in a house, and secondly he could hardly have sought to introduce a novel limitation on the old offence of affray without some discussions and justification of his innovation. I think that he used the words 'public place' loosely (and unfortunately) in order to exclude, as *Hawkins* had done, fighting in a private place where none but the contestants were present.
. . . The Court of Criminal Appeal took the view that the offence of affray was a useful part of the criminal law in modern times. I agree with that view.

The most powerful argument for the appellant is that afforded by the lapse of over a century since the error crept into the law. During that period one may assume that prosecutions and trials have been based on the hypothesis that only in respect of acts done in a public place can there be a conviction for affray. But no alteration of the surrounding law has been founded on that hypothesis, nor can it properly be regarded as an intentional development of the law of affray. The only result of it has been that during that period the citizen who has been the victim of affray in a private place had in practice been deprived of the protection of the law. That is not in itself any reason to continue the deprivation. Moreover there is no argument of principle or logic to gild the error. In riot and assault, two kindred offences which legal writers have so often treated in association with affray, there is no requirement that they should be committed in a public place. To distinguish affray in this respect is captious and illogical. There seems therefore no adequate reason to perpetuate the error."

APPEALS DISMISSED.

TAYLOR v. DIRECTOR OF PUBLIC PROSECUTIONS
[1973] 2 All E.R. 1108

A person may be guilty of affray even if, although others are fighting, he alone is fighting unlawfully to the terror of other persons, because for instance the other participants are acting in self-defence.

A fight occurred in a social club. Taylor was among those fighting. He and his two brothers were charged with affray. The defence of each of them was self-defence. The two brothers were acquitted but Taylor was convicted. He appealed to the Court of Appeal, the question being whether a man could be guilty of affray if, though others were fighting, he alone was fighting unlawfully to the terror of other persons. The Court of Appeal answered this question in the affirmative and Taylor appealed to the House of Lords.

Extracts from the Speeches of the House of Lords
Lord Hailsham of St. Marylebone, L.C.—

"From the first, as was conceded by counsel for the appellant, at least in one class of case, the offence of affray could be committed by a single person, namely, that mentioned in the Statute of Northampton (1328). This statute, however, seems to have been largely declaratory of the common law, but prescriptive of an additional remedy. It forbids amongst other things the carrying or brandishing in public of unusual or terrifying weapons. . . . The statute itself has been repealed as obsolete or unnecessary by the Criminal Law Act 1967, no doubt partly as the result of the enactment of the Prevention of Crime Act 1953. But, whether or not this example of the common law offence of affray still lives on, the fact that the crime of affray could be committed by a single person at least in this class of case is not without its importance in determining the result of the present appeal. . . .

The classical definition of affray repeated, though not always in precisely the same language, over and over again in the older textbooks was that it was fighting by two or more persons [in some public place] to the terror of the King's subjects[1] and with the omission of the words in square brackets which he demonstrated to have been added as the result of an error, Lord Gardiner, L.C., adopted this definition in *Button* v. *Director of Public Prosecutions*[2]. . . .

On this, and on some observations of Lord Goddard, C.J., in *Sharp*[3] to the effect that affray was essentially a joint offence, counsel for the appellant largely founded his submission which was to the effect that a party could only be guilty of the offence if not only he, but at least some other, was guilty of fighting unlawfully.

As the Court of Appeal[4] pointed out, this submission cannot live consistently with the decisions in *R.* v. *Scarrow*[5] or *R.* v. *Summers*[6] from which it appears fairly clearly, if they are to be supported, that a person is not to be acquitted of affray simply because his victim acts lawfully, as for instance by retreating, or simply warding off the blows aimed at him by the accused. I cannot myself see how, if this is so, it can fail to follow that if his opponent is actually fighting, but fighting lawfully, for instance, in self-defence or to effect a lawful arrest or rescue, an accused person indulging in unlawful violence against that opponent may be guilty of making an affray. Indeed, at one moment in *Scarrow*[5] Lord Parker, C.J., is reported as saying in terms:

'It may well be that if two people fight and one is acting in self-defence that man cannot be said to be guilty of an

---

[1] Cf. Blackstone, *Commentaries* (1765), bk. IV, p. 145.
[2] [1966] A.C., at p. 625; [1965] 3 All E.R., at p. 590; p. 339, *supra*.
[3] [1957] 1 Q.B., at p. 561; [1957] 1 All E.R., at p. 580.
[4] [1973] 1 All E.R. 78.
[5] (1968), 52 Cr. App. Rep. 591.
[6] (1972), 56 Cr. App. Rep. 604.

affray, but it would appear to this court that there is no reason why his attacker, whether acting alone or jointly with another attacker, should not be held guilty of the affray.'

That case was expressly followed by Edmund Davies, L.J., in *Summers*,[1] and by O'Connor, J., in delivering the judgment of the Court of Appeal[2] in the instant case. I am certain that they were right, and, though I endorse the actual decision in *Sharp*[3] to the effect that self-defence is an answer to a charge of affray, I am quite certain that the two passages in Lord Goddard's judgment in that case[4] to the effect that affray 'is of necessity a joint offence' and that if a man is 'only defending himself . . . that is not a fight and, consequently, not an affray' cannot be supported and do not represent an accurate statement of the law. It is, of course, true that before an affray of the type which consists in a fight can take place at least two persons must be present, but it does not follow from that that each of them is guilty of the affray. Making an affray consists in the unlawful participation in the fight, and one may be participating unlawfully when others are participating lawfully. . . .

From the very earliest days the offence of affray has required [the element of terror], and all the early textbooks stress the derivation of the word from the French 'effrayer', to put in terror. . . . To my mind it is essential to stress that the degree of violence required to constitute the offence of affray must be such as to be calculated to terrify a person of reasonably firm character. This should not be watered down.''

APPEAL DISMISSED.

---

[1] (1972), 56 Cr. App. Rep. 604.
[2] [1973] 1 All E.R. 78.
[3] [1957] 1 Q.B. 552; [1957] 1 All E.R. 577.
[4] [1957] 1 Q.B., at p. 561; [1957] 1 All E.R., at p. 580.

CHAPTER 8
CONSPIRACY AND ATTEMPT

Conspiracy

KAMARA v. DIRECTOR OF PUBLIC PROSECUTIONS
[1973] 2 All E.R. 1242

A conspiracy to commit a tort is criminal if the execution of the tort involves the invasion of the public domain or is intended to inflict more than nominal damage on its victim.[1]

The facts of this case are set out on p. 332, *supra*.

Extract from the Speeches of the House of Lords

Lord Hailsham of St. Marylebone, L.C.—
    "Trespass or any other form of tort can, if intended, form the element of illegality necessary in conspiracy. But in my view, more is needed. Either (1) execution of the combination must invade the domain of the public, as, for instance, when the trespass involves the invasion of a building such as the embassy of a friendly country or a publicly owned building, or (of course) where it infringes the criminal law as by breaching the Statutes of Forcible Entry and Detainer, the Criminal Damage Act 1971 or the laws affecting criminal assaults to the person. Alternatively, (2) a combination to trespass [or commit any other form of tort] becomes indictable if the execution of the combination necessarily involves and is known and intended to involve the infliction on its victim of something more than purely nominal damage. This must necessarily be the case where the intention is to occupy the premises to the exclusion of the owner's right, either by expelling him altogether . . . or otherwise effectively preventing him from enjoying his property."

---

[1] If the Criminal Law Bill is enacted a conspiracy to commit a tort will cease to be criminal, see p. 361, *infra*.

SCOTT v. COMMISSIONER OF POLICE FOR THE METROPOLIS
[1974] 3 All E.R. 1032

Conspiracy to defraud does not necessarily involve deceit by the accused of the person intended to be defrauded. A person can be convicted of conspiracy to defraud if he has agreed with one or more persons to deprive another dishonestly of something which is that other person's or of something to which he is or would or might, but for the perpetration of the fraud, be entitled.

Scott agreed with employees of cinema owners temporarily to abstract, without the permission of such cinema owners, and in return for payments to such employees, cinematograph films, without the knowledge or consent of the owners of the copyright and/or distribution rights in the films, for the purpose of making "pirate" copies and distributing them on a commercial basis. He was convicted, *inter alia*, of conspiracy to defraud and appealed unsuccessfully against this conviction to the Court of Appeal who, however, granted leave to appeal to the House of Lords.

The main contention put forward in the House of Lords by Scott's counsel was that a person could not be convicted of conspiracy to defraud unless he had deceived another.

Extracts from the Speeches of the House of Lords

Viscount Dilhorne—

". . . In the light of the cases to which I have referred, I have come to the conclusion that counsel for the appellant's main contention must be rejected. I have not the temerity to attempt an exhaustive definition of the meaning of 'defraud'. . . . 'To defraud' ordinarily means in my opinion to deprive a person dishonestly of something which is his or of something to which he is or would or might but for the perpetration of the fraud, be entitled.

In *Welham* v. *Director of Public Prosecutions*[1] Lord Radcliffe referred to a special line of cases where the person deceived is a person holding public office or a public authority and where the person deceived was not caused any pecuniary or economic loss. Forgery whereby the deceit has been

---

[1] [1961] A.C., at p. 124; [1960] 1 All E.R., at p. 808.

accomplished, had, he pointed out, been in a number of cases treated as having been done with intent to defraud despite the absence of pecuniary or economic loss. In this case it is not necessary to decide that a conspiracy to defraud may exist even though its object was not to secure a financial advantage by inflicting an economic loss on the person to whom the conspiracy was directed. But for myself I see no reason why what was said by Lord Radcliffe in relation to forgery should not equally apply in relation to conspiracy to defraud.

In this case the accused bribed servants of the cinema owners to secure possession of films in order to copy them and in order to enable them to let the copies out on hire. By so doing counsel for the appellant conceded they inflicted more than nominal damage to the goodwill of the owners of the copyright and distribution rights of the films. By so doing they secured for themselves profits which but for their actions might have been secured by those owners. . . . In the circumstances it is, I think, clear that they inflicted pecuniary loss on those owners."

Lord Diplock.—

"My Lords, I have had the advantage of reading the speech of my noble and learned friend Viscount Dilhorne. I agree with it. The authorities that he cites and others cited in the speeches in this House in the contemporaneous appeal in *Director of Public Prosecutions* v. *Withers*,[1] in my view, established the following propositions. . . .

(2) Where the intended victim of a 'conspiracy to defraud' is a private individual the purpose of the conspirators must be to cause the victim economic loss by depriving him of some property or right, corporeal or incorporeal, to which he is or would or might become entitled. The intended means by which the purpose is to be achieved must be dishonest. They need not involve fraudulent misrepresentation such as is needed to constitute the civil tort of deceit. Dishonesty of any kind is enough.

(3) Where the intended victim of a 'conspiracy to defraud' is a person performing public duties[2] as distinct from a private individual it is sufficient if the purpose is to cause him to act contrary to his public duty, and the intended

---

[1] [1975] A.C. 842; [1974] 3 All E.R. 984.

[2] Persons such as officials of banks and building societies do not fall within this category, *per* Lord Kilbrandon in *Director of Public Prosecutions* v. *Withers*, [1974] 3 All E.R., at p. 985.

means of achieving this purpose are dishonest. The purpose need not involve causing economic loss to anyone.[1]

In the instant case the intended victims of the conspiracy to defraud were private individuals. The facts bring it squarely within proposition (2) above. The dishonest means to be employed were clandestine bribery."

APPEAL DISMISSED.

SHAW v.
DIRECTOR OF PUBLIC PROSECUTIONS
[1961] 2 All E.R. 446

There is such an offence known to our law as a conspiracy to corrupt public morals.

Shaw and others produced the *Ladies' Directory* in which prostitutes advertised their services. Shaw was charged with and convicted of, *inter alia*, a conspiracy to corrupt public morals. He unsuccessfully appealed to the Court of Criminal Appeal and thence to the House of Lords.

Extracts from the Speeches of the House of Lords

Viscount Simonds.—

"Need I say, my Lords, that I am no advocate of the right of the judges to create new criminal offences? . . . But I am at a loss to understand how it can be said either that the law does not recognize a conspiracy to corrupt public morals or that, though there may not be an exact precedent for such a conspiracy as this case reveals, it does not fall generally within the words by which it is described. . . .

In the sphere of criminal law, I entertain no doubt that there remains in the courts of law a residual power to enforce the supreme and fundamental purpose of the law, to conserve not only the safety and order but also the moral welfare of the state, and that it is their duty to guard it against attacks which may be the more insidious because they are novel and unprepared for. . . . I will say a final word on an aspect of the case which was urged by counsel. No

---

[1] Cf. Lord Kilbrandon in *Director of Public Prosecutions* v. *Withers*, [1974] 3 All E.R., at p. 1009, who said: "one of the established types of conspiracy to cheat and defraud consists of deceiving public officers into committing a breach of duty".

one doubts—and I have put it in the forefront of this opinion—that certainty is a most desirable attribute of the criminal and civil law alike. Nevertheless, there are matters which must ultimately depend on the opinion of a jury. In the civil law I will take an example which comes, perhaps, nearest to the criminal law—the tort of negligence. It is for a jury to decide not only whether the defendant has committed the act complained of but whether, in doing it, he has fallen short of the standard of care which the circumstances require. Till their verdict is given, it is uncertain what the law requires. . . . There are still, as has recently been said, 'unravished remnants of the common law'. So, in the case of a charge of conspiracy to corrupt public morals, the uncertainty that necessarily arises from the vagueness of general words can only be resolved by the opinion of twelve chosen men and women. I am content to leave it to them.

The appeal . . . should, in my opinion, be dismissed."

Lord Tucker.—

"My Lords, counsel for the Crown supported the conviction and the judgment of the Court of Criminal Appeal on count 1 of the present indictment on two alternative grounds, (i) that conduct calculated and intended to corrupt public morals is indictable as a substantive offence and consequently a conspiracy to this end is indictable as a conspiracy to commit a criminal offence, alternatively (ii) a conspiracy to corrupt morals is indictable as a conspiracy to commit a wrongful act which is calculated to cause public injury. The Court of Criminal Appeal dismissed the appeal on the ground that the case fell well within the first of these propositions. I have, I hope, sufficiently indicated that I prefer to base my decision [dismissing the appeal] on the second, but, in so saying, I must not be taken as rejecting the first."

APPEAL DISMISSED.[1]

---

[1] Lord Reid dissented essentially on the ground that the creation of new heads of public policy is for Parliament.

KNULLER (PUBLISHING, PRINTING AND PROMOTIONS), LTD. v. DIRECTOR OF PUBLIC PROSECUTIONS

[1972] 2 All E.R. 898

(1) *Notwithstanding the legalisation by the Sexual Offences Act 1967 of homosexual practices in private between consenting males above the age of 21, agreements to encourage such practices continue to be conspiracies to corrupt public morals.*

(2) *There is such an offence as a conspiracy to outrage public decency, although it had not been committed on the facts of this case.*

The accused were concerned in the publication of a magazine which contained advertisements designed to attract readers who were prepared to indulge in homosexual practices with the advertisers. They were charged on an indictment containing two counts; one for a conspiracy to corrupt public morals, and the other for a conspiracy to outrage public decency. The prosecution made no point of the fact that the magazine might be read by males under the age of 21. The accused were convicted on both counts. They appealed unsuccessfully to the Court of Appeal. On their appeal to the House of Lords a majority of four to one upheld the conviction on the first count, but, though for differing reasons, a majority of three to two was for quashing the conviction on the second count.[1]

Extracts from the Speeches of the House of Lords

Lord Reid.—

"It was decided by this House in *Shaw* v. *Director of Public Prosecutions*[2] that conspiracy to corrupt public morals is a crime known to the law of England. So if the appellants are to succeed on this count, either this House must reverse that decision or there must be sufficient grounds for distinguishing this case. The appellants' main argument is that we should reconsider that decision; alternatively they submit that it can and should be distinguished.

I dissented in *Shaw's* case[2]. On reconsideration I still think that the decision was wrong and I see no reason to alter

---

[1] See note at end of case.
[2] [1962] A.C. 220; [1961] 2 All E.R. 446; p. 347, *supra*.

anything which I said in my speech. But it does not follow that I should now support a motion to reconsider the decision. I have said more than once in recent cases that our change of practice in no longer regarding previous decisions of this House as absolutely binding does not mean that whenever we think that a previous decision was wrong we should reverse it. In the general interest of certainty in the law we must be sure that there is some very good reason before we so act. We were informed that there had been at least 30 and probably many more convictions of this new crime in the ten years which have elapsed since *Shaw's* case was decided, and it does not appear that there has been manifest injustice or that any attempt has been made to widen the scope of the new crime. I do not regard our refusal to reconsider *Shaw's* case as in any way justifying any attempt to widen the scope of the decision and I would oppose any attempt to do so. But I think that however wrong or anomalous the decision may be it must stand and apply to cases reasonably analogous unless or until it is altered by Parliament.

I hold that opinion the more strongly in this case by reason of the nature of the subject-matter we are dealing with. I said in *Shaw's* case[1] and I repeat that Parliament and Parliament alone is the proper authority to change the law with regard to the punishment of immoral acts. Rightly or wrongly the law was determined by the decision in *Shaw's* case. Any alteration of the law as so determined must in my view be left to Parliament. . . .

Although I would not support reconsidering *Shaw's* case I think that we ought to clarify one or two matters. In the first place conspiracy to corrupt public morals is something of a misnomer. It really means to corrupt the morals of such members of the public as may be influenced by the matter published by the accused.

Next I think that the meaning of the word 'corrupt' requires some clarification. One of my objections to the *Shaw* decision is that it leaves too much to the jury. I recognise that in the end it must be for the jury to say whether the matter published is likely to lead to corruption. But juries, unlike judges, are not expected to be experts in the use of the English language and I think that they ought to be given some assistance. In *Shaw's* case a direction was upheld in which the trial judge said:

---

[1] *Ibid.*, at p. 457.

'And, really, the meaning of debauched and corrupt is
again, just as the meaning of the word induce is, essentially
a matter for you. After all the arguments, I wonder really
whether it means in this case and in this context much
more than to lead astray morally.'
I cannot agree that that is right. 'Corrupt' is a strong word
and the jury ought to be reminded of that, as they were in the
present case. The Obscene Publications Act 1959 appears to
use the words 'deprave' and 'corrupt' as synonymous, as I
think they are. We may regret that we live in a permissive
society but I doubt whether even the most staunch defender
of a better age would maintain that all or even most of those
who have at one time or in one way or another been led astray
morally have thereby become depraved or corrupt. I think
that the jury should be told in one way or another that
although in the end the question whether a matter is corrupt
is for them, they should keep in mind current standards of
ordinary decent people.

I can now turn to the appellant's second argument. They
say that homosexual acts between adult males in private are
now lawful so it is unreasonable and cannot be the law that
other persons are guilty of an offence if they merely put in
touch with one another two males who wish to indulge in
such acts. There is a material difference between merely
exempting certain conduct from criminal penalties and
making it lawful in the full sense. Prostitution and gaming
afford examples of this difference. So we must examine the
provisions of the Sexual Offences Act 1967 to see just how
far it altered the old law. It enables subject to limitation that
a homosexual act in private shall not be an offence but goes
no further than that. Section 4 shows that procuring is still
a serious offence and it would seem that some of the facts in
this case might have supported a charge under that section.

I find nothing in the Act to indicate that Parliament
thought or intended to lay down that indulgence in these
practices is not corrupting. I read the Act as saying that,
even though it may be corrupting, if people choose to
corrupt themselves in this way that is their affair and the law
will not interfere. But no licence is given to others to encourage the practice. So if one accepts *Shaw's* case as rightly
decided it must be left to each jury to decide in the circumstances of each case whether people were likely to be
corrupted. . . .

The second count is conspiracy to outrage public
decency. . . .

To my mind questions of public policy of the utmost importance are at stake here.

I think that the objections to the creation of this generalised offence are similar in character to but even greater than the objections to the generalised offence of conspiracy to corrupt public morals. In upholding the decision in *Shaw's* case we are, in my view, in no way affirming or lending any support to the doctrine that the courts still have some general or residual power either to create new offences or so to widen existing offences as to make punishable conduct of a type hitherto not subject to punishment. Apart from some statutory offences of limited application, there appears to be neither precedent nor authority of any kind for punishing the publication of written or printed matter on the ground that it is indecent as distinct from being obscene."

Lord Morris of Borth-y-Gest.—

"If by agreement it was arranged to insert advertisements by married people proclaiming themselves to be such and to be desirous of meeting someone of the opposite sex with a view to clandestine sexual association, would it be a justification to say that adultery is not of itself a criminal offence? A person who, as a result of reading the Ladies' Directory, decided to resort to a prostitute was committing no legal offence; but it was open to a jury to hold that those who conspired to insert the advertisements did so with the intention of corrupting the morals of those who read the advertisements. So in the present case it was open to the jury to hold that there was an intention to corrupt. . . .

It was suggested and it has been suggested that there is an element of uncertainty which attaches to the offence of conspiracy to corrupt public morals. It is said that the rules of law ought to be precise so that a person will know the exact consequences of all his actions and so that he can regulate his conduct with complete assurance. This, however, is not possible under any system of law. . . . Those who skate on thin ice can hardly expect to find a sign which will denote the precise spot where they may fall in. . . .

It has sometimes been asserted that in his speech in *Shaw's* case[1] Lord Simonds was proclaiming that the court has power to extend the sphere of the law by devising new extensions of the operation of the criminal law; his use of the

---

[1] [1962] A.C. 220; [1961] 2 All E.R. 446; p. 347, *supra*.

words 'residual power' is pointed to as a basis of what is asserted. In my view, the sustained reasoning of his speech refutes the assertion. . . . He held, in agreement with Lord Tucker, that the offence of conspiracy to corrupt public morals was an offence known to the common law. He then proceeded to demonstrate that if offending acts do reveal a conspiracy to corrupt public morals it is not to be said that no offence has been committed merely because the particular acts are novel or unprepared for or are unprecedented. . . .

In regard to count 2 the learned judge at the trial reminded the jury of all that he had said as to the nature of a conspiracy and told them that count 2 alleged an offence quite separate and distinct from that alleged in count 1. He told them that they had to be satisfied that the advertisements were lewd, disgusting and offensive and that the particular accused person was a party to an agreement to outrage public decency. He carefully reminded them that public feeling varies from one generation to another so that what would outrage public decency in one generation would pass unnoticed in the next; so the jury had to be satisfied that the advertisements did outrage public decency and that there was an agreement to outrage public decency. The matter was I think clearly and sufficiently submitted to the jury for their consideration and their decision.''

Lord Simon of Glaisdale.—

"It was argued for the Crown that it was immaterial whether or not the alleged outrage to decency took place in public, provided that the sense of decency of the public or a substantial section of the public was outraged. But this seems to me to be contrary to many of the authorities which the Crown itself relied on to establish the generic offence [a conspiracy to outrage public decency]. The authorities establish that the word 'public' has a different connotation in the respective offences of conspiracy to corrupt public morals and conduct calculated to, or conspiracy to, outrage public decency. In the first it refers to certain fundamental rules regarded as essential social control which yet lacks the force of law, in other words, when applicable to individuals 'public' refers to persons in society. In the latter offences, however, 'public' refers to places in which the offence is committed. This is borne out . . . by what is presumably the purpose of the legal rule—namely, that reasonable people may venture out in public without the risk of outrage to certain minimal accepted standards of decency. On the other hand, I do not think that it would necessarily negative the offence that the act or exhibit is superficially hid from view, if the public is expressly or impliedly invited to penetrate the cover . . . .

There are other features of the offence which should, in my view, be brought to the notice of the jury. It should be emphasised that 'outrage', like 'corrupt', is a very strong word. 'Outraging public decency' goes considerably beyond offending the susceptibilities of, or even shocking, reasonable people. Moreover the offence is, in my view, concerned with recognising minimum standards of decency, which are likely to vary from time to time. Finally, notwithstanding that 'public' in the offence is used in a locative sense, public decency must be viewed as a whole; and I think the jury should be invited, where appropriate, to remember that we live in a plural society, with a tradition of tolerance towards minorities, and that this atmosphere of toleration is itself part of public decency.

The Court of Appeal said of the direction on count 2 that it might be that it was not wholly satisfactory. I would myself go further. I regard it as essential that the jury should be carefully directed on the lines that I have ventured to suggest, on the proper approach to the meaning of 'decency' and 'outrage' and the element of publicity required to constitute the offence. The summing-up was generally a careful and fair one, but I think it was defective in these regards; and I therefore do not think it would be safe to allow the conviction on count 2 to stand."

APPEAL ALLOWED IN PART.

Note

Lord Diplock dissented on count 1 on the ground that the House had been mistaken in holding in *Shaw's* case that there was a general offence of conspiracy to corrupt public morals and the mistake should now be corrected. Lord Diplock agreed with Lord Reid on count 2 that there is no such general offence as a conspiracy to outrage public decency; but Lords Morris, Simon and Kilbrandon held that there is such an offence, although the two latter held that the jury had been misdirected and accordingly concurred in allowing the appeal on count 2.

The opinion was reiterated in all the speeches that the courts have no general or residual common law power to create new offences.

Lords Morris, Simon and Kilbrandon took the view that

Parliament had recognised the existence of the offence of conspiracy to corrupt public morals in s. 2(4) of the Theatres Act 1968, which provides that no person shall be proceeded against at common law for the offence of conspiring to corrupt public morals in respect of an agreement to present a play.

Reference was made in some of the speeches to an undertaking given in the House of Commons on July 3, 1964 that prosecutions for a conspiracy to corrupt public morals would not be initiated to circumvent the provision of s. 2(4) of the Obscene Publications Act 1959, which prohibits proceedings at common law where it is of the essence of the offence that an article was obscene, i.e. calculated to deprave or corrupt the morals of those likely to read it. The importance of the provision lies in the availability of the defence of public good under s. 4(1) of the 1959 Act in prosecutions thereunder; but Lord Kilbrandon took the view that the conspiracy in the *Knuller* case was to promote homosexual associations rather than to publish pornography.

DIRECTOR OF PUBLIC PROSECUTIONS v. WITHERS

[1974] 3 All E.R. 984

Conspiracy to effect a public mischief, in the sense of an agreement to do an act, which, although not unlawful in itself, is extremely injurious to the public, is not as such an offence known to the law.

Withers and the other appellants ran an investigation agency. In order to make reports for clients about the status and financial standing of third parties the appellants obtained confidential information from banks, building societies, government departments and local authorities by telling lies. The appellants were charged on two counts, each of which charged them with conspiracy to effect a public mischief by unlawfully obtaining private and confidential information by false representations that they were persons authorised to receive such information. The first count related to obtaining such information from the officials of certain banks and building societies and the second to obtaining such information from officers of government departments and local authorities. The appellants were convicted on both counts and appealed unsuccessfully to the Court of Appeal, but that

Court certified that the following point of law of general public importance was involved:

"Whether the learned judge was right in law in stating that if the jury were sure that one of the [appellants] agreed with another appellant to do wilfully deceitful acts themselves, or agreed to procure others to do such wilfully deceitful acts for them, and . . . that such wilfully deceitful acts would cause extreme injury to the general well-being of the community as a whole, such persons who so agreed would be guilty of the offence of conspiring to effect a public mischief."

The appellants appealed to the House of Lords.

Extracts from the Speeches of the House of Lords

Viscount Dilhorne.—

"What conclusions are to be drawn from the cases to which I have referred? I think they are these: (1) There is no separate and distinct class of criminal conspiracy called conspiracy to effect a public mischief. (2) That description has in the past been applied to a number of cases which might have been regarded as coming within well-known heads of conspiracy, e.g., conspiracy to defraud, to pervert the course of justice, etc. . . . (4) The judges have no power to create new offences. (5) Where a charge of conspiracy to effect a public mischief has been preferred, the question to be considered is whether the object or means of the conspiracy are in substance of such a quality or kind as has already been recognised by the law as criminal. (6) If they are, then one has to go on to consider, on an appeal, whether the course the trial took in consequence of the reference to public mischief was such as to vitiate the conviction.

Relating these conclusions to this appeal, it may be that, if the references to public mischief had been omitted from counts 1 and 2 of the indictment, the case might have proceeded on the basis that the conspiracy charged in each count was conspiracy to defraud, and if the accused had been then convicted, that by applying the reasoning of Lord Radcliffe in *Welham* v. *Director of Public Prosecutions*[1] and the dictum of Lord Tucker in *Board of Trade* v. *Owen*[2] . . . the convictions could have been upheld. . . .

---

[1] [1961] A.C. 103, at p. 123; [1960] 1 All E.R. 805, at p. 807.
[2] [1957] A.C., at p. 621; [1957] 1 All E.R., at p. 412.

In my opinion, it cannot be said in this case as it was in *Bailey*[1] that the reference to public mischief did not vitiate the trial. . . . If the trial had proceeded on the basis that the counts charged conspiracy to defraud, then the summing-up would have been very different. To uphold the convictions now by reliance on the Criminal Appeal Act 1968 would be to hold that no miscarriage of justice actually occurred if the appellants ought to have been convicted on a charge which was not made against them or considered at the trial at which they had been tried on another charge. So to hold would, in my opinion, amount to a miscarriage of justice. Recourse cannot, therefore, be had to the 1968 Act to uphold these convictions."

Lord Simon of Glaisdale.—

[Having reviewed a number of cases continued:]

"On this state of the authorities, and on principle, I think that the better view is that English law knows no offence of conduct by an individual effecting or tending to effect a public mischief. . . . [This] makes it incumbent to consider whether a conspiracy to commit a public mischief is a crime which is to be recognised as part of the law. . . .

All the objections which have been made to recognising a crime of conduct of an individual causing or tending to cause a public mischief seem to me to be equally cogent as regards conspiracy to effect a public mischief. In effect the concept enjoins an English criminal court to act like a 'people's court' in a totalitarian regime, and to declare punishable and to punish conduct held at large to be 'extremely injurious to the public'. No doubt the word 'extremely' imposes some restraint, and the matter is in general finally for the jury. But the objection remains. . . . Does, then, the fact that in a conspiracy more than one person is concerned overcome or outweigh the objection?

This was undoubtedly a potent factor in many of the older cases of conspiracy. It was considered, for example, of conspiracy to cheat that a potential victim might be expected to look after himself against the machinations of one where he would be helpless against many. And in the case of conspiracy to trespass (however limited by *Kamara* v. *Director of Public Prosecutions*[2]), numbers might make all the practical difference. . . . Although some conduct which

---

[1] [1956] N.I. 15.
[2] [1974] A.C. 104; [1973] 2 All E.R. 1242; p. 344, *supra*.

causes or tends to cause extreme injury to the public may be more heinous and more damaging when committed by numbers, not all such conduct will be so; nor may some such conduct when committed by numbers be necessarily more heinous and damaging than other such conduct when committed by an individual.

If, therefore, the matter fell purely for decision on principle I would hold that a crime of conspiracy to effect a public mischief is so contrary to the spirit of our law and so devoid of juridical cogency that it should not be countenanced. But there is considerable authority supporting the existence of such a crime; and your Lordships are no more free to abrogate an offence known to the law than to create an offence previously unknown: both tasks are for the legislature as whole. . . .

The principal constraint on your Lordships' freedom in this branch of the law is constituted by Lord Tucker's speech in *Shaw* v. *Director of Public Prosecutions*,[1] with which the rest of the majority agreed. It is necessary to examine carefully his ratio decidendi. There were three avenues by any one of which he could have reached his conclusion: (a) that the law recognised an offence when committed by an individual of corrupting public morals, so that an agreement to corrupt public morals is a criminal conspiracy as an agreement to commit a crime; (b) that an examination of the authorities shows that the law has consistently recognised an offence of conspiracy to corrupt public morals; (c) that a conspiracy to corrupt public morals is a sub-genus of the genus conspiracy to commit a public mischief, which the law recognises. Lord Tucker expressly did not reject (a) and undoubtedly relied on (c). He . . . said:[2] 'Can it be doubted that a conspiracy to corrupt public morals is a conspiracy to effect a public mischief?' [His Lordship then quoted the extract from Lord Tucker's speech which is set out at p. 348, *supra*, and continued:] But he had earlier demonstrated a continuous history of the offence of conspiracy to corrupt public morals and had given reasons for recognising its continued existence.[3] . . . In other words, I think that in stating his conclusion Lord Tucker was running together two *rationes decidendi* (what I have signified by (b) and (c)), while not rejecting a third, (a).

If that is right, this is one of those cases where your

---

[1] [1962] A.C. 220; [1961] 2 All E.R. 446; p. 347, *supra*.
[2] [1962] A.C., at p. 285; [1961] 2 All E.R., at p. 463.
[3] [1962] A.C., at pp. 285–289; [1961] 2 All E.R., at p. 463–466.

Lordships have, in my respectful submission, a genuine choice as to which rule of law to apply. If one of Lord Tucker's rationes decidendi, (c), is applied in accordance with *Mirehouse* v. *Rennell*,[1] it leads to the conclusion that the law recognises a generic offence of conspiracy to effect a public mischief, that being descriptive of an agreement to perpetrate conduct which is extremely injurious to the public. But your Lordships would be then accepting a juridical situation the practical effect of which is to permit the forensic creation of new criminal offences or the forensic extension of the ambit of old ones, contrary to what was plainly endorsed in *Knuller's* case.[2] Although, no doubt, the line between, on the one hand, applying to new circumstances a rule which defines an existing offence and, on the other, the extension of an existing offence, is one which is often difficult to draw, I have no doubt that the recognition of the generic offence of conspiracy to effect a public mischief would give an uncontrollable dynamism to this branch of the law. This very case illustrates how the generic offence could penetrate into a sphere (privacy) of great delicacy and controversy and where Parliament has assumed cognisance and as yet taken no action. So, although I think that the learned judge was, on the authorities, bound to direct the jury as he did, and the Court of Appeal to uphold the conviction, your Lordships are, in my judgment, free to declare that no such generic offence as conspiracy to effect a public mischief is known to our law, and should do so . . . ."

APPEALS ALLOWED.

R. v. McDONNELL
[1966] 1 All E.R. 193

The one man responsible for the affairs of a limited company cannot be convicted of conspiring with that company.

McDonnell was charged with conspiracy to defraud. The other party to the alleged conspiracy was a limited company for whose affairs McDonnell was in fact solely responsible as director. On a motion to quash the indictment it was held by Nield, J., that the charge would not lie.

[1] (1833), 1 Cl. & Fin. 527.
[2] P. 349, *supra*.

Extracts from the Judgment

Nield, J.—

"I turn to the last of these points, which is much the most substantial, namely the submission by counsel for the defendant that in the particular circumstances of this case there can be no conspiracy, for the reason that there are not two persons and two minds involved. . . . I have reached the conclusion that I should express the opinion or anticipatory ruling that these charges of conspiracy cannot be sustained on the footing that in the particular circumstances here, where the sole responsible person in the company is the defendant himself, it would not be right to say that there were two persons or two minds. If it were otherwise, I feel that it would offend against the basic concept of a conspiracy, namely an agreement of two or more to do an unlawful act, and I think that it would be artificial to take the view that each of these companies can be regarded as a separate person or a separate mind, in view of the admitted fact that this defendant acts alone so far as these companies are concerned.

It is interesting to observe that in the Canadian case[1] an earlier edition of Mr. Glanville Williams' book was referred to. I have been shown the later edition, and the learned author there expresses under the heading: 'Crimes for which a corporation can be convicted', this opinion:[2]

'Probably (thereby being cautious) a company and its director cannot be convicted of conspiracy when the only human being who broke the law or intended to do so was the one director.' "

MOTION UPHELD.

Note on the reform of the law of conspiracy

Following consultation on its Working Papers on the subject,[3] the Law Commission published its report on conspiracy, *Criminal Law: Report on Conspiracy and Criminal Law Reform*, in March 1976. The Report contained a draft Bill which, with some amendments, was introduced into the House of Lords in November 1976 as part of the Criminal Law Bill. The Bill also gives effect

---

[1] R. v. *Electrical Contractors Assocn. of Ontario and Dent*, [1961] O.R. 265.

[2] *Criminal Law: The General Part* (2nd Edn., 1961) p. 861.

[3] Law Commission Working Papers, No. 50, 54, 57 and 63.

to most of the recommendations of the James Committee on the distribution of criminal offences between the Crown Court and magistrates' courts.[1]

The Law Commission Report endorsed the provisional proposal in Working Paper No. 50 that only conspiracy to commit an offence should be criminal and clause 1 of the Bill provides a statutory offence to this effect. The common law offence of conspiracy, which, as has been seen, extends to agreements for purposes which do not necessarily involve the commission of an offence, e.g. to commit a tort, is to be abolished by clause 5(1). One exception to this abolition was proposed by the Law Commission; pending the conclusion of the Law Commission's consultation, and the finalisation of its views, on offences involving fraud, the common law offence of conspiracy to cheat and defraud is temporarily kept in being. However, the Criminal Law Bill provides a second exception, conspiracy to corrupt public morals or to outrage public decency. This exception is discussed at p. 367, *infra*.

Clauses in other parts of the Bill, *inter alia*, abolish the common law offences of forcible entry and detainer and repeal the Forcible Entry Acts 1381–1623. The Bill provides new substantive offences which will fill the gaps, where desirable, left by the disappearance of these offences and of conspiracy to trespass.

The contents of the Criminal Law Bill, which relate to conspiracy are set out below. When this edition went to press the Bill had just passed the Report stage in the House of Lords and is set out as it stood at that time. If the Criminal Law Bill is enacted it will come into force on such day or days as the Secretary of State appoints.

CRIMINAL LAW BILL

Part I

Conspiracy

Clause 1.—The offence of conspiracy
(1) Subject to the following provisions of this Part of this Act, if a person agrees with any other person or persons that a course of conduct shall be pursued which will necessarily amount to or involve the commission of any offence or offences by one or more of the parties to the agreement if

---

[1] Cross and Jones, *Introduction to Criminal Law*, 8th ed., Appendix.

the agreement is carried out in accordance with their intentions, he is guilty of conspiracy in relation to the offence or offences in question.[1]

(2) Where in pursuance of any agreement the acts in question in relation to any offence are to be done in contemplation or furtherance of a trade dispute (within the meaning of the Trade Union and Labour Relations Act 1974) that offence shall be disregarded for the purposes of subsection (1) above provided that it is a summary offence for which imprisonment may not be imposed otherwise than by way of committal in default of payment of a fine or for want of sufficient distress to satisfy a fine.

(3) In this part of this Act "offence" means an offence triable in England and Wales, except that it includes murder notwithstanding that the murder in question would not be so triable if committed in accordance with the intentions of the parties to the agreement.

Clause 2.—Exemptions from liability for conspiracy

(1) A person shall not by virtue of section 1 above be guilty of conspiracy in relation to any offence if he is an intended victim of that offence.

(2) A person shall not by virtue of section 1 above be guilty of conspiracy in relation to any offence or offences if the only other person or persons with whom he agrees are (both initially and at all times during the currency of the agreement) persons of any one or more of the following descriptions, that is to say—

(*a*) his spouse;
(*b*) a person under the age of criminal responsibility; and
(*c*) an intended victim of that offence or of each of those offences.

(3) A person is under the age of criminal responsibility for the purposes of subsection (2) (*b*) so long as it is conclusively presumed, by virtue of section 50 of the Children and Young Persons Act 1933,[2] that he cannot be guilty of any offence.

---

[1] By clause 3 conspiracies to commit an indictable offence will be subject *generally* to the same maximum punishment as the indictable offence or one year's imprisonment whichever is greater. Conspiracy to commit a summary offence will be punishable *generally* with a maximum of one year's imprisonment.

[2] P. 72, *supra.*

Clause 4.—Restrictions on the institution of proceedings for conspiracy

(1) Proceedings under section 1 above for conspiracy in relation to any offence or offences shall not be instituted against any person except by or with the consent of the Director of Public Prosecutions if the offence or (as the case may be) each of the offences in question is a summary offence.

(2) Any prohibition by or under any enactment on the institution of proceedings for any offence otherwise than by, or on behalf of or with the consent of, the Director of Public Prosecutions or any other person shall apply also in relation to proceedings under section 1 above for conspiracy in relation to that offence.

(3) Where—

(a) an offence has been committed in pursuance of any agreement; and

(b) proceedings may not be instituted for that offence because any time limit applicable to the institution of any such proceedings has expired,

proceedings under section 1 above for conspiracy in relation to that offence shall not be instituted against any person on the basis of that agreement.

Clause 5.—Abolition, savings, consequential amendment and repeals

(1) Subject to the following provisions of this section, the offence of conspiracy at common law is hereby abolished.

(2) Subsection (1) above shall not affect the offence of conspiracy at common law so far as relates to conspiracy to cheat and defraud, and section 1 above shall not apply in any case where the agreement in question amounts to a conspiracy to cheat and defraud at common law.

(3) Subsection (1) above shall not affect the offence of conspiracy at common law if and in so far as it may be committed by entering into an agreement to engage in conduct which—

(a) tends to corrupt public morals or outrages public decency; but

(b) would not amount to or involve the commission of an offence if carried out by a single person otherwise than in pursuance of an agreement.

(4) Subsection (1) above shall not affect—

(*a*) any proceedings commenced before the time when this Part of this Act comes into force;

(*b*) any proceedings commenced after that time against a person charged with the same conspiracy as that in issue in any proceedings commenced before that time; or

(*c*) any proceedings commenced after that time in respect of a trespass committed before that time;

but a person convicted of conspiracy to trespass in any proceedings brought by virtue of paragraph (*c*) above shall not in respect of that conviction be liable to imprisonment for a term exceeding one year.

(5) Sections 1 and 2 above shall apply to things done before as well as to things done after the time when this Part of this Act comes into force, but in the application of section 3 above to a case where the agreement in question was entered into before that time—

(*a*) subsection (2) shall be read without the reference to murder in paragraph (*a*); and

(*b*) any murder intended under the agreement shall be treated as an indictable offence for which a maximum term of imprisonment on conviction on indictment of ten years is provided.

(6) The rules laid down by sections 1 and 2 above shall apply for determining whether a person is guilty of an offence of conspiracy under any enactment other than section 1 above, but conduct which is an offence under any such other enactment shall not also be an offence under section 1 above.

(7) The fact that the person or persons who, so far as appears from the indictment on which any person has been convicted of conspiracy, were the only other parties to the agreement on which his conviction was based have been acquitted of conspiracy by reference to that agreement (whether after being tried with the person convicted or separately) shall not be a ground for quashing his conviction unless under all the circumstances of the case his conviction is inconsistent with the acquittal of the other person or persons in question.

(8) Any rule of law or practice inconsistent with the provisions of subsection (7) above is hereby abolished.

. . . .

Comment on the Conspiracy Provisions in the Criminal Law Bill

Clause 1

This clause gives effect to the central recommendations of Part I of the Law Commission's Report that there should be a statutory offence of conspiracy which would be committed only when there was an agreement to commit a criminal offence.

Subsection (1) requires that the parties must agree that a course of conduct shall be pursued which if carried out will *necessarily* amount to an offence; so, for example, an agreement to beat up a nightwatchman will be a conspiracy to cause grievous bodily harm and not a conspiracy to murder, notwithstanding that, if the agreement were carried out and the watchman died, there would be an offence of murder.

The wording of the subsection is such that a person will not be guilty of conspiracy unless he and at least one other party to the agreement intend that the actual act or omission involved in the *actus reus* of the substantive offence should be performed, intend to cause any result required for the completion of that *actus reus* and have any other *mens rea* required for the substantive offence. However, as the Bill stands, a person, who agrees with another to pursue a course of conduct which in fact constitutes the *actus reus* of an offence which is one of strict liability as to a particular fact, will be guilty of that offence even though he was ignorant of that fact. In other words, the Bill would make conspiracy to commit a strict liability offence itself a strict liability offence, a situation which was rejected in the case of the common law offence of conspiracy by the House of Lords in *Churchill* v. *Walton*.[1]

The Bill originally contained a provision whose effect would have been to avoid the above result. However, it was regarded as over-elaborate by the House of Lords and was withdrawn. It is anticipated that a new subsection will be inserted into clause 1 at a later stage in Parliament which will provide that, where liability for any offence may be incurred without knowledge on the part of the person committing it of any particular fact which is an element of the offence, a person shall nevertheless not be guilty of conspiracy in relation to that offence unless he and at least one other party to the agreement intend or know that that fact shall or will exist when the conduct constituting the offence is to take place.[2] If such a provision is inserted its effect will be that, while a person may be guilty of taking an unmarried girl

---

[1] [1967] 2 A.C. 224.
[2] H. L. Deb., 5th Ser., Vol. 380, 539–556.

under the age of 16 out of the possession of her parents even though he did not know that she was under 16, it will not be possible to convict two persons of conspiracy to commit such an offence without showing that they knew she was under 16. In substance this would put into statutory form the decision in *Churchill* v. *Walton.*

Subsection (2) re-enacts the provisions of s. 3 of the Conspiracy and Protection of Property Act 1875, which is now repealed by clause 5(10).

The effect of the first part of subs. (3) is to provide a general rule that, where there is an agreement to pursue a course of conduct outside England and Wales, this will be conspiracy only where that conduct would constitute an offence triable in England and Wales. This is in effect the common law position as stated in *Board of Trade* v. *Owen.*[1] The subsection goes on to provide the only exception to the general rule. It relates to conspiracy to murder, which under section 4 of the Offences against the Person Act 1861 is an offence even where the murder is to be committed abroad by a person who is not a British subject. This section is repealed in so far as it relates to conspiracy to murder by clause 5(9), but its effect is preserved by the present subsection.

Clause 2

As originally drafted, subsection (1) also provided that a person who himself would not be guilty of the offence it was conspired to commit, by reason of his not being within the description of person capable of committing the offence or by virtue of any exemption from prosecution, could not be guilty of conspiracy to commit that offence. This provision, which was rejected by the House of Lords, would have reversed the effect of the decision in *Whitchurch.*[2] In that case a woman who was not pregnant, was found guilty of conspiracy with a man to procure her miscarriage contrary to s. 58 of the Offences against the Person Act 1861, although that section requires her to be with child before she can contravene it.

It is questionable whether it is right to preserve the old rule (as subs. (2)(*a*) does) that a husband and wife cannot be guilty of conspiring together unless a third person is also a party to the conspiracy. The rule, which is supposedly based on the fiction that husband and wife are one, is a historical anachronism in days of emancipation. By way of contrast, one spouse can be convicted as an accomplice to the other's crime or of inciting the other to commit a crime.

---

[1] [1957] A.C. 602, 634.
[2] (1890), 24 Q.B.D. 420.

Clause 5

Subject to subsection (4), subsection (1) abolishes the offence of conspiracy at common law save for:

(subs. (2)) conspiracy to cheat and defraud; see p. 345, *supra*;
(subs. (3)) "the offence of conspiracy at common law *if and in so far as* it may be committed by entering into an agreement to engage in conduct which—

    (*a*) tends to corrupt' public morals or outrages public decency; *but*

    (*b*) *would not amount to or involve the commission of an offence if carried out by a single person otherwise than in pursuance of an agreement.*"[1]

Subsection (3) raises the problem of whether substantive common law offences of corrupting public morals and outraging public decency exist. If they do, and the agreed conduct amounts to or involves such an offence, the conspiracy will be a statutory offence under clause 1 of the Bill and subsection (3) will be redundant. On the other hand, if corrupting public morals or outraging public decency or both, is not a substantive offence then, no statutory offence of conspiracy under clause 1 having been committed, it will be necessary to fall back on the common law offence of conspiracy. The same would be the case if, although corrupting public morals or outraging public decency is an offence, such corruption or outraging has a wider meaning when it is the object of a conspiracy charge, rather than a charge of the substantive offence, and the agreed conduct fell solely within that wider meaning.

In *Knuller* v. *Director of Public Prosecutions*[2] the majority of the House of Lords said (*obiter*) that there is a substantive common law offence of outraging public decency. Whether there is a substantive common law offence of corrupting public morals is more doubtful. The decision of the House of Lords in *Shaw* v. *Director of Public Prosecutions*[3] was based on the ground that conspiracy to corrupt public morals is indictable as a conspiracy to commit a wrongful act which is calculated to cause public injury. However, their Lordships did not expressly reject an alternative ground which had been argued by the prosecution, that conduct calculated and intended to corrupt public morals was a substantive common law offence and consequently a

---

[1] Italics supplied.
[2] [1973] A.C. 435; [1972] 2 All E.R. 898; p. 349, *supra*.
[3] [1962] A.C. 220; [1961] 2 All E.R. 446; p. 347, *supra*.

conspiracy for this end was a conspiracy to commit an offence. In fact, Lord Tucker said he was not to be taken as rejecting this alternative ground.[1]

In its Report the Law Commission recognised that offences of corrupting public morals and outraging public decency might well exist as substantive common law offences[2] and recommended the abolition of any such common law offences as may exist. Clause 22(1) of the *draft* Bill read:

> "Any distinct offence under the common law whose substance consists in the fact that conduct constituting the offence tends to corrupt, undermine or otherwise injure public morals or affronts or outrages public decency is hereby abolished."

Without prejudice to this subsection, clause 22 went on to abolish the common law offences of indecent exposure, public exhibition of indecent acts and things, obscene libel and keeping a disorderly house. Most of such conduct which might be prosecutable under these heads is already covered by statute. To fill the gap left by these abolitions, the Law Commission proposed a number of statutory offences, dealing with obscene films, obscene performances and displays and certain related matters.[3]

None of these abolitions or proposals have been incorporated into the Bill. The Government has decided not to introduce legislation on these matters at the same time as the other items in the Law Commission Report because this would have raised more fundamental questions about the general law of obscenity than it was the task of the Law Commission to examine. The Government considers that legislation on these questions should not be brought forward until a broader look has been taken at the subject and has therefore appointed a committee to undertake a fundamental review of the laws of obscenity, indecency and censorship.

This is why clause 5(3) is in the present Bill. Its inclusion would seem to be unfortunate partly because the Law Commission's proposals on obscenity and indecency seemed to be a sensible "middle-way" between the somewhat extreme opposing views held in this area and partly because of the uncertainty as to whether corruption of public morals or outraging of public decency are separate substantive offences and, if they are, what their ambit is.

---

[1] [1962] A.C., at p. 290; p. 348, *supra*.
[2] Para. 3.21–323.
[3] Para. 3.33–3.148.

Subsection (6) applies the rules in clauses 1 and 2 to any specific statutory offence of conspiracy (such as conspiracy to cause an explosion contrary to s. 3 of the Explosive Substances Act 1883, or conspiracy to commit an offence contrary to para. 1 of Part II of Sch. 5 of the Exchange Control Act 1947) for determining whether a person is guilty of any such conspiracy, and ensures that such a conspiracy is not also an offence under s. 1.

Subsections (7) and (8) provide that, for the future, the acquittal of one party to an agreement upon which a conviction for conspiracy is based shall not be a ground *in itself* for questioning the conviction of the other party to the agreement, unless under the circumstances of the case his conviction is inconsistent with the acquittal of the other person in question.

Clauses 6–12 contain provisions to fill the gaps left by the abolition of conspiracy to trespass (clause 5(1)) and the various offences of forcible entry and detainer (clause 13). The following new offences are created: violence for securing entry to any premises (clause 6); adverse occupation of residential premises (clause 7); trespassing with a weapon of offence (clause 8); trespassing on the premises of foreign missions, etc. (clause 9).

Attempt

Note

In Law Commission Working Paper No. 50, *Inchoate Offences*, a number of provisional proposals are made for the reform of the law relating to attempt. These are summarised in Cross and Jones, *Introduction to Criminal Law*, 8th ed., paras. 17.22–17.35.

R. v. MOHAN
[1975] 2 All E.R. 193

A person cannot be convicted of attempt unless he intends to bring about any consequence required by the definition of the offence attempted. Only a direct intention suffices for this purpose.

See p. 5, *supra*.

GARDNER v. AKEROYD

[1952] 2 Q.B. 743

On a charge of attempt, even where the offence attempted is one of strict liability, the accused cannot be convicted unless he knew of the existence of the circumstances required by the actus reus of the offence attempted.

Akeroyd was a butcher who employed M as an assistant. Ministry of Food inspectors visited the shop and found parcels of meat made up for delivery bearing price tickets, some of which disclosed prices in excess of the permitted maximum, contrary to art. 2 of the Meat (Prices) (Great Britain) Order 1951.[1] The parcels and tickets had been prepared by M in the absence of Akeroyd and without his knowledge. Both men were charged under reg. 90 (1) of the Defence Regulations which stated: "Any person who attempts to commit, or does any act preparatory to the commission of, an offence against any of these regulations shall be guilty of an offence against that regulation". M was convicted but the informations against Akeroyd were dismissed by the magistrates. The prosecutor appealed to the Divisional Court against these dismissals.

Extracts from the Judgments of the Divisional Court

Parker, J.—

". . . It is, I think, clear that, if the parcels had been delivered, the respondent would have committed the full offence of selling meat at a price exceeding the maximum price, contrary to art. 2 of the Order of 1951. The prohibition in that article is absolute, and it would have been no answer for the respondent to show that this had been done in his absence without his knowledge and intent. It is contended on behalf of the prosecutor that the words in reg. 90(1) equally import an absolute prohibition against doing an act preparatory to such a sale. In considering the validity of this contention it is important to consider the general rule referred to by Goddard, L.C.J., in *Harding v. Price.*[2] *Prima*

---

[1] The order was made under reg. 55AB of the Defence Regulations. Article 2 provided: "No person shall sell or buy by retail any meat at a price exceeding the maximum price applicable in accordance with the schedule to this order."

[2] [1948] 1 K.B. 695; [1948] 1 All E.R. 283; p. 55, *supra*.

facie, therefore, the respondent commits no offence unless *mens rea* is present. . . . So far as an attempt is concerned, knowledge and intent are clearly necessary. . . . If *mens rea* is necessary in the case of an attempt then it would have been all the more necessary in the case of the doing of an act preparatory to the commission of an offence. . . ."

Goddard, L.C.J. (who agreed)—

". . . Does, then, this doctrine of vicarious liability extend to an attempt? For, if it does not, it cannot apply to a mere preparatory act. . . . There is no case to be found in the books where it has been applied to an attempt, and, for my part, I refuse so to extend and apply it. . . ."

APPEAL DISMISSED.

Note

Contrast *R.* v. *Collier*[1] where Streatfeild, J., tacitly envisaged strict liability in attempts.

R. v. ROBINSON

[1915] 2 K.B. 342

There must be some act beyond mere preparation for the commission of an offence to constitute an attempt. Thus, faking a burglary in order to make a false insurance claim, which was never made, has been held not to constitute an attempt to obtain property by false pretences (deception).

Robinson was convicted of attempting to obtain money by false pretences.

The evidence was that he was a jeweller, and that his stock was insured at Lloyd's. He was found tied to a chair in his shop by a policeman who came from the street in response to his call for assistance. He stated that he had been attacked by thieves who had left him tied up on the previous night. The safe in which he placed his jewellery at night was empty. As the police were not satisfied with his story, he was taken to the police station, and the jewellery was found in a recess behind his safe. He later admitted that he had done what he did for the purpose of making a claim against Lloyd's on the insurance policy relating to his jewellery.

---

[1] [1960] Crim. L. R. 204.

He successfully appealed to the Court of Criminal Appeal against his conviction on the ground that it was not warranted by the evidence.

Extract from the Judgment of the Court of Criminal Appeal

Lord Reading, C.J.—

". . . It seems to the Court upon consideration of the authorities that there is no real difficulty in formulating the principle of law which is applicable to cases of this kind. A safe guide is to be found in the statement of the law which is laid down by Parke, B., in *R.* v. *Eagleton*[1]: 'The mere intention to commit a misdemeanour is not criminal. Some act is required, and we do not think that all acts towards committing a misdemeanour are indictable. Acts remotely leading towards the commission of the offence are not to be considered as attempts to commit it, but acts immediately connected with it are.' The difficulty lies in the application of that principle to the facts of the particular case. In some cases it is a difficult matter to determine whether an act is immediately or remotely connected with the offence of which it is alleged to be an attempt. In other cases the question is easier of solution, as for instance in *R.* v. *Button.*[2] There upon the evidence there was a false pretence made directly to the race authorities with the intent to make them part with the prize, and one which, but for the fact of the fraud being discovered, would necessarily have had that effect. In the present case the real difficulty lies in the fact that there is no evidence of any act done by the appellant in the nature of a false pretence which ever reached the minds of the underwriters, though they were the persons who were to be induced to part with the money. The evidence falls short of any communication of such a pretence to the underwriters or to any agent of theirs. The police were not acting on behalf of the underwriters. In truth what the appellant did was preparation for the commission of a crime, not a step in the commission of it. It consisted in the preparation of evidence which might indirectly induce the underwriters to pay; for if the police had made a report that a burglary had taken place,—and that was presumably what the appellant intended,—it may very well be that the underwriters would

---

[1] (1855), Dears C.C. 515, at p. 538.
[2] [1900] 2 Q.B. 597; p. 373, *infra*.

have paid without further inquiry. But there must be some act beyond mere preparation if a person is to be charged with an attempt. Applying the rule laid down by Parke, B., we think that the appellant's act was only remotely connected with the commission of the full offence, and not immediately connected with it. If we were to hold otherwise we should be going further than any case has ever yet gone, and should be opening the door to convictions for acts which are not at present criminal offences. We think the conviction must be quashed, not on the technical ground that no information or evidence as to the property lost was given to the underwriters as required by the policy but upon the broad ground that no communication of any kind of the false pretence was made to them."

APPEAL ALLOWED.[1]

R. v. BUTTON
[1900] 2 Q.B. 597

On a charge of attempt the accused may be convicted if he does acts sufficiently proximate to the commission of the substantive offence.

The appellant was charged with attempting to obtain money by false pretences. He was a good runner, and entered for two races at Lincoln in the name of Sims, a moderate runner. The appellant stated that he had not previously won a race which was untrue. In consequence he received a handicap in each of the races in which he ran and which he won. He did not claim the money prizes because questions were raised as to whether he really was Sims. In his summing up to the jury, the trial judge directed them to acquit if they were of opinion that the whole transaction was entered into by the appellant as a joke. The jury returned a verdict of guilty, and a case was reserved for the opinion of the Court for Crown Cases Reserved who held that the appellant had been rightly convicted.

---

[1] Presumably Robinson could now be convicted of an offence under s. 5 (2) of the Criminal Law Act 1967 (causing wasteful employment of the police).

Extracts from the Judgments of the Court for Crown Cases Reserved

Mathew, J.—

". . . It was also contended that his coming in first in the races was owing to his own good running; but it was also owing, in part at least, to the false pretences, for by means of the false pretences he obtained a longer start than he would have had if his true name and performances had been known. It is also said that some other act had to be done in order to make the offence complete, and that he could not rightly be convicted because it was not shewn that he had applied for the prizes, and that the criminal intention was exhausted. The argument is exceedingly subtle, but unsound. In fact, he was found out before he had the opportunity of applying for the prizes, as no doubt he otherwise would have done. The pretences which the prisoner made were not too remote, and the conviction was good."

Wright, J.—

". . . I am of the same opinion. If nothing more had been shewn than that the defendant had entered for the races in a false name, the case would have been different. If he did not run or claim the prize it would be difficult to say that there was an actual attempt to obtain it. But here in effect he did claim the prize."

CONVICTION AFFIRMED.

DAVEY v. LEE

[1967] 2 All E.R. 423

The actus reus *necessary to constitute an attempt to commit a crime is complete if the prisoner does an act as a step towards the commission of a specific crime, which is immediately and not merely remotely connected with the commission of it, and the doing of which cannot reasonably be regarded as having any other purpose than the commission of the specific crime.*

The accused were charged and convicted of attempting to steal metal from the Electricity Board. They ran away after being detected in endeavouring to break into the property of the Electricity Board near a point at which there was a copper store. They had cut the wire fence and were getting over it. There were other stores and buildings on the property, and it was argued on behalf of the accused that the acts proved against them were not sufficiently proximate to the stealing of the copper. The accused unsuccessfully appealed to Quarter Sessions and then by way of case stated to the Divisional Court.

Extract from the Judgments of the Divisional Court

Lord Parker, C.J.—

"The real point taken by counsel for the appellants is that an intention to steal is not sufficient to constitute an attempt, but that there must be acts which have moved further than being merely preparatory acts. What amounts to an attempt has been described variously in the authorities, and, for my part, I prefer to adopt the definition given in *Stephen's Digest of Criminal Law* (5th edn., 1894), art. 50, where it says that:

'An attempt to commit a crime is an act done with intent to commit that crime, and forming part of a series of acts which would constitute its actual commission if it were not interrupted.'

As a general statement that seems to me to be right, though it does not help to define the point of time at which the series of acts begins. That, as *Stephen* said, depends on the facts of each case. A helpful definition is given in para. 4104 in *Archbold's Pleading, Evidence and Practice* (36th edn.), where it is stated in this form:

'It is submitted that the *actus reus* necessary to constitute an attempt is complete if the prisoner does an act which is a step towards the commission of the specific crime, which is immediately and not merely remotely connected with the commission of it, and the doing of which cannot reasonably be regarded as having any other purpose than the commission of the specific crime.'

It seems to me that the facts of this case fully come within that test, and that the magistrates were undoubtedly right in the view they formed. I would dismiss this appeal."

APPEAL DISMISSED

JONES v. BROOKS
(1968), 52 Cr. App. Rep. 614

Where the act alleged to constitute an attempt to commit a crime is equivocal, evidence of the accused's intention is admissible in order to explain the object of the act.

Two brothers, Brooks, were charged with attempting to take and drive away a motor car. They were seen trying the doors of various cars, and subsequently admitted that they intended to drive home a car into which they could effect an entry. The magistrates dismissed the charge on the ground that the acts of the accused were equivocal, but they stated a case for the opinion of a Divisional Court which was of opinion that the magistrates should have convicted.

Extracts from the Judgments of the Divisional Court

Lord Parker, C.J.—

"Quite recently this Court in *Davey and Others* v. *Lee*[1], to which the magistrates were referred, adopted and approved the definition which appears in the current (36th) edition of *Archbold* in paragraph 4104 to this effect, that the *actus reus* necessary to constitute an attempt must be immediately, and not merely remotely, connected with the commission of the offence.

Ignoring entirely the expressed intention that these two respondents admitted, it is quite clear that the attempt to open this door was equivocal in the sense that it might have been a step towards the commission of a number of different crimes, not merely taking and driving away, but stealing either the car or some contents of the car, or indeed for the purely innocent purpose of going to sleep in it. If the expressed intention here is to be disregarded entirely, then quite clearly, in my judgment, the justices were right in saying that it had not been shown that the step in attempting to open the door was a step towards the commission of the specific crime of taking and driving away. It was submitted to the justices, and to this Court, that the expressed intention of these respondents does not enter into this matter at all except at a later stage in considering *mens rea*.

I am quite unable to accept that contention. Of course,

---

[1] [1968] 1 Q.B. 366; [1967] 2 All E.R. 423; p. 374, *supra.*

an expressed intention alone does not amount to an attempt; there must be an *actus reus* which is sufficiently proximate to the expressed intention. But that does not mean to say that the courts should disregard entirely as part of the surrounding circumstances and the evidence in the case the expressed intention of the respondents, both at the time and after the *actus reus*. It seems to me that that intention is relevant when the act concerned is equivocal in order to see towards what the act is directed. Once that is decided, then it still remains for the prosecution to show that the act itself is sufficiently proximate to amount to an attempt to commit the crime which it was the intention of the respondents to commit.

Looked at in this way, I have no doubt that the specific crime being isolated by the expressed intention as one to take and drive away, the insertion of the key into the door and seeking to open the door of the car was an act sufficiently proximate."

Bridge, J.—

"If the argument for the respondents is pressed to its logical conclusion, it would seem to lead to the result that there can never be *actus reus* sufficient to constitute an attempt to commit a crime unless the act itself viewed independently of any other circumstances in the case leads irresistibly to the conclusion that the person accused of the act had a guilty mind."

APPEAL ALLOWED. CASE REMITTED TO MAGISTRATES WITH DIRECTION TO CONVICT.

HOPE v. BROWN
[1954] 1 All E.R. 330

In assessing whether a proximate act has been committed it may be relevant to consider whether the accused has reached a stage where the chances of repentance are slight.

The accused was charged with an attempt to sell meat at a price in excess of that permitted by legislation which was then in force. He was a butcher and his refrigerator contained packets of meat bearing tickets specifying the contents and correct price. In the drawer there were found duplicate tickets specifying excessive prices and the accused admitted that he had instructed his employee to change the tickets before selling the meat to customers. The magistrates held that the accused was not guilty and the prosecutor unsuccessfully appealed by way of case stated to the Divisional Court.

Extract from the Judgments of the Divisional Court

Lord Goddard, C.J.—

"In the present case, what remained to be done before there could be an attempt was the affixing to the meat of the false tickets. Until that was done, in my opinion, the matter remained simply what I may call in embryo and in intention. The girl, no doubt, and not the respondent himself, would have affixed the tickets, but that was because she was instructed to do so. Her act would have been the act of the respondent, but until she had affixed the tickets, it seems to me that one cannot say that an offence was committed. The preparation of the false tickets and putting them in the drawer is too remote from the actual transaction which would be necessary to constitute the attempt. It is obvious that there might be a sudden change of heart, or an intervention by the master, or something of that sort, which would have prevented any attempt being made to sell this meat to the customers. The court has always said, in cases where it has been found that there has been an attempt, that the crime would have been committed but for the intervention of someone, but no crime would have been committed in the present case until the meat had been sold to the customer with the false ticket.

Therefore, I think the mere fact that the respondent prepared a false ticket is not enough. No doubt, this charge was preferred because of the decision in *Gardner* v. *Akeroyd*,[1] but that case turned on whether the proprietor of a butcher's business could be made vicariously liable for the act of an assistant in the shop which was preparatory to an illegal sale, but did not amount to an attempt, and we held that the doctrine of vicarious liability could not be so extended. Giving judgment in that case, I said: 'Now, applying the doctrine laid down in *R.* v. *Eagleton*,[2] I should have no hesitation in holding that the servant in this case was guilty of, and could properly have been charged with, an attempt as the facts proved were clearly immediately connected with what would have been a substantive offence had not the enforcement officer intervened before the goods had been

---

[1] [1952] 2 Q.B. 743; [1952] 2 All E.R. 306; p. 370, *supra*.
[2] (1855), Dears. C.C. 376.

actually sold.' But there the false tickets had already been affixed to the meat, while in the present case they had not. For these reasons I think the enforcement officers struck too soon. In my opinion, the justices came to a right decision in point of law and this appeal fails.''

APPEAL DISMISSED.

HAUGHTON v. SMITH
[1973] 3 All E.R. 1109

Assuming the proximity test is passed, a person whose attempt to commit an offence fails through ineptitude, inefficiency or insufficient means can be convicted of a criminal attempt; but a person who attempts to commit an offence which is physically impossible of achievement, whatever means are adopted, or who has, or could have, achieved his object in physical terms, mistakenly believing that this object amounts to an offence, is not guilty of a criminal attempt.

Corned beef was stolen in Liverpool. Later, a lorry travelling south was stopped by the police and found to be carrying the stolen beef. The police decided to set a trap for those who were to take delivery of the stolen beef. Accordingly three policemen accompanied the driver to his rendezvous where Smith, who was acting in concert with those who had planned to dispose of the beef, came on the scene and directed the lorry where to go. Smith was convicted of attempted handling of stolen goods but appealed successfully to the Court of Appeal. The prosecution's appeal to the House of Lords was dismissed.

Extracts from the Speeches of the House of Lords

Lord Hailsham of St. Marylebone, L.C.—
   "... The completed offence of handling was not charged since the prosecution were of the opinion that, by the time the goods were handled, they were no longer to be treated as stolen, because in the view taken, they were restored to lawful custody within the meaning of s. 24(3) of the Theft Act 1968[1] after the police had prepared the trap. Whether this was in truth so, is, I think, open to question, but it is

---
[1] See pp. 299–300, *supra.*

not possible to go back on this concession now, or even to enquire how wise it was to have made it. . . . At the trial, the respondent told a story which was not believed by the jury, but his counsel took advantage of the position in which the prosecution had placed itself to submit to the court the formidable argument that a man could hardly be convicted of attempting to handle stolen goods when the goods were not stolen at the time of the attempted handling. This submission failed before the trial judge, but it succeeded before the Court of Appeal[1] and, in my opinion, it succeeds here too.

. . . In my view, it is plain that, in order to constitute the offence of handling, the goods specified in the particulars of offence must not only be believed to be stolen, but actually continue to be stolen goods at the moment of handling. Once this is accepted as the true construction of the section, I do not think that it is possible to convert a completed act of handling, which is not itself criminal because it was not the handling of stolen goods, into a criminal act by the simple device of alleging that it was an attempt to handle stolen goods on the ground that at the time of handling the accused falsely believed them still to be stolen. In my opinion, this would be for the courts to manufacture a new criminal offence not authorised by the legislature.

This would be enough to decide the result of this appeal, but both counsel invited us to take a wider view of our obligations, and, once the question was discussed by the Court of Appeal in general terms and since I believe that the result of our decision is to overrule a number of decided cases, at least to some extent, I feel bound to accede to this invitation. . . .

From the . . . definitions [of attempt given in *R.* v. *Eagleton*[2] and *Davey* v. *Lee*[3]], I derive the following propositions relevant to the present appeal.

(1) There is a distinction between the intention to commit a crime and an attempt to commit it. Thus, in this case, the respondent intended to commit a crime under s. 22 of the Theft Act 1968. But this dishonest intention does not amount to an attempt. This distinction has not always been observed, in the discussion of cases on the law affecting attempts.

---

[1] [1973] 2 All E.R. 896.
[2] (1855), Dears. C.C. 515, at p. 538; [1843–60] All E.R. Rep. 363, at p. 367, *per* Parke, B.
[3] [1968] 1 Q.B. 366, at p. 370; [1967] 2 All E.R. 423, at p. 425, *per* Lord Parker, C.J. See p. 375, *supra*.

(2) In addition to the intention, or *mens rea*, there must be an overt act of such a kind that it is intended to form and does form part of a series of acts which would constitute the actual commission of the offence if it were not interrupted. In the present case the series of acts would never have constituted and in fact did not constitute an actual commission of the offence, because at the time of the handling the goods were no longer stolen goods.

(3) The act relied on as constituting the attempt must not be an act merely preparatory to commit the completed offence, but must bear a relationship to the completion of the offence referred to in *R*. v. *Eagleton*[1] as being 'proximate' to the completion of the offence and in *Davey* v. *Lee*[2] as being 'immediately and not merely remotely connected' with the completed offence. I do not think that the present case turns on the test of proximity at all, although, as will be seen many of the arguments canvassed involve a discussion of it. Obviously whenever the test of proximity becomes crucial in a particular case, difficult questions of fact and degree will arise which will call for considerable skill on the part of the trial judge in directing the jury. I do not think these problems arise here.

In his discussion in the present case of the legal implications of inchoate, but uncompleted, sequences of actions in cases which might or might not amount to criminal attempts, Lord Widgery, C.J., attempted to analyse them into two categories namely[3]:

'(1) . . . the type of case where the accused has embarked on a course of conduct which, if completed, will result in an offence but for some reason breaks off that course of conduct and never completes the action required to amount to the offence.'

In this first class of case, Lord Widgery, C.J., classified the—

'pickpocket who puts his hand in a man's pocket only to find it empty; the burglar who is disturbed by the police when he is in the process of trying to break open the window; the safebreaker who finds when he gets to the safe, it is too difficult for him and he cannot open it.'

---

[1] (1855), Dears. C.C. 515, at p. 538; [1843–60] All E.R. Rep. 363, at 367, *per* Parke, B.
[2] [1968] 1 Q.B. 366; [1967] 2 All E.R. 423.
[3] [1973] 2 All E.R., at p. 899.

'In general', . . . he 'thought a charge of attempt can properly be laid in that type of case.' But it was otherwise, he thought, in a second class of case which he described as follows:

> '(2) . . . where the accused has meticulously and in detail followed every step of his intended course believing throughout that he was committing a criminal offence and when in the end it is found he had not committed a criminal offence because in law that which he planned and carried out does not amount to a criminal offence at all.'

Lord Widgery, C.J., placed the present case in this second class and, after discussing a number of divergent authorities, came to the conclusion that in such a case a criminal attempt had not been committed.

With respect, I do not altogether agree that this dual classification is adequate, and if it were, I am not quite sure why all the examples given should be classified as they were. I note that in the New Zealand case of *R.* v. *Donnelly*,[1] which, except insofar as it relates to the construction of the relevant New Zealand statutes, is very much on all fours with this, Turner, J., adopts a six-fold classification. He says:[2]

> 'He who sets out to commit a crime may in the event fall short of the complete commission of that crime for any one of a number of reasons. *First*, he may, of course, simply change his mind before committing any act sufficiently overt to amount to an attempt. *Second*, he may change his mind, but too late to deny that he had got so far as an attempt. *Third*, he may be prevented by some outside agency from doing some act necessary to complete commission of the crime—as when a police officer interrupts him while he is endeavouring to force the window open, but before he has broken into the premises. *Fourth*, he may suffer no such outside interference, but may fail to complete the commission of the crime through ineptitude, inefficiency or insufficient means. The jemmy which he has brought with him may not be strong enough to force the window open. *Fifth*, he may find that what he is proposing to do is after all impossible—not because of insufficiency of means, but because it is for some reason physically not possible, what-

---

[1] [1970] N.Z.L.R. 980.
[2] *Ibid.*, at pp. 990, 991.

ever means be adopted. He who walks into a room intending to steal, say a specific diamond ring, and finds that the ring is no longer there but has been removed by the owner to the bank, is thus prevented from committing the crime which he intended, and which, but for the supervening physical impossibility imposed by events he would have committed. *Sixth*, he may without interruption efficiently do every act which he set out to do, but may be saved from criminal liability by the fact that what he has done, contrary to his own belief at the time, does not after all amount in law to a crime.'

On the whole, though I hope it will never be subjected to too much analysis, as it is merely a convenient exposition and illustration of classes of case which can arise, I find this classification more satisfactory than Lord Widgery, C.J.'s dual classification. Applying the three principles derived from my primary definitions, I would seek to obtain the following results. (1) In the first case no criminal attempt is committed. At the relevant time there was no *mens rea* since there had been a change of intention, and the only overt acts relied on would be preparatory and not immediately connected with the completed offence. (2) In the second case there is both *mens rea* and an act connected immediately with the offence. An example would be an attempted rape where the intended victim was criminally assaulted, but the attacker desisted at the stage immediately before he had achieved penetration. It follows that there is a criminal attempt. (3) The third case is more difficult because, as a matter of fact and degree, it will depend to some extent on the stage at which the interruption takes place, and the precise offence the attempt to commit which is the subject of the charge. In general, however, a criminal attempt is committed, assuming that the proximity test is passed. (4) In the fourth case there is ample authority for the proposition that, assuming the proximity test is passed, a criminal attempt is committed. But here casuistry is possible. Examples were given in argument of shots at an intended victim which fail because he is just out of range or because, as in the case of the well-known popular novel, *The Day of the Jackal*, the intended victim moves at the critical moment, or when a dose of poison insufficient to kill is administered with intent to murder. In all these cases the attempt is clearly criminal. (5) The fifth case is more complicated. It is clear that an attempt to obtain money by a false

pretence which is not in fact believed, is criminal notwithstanding that the consequences intended were not achieved:
see *R. v. Hensler.*[1] The same would be true of an attempted
murder when the victim did not actually die for whatever
reason. But I do not regard these as true, or at least not as
typical, examples of the fifth class. They belong rather to
the fourth, since the criminal had done all that he intended
to do, and all that was necessary to complete the crime was
an act or event wholly outside his control. . . . [I]n general I
would consider that 'attempts' in Turner, J.'s fifth class of
case are not indictable in English law. . . . In addition to the
reported cases, we postulated in argument a number of real
and imaginary instances of this class. In *The Empty Room*,
Sherlock Holmes's enemy, Colonel Maron, was induced to
fire at a wax image of the detective silhouetted in the window,
though Holmes prudently rejected Inspector Lestrade's
advice to prefer a charge of attempted murder and so the
matter was never tested; in *R. v. White*,[2] a man who put a
small quantity of cyanide in a wine glass, too small to kill, was
held guilty of attempted murder. This was an example of the
fourth of Turner, J.'s cases and therefore criminal. But
quaere, what would have been the position if the glass administered had contained pure water, even though the
accused believed falsely that it contained cyanide? We
discussed the situation when a would-be murderer attempts
to assassinate a corpse, or a bolster in a bed, believing it to
be the living body of his enemy, or when he fires into an
empty room believing that it contained an intended victim;
and we had our attention drawn to an American case where
the accused fired at a peephole in a roof believed to be in use
by a watching policeman who was in fact a few yards away.
In most of these cases, a statutory offence of some kind (e.g.
discharging a firearm with intent to endanger life) would be
committed in English law, but in general I would think that
a charge of an attempt to commit the common law offence of
murder would not lie since, if the contemplated sequence of
actions had been completed (as in some of the supposed
instances they were) no substantive offence could have been
committed of the type corresponding to the charge of
attempt supposed to be laid. . . .

    Turner, J.'s sixth class of case was where a man effici-
ently does—

---

[1] (1870), 22 L.T. 691.
[2] [1910] 2 K.B. 124; [1908–10] All E.R. Rep. 340.

'without interruption . . . every act which he set out do to, but may be saved from criminal liability by the fact that what he has done, contrary to his own belief at the time, does not after all amount in law to a crime.'

This is really equivalent to Lord Widgery, C.J.'s second class. I have already explained that I consider that the present appeal fails on the proper construction of s. 22 of the Theft Act 1968. But I think that this is a special example of a wider principle, and I agree with Turner, J.'s conclusion about it.

In *R. v. Collins*[1] Bramwell, B., put the rhetorical question:

'Suppose a man takes away an umbrella from a stand with intent to steal it, believing it not to be his own, but it turns out to be his own, could he be convicted of attempting to steal?'

In *R. v. Villensky*[2] Lord Coleridge, C.J., in circumstances not unlike the present, following *R. v. Dolan*,[3] held that prisoners could not be indicted under the old law for receiving stolen goods, and made no reference to the possibility of a conviction for attempt.

In *R. v. Williams*[4] the same Lord Chief Justice said that a boy below the age at which he could be properly indicted for rape could not be convicted on the same facts for an attempt. I do not agree with the contrary opinion of Hawkins, J., in the same case, even though it was possibly supported by the rest of the court. . . .

I agree with the decision in *R. v. Percy Dalton (London), Ltd.*,[5] and particularly with the quotation from Birkett, J.,[6] . . . where he said:

'Steps on the way to the commission of what would be a crime, if the acts were completed, may amount to attempts to commit that crime, to which, unless interrupted, they would have led; but steps on the way to the doing of something which is thereafter done, and which is no crime, cannot be regarded as attempts to commit a crime.'

I would add to the last sentence a rider to the effect that equally steps on the way to do something which is thereafter

---

[1] (1864), 9 Cox C.C. 497, at p. 498.
[2] [1892] 2 Q.B. 597.
[3] (1855), Dears. C.C. 436.
[4] [1893] 1 Q.B. 320, at p. 321.
[5] [1949] L.J.R. 1626.
[6] *Ibid.*, at p. 1630.

not completed, but which if done would not constitute a crime cannot be indicted as attempts to commit that crime. It is, of course, true that, at least in theory, some villains will escape by this route. But in most cases they can properly be charged with something else—statutory offences like breaking and entering with intent, etc., or loitering with intent, etc., using an instrument with intent, etc., discharging or possessing a firearm with intent, etc., or as here, common law offences like conspiring to commit the same offence as that the attempt to commit which is charged, or even committing a substantive offence of a different kind, as here, stealing or attempting to steal.''

APPEAL DISMISSED.

CHAPTER 9
GENERAL DEFENCES

Duress

R. v. GILL
[1963] 2 All E.R. 688

The defence of duress is not available to someone who had an obvious safe avenue of escape before committing the offence in question.

See p. 19, *supra*.

R. v. HUDSON AND R. v. TAYLOR
[1971] 2 All E.R. 244

(1) *An avenue of escape must be reasonably open to the accused in order to be regarded as safe. In deciding whether it was the accused's age, the circumstances of the case and any risks involved should be taken into account.* (2) *Although the threat must be operative at the time the offence was committed, the defence of duress may be available even though the harm threatened might not occur until later.*

Miss Hudson and Miss Taylor gave false evidence at a criminal trial, and they were charged with perjury. Their defence was that a man who was present at the trial at which the false evidence was given had together with others threatened to cut them up unless they gave it. The recorder held that duress was no defence because the accused had not been subject to the threat of immediate physical violence when they gave the false evidence. The accused were convicted, but successfully appealed to the Court of Appeal.

Extract from the Judgment of the Court of Appeal

Widgery, L.J.—

"Despite the concern expressed in 2 Stephen's *History of the Criminal Law in England*,[1] that it would be—

'. . . a much greater misfortune for society at large if criminals could confer impunity upon their agents by threatening them with death or violence if they refused to execute their commands . . .'

it is clearly established that duress provides a defence in all offences including perjury (except possibly treason or murder as a principal)[2] if the will of the accused has been overborne by threats of death or serious personal injury so that the commission of the alleged offence was no longer the voluntary act of the accused. This appeal raises two main questions: first, as to the nature of the necessary threat and, in particular, whether it must be 'present and immediate'; secondly, as to the extent to which a right to plead duress may be lost if the accused has failed to take steps to remove the threat as, for example, by seeking police protection.

It is essential to the defence of duress that the threat shall be effective at the moment when the crime is committed. The threat must be a 'present' threat in the sense that it is effective to neutralise the will of the accused at the time. Hence an accused who joins a rebellion under the compulsion of threats cannot plead duress if he remains with the rebels after the threats have lost their effect and his own will has had a chance to re-assert itself (*McGrowther's* case[3] and *A.-G.* v. *Whelan*[4]). Similarly a threat of future violence may be so remote as to be insufficient to overpower the will at the moment when the offence was committed, or the accused may have elected to commit the offence in order to rid himself of a threat hanging over him and not because he was driven to act by immediate and unavoidable pressure. In none of these cases is the defence of duress available because a person cannot justify the commission of a crime merely to secure his own peace of mind.

When, however, there is no opportunity for delaying tactics, and the person threatened must make up his mind whether he is to commit the criminal act or not, the existence at that moment of threats sufficient to destroy his will ought

---

[1] Vol. 2, p. 107.
[2] See *Abbott* v. *R.*, p. 390, *infra*.
[3] (1746), Fost. 13.
[4] [1934] I.R. 518.

to provide him with a defence even though the threatened injury may not follow instantly, but after an interval. This principle is illustrated by *Subramaniam* v. *R.*,[1] when the appellant was charged in Malaya with unlawful possession of ammunition and was held by the Privy Council to have a defence of duress, fit to go to the jury, on his plea that he had been compelled by terrorists to accept the ammunition and feared for his safety if the terrorists returned.

In the present case the threats of Farrell were likely to be no less compelling, because their execution could not be effected in the court room, if they could be carried out in the streets of Salford the same night. Insofar, therefore, as the recorder ruled as a matter of law that the threats were not sufficiently present and immediate to support the defence of duress we think that he was in error. He should have left the jury to decide whether the threats had overborne the will of the appellants at the time when they gave the false evidence.

Counsel for the Crown, however, contends that the recorder's ruling can be supported on another ground, namely, that the appellants should have taken steps to neutralise the threats by seeking police protection either when they came to court to give evidence, or beforehand. He submits on grounds of public policy that an accused should not be able to plead duress if he had the opportunity to ask for protection from the police before committing the offence and failed to do so. The argument does not distinguish cases in which the police would be able to provide effective protection, from those when they would not, and it would, in effect, restrict the defence of duress to cases where the person threatened had been kept in custody by the maker of the threats, or where the time interval between the making of the threats and the commission of the offence had made recourse to the police impossible. We recognise the need to keep the defence of duress within reasonable bounds but cannot accept so severe a restriction on it. The duty, of the person threatened, to take steps to remove the threat does not seem to have arisen in an English case but in a full review of the defence of duress in the Supreme Court of Victoria (*R.* v. *Hurley, R.* v. *Murray*[2]), a condition of raising the defence was said to be that the accused 'had no means, with safety, to himself, of preventing the execution of the threat'.

In the opinion of this court it is always open to the

[1] [1956] 1 W.L.R. 965.
[2] [1967] V.R. 526.

Crown to prove that the accused failed to avail himself of some opportunity which was reasonably open to him to render the threat ineffective, and that on this being established the threat in question can no longer be relied on by the defence. In deciding whether such an opportunity was reasonably open to the accused the jury should have regard to his age and circumstances, and to any risks to him which may be involved in the course of action relied on."

APPEAL ALLOWED.

ABBOTT v. R.
[1976] 3 All E.R. 140

Although the defence of duress is available to a person who aids and abets murder, it is not available to a perpetrator of murder.

Abbott was a member of a commune which occupied a house in Trinidad. The commune was presided over by a man called Malik, whom Abbott had reason to regard as a dangerous man. On the directions of Malik, Abbott took an active part in killing a young woman, Gale Benson. He had held her while others tried to kill her with a cutlass and had then, with three other men, buried her dying body. At his trial for murder Abbott claimed that he had acted as he had done because Malik had threatened to kill Abbott and his mother unless his instructions were obeyed. Abbott was convicted of murder and appealed on the ground that the trial judge had failed to direct the jury to consider whether, on the evidence, he was entitled to be acquitted on the ground that he had acted under duress. The Court of Appeal of Trinidad and Tobago dismissed Abbott's appeal and he appealed to the Privy Council.

Extracts from the Advice of the Privy Council, and from the Dissenting Judgment

Lord Salmon.—

". . . [I]t is necessary first to examine *Lynch* v. *Director of Public Prosecutions for Northern Ireland*.[1] By a majority of three to two the House of Lords held that if duress was

---

[1] [1975] A.C. 653; [1975] 1 All E.R. 913.

relied on and there was any material to support it, it would afford a complete defence to anyone charged with murder as a principal in the second degree unless the Crown satisfied the jury beyond reasonable doubt that the accused had not acted under duress.

The short facts as stated in evidence by the accused in *Lynch* v. *Director of Public Prosecutions for Northern Ireland* were that he was ordered by a well-known member of the I.R.A. who was reputed to be a ruthless gunman to drive him and two others to a particular road. Lynch firmly believed that he would be shot if he refused. So he drove the three men according to the orders which he had received. To Lynch's knowledge one of them was carrying a rifle, another had a gun in his pocket and all three were wearing balaclava helmets. In the course of the journey he suspected strongly from their conversation that they were about to shoot a policeman. He was right. At a certain point on the journey he was told to stop the car. He obeyed. The other three men, pulling the balaclava helmets over their faces, jumped out of the car and ran across the road. Three shots rang out. They ran back to the car and jumped in, ordering Lynch to return to their starting point. He did so. The rest of the evidence established that these three men driven by Lynch had murdered a policeman when they jumped out of the car driven by Lynch.

The trial judge refused to leave duress to the jury on the ground that it afforded no defence to murder and Lynch's appeal was dismissed by the Court of Appeal.[1] Lynch then appealed to the House of Lords with the result which has already been stated. On his retrial the jury rejected the defence of duress and he was again convicted of murder.

Whilst their Lordships feel bound to accept the decision of the House of Lords in *Lynch* v. *Director of Public Prosecutions for Northern Ireland* they find themselves constrained to say that had they considered (which they do not) that that decision was an authority which required the extension of the doctrine to cover cases like the present, they would not have accepted it.

Their Lordships will now consider the question whether *Lynch* v. *Director of Public Prosecutions for Northern Ireland* can properly be regarded as any authority for the proposition advanced on behalf of the appellant that duress affords him a complete defence although he was a principal in the first

---

[1] I.e. the Court of Appeal in Northern Ireland.

degree, having clearly taken an active, prominent and indispensable part in the actual killing of Gale Benson.

The majority of the noble and learned Lords who decided *Lynch* v. *Director of Public Prosecutions for Northern Ireland* certainly said nothing to support the contention now being made on behalf of the appellant. At best, from the appellant's point of view, they left the point open. Indeed, there are passages in some of their speeches which suggest that duress can be of no avail to a charge of murder as principal in the first degree. Lord Morris of Borth-y-Gest said:[1] 'It may be that the law must deny such a defence [i.e. duress] to an actual killer, and that the law will not be irrational if it does so.' He went on to explain the difference between the situation in which a man under a real threat of death or serious violence (a) carries a gun or drives a car to a place with the knowledge that at such place those exercising the duress plan to kill and (b) the man who under the same threat is the actual killer. Of the former he said:[1]'The final and fatal moment of decision has not arrived. He saves his own life at a time when the loss of another life is not a certainty.' Of the latter he said:[1]

'. . . the person is told that to save his life he himself must personally . . . pull the trigger or otherwise . . . do the act of killing. There, I think, before allowing duress as a defence it may be that the law will have to call a halt.'

Of the dissenting judgment of Bray, C.J., in *R.* v. *Brown*[2] he said:[3]

'In a closely reasoned judgment, the persuasive power of which appeals to me, [Bray, C.J.] held that it was wrong to say that no type of duress can ever afford a defence to any type of complicity in murder though he drew a line of limitation when he said: "I repeat also that as at present advised I do not think duress could constitute a defence to one who actually kills or attempts to kill the victim."'

Lord Wilberforce said:[4]
'Indeed to justify the deliberate killing by one's own hand of another human being may be something that no pressure or threat even to one's own life . . . can justify—no such

[1] [1975] A.C., at p. 671; [1975] 1 All E.R., at pp. 918, 919.
[2] [1968] S.A.S.R. 467.
[3] [1975] A.C., at p. 677; [1975] 1 All E.R., at pp. 923, 924.
[4] [1975] A.C., at pp. 680, 683; [1975] 1 All E.R., at pp. 926, 927 and 929.

case ever seems to have reached the courts. But if one accepts the test of heinousness, this does not, in my opinion, involve that all cases of what is murder in law must be treated in the same way. Heinousness is a word of degree, and that there are lesser degrees of heinousness, even of involvement in homicide, seems beyond doubt. An accessory before the fact, or an aider or abettor, may (not necessarily must) bear a less degree of guilt than the actual killer: and even if the rule of exclusion is absolute, or nearly so in relation to the latter, it need not be so in lesser cases. . . . The conclusion which I deduce is that although, in a case of actual killing by a first degree principal the balance of judicial authority at the present time is against the admission of the defence of duress, in the case of lesser degrees of participation, the balance is, if anything, the other way."

It seems to their Lordships that if one adds these passages from the speeches of Lord Morris of Borth-y-Gest and Lord Wilberforce to those of Lord Simon of Glaisdale and Lord Kilbrandon, who dissented in *Lynch* v. *Director of Public Prosecutions for Northern Ireland*, the majority of the House was of the opinion that duress is not a defence to a charge of murder against anyone proved to have done the actual killing. However this may be, their Lordships are clearly of the opinion that in such a case, duress, as the law now stands, affords no defence. For reasons which will presently be explained their Lordships, whilst loyally accepting the decision in *Lynch's* case, are certainly not prepared to extend it.

When Lord Simon of Glaisdale and Lord Kilbrandon stated in their dissenting speeches in *Lynch* v. *Director of Public Prosecutions for Northern Ireland* that the drawing of an arbitrary line between murder as a principal in the first degree and murder as a principal in the second degree cannot be justified either morally or juridically, they clearly meant that since, rightly, it had always been accepted that duress was not a defence to a charge of murder as a principal in the first degree, the cases and dicta (e.g. Bray, C.J., in *R.* v. *Brown*[1] and *R.* v. *Kray*[2]) which suggested that duress could amount to a defence to a charge of murder in the second degree should not be followed. The noble and learned Lords were clearly not conceding that if, contrary to their view, duress

---

[1] [1968] S.A.S.R., at p. 499.
[2] (1969), 53 Cr. App. Rep. 412.

was capable of being a defence to a charge of murder as a principal in the second degree it should therefore be capable of being a defence to a charge of murder as a principal in the first degree.

No doubt the facts might be such that murder by a principal in the second degree may sometimes be as heinous a crime as murder by a principal in the first degree. On the other hand, as pointed out by the majority in *Lynch* v. *Director of Public Prosecutions for Northern Ireland* the facts may often be such that murder by a principal in the second degree involves only a comparatively slight participation in the crime, not nearly so heinous or blameworthy as the act of the man who did the actual killing.

If duress affords a defence, as *Lynch* v. *Director of Public Prosecutions for Northern Ireland* decides, to all murderers who are principals in the second degree, it may be that ... some villainous murderers in this class will be lucky in that *Lynch's* case will allow them to escape conviction and go free. This does not however seem to their Lordships to afford any sound reason for changing the law by ruling that duress should allow the man who does the actual killing to go free. ...

Prior to the present case it has never been argued in England or any other part of the Commonwealth that duress is a defence to a charge of murder by a principal in the first degree. The only case in which such a view was canvassed is *State* v. *Goliath*;[1] this was a case decided under a mixture of Roman–Dutch and English law after South Africa had left the Commonwealth. From time immemorial it has been accepted by the common law of England that duress is no defence to murder, certainly not to murder by a principal in the first degree. Hale stated:[2]

'Again, if a man be desperately assaulted, and in peril of death, and cannot otherwise escape, unless to satisfy his assailant's fury he will kill an innocent person then present, the fear and actual force will not acquit him of the crime and punishment of murder, if he commit the fact; for he ought rather to die himself, than kill an innocent.'

Blackstone stated[3] that a man under duress 'ought rather to die himself than escape by the murder of an innocent' ....

Counsel for the appellant has argued that the law now presupposes a degree of heroism of which the ordinary man

---

[1] 1972 (3) S.A. 1.
[2] *Pleas of the Crown* (1800), vol. 1, p. 51.
[3] *Commentaries on the Laws of England* (1766), vol. 4, p. 30.

is incapable and which therefore should not be expected of him and that modern conditions and concepts of humanity have rendered obsolete the rule that the actual killer cannot rely on duress as a defence. Their Lordships do not agree. . .

We have been reminded that it is an important part of the judge's role to adapt and develop the principles of the common law to meet the changing needs of time. We have been invited to exercise this role by changing the law so that on a charge of murder in the first degree, duress shall entitle the killer to be acquitted and go scot-free. Their Lordships certainly are very conscious that the principles of the common law must not be allowed to become sterile. The common law, as has often been said, is a living organism. . . . Their Lordships, however, are firmly of the opinion that the invitation extended to them on behalf of the appellant goes far beyond adapting and developing the principles of the common law. What has been suggested is the destruction of a fundamental doctrine of our law which might well have far-reaching and disastrous consequences for public safety, to say nothing of its important social, ethical and maybe political implications. Such a decision would be far beyond their Lordships' powers even if they approved—as they certainly do not—of this revolutionary change in the law proposed on behalf of the appellant. Judges have no power to create new criminal offences nor, in their Lordships' opinion, for the reasons already stated, have they the power to invent a new defence to murder which is entirely contrary to fundamental legal doctrine, accepted for hundreds of years without question. If a policy change of such a fundamental nature were to be made it could, in their Lordships' view, be made only by Parliament. Whilst their Lordships strongly uphold the right and indeed the duty of the judges to adapt and develop the principles of the common law in an orderly fashion, they are equally opposed to any usurpation by the courts of the functions of Parliament. . . .

Their Lordships, however, consider that the law relating to duress is in an unsatisfactory state. . . .

Any murderer who kills under duress would be less, in many cases far less, blameworthy than another who has killed of his own free will. Should not the law recognise this factor? A verdict of guilty of murder carries with it a mandatory sentence, in this country life imprisonment, in other parts of the Commonwealth death. There is much to be said for the view that on a charge of murder, duress, like provocation, should not entitle the accused to a clean acquittal but should reduce murder to manslaughter and thus give the court power to pass whatever sentence might be appropriate in all the circumstances of the case.

For the reasons given earlier in this judgment their Lordships will humbly advise Her Majesty that this appeal should be dismissed.''

Dissenting judgment of

Lord Wilberforce and Lord Edmund-Davies.—

"The question raised by this appeal is not whether the appellant should be acquitted of the murder of Gale Benson, but rather whether a new trial should be ordered so that he may have the opportunity, hitherto denied him, of being heard on his plea that his participation in the acts resulting in her death was due to his having acted under duress. . . .

The appellant is under sentence of death, and subject to the discretion of the executive there is no reason to think that the sentence will not be carried out, following on the dismissal of his appeal. Accordingly, even were it permissible and proper in cases of lesser gravity to leave the law to take its course and allow the legislature breathing space to consider possible amendments of a law which the majority of their Lordships themselves describe as being 'in an unsatisfactory condition', this is emphatically not such a case. For the appellant the time to declare what the law is brooks of no delay.

. . . The sole question of law is whether it is open to [a perpetrator of murder] to plead that he acted under duress. For the purpose of this appeal, it is unnecessary to consider what *sort* of duress or how *much* duress. If the Crown is right, there is no let-out for any principal in the first degree, even if the duress be so dreadful as would be likely to wreck the morale of most men of reasonable courage, and even were the duress directed not against the person threatened but against other innocent people (in the present case, the appellant's mother) so that considerations of mere self-perservation are not operative. That is indeed 'a blue print for heroism' (*State* v. *Goliath*[1]). The question is whether it is also the common law, which, being indivisible, has to be applied in Trinidad and Tobago as in Great Britain. In our opinion it is not.

The starting-point in this appeal must be the decision of the House of Lords in *Lynch* v. *Director of Public Prose-*

---

[1] 1972 (3) S.A. 1.

cutions for Northern Ireland[1], which decision was not available to the trial judge in this case or to the Court of Appeal. This established that on a murder charge the defence of duress is open to a person accused as a principal in the second degree. Not only has the actual decision in *Lynch's* case to be respected but also its implications, for it was based on a consideration in some depth of topics scarcely adverted to by their Lordships in the present appeal. The question that immediately arises is whether any acceptable distinction can invariably be drawn between a principal in the first degree to murder and one in the second degree, with the result that the latter *may* in certain circumstances be absolved by his plea of duress, while the former may never even advance such a plea.

The simple fact is that *no* acceptable basis of distinction has even now been advanced. In *Lynch v. Director of Public Prosecutions for Northern Ireland* Lord Simon of Glaisdale and Lord Kilbrandon, who dissented, adverted to the absence of any valid distinction as a ground for holding that duress should be available to *neither*, the former saying:[2]

'How can an arbitrary line drawn between murder as a principal in the first degree and murder as a principal in the second degree be justified either morally or juridically?'

. . . Of those of their Lordships who are in a minority in the in the present appeal, Lord Wilberforce found[3]—

'. . . no convincing reason, on principle, why, if a defence of duress in the criminal law exists at all, it should be absolutely excluded in murder charges whatever the nature of the charge; hard to establish, yes, in case of direct killing so hard that perhaps it will never be proved; but in other cases to be judged, strictly indeed, on the totality of facts. Exclusion, if not arbitrary, must be based either on authority or policy.'

Lord Edmund-Davies[4] expressed agreement with the observation in Smith and Hogan[5] that—

'The difficulty about adopting a distinction between the principal and secondary parties as a rule of law is that the contribution of the secondary party to the death may be no less significant than that of the principal.'

---

[1] [1975] A.C. 653; [1975] 1 All E.R. 913.
[2] [1975] A.C., at p. 687; [1975] 1 All E.R., at p. 932.
[3] [1975] A.C., at p. 681; [1975] 1 All E.R., at p. 927.
[4] [1975] A.C., at p. 715; [1975] 1 All E.R., at p. 956.
[5] *Criminal Law*, 3rd ed., p. 166.

Little advantage is to be gained by referring all over again to the many cases cited in *Lynch* v. *Director of Public Prosecutions for Northern Ireland*. But mention must obviously be made of *R.* v. *Brown*,[1] where Bray, C.J., ended his illuminating judgment with the words: '. . . as at present advised I do not think duress could constitute a defence to one who actually kills or attempts to kill the victim.' But he adduced no reason, and when *Lynch's* case was before the Court of Criminal Appeal of Northern Ireland, Lowry, C.J., said:

> 'We find it difficult to justify the distinction drawn by Bray, C.J., but not apparently reflected in any other way, between principals in the first and second degree in murder, and, by way of contrast, we note the case of *R.* v. *Farduto*.[2] . . . That case was admittedly decided under the Canadian Criminal Code, but it also discussed the common law and, in upholding the conviction, made no distinction, with regard to duress as a defence to murder, between principals in the first and second degree.' . . .

As to South Africa, it is noteworthy that, although in *R.* v. *Hercules*[3] duress was treated as a mitigating factor reducing murder to manslaughter, in *State* v. *Goliath*[4] it was held to be a complete defence, Rumpff, J., saying:

> 'It is generally accepted . . . that for the ordinary person in general his life is more valuable than that of another. Only those who possess the quality of heroism will intentionally offer their lives for another. Should the criminal law then state that compulsion could never be a defence to a charge of murder, it would demand that a person who killed another under duress, whatever the circumstances, would have to comply with a higher standard than that demanded of the average person. I do not think that such an exception to the general rule which applies in criminal law is justified.'

Great stress has been laid by the majority of their Lordships on the apparent unanimity with which great writers of the past have rejected duress as a defence. But, on any view, they have to be read with circumspection in these days, for the criminal courts have long accepted duress as an available defence to a large number of crimes from which

---

[1] [1968] S.A.S.R., at p. 499.
[2] (1912), 10 D.L.R. 669.
[3] 1954 (3) S.A. 826.
[4] 1972 (3) S.A. 1.

those same writers withheld it. . . . Their work needs to be
looked at with a fresh eye and with a readiness to regard it as
at least conceivable that what Hale and others propounded
as the law in their day does not necessarily hold good today.
This is in fact what the courts, in the cases cited in *Lynch's*
case, have been doing continuously over the last century. In
the result, it is inaccurate to treat *Lynch's* case as having
invented an entirely new defence contrary to fundamental
legal doctrine. As Lord Wilberforce said:[1]

'The House is not inventing a new defence; on the contrary,
it would not discharge its judicial duty if it failed to define
the law's attitude to this particular defence in particular
circumstances.'

And, *Lynch's* case having been decided as it was, it is still
less permissible to claim that the acceptance of the appellant's
submissions threatens, in their Lordships' words, 'the
destruction of a fundamental doctrine of our law'.

Something must be said about the significance attached
by the majority of their Lordships to the absence of any
direct decision that it is open to principals in the first degree
to murder to advance a plea of duress. As to this, two
observations need to be made: (i) There is little use in looking
back earlier than 1838,[2] for until then an accused could not
give evidence on his own behalf; and to advance such a
plea without any opportunity of explaining to the jury
why he acted as he did would be to attempt something
foredoomed to failure. It is significant, too, that the in-
creasingly humane attitude of the courts in relation to duress
has developed since the gag on accused persons was removed.
(ii) As was pointed out in *Lynch* v. *Director of Public Prosecutions for Northern Ireland*, the balance of such judicial
authority as exists was against the admission of the defence
of duress in cases of first degree murder. But this balance was
a weak one and one which both of us thought might have to
yield in an actual case. While there are in the law reports
a number of *obiter dicta* (that is in cases where murder was
not charged) to the effect that duress is not available in
murder, apparently in only one case has it been directly so
held. The one exception is nearly 140 years old, *R.* v. *Tyler
and Price*,[3] where Lord Denman, C.J., using unqualified

---

[1] [1975] A.C., at p. 685; [1975] 1 All E.R., at p. 930.
[2] *R.* v. *Tyler and Price* (1838), 8 C. & P. 616.
[3] (1838), 8 C. & P., at p. 620.

terms which certainly cannot be regarded as accurately stating the law of today, said: 'It cannot be too often repeated that the apprehension of personal danger does not furnish any excuse for assisting in doing any act which is illegal.' Apart from the unqualified and therefore unacceptable generality of those words, the decision is for additional reasons an unsatisfactory guide to the proper outcome of the present appeal: see *Lynch's* case.[1]. . .

Lynch v. *Director of Public Prosecutions for Northern Ireland* having been decided as it was, the most striking feature of the present appeal is the lack of any indication, in the judgment of the majority, *why* a flat declaration that in no circumstances whatsoever may the actual killer be absolved by a plea of duress makes for sounder law and better ethics. In truth, the contrary is the case. For example, D attempts to kill P but, though injuring him, fails. When charged with attempted murder he may plead duress (*R.* v. *Fegan*[2] and several times referred to in *Lynch's* case). Later P dies and D is charged with his murder: if the majority of their Lordships are right, he now has no such plea available. . . . It is not the mere lack of logic that troubles one. It is when one stops to consider why duress is *ever* permitted as a defence even to a charge of great gravity that the lack of any moral reason justifying its *automatic* exclusion in such cases as the present becomes so baffling—and so important. . . .

To hold that a principal in the first degree in murder is never in any circumstances to be entitled to plead duress, whereas a principal in the second degree may, is to import the possibility of grave injustice into the common law. Such a conclusion should not be arrived at unless supported by compelling authority or by the demands of public policy shown to operate differently in the two cases. There are no authorities compelling this Board so to hold, nor are there reasons of public policy present in this case which are lacking in the case of principals in the second degree. It has to be said with all respect that the majority opinion of their Lordships amounts, in effect, to side-stepping the decision in *Lynch* v. *Director of Public Prosecutions for Northern Ireland* and, even were that constitutionally appropriate, to do it without advancing cogent grounds.

For these reasons, those of their Lordships who are in the minority would have humbly advised Her Majesty that the

---

[1] [1975] A.C., at pp. 713, 714; [1975] 1 All E.R., at p. 954, 955.
[2] (1974), September 20th, unreported.

appeal should be allowed and that a new trial should be ordered."

APPEAL DISMISSED.

Note

If the provisional proposals in Law Commission Working Paper No. 55, *General Principles: Defences of General Application,*[1] were enacted the defences of duress and necessity (see next case) would be available to a perpetrator of murder.

The statutory defence of marital coercion (whose abolition is proposed in the Working Paper) does not apply on a charge of murder, whether as perpetrator or accomplice. This defence is provided by s. 47 of the Criminal Justice Act 1925, which abolished the presumption that a wife who committed a crime in the presence of her husband did so under such compulsion as to entitle her to an acquittal. Section 47 provides:

"Any presumption of law that an offence committed by a wife in the presence of her husband is committed under the coercion of the husband is hereby abolished, but on a charge against a wife, for any offence other than treason or murder, it shall be a good defence to prove that the offence was committed in the presence of, and under the coercion of, the husband."

This defence may embrace a wider range of threats than suffice for duress. It does not prejudice a plea of duress by a wife instead.

Necessity

R. v. DUDLEY AND STEPHENS
(1884), 14 Q.B.D. 273

A man who, in order to escape death from hunger, kills another for the purpose of eating his flesh, is guilty of murder although, at the time of the act, he is in such circumstances that he believes, and has reasonable grounds for believing, that it affords the only chance of saving his life.

Dudley and Stephens were charged at the Devon Assizes with the murder of a boy, and the following is the effect of the special verdict which was found by the jury at the trial

---

[1] The proposals are summarised in Cross and Jones, *Introduction to Criminal Law*, 8th ed., para. 18.7 and 18.17.

before Huddleston, B. The prisoners, the deceased and a fourth person were shipwrecked, and cast adrift in an open boat a thousand miles from land. After eighteen days, by which time they had been without food for seven days, and without water for five days, the prisoners decided to kill the deceased in order that they might eat his body. On the 20th day, Dudley, with the assent of Stephens (the fourth man refusing to assent), knifed the deceased who, on account of his youth, was in a weaker state than any other member of the party, and who in no way assented to his death. The three survivors lived on the flesh of the deceased for a further four days, after which they were picked up by a passing ship. At the time the boy was killed, there was no reasonable prospect of relief, and there was every probability that, unless the prisoners ate the deceased, or one of the other members of the party, they would have died of starvation.

On these findings, Huddleston, B., adjourned the case for argument before five judges at the Royal Courts of Justice where the accused were held guilty of murder.

Extracts from the Judgment of the Five Judges

Lord Coleridge, C.J.—

". . . it appears sufficiently that the prisoners were subject to terrible temptation, to sufferings which might break down the bodily power of the strongest man, and try the conscience of the best. Other details yet more harrowing, facts still more loathsome and appalling, were presented to the jury, and are to be found recorded in my learned Brother's notes. But nevertheless this is clear, that the prisoners put to death a weak and unoffending boy upon the chance of preserving their own lives by feeding upon his flesh and blood after he was killed, and with the certainty of depriving *him* of any possible chance of survival. . . .

There remains to be considered the real question in the case—whether killing under the circumstances set forth in the verdict be or be not murder. The contention that it could be anything else was, to the minds of us all, both new and strange, and we stopped the Attorney-General in his negative argument in order that we might hear what could be said in support of a proposition which appeared to us to be at once dangerous, immoral, and opposed to all legal principle and analogy. All, no doubt, that can be said has

been urged before us, and we are now to consider and
determine what it amounts to. First it is said that it follows
from various definitions of murder in books of authority,
which definitions imply, if they do not state, the doctrine,
that in order to save your own life you may lawfully take
away the life of another, when that other is neither attempting
not threatening yours, nor is guilty of any illegal act whatever towards you or any one else. But if these definitions be
looked at they will not be found to sustain this contention.
. . . Decided cases there are none. . . . The American case
cited by my Brother Stephen in his *Digest*, from Wharton
on *Homicide*, in which it was decided, correctly indeed, that
sailors had no right to throw passengers overboard to save
themselves, but on the somewhat strange ground that the
proper mode of determining who was to be sacrificed was to
vote upon the subject by ballot, can hardly, as my Brother
Stephen says, be an authority satisfactory to a court in this
country. . . .

Now, except for the purpose of testing how far the
conservation of a man's own life is in all cases and under all
circumstances, an absolute, unqualified, and paramount duty,
we exclude from our consideration all the incidents of war.
We are dealing with a case of private homicide, not one
imposed upon men in the service of their Sovereign and in the
defence of their country. Now it is admitted that the deliberate killing of this unoffending and unresisting boy was
clearly murder, unless the killing can be justified by some
well-recognised excuse admitted by the law. It is further
admitted that there was in this case no such excuse, unless
the killing was justified by what has been called 'necessity'.
But the temptation to the act which existed here was not
what the law has ever called necessity. Nor is this to be
regretted. Though law and morality are not the same, and
many things may be immoral which are not necessarily
illegal, yet the absolute divorce of law from morality would
be of fatal consequence; and such divorce would follow if
the temptation to murder in this case were to be held by law
an absolute defence of it. It is not so. To preserve one's life
is generally speaking a duty, but it may be the plainest and
the highest duty to sacrifice it. War is full of instances in
which it is a man's duty not to live, but to die. The duty, in
case of shipwreck, of a captain to his crew, of the crew to
the passengers, of soldiers to women and children, as in
the noble case of the *Birkenhead*; these duties impose on men
the moral necessity, not of the preservation, but of the

sacrifice of their lives for others, from which in no country, least of all, it is to be hoped, in England, will men ever shrink, as indeed, they have not shrunk. . . . It would be a very easy and cheap display of common place learning to quote from Greek and Latin authors, from Horace, from Juvenal, from Cicero, from Euripides, passage after passage, in which the duty of dying for others has been laid down in glowing and emphatic language as resulting from the principles of heathen ethics; it is enough in a Christian country to remind ourselves of the Great Example whom we profess to follow. . . .

It must not be supposed that in refusing to admit temptation to be an excuse for crime it is forgotten how terrible the temptation was; how awful the suffering; how hard in such trials to keep the judgment straight and the conduct pure. We are often compelled to set up standards we cannot reach ourselves, and to lay down rules which we could not ourselves satisfy.[1] But a man has no right to declare temptation to be an excuse, though he might himself have yielded to it, nor allow compassion for the criminal to change or weaken in any manner the legal definition of the crime. It is therefore our duty to declare that the prisoner's act in this case was wilful murder, that the facts as stated in the verdict are no legal justification of the homicide; and to say that in our unanimous opinion the prisoners are upon this special verdict guilty of murder.''[2]

THE PRISONERS WERE SENTENCED TO DEATH, BUT THEIR SENTENCE WAS COMMUTED TO SIX MONTHS' IMPRISONMENT.

Comment on R. v. Dudley and Stephens

The American case mentioned in Lord Coleridge's judgment in *Dudley and Stephens* is *U.S.* v. *Holmes* (26 Fed. Cas. 360).

---

[1] This is particularly so in the law of homicide. *Cf.* the rule that duress is not a defence to a perpetrator of murder and the fact that someone whose murder charge is reduced to manslaughter on account of provocation is often severely punished although, *ex hypothesi*, the provocation might have caused a reasonable man, i.e. an average man, to do what the accused did.

[2] Grove, J., who was one of the judges in the above case, pointed out (14 Q.B.D. 288) that, if the defence of necessity were allowed to prevail on such facts, it would mean that one of the three survivors might be killed by the others, of whom the stronger might kill the weaker, with the result that three lives might ultimately be taken in order to save one. Stephen, J., who was not one of the judges in the above case, subsequently indicated his approval of the actual decision, although he disagreed with some of the arguments advanced by Lord Coleridge in his judgment (*Digest of Criminal Law*, 9th edn., p. 10, n. 2).

After a shipwreck in 1842, a number of members of the crew and passengers were adrift in an open boat which was too full to remain afloat. Holmes was a member of the crew, and, acting under orders, he threw some of the passengers overboard. He was charged with manslaughter and convicted. The sentence was six months hard labour and a fine of twenty dollars. Points made by the judge were (1) provided enough members of the crew were left to navigate the boat, the crew should perish first because of the duty of protection owed to passengers, and (b) subject to the above point, lots should have been drawn. It is not without significance that the charge was only one of manslaughter for it is arguable that, at the very least, this is the proper verdict on facts such as those of *Dudley and Stephens*.

Section 25 of the Queensland Criminal Code reads as follows:

"Subject to the express provisions of this Code relating to acts done upon compulsion or provocation or in self-defence, a person is not criminally responsible for an act or omission done or made under such circumstances of sudden or extraordinary emergency that an ordinary person possessing ordinary powers of self-control could not reasonably be expected to act otherwise."

The emergency in *Dudley and Stephens* was certainly "extraordinary" although there is room for argument whether it was "sudden" within the meaning of the above provision. However, s. 25 does show that under some legal systems, extreme necessity may be a defence, even to a charge of intentional killing. The provision would certainly apply to the case of two shipwrecked mariners who arrived simultaneously at a plank large enough for only one. If the stronger pushed the weaker off the plank with the result that he was drowned, he would have a defence in Queensland but not, on the literal construction of Lord Coleridge's words, in England.

Self-Defence and Prevention of Crime

CRIMINAL LAW ACT 1967

"Section 3.—Use of force in making arrest, etc.

(1) A person may use such force as is reasonable in the circumstances in the prevention of crime, or in effecting or assisting in the lawful arrest of offenders or suspected offenders or of persons unlawfully at large.

(2) Subsection (1) above shall replace the rules of the common law on the question when force used for a purpose mentioned in the subsection is justified by that purpose."

Note

A person acting in self-defence or defence of his property is invariably engaged in the prevention of crime, but the above section may be confined to the prevention of crime against persons other than the accused. It has not been applied directly in cases on self-defence reported since the Act came into force. However, some of these cases, e.g. *McInnes*, p. 186, *supra*, suggest that the test of reasonableness will be applied to the exclusion of some of the supposed old rules such as that the person attacked must retreat as far as he can before resorting to force; all that he need do is manifest an unwillingness to fight.

A number of cases concerning the operation of these defences in particular offences have been set out on earlier pages of this book. See *Driscoll*, p. 146; *Kenlin* v. *Gardiner*, p. 147; *Fennell*, p. 149; *Rose*, p. 182; *Palmer* v. *R.*, p. 183; *McInnes*, p. 186.

CHAPTER 10
PARTICIPATION

Preliminary Note

Terminology

Many of the cases in this chapter were decided before the Criminal Law Act 1967 came into force. That Act abolished the distinction between felonies and misdemeanours. A fairly precise terminology had formerly been in use with regard to the different parties to a felony. The actual offender was a "principal in the first degree"; he was the one who actually did the criminal act, although allowance had to be made for the possibility of joint principals to cover cases in which the act was performed by both of them whether by agreement or otherwise, and of innocent agency, where the person who did the criminal act under the instigation of the principal offender was himself not committing any crime. All other parties to a felony were secondary parties, and it was a debatable point whether they could be liable where there was no principal in the first degree. The possible secondary parties were: "principals in the second degree", i.e. those present at and encouraging or assisting in the commission of the felony by, for example, keeping watch, or handing the lethal weapon to a murderer; "accessories before the fact", i.e. those who had given encouragement or assistance but not actually present at the commission of the felony; and "accessories after the fact", i.e. those who assisted the felon after he had committed the crime.

The position was different in the case of misdemeanours. Section 8 of the Accessories and Abettors Act 1861 provided:

> "Whosoever shall aid, abet, counsel, or procure the commission of any misdemeanour, whether the same be a misdemeanour at common law or by virtue of any Act passed or to be passed, shall be liable to be tried, indicted, and punished as a principal offender."

Section 1 of the Criminal Law Act 1967 abolished the distinctions between felonies and misdemeanours and provided that henceforth the law applicable to misdemeanours should apply wherever a distinction had been made previously. One result was to abolish liability for a felony as an accessory after the fact, since such liability has never existed in the case of a misdemeanour. However, those who assist persons who have committed an arrestable offence may commit the separate offence of assisting offenders, which is provided by s. 4 of the Criminal Law Act 1967. Apart from this and the abolition of the old terminology in the case of felonies, the Criminal Law Act 1967 has not affected the substantive law with regard to the liability of the other secondary parties described above. Thus, a person whose participation in a felony before the Act of 1967 would have made him a principal in the second degree or an accessory before the fact would now be tried, indicted and punished as a principal offender, as in the case of participation in a misdemeanour before and after the Act.

The extent to which the old terminology will survive is perhaps debatable. In the case of a misdemeanour, those who would if the crime were a felony have been principals in the second degree, or accessories before the fact were said to be guilty of "aiding and abetting". Strictly speaking, this term was only appropriate to those who would have been principals in the second degree in the case of a felony; those who would, in the case of a felony, have been accessories before the fact, were guilty of "counselling or procuring" the commission of the misdemeanour. "Aiding and abetting" is, moreover, sometimes used to cover the activities of a principal offender in cases in which there are more than one.

In the headnotes to the cases in this chapter "perpetrator" will be used to describe the principal offender and "accomplice" to describe an aider and abettor.

The Law Commission

The Law Commission's Working Paper No. 43, published in 1972, makes tentative suggestions for reform of the law relating to complicity and liability for the acts of others. References to some of these suggestions are made in footnotes at appropriate points. Unfortunately the paper does not consider the possibility of divorcing the liability of those who aid in the commission of crimes from the notion that they must be considered as parties to the crime.[1]

ATTORNEY-GENERAL'S REFERENCE
(No. 1 of 1975)
[1975] 2 All E.R. 684

"To procure" means to produce by endeavour. An offence cannot be procured unless there is a causal link between the steps taken by the alleged procurer and the commission of the

---

[1] See Cross and Jones, *Introduction to Criminal Law*, 8th ed., para. 9.23, and the article in 85 Law Quarterly Review 252 there cited.

offence. In the case of procuring, at least, a shared intention is not necessary.

This case concerned a reference by the Attorney-General under s. 36 of the Criminal Justice Act 1972, under which the Attorney-General may refer to the Court of Appeal a point of law arising at a trial on indictment where the person tried has been acquitted. The opinion of the Court of Appeal does not affect the acquittal but provides authoritative guidance for the future. The point of law involved in this reference is set out below.

Extracts from the Opinion of the Court of Appeal

Lord Widgery, C.J.—
"This case comes before the court on a reference from the Attorney-General under s. 36 of the Criminal Justice Act 1972, and by his reference he asks the following question:

'Whether an accused who surreptitiously laced a friend's drinks with double measures of spirits when he knew that his friend would shortly be driving his car home, and in consequence his friend drove with an excess quantity of alcohol in his body and was convicted of the offence under the Road Traffic Act 1972 s. 6(1) is entitled to a ruling of no case to answer on being later charged as an aider and abettor, counsellor and procurer, on the ground that there was no shared intention between the two, that the accused did not by accompanying him or otherwise positively encourage the friend to drive, or on any other ground.'

. . . The language in the section which determines whether a 'secondary party', as he is sometimes called, is guilty of a criminal offence committed by another embraces the four words 'aid, abet, counsel or procure'. The origin of those words is to be found in s. 8 of the Accessories and Abettors Act 1861 which provides:

'Whosoever shall aid, abet, counsel, or procure the commission of any misdemeanour, whether the same be a misdemeanour at common law or by virtue of any Act passed or to be passed, shall be liable to be tried, indicted, and punished as a principal offender.'

Thus, in the past, when the distinction was still drawn between felony and misdemeanour, it was sufficient to make a person guilty of a misdemeanour if he aided, abetted, counselled or procured the offence of another. When the difference between felonies and misdemeanours was abolished in 1967, s. 1 of the Criminal Law Act 1967 in effect provided that the same test should apply to make a secondary party guilty either of treason or felony.

Of course it is the fact that in the great majority of instances where a secondary party is sought to be convicted of an offence there has been a contact between the principal offender and the secondary party. Aiding and abetting almost inevitably involves a situation in which the secondary party and the main offender are together at some stage discussing the plans which they may be making in respect of the alleged offence, and are in contact so that each knows what is passing through the mind of the other.

In the same way it seems to us that a person who counsels the commission of a crime by another, almost inevitably comes to a moment when he is in contact with that other, when he is discussing the offence with that other and when, to use the words of the statute, he counsels the other to commit the offence.

The fact that so often the relationship between the secondary party and the principal will be such that there is a meeting of minds between them caused the trial judge in the case from which this reference is derived to think that this was really an essential feature of proving or establishing the guilt of the secondary party and, as we understand his judgment, he took the view that in the absence of some sort of meeting of minds, some sort of mental link between the secondary party and the principal, there could be no aiding, abetting or counselling of the offence within the meaning of the section.

So far as aiding, abetting and counselling is concerned we would go a long way with that conclusion. It may very well be, as I said a moment ago, difficult to think of a case of aiding abetting or counselling when the parties have not met and have not discussed in some respects the terms of the offence which they have in mind. But we do not see why a similar principle should apply to procuring.[1] We approach s. 8 of the

---

[1] It had already been established, see *Mohan* v. *R.* (p. 413, *infra*), that in the case of an aider and abettor it is unnecessary that there should be any agreement between the parties, but in cases such as *Mohan* v. *R.* the parties did at least have a shared intention. The importance of the present case is that it shows that, at least in a case of procuring, it is no defence for the accomplice to show that there was not even a shared intention between him and the perpetrator.

1861 Act on the basis that the words should be given their ordinary meaning, if possible. We approach the section on the basis also that if four words are employed here, 'aid, abet, counsel or procure', the probability is that there is a difference between each of those four words and the other three, because, if there were no such difference, then Parliament would be wasting time in using four words where two or three would do. Thus, in deciding whether that which is assumed to be done under our reference was a criminal offence we approach the section on the footing that each word must be given its ordinary meaning.[1]

To procure means to produce by endeavour. You procure a thing by setting out to see that it happens and taking the appropriate steps to produce that happening. We think that there are plenty of instances in which a person may be said to procure the commission of a crime by another even though there is no sort of conspiracy between the two, even though there is no attempt at agreement or discussion as to the form which the offence should take. In our judgment the offence described in this reference is such a case.

If one looks at the facts of the reference: the accused surreptitiously laced his friend's drink. This is an important element and, although we are not going to decide today anything other than the problem posed to us, it may well be that in similar cases where the lacing of the drink or the introduction of extra alcohol is known to the driver quite different considerations may apply. We say that because where the driver has no knowledge of what is happening, in most instances he would have no means of preventing the offence from being committed. If the driver is unaware of what has happened, he will not be taking precautions. He will get into his car seat, switch on the ignition and drive home and, consequently the conception of another procuring the commission of the offence by the driver is very much stronger where the driver is innocent of all knowledge of what is happening as in the present case where the lacing of the drink was surreptitious.

The second thing which is important in the facts set out in our reference is that following and in consequence of the introduction of the extra alcohol, the friend drove with an excess quantity of alcohol in his blood. Causation here is important. You cannot procure an offence unless there is a

---

[1] But see *Lynch* v. *Director of Public Prosecutions for Northern Ireland*, pp. 436 and 437, *infra*.

causal link between what you do and the commission of the offence, and here we are told that in consequence of the addition of this alcohol the driver, when he drove home, drove with an excess quantity of alcohol in his body.

Giving the words their ordinary meaning in English, and asking oneself whether in those circumstances the offence has been procured, we are in no doubt that the answer is that it has. It has been procured because, unknown to the driver and without his collaboration, he has been put in a position in which in fact he has committed an offence which he would never have committed otherwise. We think that there was a case to answer and that the trial judge should have directed the jury that an offence is committed if it is shown beyond reasonable doubt that the accused knew that his friend was going to drive, and also knew that the ordinary and natural result of the additional alcohol added to the friend's drink would be to bring him above the recognised limit of 80 milligrammes per 100 millilitres of blood.

It was suggested to us that, if we held that there may be a procuring on the facts of the present case, it would be but a short step to a similar finding for the generous host, with somewhat bibulous friends, when at the end of the day his friends leave him to go to their own homes in circumstances in which they are not fit to drive and in circumstances in which an offence under the Road Traffic Act 1972 is committed. The suggestion has been made that the host may on those circumstances be guilty with his guests on the basis that he has either aided, abetted, counselled or procured the offence.

The first point to notice in regard to the generous host is that that is not a case in which alcohol is being put surreptitiously into the glass of the driver. That is a case in which the driver knows perfectly well how much he has to drink and where to a large extent it is perfectly right and proper to leave him to make his own decision.

Furthermore, we would say that if such a case arises, the basis on which the case will be put against the host is, we think, bound to be on the footing that he has supplied the tool with which the offence is committed. This of course is a reference back to such cases as those where oxy-acetylene cutting equipment was bought by a man knowing it was to be used by another for a criminal offence.[1] There is ample and

---

[1] *R.* v. *Bainbridge*, [1960] 1 Q.B. 129; [1959] 3 All E.R. 200; p. 437, *infra*.

clear authority as to the extent to which supplying the tools for the commission of an offence may amount to aiding and abbetting for present purposes.

Accordingly, so far as the generous host type case is concerned we are not concerned at the possibility that difficulties will be created, as long as it is borne in mind that in those circumstances the matter must be approached in accordance with well-known authority governing the provision of the tools for the commission of an offence, and never forgetting that the introduction of the alcohol is not there surreptitious, and that consequently the case for saying that the offence was procured by the supplier of the alcohol is very much more difficult."

DETERMINATION ACCORDINGLY.

MOHAN v. R.
[1967] 2 All E.R. 58

Two persons may be convicted of aiding and abetting each other to commit a crime though there was no agreement between them.

The two appellants were charged and convicted of the murder of one Mootoo. The evidence was that one of them quarrelled with Mootoo and chased him towards his house. The other appellant then appeared, and Mootoo suffered wounds at the hands of each appellant. It was not clear which of the two inflicted the fatal wound. There was no evidence of any prearranged plan between the appellants, but the Judicial Committee of the Privy Council recommended that their convictions should be affirmed.

Extract from the Advice of the Privy Council

Lord Pearson.—

"It is impossible on the facts of this case to contend that the fatal blow was outside the scope of the common intention. The two appellants were attacking the same man at the same time with similar weapons and with the common intention that he should suffer grievous bodily harm. Each of the appellants was present and aiding and abetting the other of them in the wounding of Mootoo.

That is the feature which distinguishes this case from cases in which one of the accused was not present or not participating in the attack or not using any dangerous weapon, but may be held liable as a conspirator or an accessory before the fact or by virtue of a common design, if it can be shown that he was party to a prearranged plan in pursuance of which the fatal blow was struck. In this case one of the appellants struck the fatal blow, and the other of them was present aiding and abetting him. In such a case the prosecution do not have to prove that the accused were acting in pursuance of a prearranged plan.

In *R.* v. *Kupferberg*[1] the accused had in an earlier trial been acquitted on a charge of conspiracy, and in a later trial he was charged and convicted of aiding and abetting. Lawrence, J., in giving the judgment of the Court of Criminal Appeal, said that:

'Mr. Purchase had also contended that the acquittal on the count charging conspiracy, which was framed on the same clause of the regulations as the charge of aiding and abetting of which the appellant had been found guilty, entitled the appellant to plead autrefois acquit. That was not so, because conspiracy was not the same as aiding and abetting. The two offences had different ingredients: previous agreement was necessary in the one, but not in the other.' "

APPEAL DISMISSED.

R. v. ANDERSON AND MORRIS
[1966] 2 All E.R. 644

Where two persons embark on a joint enterprise, each is liable criminally for acts done in pursuance of the joint enterprise, including unusual consequences arising from the execution of the joint enterprise; but if one of them goes beyond what has been tacitly agreed as part of the joint enterprise the other is not liable for the consequence of the unauthorised act.

Anderson and Morris agreed to attack one Welch. There was evidence that Anderson had a knife with him and stabbed Welch to death with it. The jury were directed that, if they were satisfied that Anderson and Morris had a common design to attack Welch, although they were not satisfied that Morris intended to kill Welch or cause him

---

[1] (1918), 34 T.L.R. 587.

grievous bodily harm, they might convict Anderson of murder and Morris of manslaughter. Anderson was convicted of murder, and a new trial was ordered by the Court of Criminal Appeal because of the adduction of fresh evidence before that Court. Morris was convicted of manslaughter, and he successfully appealed to the Court of Criminal Appeal on the ground that the jury had been misdirected in his case.

Extracts from the Judgment of the Court of Criminal Appeal

Lord Parker, C.J.—

"Counsel for the applicant Morris . . . [puts] . . . the principle of law to be invoked in this form: that where two persons embark on a joint enterprise each is liable for the acts done in pursuance of that joint enterprise, that that includes liability for unusual consequences if they arise from the execution of the agreed joint enterprise but (and this is the crux of the matter) that if one of the adventurers goes beyond what has been tacitly agreed as part of the common enterprise, his co-adventurer is not liable for the consequences of that unauthorised act. Finally, he says it is for the jury in every case to decide whether what was done was part of the joint enterprise, or went beyond it and was in fact an act unauthorised by that joint enterprise. In support of that, he refers to a number of authorities to which this court finds it unnecessary to refer in detail. . . . In R. v. Smith[1] the co-adventurer who in fact killed was known by the accused to have a knife, and it was clear on the facts of that case that the common design involved an attack on a man, in that case a barman, in which the use of the knife would not be outside the scope of the concerted action. Reference was there made to the fact that the case might have been different if in fact the man using the knife had used a revolver, a weapon which he had, unknown to Smith. . . . Counsel for the Crown, on the other hand, while recognising that he cannot go beyond this long string of decided cases, has said that they are really all part and parcel of a much wider principle which he would put in this form, that if two or more persons engage in an unlawful act and one suddenly develops an intention to kill whereby death results, not only is he guilty of murder, but all those who have engaged in the unlawful act are guilty of manslaughter.

---

[1] [1963] 3 All E.R. 597.

He recognises that the present trend of authority is against that proposition, but he goes back to *R. v. Salisbury*[1] in 1553. In that case a master had lain in wait to attack a man, and his servants who had no idea of what his, the master's idea was, joined in the attack, whereby the man was killed. It was held there that those servants were themselves guilty of manslaughter. The court is by no means clear on the facts as reported that that case is really on all fours, but it is in the opinion of the court quite clear that that principle is wholly out of touch with the position today. It seems to this court that to say that adventurers are guilty of manslaughter when one of them has departed completely from the concerted action of the common design and has suddenly formed an intent to kill and has used a weapon and acted in a way which no party to that common design could suspect is something which would revolt the conscience of people today. Counsel for the Crown in his attractive argument points to the fact that it would seem to be illogical that, whereas if two people had formed a common design to do an unlawful act and death resulted by an unforseen consequence, they should be held, as they would undoubtedly be held, guilty of manslaughter; yet if one of them in those circumstances had in a moment of passion decided to kill, the other would be acquitted altogether. The law, of course, is not completely logical, but there is nothing really illogical in such a result, in that it could well be said as a matter of common-sense that in the latter circumstances the death resulted or was caused by the sudden action of the adventurer who decided to kill and killed. Considered as a matter of causation, there may well be an overwhelming supervening event which is of such a character that it will relegate into history matters which would otherwise be looked on as causative factors. Looked at in that way, there is really nothing illogical in the result to which counsel for the Crown points."

APPEAL ALLOWED.

R. v. BUCK AND BUCK

(1960), 44 Cr. App. Rep. 213

Someone who procures the commission of an unlawful abortion which proves fatal may be convicted as an accomplice to involuntary manslaughter.

---

[1] (1553), 1 Plowd. 100.

The accused woman was charged with manslaughter and the accused man was charged with being an accessory before the fact. The deceased had met her death in consequence of an abortion performed by the woman in relation to which the man had acted as go-between. It was submitted on behalf of the accused that it was no longer manslaughter to kill someone by an unlawful act, whatever its nature, in the absence of proof of criminal negligence, and that there could not be an accessory before the fact to involuntary manslaughter. These submissions were overruled by the trial judge who held, in relation to the accused woman, that to kill someone in consequence of an illegal abortion was at least manslaughter although there was no evidence of criminal negligence.[1] The extracts from the trial judge's judgment which follow are concerned with the liability of the accused man as an accomplice to involuntary manslaughter.

Extracts from the Judgment

Edmund Davies, J.—

"The second submission, I recall, was that there cannot be any accessory before the fact to involuntary manslaughter and that, despite the fact that I have overruled the first submission, the male defendant therefore ought not to be convicted of being accessory before the fact to manslaughter by criminal abortion. Mr. Chapman submitted that procuring a manslaughter is impossible in law. Procuring an abortion there may be, but even though death results from that criminal abortion, nevertheless there cannot be procuring of manslaughter. The authorities on the matter are not many. . . .

In *R. v. Gaylor* (1857), Dears & B. 288, the prisoner was convicted of manslaughter and I quote from the short headnote: 'It appeared that the prisoner procured sulphate of potash and gave it to his wife intending her to take it for the purpose of procuring abortion; and that she, believing herself to be pregnant, although in reality she was not, took the sulphate of potash in the absence of the prisoner, and died from its effects.' It was held that the conviction of the husband for manslaughter was right. Mr. Chapman has criticised this report and particularly the intervention of Erle, J., at page 293 as affording, perhaps, unreliable guidance to the courts in those days; but I note that that

---

[1] On the basis, of course, of the doctrine of constructive manslaughter, see pp. 227, *supra*.

great judge Bramwell, B. at page 291 said this: 'Suppose a man, for mischief, gives another a strong dose of medicine, not intending any further injury than causing him to be sick and uncomfortable, and death ensues, would not that be manslaughter? Suppose, then, another had counselled him to do it, would not he who counselled be an accessory before the fact?' Obviously, the learned Baron took the answers to both those questions to be clearly in the affirmative. . . .

I hold that, where criminal abortion is proved to have taken place and death is proved to have resulted from that criminal abortion there must, at least, be a conviction of manslaughter. In my judgment, further, there can be an accessory before the fact to involuntary manslaughter or, to bring the matter more directly to bear on the present case, a man or woman who procures another person to commit a criminal abortion is guilty of being an accessory before the fact to manslaughter if death results from that abortion."

SUBMISSIONS OVERRULED.

Note on R. v. Buck and Buck

This decision has been affirmed by the Court of Criminal Appeal in *Creamer*[1] where the appellant's conviction of being an accessory before the fact to manslaughter was affirmed when the deceased's death was caused by an abortion arranged by the appellant. In the course of his judgment Lord Parker, C.J., said:

"It is the accident of death resulting which makes him guilty of manslaughter as opposed to some lesser offence, such as assault or, in the present case, abortion. This can no doubt be said to be illogical, since the culpability is the same, but, nevertheless, it is an illogicality which runs throughout the whole of our law, both the common law and the statute law. A comparatively recent example is clearly that of dangerous driving and causing death by dangerous driving." For another example of this illogicality, see *Mowatt*, p. 167, *supra*.

R. v. TYLER AND PRICE
(1838), 8 C. & P. 616

(1) *A person cannot be convicted of aiding and abetting the commission of an offence where the criminal act is done by a person who is insane because no crime is committed by the latter.*

---

[1] [1966] 1 Q.B. 72; [1965] 3 All E.R. 257.

(2) *A person may be convicted as a perpetrator if he encourages or assists in the commission of criminal acts by an insane person.*

Tyler and Price were tried on an indictment containing two counts. The first charged them with aiding and abetting one Thom (since deceased) in the murder of a constable, Nicholas Meares, and the second charged them with the murder of the constable as principals in the first degree.

It appeared that Thom, who described himself as the saviour of the world, had created a number of disturbances in the neighbourhood of Canterbury, and that a warrant had been issued for his arrest. Thom assembled a number of people, including the accused, for the purpose of preventing his apprehension, and he shot the constable who was sent with others to arrest him. Acting on the orders of Thom, who was subsequently shot himself, the accused threw the body of the constable, while he was still alive, into a ditch.

Extracts from the Summing-up to the Jury

Lord Denman, C.J.—

"In order to make out that part of the charge which imputes to Thom the act of murder, and that these persons were guilty of aiding and abetting him to commit the murder, it would be necessary to shew that Thom was a person capable of committing that murder. In order to make out the malicious intention imputed in the indictment to the act of Thom, he must be shewn to have been of sound mind at the time when he committed it, for it is a maxim of law, that persons not of sound mind cannot be held responsible for their acts. It seems to me, therefore, that if it appears in evidence that Thom was not, at the time of committing the act, of sound mind, you must acquit the prisoners upon the first count of the indictment, for there will be no foundation on which the accessory crime can rest. . . . [I]f Thom was now on his trial, it could hardly be said, from the evidence, that he could be called on to answer for his criminal acts; that, therefore, simplifies the question you will have to decide, and confines it to the second count of the indictment. There these persons are themselves charged with having committed the offence; and if they were aware of the malignant purpose entertained by Thom, and shared in that purpose with him, and were present aiding and abetting, and assisting him in the commission of acts fatal to life, in the course of accomplishing this purpose, then no doubt they are guilty as principals on this second count. . . . If any man is found aiding another, of whose ill intentions he is thoroughly apprised, he is responsible. It will be for you to say whether, from what was done by these men both before and after the killing of Nicholas Meares, they did not intend this general resistance to the law. . . . You will, therefore, say whether these two men were so far cognisant of an illegal purpose in Thom, and joined in his acts, that they are guilty of the murder which the hand of Thom committed. You will say whether they were abetting Thom in the blow he gave the deceased; for if they were, the blow of Thom was the blow of them all, and they are answerable for it. If you think that they kept together with the knowledge of any general purpose of resistance to the law, then they are guilty. . . . You will, therefore, . . . say whether you find that Thom was a dangerous and mischievous person; that these two prisoners knew he was so, and yet kept with him, aiding and abetting him by their presence, and concurring in his acts: and if you do so, you will find them guilty, for they are then liable as principals for what was done by his hand."

VERDICT—NOT GUILTY ON THE FIRST COUNT, BUT GUILTY ON THE SECOND COUNT.

R. v. BOURNE

(1952), 36 Cr. App. Rep. 125

A husband who compels his wife to commit buggery per vaginam *with a dog can be convicted as an accomplice although the wife is entitled to be acquitted with the reults that there is no perpetrator.*

Bourne was charged, *inter alia*, with aiding and abetting his wife to commit buggery with a dog. There was evidence that he had, on two occasions, compelled his wife to submit herself to intercourse *per vaginam* with a dog. Bourne was convicted and appealed unsuccessfully to the Court of Criminal Appeal.

Extracts from the Judgment of the Court of Criminal Appeal

Lord Goddard, C.J.—

". . . in fact we have allowed Mr. Green to argue this case on the footing that the wife would have been entitled to be acquitted on the ground of duress. The learned judge left no question to the jury on duress, but the jury have found that she did not consent. Assuming that she could have set up duress, what does that mean? It means that she admits that she has committed the crime but prays to be excused from punishment for the consequences of the crime by reason of the duress, and no doubt in those circumstances the law would allow a verdict of Not Guilty to be entered. . . . There may be certain doctrines with regard to murder which do not apply to other cases, but I am willing to assume for the purpose of this case, and I think my brethren are too, that if this woman had been charged herself with committing the offence, she could have set up the plea of duress, not as showing that no offence had been committed, but as showing that . . . her will was overborne by threats of imprisonment or violence so that she would be excused from punishment. But the offence of buggery whether with man or beast does not depend upon consent; it depends on the act, and if an act of buggery is comitted, the felony is committed.

A point is raised here that the appellant was charged with being not merely an accessory before the fact but with being an aider and abettor. So he was, because the charge is: 'you being present aided and abetted, counselled and procured.' The only questions that were left to the jury by the learned judge, and he was not asked to leave any more, were these: (1) 'Did the prisoner on a day in or about the month of September, 1949, in the County of Stafford cause his wife Adelaide Bourne to have carnal knowledge of a dog?' and the jury have found that he did. (2) 'Are you satisfied that she did not consent to having such carnal knowledge?' The answer of the jury was: 'Yes, we are satisfied she did not consent.' Then the same two questions were asked with regard to the other day on which an offence was alleged to have been committed.

In the opinion of the court, there is no doubt that the appellant was properly indicted for being a principal in the second degree to the commission of the crime of buggery. That is all that it is necessary to show. The evidence was, and the jury by their verdict have shown they accepted it, that he caused his wife to have connection with a dog, and if he caused his wife to have connection with a dog he is guilty, whether you call him an aider and abettor or an accessory, as a principal in the second degree. For that reason, this appeal fails and is dismissed."

APPEAL DISMISSED.

R. v. COGAN AND LEAK
[1975] 2 All E.R. 1059

A husband who procures another man to have sexual intercourse with his, the husband's, wife without her consent, the other man believing that she is consenting and therefore entitled to be acquitted, can be convicted as the perpetrator of rape through the innocent agency of the other man, although he could not have been convicted of rape if he personally had had intercourse with his wife without her consent.

One evening Leak came home with Cogan. He told his wife that Cogan wanted to have sexual intercourse with her and that he, Leak, was going to see that she did. He then made his wife go upstairs and undressed her, whereupon Cogan entered the room. Initially, Cogan refused Leak's invitations to have intercourse with his wife but, after Leak had had intercourse with her in his presence, he accepted a further invitation and had intercourse with Mrs. Leak. There was ample evidence that Mrs. Leak had not consented to intercourse with Cogan and subsequently the jury so found. Cogan was charged with rape and Leak, *inter alia*, with aiding and abetting the rape by Cogan. At the trial Cogan gave evidence that he believed Mrs. Leak had consented to intercourse with him. The trial judge directed the jury that Cogan's mistake had to be based on reasonable grounds. The jury found Cogan guilty, but went on to say that Cogan had believed Mrs. Leak was consenting although he had no reasonable grounds for his belief. The jury also found Leak guilty.

Both men appealed to the Court of Appeal who allowed Cogan's appeal on the ground that the subsequent decision of the House of Lords in *Director of Public Prosecutions* v.

Morgan[1] applied and the jury should have been directed to acquit Cogan if he had believed that Mrs. Leak was consenting, whether or not he had reasonable grounds for his belief. The extracts which follow are concerned with Leak's appeal against conviction for aiding and abetting rape.

Extracts from the Judgment of the Court of Appeal

Lawton, L.J.—

"Leak's appeal against conviction was based on the proposition that he could not be found guilty of aiding and abetting Cogan to rape his wife if Cogan was acquitted of that offence as he was deemed in law to have been when his conviction was quashed: see s. 2(3) of the Criminal Appeal Act 1968. . . .

The only case which counsel for Leak submitted had a direct bearing on the problem of Leak's guilt was *Walters* v. *Lunt*.[2] In that case the respondents had been charged under the Larceny Act 1916, s. 33(1),[3] with receiving from a child aged seven years, certain articles knowing them to have been stolen. In 1951 a child under eight years was deemed in law to be incapable of committing a crime;[4] it followed that at the time of receipt by the respondents the articles had not been stolen and that the charge had not been proved. That case is very different from this because here one fact is clear—the wife had been raped. Cogan had had sexual intercourse with her without her consent. The fact that Cogan was innocent of rape because he believed that she was consenting does not affect the position that she was raped.

Her ravishment had come about because Leak had wanted it to happen and had taken action to see that it did by persuading Cogan to use his body as the instrument for the necessary physical act. In the language of the law the act of sexual intercourse without the wife's consent was the *actus reus*; it had been procured by Leak who had the appropriate *mens rea*, namely his intention that Cogan should have sexual intercourse with her without her consent. In our judgment it is irrelevant that the man whom Leak had procured to do the physical act himself did not intend to

---

[1] [1976] A.C., at p. 192; [1975] 2 All E.R. 347. See p. 22, *supra*.

[2] [1951] 2 All E.R. 645.

[3] This section was repealed by the Theft Act 1968. The relevant offence is now handling stolen goods (Theft Act 1968, s. 22; see p. 299, *supra*.).

[4] By the Children and Young Persons Act 1963, s. 16, the minimum age of criminal responsibility is now ten.

have sexual intercourse with the wife without her consent. Leak was using him as a means to procure a criminal purpose.

Before 1861 a case such as this, pleaded as it was in the indictment, might have presented a court with problems arising from the old distinctions between principals and accessories in felony. Most of the old law was swept away by s. 8 of the Accessories and Abettors Act 1861 and what remained by s. 1 of the Criminal Law Act 1967. The modern law allowed Leak to be tried and punished as a principal offender. In our judgment he could have been indicted as a principal offender. It would have been no defence for him to submit that if Cogan was an 'innocent' agent, he was necessarily in the old terminology of the law a principal in the first degree, which was a legal impossibility as a man cannot rape his own wife during cohabitation. The law no longer concerns itself with niceties of degrees in participation in crime; but even if it did, Leak would still be guilty. The reason a man cannot by his own physical act rape his wife during cohabitation is because the law presumes consent from the marriage ceremony: see Hale.[1] There is no such presumption when a man procures a drunken friend to do the physical act for him. Hale, C.J., put this case in one sentence:

'tho in marriage she hath given up her body to her husband, she is not to be by him prostituted to another.'

Had Leak been indicted as a principal offender, the case against him would have been clear beyond argument. Should he be allowed to go free because he was charged with 'being aider and abettor to the same offence'? If we are right in our opinion that the wife had been raped (and no one outside a court of law would say that she had not been), then the particulars of offence accurately stated what Leak had done, namely he had procured Cogan to commit the offence. This would suffice to uphold the conviction. We would prefer, however, to uphold it on a wider basis. In our judgment convictions should not be upset because of mere technicalities of pleading in an indictment. Leak knew what the case against him was and the facts in support of that case were proved. But for the fact that the jury thought that Cogan in his intoxicated condition might have mistaken the wife's sobs and distress for expressions of her consent, no question of any kind would have arisen about the form of pleading. By his written statement Leak virtually admitted what he

---

[1] *Pleas of the Crown*, Vol. 1, p. 629.

had done. As Judge Chapman said in *R. v. Humphreys and Turner*[1];

'It would be anomalous if a person who admitted to a substantial part in the perpetration of a misdemeanour as aider and abettor could not be convicted on his own admission merely because the person alleged to have been aided and abetted was not or could not be convicted.'

In the circumstances of this case it would be more than anomalous: it would be an affront to justice and to the common sense of ordinary folk. It was for these reasons that we dismissed the appeal against conviction.''

COGAN'S APPEAL AGAINST CONVICTION ALLOWED.

LEAK'S APPEAL AGAINST CONVICTION DISMISSED.

Comment on R. v. Tyler and Price, R. v. Bourne and R. v. Cogan and Leak

At first sight Lord Denman's statement that, if Thom was of unsound mind at the material time, there was no foundation on which the accessory crime could rest, appears to be quite inconsistent with the conclusion that Bourne could be convicted as a principal in the second degree although, had she been tried, Mrs. Bourne would have been acquitted. As a matter of substantive law, the statement and the conclusion can be reconciled on the ground that there is a difference between the defences of insanity and duress. In the case of insanity, it is established that the accused did not know the nature and quality of his act, or, if he did know this much, he did not know that he was doing wrong. In the case of duress, on the other hand, the accused admits that he knew what he was doing and that it was wrong, but claims that he acted as he did in order to avoid threats. Duress is thus a plea in confession and avoidance, and the person responsible for the threats can be said to have aided and abetted the accused because he caused the accused knowingly to commit wrongful acts.

In most cases of duress, it is possible to hold that the person acting under it was an innocent agent and thus to hold that the person responsible for the duress was the perpetrator. The problem in *Bourne* was that a man cannot personally commit the form of buggery in issue there. The operation of the decision in *Bourne* can be illustrated from the offence of bigamy: A, a bachelor, compels B, a married woman, to go through a form

---

[1] [1965] 3 All E.R. 689, at p. 692.

of marriage with him. *Bourne* shows that, although B is acquitted, A can be convicted as an accomplice to bigamy despite the fact that, not being married, he cannot personally commit the *actus reus* of that offence.

Even if *Bourne* and *Tyler and Price* can be reconciled on the lines suggested above, there is still difficulty in cases where the person actually committing the *actus reus* lacks the necessary *mens rea* and the instigator is, by definition, incapable of personally committing the offence. To illustrate again from bigamy: A, a bachelor, persuades B, a married woman, to go through a form of marriage with him. B's husband has been absent for more than seven years and B does not know that he is alive. A knows that B's husband is alive. B must be acquitted but what about A?

According to the main ground of the decision in *Cogan and Leak*, where neither *Tyler and Price* nor *Bourne* was cited, A can be convicted as a perpetrator of bigamy through an innocent agent (and it is implicit that the court would have taken the same view in a case like *Bourne*). However, if, as Leak (and A) did, the procurer of an innocent agent lacks a characteristic, e.g. "being married" or "not being the husband", required for the personal commission of the *actus reus* of the particular offence it is difficult to see how he can be convicted of it as a perpetrator through an innocent agent. According to the view taken in *Tyler and Price* A cannot be convicted of aiding and abetting bigamy. However, as its alternative ground for its decision in *Cogan and Leak* the Court of Appeal held that Leak could be convicted of aiding and abetting rape although the man who had intercourse lacked the necessary *mens rea*. Pursuant to this, A in the above example could be convicted of aiding and abetting bigamy. This solution seems preferable but the only way of reconciling it with *Tyler and Price* appears to be that it is a special rule which applies where the procurer of an innocent agent lacks a characteristic required for the personal commission of the *actus reus* in question.

R. v. CONEY
(1882), 8 Q.B.D. 534

Mere presence at the commission of a crime does not render a person liable as an accomplice.

Two persons fought with bare fists in a ring in the presence of a crowd including the prisoners who were charged with aiding and abetting the fight. There was no evidence that they said or did anything to assist or encourage the pugilists, but the Chairman of the Berkshire Quarter Sessions directed the jury that mere presence at an unlawful fight was, if unexplained, conclusive proof of aiding and abetting. The prisoners were accordingly convicted, but the Chairman stated a case for the opinion of the Court for Crown Cases Reserved. This court quashed the conviction by a majority of 8 to 3 judges.

Extracts from the Judgments of the Court for Crown Cases Reserved

Cave, J.—

". . . For the defence it was first contended that inasmuch as Burke and Mitchell had agreed to fight there was no assault. I am, however, of opinion that this is not so. With regard to an action for an assault, in the case of *Boulter* v. *Clark*[1] it was held by Parker, C.B., that it was no defence to allege that the plaintiff and defendant fought together by consent, the fighting itself being unlawful, and in *Matthew* v. *Ollerton*[2] it was held that if one license another to beat him, such licence is no defence, because it is against the peace. . . . It was next contended that the chairman was wrong in directing the jury in the words of Littledale, J., in *R.* v. *Murphy*[3] that if the prisoners were not merely casually passing by, but stayed at the place, they encouraged it by their presence, although they did not say or do anything.

Now it is a general rule in the case of principals in the second degree that there must be participation in the act, and that, although a man is present whilst a felony is being committed, if he takes no part in it, and does not act in concert with those who commit it, he will not be a principal in the second degree merely because he does not endeavour to prevent the felony, or apprehend the felon. . . .

Where presence may be entirely accidental, it is not even evidence of aiding and abetting. Where presence is *prima facie* not accidental it is evidence, but no more than evidence, for the jury. . . .

In *R.* v. *Young*,[4] the prisoners were indicted for the murder of Mirfin, who was killed in a duel by one Eliot. In summing up, Vaughan, J., said, 'There is no difficulty as

---

[1] (1747), Bull. N.P. 16.
[2] (1693), Comb. 218.
[3] (1833), 6 C. & P. 103.
[4] (1838), 8 C. & P. 644.

to the law upon this subject. Principals in the first degree are those by whom the death wound is inflicted. Principals in the second degree, those who are present at the time it is given, aiding and abetting, comforting and assisting the persons actually engaged in the contest—mere presence alone will not be sufficient to make a party an aider and abettor, but it is essential that he should by his countenance and conduct in the proceeding, being present, aid and assist the principals. If either of the prisoners sustained the principal by his advice or presence, or if you think he went down for the purpose of encouraging and forwarding the unlawful conflict, although he did not do or say anything; yet, if he was present and was assisting and encouraging when the pistol was fired, he will be guilty of the offence imputed by the indictment.'[1] In that direction I entirely concur, but I believe if a similar direction had been given in the present case the prisoners would have been acquitted. . . ."

CONVICTION QUASHED.

R. v. CLARKSON AND OTHERS
[1971] 3 All E.R. 344

Non-accidental presence at the commission of a crime can constitute aiding and abetting if there can be inferred (i) actual encouragment and (ii) an intention to encourage on the part of the person in question.

A girl went to a party in British army barracks in Germany. In a room there she was raped by at least three soldiers. At some time after the raping had begun a number of men, including Clarkson and Carroll, entered the room and remained there while the girl was raped. Some of the men actively assisted by holding the girl down but there was no evidence that Clarkson or Carroll had done any positive act to assist. A number of soldiers in the room at the time were tried subsequently by court-martial, Clarkson and Carroll being convicted of aiding and abetting rape. Both men appealed to the Courts-Martial Appeal Court.

---

[1] Cf. *Wilcox* v. *Jeffery*, [1951] 1 All E.R. 464.

Extracts from the Judgment of the Courts-Martial Appeal Court

Megaw, L.J.—

"As has been said, there was no evidence on which the prosecution sought to rely that either the appellant Clarkson or the appellant Carroll had done any physical act or uttered any word which involved direct physical participation or verbal encouragement. . . . Therefore, if there was here aiding and abetting by the appellants Clarkson or Carroll it could only have been on the basis of inferences to be drawn that by their presence they, each of them separately as concerns himself, encouraged those who were committing rape. Let it be accepted, and there was evidence to justify this assumption, that the presence of those two appellants in the room where the offence was taking place was not accidental in any sense and that it was not by chance, unconnected with the crime, that they were there. Let it be accepted that they entered the room when the crime was committed because of what they had heard, which indicated that a woman was being raped, and they remained there.

R. v. *Coney*[1] decided that non-accidental presence at the scene of the crime is not conclusive of aiding and abetting. The jury has to be told by the judge, or as in this case the court-martial has to be told by the judge-advocate, in clear terms what it is that has to be proved before they can convict of aiding and abetting; what it is of which the jury or the court-martial, as the case may be, must be sure as matters of inference before they can convict of aiding and abetting in such a case where the evidence adduced by the prosecution is limited to non-accidental presence. What has to be proved is stated by Hawkins, J., in a well-known passage in his judgment in *R.* v. *Coney*[2] where he said:

'In my opinion, to constitute an aider and abettor some active steps must be taken by word, or action, with the intent to instigate the principal, or principals. Encouragement does not of necessity amount to aiding and abetting, it may be intentional or unintentional, a man may unwittingly encourage another in fact by his presence, by misinterpreted words, or gestures, or by his silence, or non-interference, or he may encourage intentionally by expressions, gestures, or actions intended to signify approval. In the latter case he aids and abets, in the former

[1] (1882), 8 Q.B.D. 534.
[2] *Ibid.*, at pp. 557, 558.

he does not. It is no criminal offence to stand by, a mere passive spectator of a crime, even of a murder. Non-interference to prevent a crime is not itself a crime. But the fact that a person was voluntarily and purposely present witnessing the commission of a crime, and offered no opposition to it, though he might reasonably be expected to prevent and had the power so to do, or at least to express his dissent, might under some circumstances, afford cogent evidence upon which a jury would be justified in finding that he wilfully encouraged and so aided and abetted. But it would be purely a question for the jury whether he did so or not.'

It is not enough, then, that the presence of the accused has, in fact, given encouragement. It must be proved that the accused intended to give encouragement; that he *wilfully* encouraged. In a case such as the present, more than in many other cases where aiding and abetting is alleged, it was essential that that element should be stressed; for there was here at least the possibility that a drunken man with his self-discipline loosened by drink, being aware that a woman was being raped, might be attracted to the scene and might stay on the scene in the capacity of what is known as a voyeur; and, while his presence and the presence of others might in fact encourage the rapers or discourage the victim, he himself, enjoying the scene or at least standing by assenting, might not intend that his presence should offer encouragement to rapers or would-be rapers or discouragement to the victim; he might not realise that he was giving encouragement; so that, while encouragement there might be, it would not be a case in which, to use the words of Hawkins, J., the accused person 'wilfully encouraged'.

A further point is emphasised in passages in the judgment of the Court of Criminal Appeal in *R. v. Allan*[1]. That was a case concerned with participation in an affray. Edmund Davies, J., giving the judgment of the court, said:

'In effect, it amounts to this: that the learned judge thereby directed the jury that they were in duty bound to convict an accused who was proved to have been present and witnessing an affray if it was also proved that he nursed an intention to join in if help was needed by the side which he favoured, and this notwithstanding that he did nothing by words or deeds to evince his intention and

---

[1] [1965] 1 Q.B. 130, at pp. 135, 138; [1963] 2 All E.R. 897, at pp. 898–901.

outwardly played the rôle of a purely passive spectator. It was said that, if that direction is right, where A and B behave themselves to all outward apperances in an exactly similar manner, but it be proved that A had the intention to participate if need be, whereas B had no such intention, then A must be convicted of being a principal in the second degree to the affray, whereas B should be acquitted. To do that, it is objected, would be to convict A on his thoughts, even though they found no reflection in his actions.'

The other passage in the judgment is this:

'In our judgment, before a jury can properly convict an accused person of being a principal in the second degree to an affray, they must be convinced by the evidence that, at the very least, he by some means or other encouraged the participants. To hold otherwise would be, in effect, as counsel for the appellants rightly expressed it, to convict a man on his thoughts, unaccompanied by any physical act other than the fact of his mere presence.'

From that it follows that mere intention is not in itself enough. There must be an intention to encourage; and there must also be encouragement in fact, in cases such as the present case. . . . [T]his court has come to the conclusion that the court-martial might have misunderstood the relevant principles that ought to be applied. It might have been left under the impression that it could find the two appellants guilty on the basis of their continuing, non-accidental, presence, even though it was not sure that the necessary inferences to be drawn from the evidence included (i) an intention to encourage and (ii) actual encouragement. While we have no doubt that those inferences could properly have been drawn in respect of each appellant on each count, so that verdicts of guilty could properly have been returned, we cannot say that the court-martial, properly directed, would necessarily have drawn those inferences. Accordingly the convictions of the appellants Clarkson and Carroll must be quashed.

APPEALS OF CLARKSON AND CARROLL ALLOWED.

NATIONAL COAL BOARD v. GAMBLE
[1959] 1 Q.B. 11

Someone who knowingly assists another to commit an offence aids and abets him to do so, even though he is indifferent as to whether the offence is committed.

Mallender, a servant of a firm of hauliers, drove a lorry to one of the Board's quarries in order to take delivery of a quantity of coal which the Board had contracted to supply to an electricity authority. After the lorry had been loaded, it was weighed on a weighbridge and Haslam, a servant of the Board, informed Mallender that the lorry was four tons over weight. Mallender said that he would take the risk, and Haslam allowed him to drive away after handing over the weight ticket. He need not have done so because the property in the coal had not previously passed to the electricity authority. The Board was charged and convicted before the magistrates with aiding and abetting Mallender to commit an offence against the Motor Vehicles (Construction and Use) Regulations 1955. The magistrates stated a case for the opinion of the Divisional Court where their decision was affirmed by a majority.

Extracts from the Judgments of the Divisional Court
Devlin, J.—

"A person who supplies the instrument for a crime or anything essential to its commission aids in the commission of it; and if he does so knowingly and with intent to aid, he abets it as well and is therefore guilty of aiding and abetting. I use the word 'supplies' to comprehend giving, lending, selling or any other transfer of the right of property. In a sense a man who gives up to a criminal a weapon which the latter has a right to demand from him aids in the commission of the crime as much as if he sold or lent the article. But this has never been held to be aiding in law; see *R.* v. *Lomas*[1] and *R.* v. *Bullock*.[2] The reason, I think, is that in the former case there is in law a positive act and in the latter only a negative one. In the transfer of property there must be either a physical delivery or a positive act of assent to a taking. But a man who hands over to another his own property on demand,

---

[1] (1913), 110 L.T. 239.
[2] [1955] 1 All E.R. 15; [1955] 1 W.L.R. 1.

although he may physically be performing a positive act, in law is only refraining from detinue. Thus in law the former act is one of assistance voluntarily given and the latter is only a failure to prevent the commission of the crime by means of a forcible detention, which would not even be justified except in the case of felony. Another way of putting the point is to say that aiding and abetting is a crime that requires proof of *mens rea*, that is to say, of intention to aid as well as of knowledge of the circumstances, and that proof of the intent involves proof of a positive act of assistance voluntarily done.

These considerations make it necessary to determine at what point the property in the coal passed from the board and what the board's state of knowledge was at that time. If the property had passed before the board knew of the proposed crime, there was nothing they could legally do to prevent the driver of the lorry from taking the overloaded lorry out onto the road. If it had not, then they sold the coal with knowledge that an offence was going to be committed.

The board called no evidence, so that a good deal was left to inference; but the conclusions of fact reached by the magistrates have not been seriously disputed. . . .

I think that the delivery of the coal was not completed until after the ascertained weight had been assented to and some act was done signifying assent and passing the property. The property passed when Haslam asked Mallender whether he intended to take the load and Mallender said he would risk it and when the mutual assent was, as it were, sealed by the delivery and acceptance of the weighbridge ticket. Haslam could therefore after he knew of the overload have refused to transfer the property in the coal.

This is the conclusion to which the justices came. Mr. Thompson [counsel for the appellant] submits on behalf of the board that it does not justify a verdict of guilty of aiding and abetting. He submits, first, that even if knowledge of the illegal purpose had been acquired before delivery began, it would not be sufficient for the verdict; and secondly, that if he is wrong about that, the knowledge was acquired too late, and the board was not guilty of aiding and abetting simply because Haslam failed to stop the process of delivery after it had been initiated.

On his first point Mr. Thompson submits that the furnishing of an article essential to the crime with knowledge of the use to which it is to be put does not of itself constitute

aiding and abetting; there must be proved in addition a
purpose or motive of the defendant to further the crime or
encourage the criminal. Otherwise, he submits, there is no
mens rea.

I have already said that in my judgment there must be
proof of intent to aid. I would agree that proof that the
article was knowingly supplied is not conclusive evidence of
intent to aid. *R.* v. *Fretwell*[1] is authority for that. *R.* v.
Steane,[2] in which the defendant was charged with having
acted during the war with intent to assist the enemy contrary
to the Defence Regulations then in force, makes the same
point. But *prima facie*—and *R.* v. *Steane* makes this clear
also—a man is presumed to intend the natural and probable
consequences of his acts, and the consequence of supplying
essential material is that assistance is given to the criminal.
It is always open to the defendant, as in *R.* v. *Steane,* to
give evidence of his real intention. But in this case the
defence called no evidence. The *prima facie* presumption is
therefore enough to justify the verdict, unless it is the law
that some other mental element besides intent is necessary
to the offence.

This is what Mr. Thompson argues, and he describes the
additional element as the purpose or motive of encouraging
the crime. No doubt evidence of an interest in the crime or of
an express purpose to assist it will greatly strengthen the case
for the prosecution. But an indifference to the result of the
crime does not of itself negative abetting. If one man deliberately sells to another a gun to be used for murdering a third,
he may be indifferent about whether the third man lives or
dies and interested only in the cash profit to be made out of
the sale, but he can still be an aider and abettor. To hold otherwise would be to negative the rule that *mens rea* is a matter of
intent only and does not depend on desire or motive.

The authorities, I think, support this conclusion, though
none has been cited to us in which the point has been specifically argued and decided."

APPEAL DISMISSED.[3]

---

[1] (1862), Le. & Ca. 161.
[2] [1947] K.B. 997; [1947] 1 All E.R. 813; p. 9, *supra.*
[3] The National Coal Board desired to obtain a decision on principle
and therefore invited the court to identify the Board with Haslam without
going into any question of vicarious liability. The court accepted this
invitation. Thus, the above decision does not conflict with the rule that
the doctrine of vicarious liability does not extend to aiding and abetting
(see p. 447, *infra*).

LYNCH v. DIRECTOR OF PUBLIC PROSECUTIONS FOR NORTHERN IRELAND

[1975] 1 All E.R. 913

A person who knowingly assists another to commit an offence can be convicted as an accomplice even though he is unwilling that the offence be committed.

The facts as stated in evidence by Lynch were that he was ordered by a well-known member of the I.R.A. who was reputed to be a ruthless gunman to drive him and two others in a hi-jacked car. Lynch, firmly believing that he would be shot if he refused, drove the three men according to the orders he received. In the course of their journey he suspected strongly that they were about to shoot a policeman. His suspicions were correct. At a certain point he was told to stop the car. The three men got out, ran across the road and shot and fatally wounded an off-duty policeman who was working on his car. Lynch then drove the men away after being ordered to do so.

Lynch was charged with murder, the case being that he was a principal in the second degree.[1] He was convicted and appealed unsuccessfully to the Court of Appeal of Northern Ireland, who held that duress could not be a defence to a charge of murder. The Court gave Lynch leave to appeal to the House of Lords, certifying that two points of law of general public importance were involved in their decision. The first question certified was whether on a charge of murder the defence of duress is open to a person "who is accused as a principal in the second degree (aider and abettor)". The House gave an affirmative answer to this question (see p. 390, *supra*). The second question certified is set out below.

Extracts from the Speeches of the House of Lords

Lord Simon of Glaisdale.—
"The second certified question reads:
'(2) Where a person charged with murder as an aider and

---

[1] The use of this terminology is rather surprising since the Criminal Law Act (Northern Ireland) 1967, s. 1 is identical to the Criminal Law Act 1967, s. 1, p. 407, *supra*.

abettor is shown to have intentionally done an act which assists in the commission of the murder with knowledge that the probable result of his act, combined with the acts of those whom his act is assisting, will be the death or serious bodily injury of another, is his guilt thereby established without the necessity of proving his willingness to participate in the crime?'

. . . I find myself entirely convinced by the judgment delivered by Lowry, C.J., on behalf of the majority of the court on this issue. I would merely emphasise that the majority did not hold that the crime of aiding and abetting a crime required no proof of *mens rea*: they held that the *mens rea* did not involve a 'specific intent'.

I respectfully agree. As regards the *actus reus*, 'aiding' and 'abetting' are, as Smith and Hogan[1] note, synonymous. But the phrase is not a pleonasm; because 'abet' clearly imports *mens rea*, which 'aid' might not. As Devlin, J., said in *National Coal Board* v. *Gamble*:[2]

'A person who supplies the instruments for a crime or anything essential to its commission aids in the commission of it; and if he does so knowingly and with intent to aid, he abets it as well and is therefore guilty of aiding and abetting.'

The *actus reus* is the supplying of an instrument for a crime or anything essential for its commission. On Devlin, J.'s, analysis the *mens rea* does not go beyond this. The act of supply must be voluntary . . ., and it must be foreseen that the instrument or other object or service supplied will probably be used for the commission of a crime. The definition of the crime does not in itself suggest any ulterior intent; and whether anything further in the way of *mens rea* was required was precisely the point at issue in *Gamble's* case.[2] Slade, J., thought the very concept of aiding and abetting imported the concept of motive. But Lord Goddard, C.J., and Devlin, J., disagreed with this. So do I. Slade, J., thought that abetting involved assistance or encouragement, and that both implied motive. So far as assistance is concerned, this is clearly not so. One may lend assistance without any motive, or even with the motive of bringing about a result directly contrary to that in fact assisted by one's efforts. . . . As for encouragement, at most it is only one way of abetting."

---

[1] *Criminal Law*, 3rd ed., p. 93.
[2] [1959] 1 Q.B. 11, at p. 20; [1958] 3 All E.R. 203, at p. 207; p. 432, *supra*.

Lord Morris of Borth-y-Gest.—

"In regard to the matters discussed in the judgments on [the second certified question] I am content to say that I am in general agreement with the conclusion reached by the majority as expressed in the judgment of Lowry, C.J. The words 'aid' and 'abet' are, I think, synonymous. If in the present case the jury were satisfied that the car was driven towards the garage in pursuance of a murderous plan and that the appellant knew that that was the plan and intentionally drove the car in execution of that plan he could be held to have aided and abetted even though he regretted the plan or indeed was horrified by it. However great his reluctance he would have intended to aid and abet. But if that intention and all that he did only came about because of the compulsion of duress of the nature that I have described he would, in my view, have a defence."

APPEAL ALLOWED: NEW TRIAL ORDERED.

R. v. BAINBRIDGE
[1960] 1 Q.B. 129

A person can be convicted as an accomplice if he assisted the perpetrator with knowledge of his intention to commit an offence of the kind actually committed. It is unnecessary for the prosecution to prove that the particular time and place of the intended offence was know to the accomplice.

Bainbridge was convicted as an accessory before the fact to office-breaking.[1] He had purchased oxygen cutting-equipment and handed it to some people who used it for the purpose of breaking into and stealing from a bank. He said that he merely suspected that the equipment would be used for some illegal purpose and did not know that it was to be used for breaking into the bank at which the crime was committed. The trial judge directed the jury that it was sufficient for the prosecution to prove that the accused knew that a crime of the type which was in fact committed was intended. Bainbridge unsuccessfully appealed to the Court of Criminal Appeal.

---

[1] Bainbridge's crime would now be aiding and abetting burglary.

Extract from the Judgment of the Court of Criminal Appeal

Lord Parker, C.J.—

"The court fully appreciates that it is not enough that it should be shown that a man knows that some illegal venture is intended. To take this case, it would not be enough if he knew—he says he only suspected—that the equipment was going to be used to dispose of stolen property. That would not be enough. Equally, this court is quite satisfied that it is unnecessary that knowledge of the particular crime which was in fact committed should be shown to his knowledge to have been intended, and by 'particular crime' I am using the words in the same way in which Mr. Simpson [counsel for the appellant] used them, namely, on a particular date and particular premises.

It is not altogether easy to lay down a precise form of words which will cover every case that can be contemplated but, having considered the cases and the law this court is quite clear that the direction of Judge Aarvold in this case cannot be criticised. Indeed, it might well have been made with the passage in *Foster's Crown Cases* (3rd ed. (1809), at p. 369) in mind, because there the author says: 'If the principal totally and substantially varieth, if being solicited to commit a felony of one kind he wilfully and knowingly committeth a felony of another, he will stand single in that offence, and the person soliciting will not be involved in his guilt. For on his part it was no more than a fruitless ineffectual temptation,' the converse, of course, being that if the principal does not totally and substantially vary the advice or the help and does not wilfully and knowingly commit a different form of felony altogether, the man who has advised or helped, aided or abetted, will be guilty as an accessory before the fact.

Judge Aarvold in this case, in the passage to which I have referred, makes it clear that there must be not merely suspicion but knowledge that a crime of the type in question was intended, and that the equipment was bought with that in view. In his reference to the felony of the type intended it was, as he stated, the felony of breaking and entering premises and the stealing of property from those premises. The court can see nothing wrong in that direction."

APPEAL DISMISSED.

FERGUSON v. WEAVING
[1951] 1 K.B. 814

A person cannot be convicted of aiding, abetting, counselling or procuring the commission of an offence if he is personally unaware of the facts constituting it.

S. 4 of the Licensing Act 1921 prohibited the sale or consumption of intoxicants otherwise than during permitted hours. Customers of a public house managed by the respondent were found consuming liquor on the respondent's premises outside permitted hours,[1] and were convicted of an offence under the section. The respondent was charged with counselling and procuring the offence, although there was no evidence that she knew that the liquor was being consumed out of hours, as it was served by waiters employed by her who had failed to collect the customers' glasses in time. The charge was dismissed and the prosecutor appealed unsuccessfully to the Divisional Court.

Extracts from the Judgment of the Divisional Court
Lord Goddard, C.J.—

". . . It is well known that the words 'aid and abet' are apt to describe the action of a person who is present at the time of the commission of an offence and takes some part therein. He is then described as an 'aider and abettor'. The words 'counsel and procure' are appropriate to a person who, though not present at the commission of the offence, is an accessory before the fact. That all these words may be used together to charge a person who is alleged to have participated in an offence otherwise than as a principal in the first degree was established by *In re Smith*.[2] Whether where the words 'counsel and procure' alone are used, there must be a proof of something more than would establish a case of being an accessory before the fact is not one which we feel necessary to decide in this case. The main point that was argued is one of general importance with regard to offences under the Licensing Acts, and as we are satisfied that the licensee cannot be convicted as a participant, to

---

[1] See now Licensing Act 1964, s. 100.
[2] (1858), 3 H. & N. 227.

use a compendious expression, in the offence charged against
the persons who consumed the intoxicating liquor, we give
no decision upon it. . . . There can be no doubt that this
court has more than once laid it down in clear terms that
before a person can be convicted of aiding and abetting the
commission of an offence, he must at least know the essential
matters which constitute the offence: see, for instance,
Johnson v. *Youden*.[1] The magistrate in this case has
acquitted the licensee of any knowledge of the matters which
constituted the principal offence, but it is said that the cases
establish that the knowledge of her servants must be imputed to her, and that there are many cases in which a
licensee has been convicted although he himself did not know
the facts constituting the offence is, of course, beyond question. There are certain offences under the Licensing Acts
which arise because the statute imposes an absolute prohibition, for instance, the offence of selling liquor to a drunken
person. In *Cundy* v. *Le Cocq*[2] it was held that the prohibition
against selling to such a person imposed by s. 13 of the
Licensing Act 1872 now replaced by s. 75 of the Licensing
(Consolidation) Act 1910[3] is absolute and that knowledge
of the condition of the person served is not necessary to
constitute the offence. On the other hand there are many
offences in which it is necessary to show either that the licensee
suffered or permitted the offence to take place, or that
he knowingly permitted matters which constituted an
offence. There is no material difference between permitting
or suffering something and knowingly allowing it to take
place, for, as was said in *Somerset* v. *Hart*:[4] 'How can a man
suffer a thing to be done when he does not know of it?'
The difference between an absolute prohibition and a prohibition against permitting or suffering was pointed out by
Collins, J., in *Somerset* v. *Wade*,[5] where, under other words
in the same section as was under consideration in *Cundy*
v. *Le Cocq*[2] the licensee was prosecuted, not for selling to a
drunken person, but for permitting drunkenness on licensed
premises. As it was there proved that the licensee did not
know that the person in question was drunk the court held
he could not be convicted of permitting drunkenness, though

---

[1] [1950] 1 K.B. 544; [1950] 1 All E.R. 300.
[2] (1884), 13 Q.B.D. 207; p. 47, *supra*.
[3] See now s. 172 (3) of the Licensing Act 1964.
[4] (1884), 12 Q.B.D. 360, at p. 362.
[5] [1894] 1 Q.B. 574.

they approved the decision in *Cundy* v. *Le Cocq*[1] because the prohibition against selling to a drunken person is absolute.

We now turn to the cases in which knowledge has been imputed to a licensee because of the knowledge of his manager or servant. It is unnecessary to go through them all because the principle which applies was laid down, not for the first time, in *Linnett* v. *Metropolitan Police Commissioner.*[2] All the cases on the subject were quoted, and, in giving judgment, I said:[3] 'The principle underlying these decisions does not depend upon the legal relationship existing between master and servant or between principal and agent; it depends on the fact that the person who is responsible in law, as, for example, a licensee under the Licensing Acts, has chosen to delegate his duties, powers and authority to another.'

We will assume for the purpose of this case that the licensee had delegated to the waiters the conduct and management of the concert room, and if the Act had made it an offence for a licensee knowingly to permit liquor to be consumed after hours, then the fact that she had delegated the management and control of the concert room to the waiters would have made their knowledge her knowledge.[4] In this case there is no substantive offence in the licensee at all. The substantive offence is committed only by the customers. She can aid and abet the customers if she knows that the customers are committing the offence, but we are not prepared to hold that knowledge can be imputed to her so as to make her, not a principal offender, but an aider and abettor. So to hold would be to establish a new principle in criminal law and one for which there is no authority. If Parliament had desired to make a licensee guilty of an offence by allowing persons to consume liquor after hours it would have been perfectly easy so to provide in the section. But a doctrine of criminal law that a licensee who has knowledge of the facts is liable as a principal in the second degree is no reason for holding that if she herself had no knowledge of the facts but that someone in her employ and to whom she may have entrusted the management of the room did know them, this makes her an aider and abettor. As no duty is imposed on her by the section to prevent the consumption of liquor after hours there was no duty in this respect that she could delegate to her employees. While it may be that the waiters

---

[1] (1884), 13 Q.B.D. 207; p. 47, *supra.*
[2] [1946] K.B. 290; [1946] 1 All E.R. 380.
[3] *Ibid.*, at p. 294.
[4] See note 2, p. 445, *infra.*

could have been prosecuted for aiding and abetting the consumers, as to which we need express no opinion, we are clearly of opinion that the licensee could not be. To hold the contrary would, in our opinion, be an unwarranted extension of the doctrine of vicarious responsibility in criminal law."

APPEAL DISMISSED.

Vicarious Liability

GRIFFITHS v. STUDEBAKER, LTD.

[1924] 1 K.B. 102

A statute may be so construed as to render an employer (or principal) criminally vicariously liable for the acts of his employee (or agent).

A car belonging to the respondents and bearing a limited trade licence was driven in the course of his employment by one of the respondents' employees who was giving a trial run for prospective purchasers of the car. Unknown to any responsible officer of the respondents, and thus to the respondents, and contary to their express orders there were more than two passengers in the car.

The respondents were charged with using on a public road a motor vehicle under a limited trade licence and carrying thereon more than two persons in addition to the driver, in contravention of the Road Vehicles (Trade Licences) Regulations 1922, and the employee with aiding and abetting the commission of this offence. The magistrates dismissed the informations and the prosecutor appealed to the Divisional Court.

Extracts from the Judgments of the Divisional Court

Lord Hewart, C.J.—

"It is said on behalf of the respondents that if the question were one of civil liability they would no doubt be liable for the acts of their servant, but that they are not liable to be convicted, inasmuch as they took precautions to prevent the breach of the Regulations which was committed. This argument approaches the matter from the wrong standpoint. The respondents received a limited trade licence in respect of this car, and by virtue of that licence they could use it for particular purposes if they observed certain conditions; if they failed to observe those conditions and used the car they contravened the Regulations. It is said that they did not commit the breach alleged, as the act complained of was that of their servant. Two observations may be made upon that argument. It is quite clear that the limited company as a company could not drive the car, and secondly, it is not disputed that the employee who was driving the car on the day in question was in fact upon the respondents' business and was acting within the scope of his employment; in short, he was doing the very thing which for the advantage of the respondents he was employed to do. The only respect in which he fell short of the requirements of his employers was that, contrary to their wish, expressed in certain ways, he was carrying an excessive number of persons in the car. In those circumstances it seems clear to me that the act of the driver was the act of the respondents. . . . It would be fantastic to suppose that a manufacturer, whether a limited company, a firm, or an individual, would, even if he could, always show cars to prospective purchasers himself; and it would defeat the scheme of this legislation if it were open to an employer, whether a company, a firm, or an individual, to say that although the car was being used under the limited licence in contravention of the conditions upon which it was granted: 'My hand was not the hand that drove the car.' On these facts there ought to have been a conviction of the respondents and also of the driver as an aider and abettor."

APPEAL ALLOWED.

VANE v. YIANNOPOULLOS
[1964] 3 All E.R. 820

A licensee is not vicariously liable for knowingly supplying liquor to a customer to whom he is not permitted to supply it, when he retains control of the licensed premises and has no guilty knowledge himself.

The respondent was the holder of a restaurant licence under which he was not permitted to supply liquor to customers who did not consume a meal. He instructed his waitress not to supply liquor to customers who did not eat meals and on the occasion in question had withdrawn to the basement. The waitress knowingly supplied liquor to customers who did not consume a meal. The Divisional Court held that the respondent was not guilty of an offence under s. 22 (1) (a) of the Licensing Act 1961 which punishes the holder of a justices' on-licence who 'knowingly sells or supplies intoxicating liquor to persons to whom he is not permitted by the conditions of the licence to sell or supply' it (see now s. 161 (1) of the Licensing Act 1964). The appellant unsuccessfully appealed to the House of Lords. The House of Lords decided in favour of the respondent on the construction of the relevant legislation and reservations were expressed about the validity of the principle of delegation under which the delegator may be held guilty of licensing offences in the absence of guilty knowledge or connivance on his part.

Extracts from the Speeches of the House of Lords

Lord Reid.—

"The appellant maintains that under this section there is vicarious responsibility, so that the licence holder must be held guilty if a servant employed to sell liquor sells knowingly to a person to whom the licence holder is not permitted to sell, and that it is no defence that the accused had forbidden the servant so to sell and did not know of or connive at the sale. The appellant does not dispute that it is the general rule in criminal cases that an accused person cannot be convicted unless he has *mens rea*; but he maintains that the authorities have established a principle of interpretation of the provisions of the Licensing Acts that, where a licence holder is prohibited from doing or suffering certain things, vicarious responsibility must be inferred, so that the knowledge of the servant must be imputed to the licence holder whatever be the terms of the section under which he is prosecuted. His counsel frankly agreed that, but for this principle, a man charged with knowingly selling could not be convicted unless it was shown that he knew what his servant was doing or at least connived or shut his eyes to facts indicating that the servant was doing wrong or disobeying his orders.

. . . There are four cases since 1903 where the word 'knowingly' did occur in the relevant section, but they do not support the contention of the appellant in this case. There the courts adopted a construction which on any view I find it hard to justify. They drew a distinction between acts done by a servant without the knowledge of the licence holder while the licence holder was on the premises and giving general supervision to his business, and acts done without the knowledge of the licence holder but with the knowledge of a person whom the licence holder had left in charge of the premises. In the latter case they held that the knowledge of the person left in charge must be imputed to the licence holder. If that distinction is valid then I agree with the Divisional Court that, on the facts of this case, there was not that 'delegation' by the accused necessary to make him answerable for the servant having acted against the orders of the accused.

Counsel for the appellant strenuously argued that this distinction is illogical and not warranted by any statutory provision. He maintained that if a licence holder entrusts to his wine waiter the duty of selling intoxicating liquor that is sufficient delegation and that, if the wine waiter disobeys his orders and sells to persons to whom he ought not to sell, there is nothing to justify the licence holder being acquitted, if he happens to have been in some other part of the premises, but held vicariously liable if he happens to have gone out leaving the wine waiter in charge. If this were a new distinction recently introduced by the courts I would think it necessary to consider whether a provision that the licence holder shall not knowingly sell can ever make him vicariously liable by reason of the knowledge of some other person; but this distinction has now been recognised and acted on by the courts for over half a century.[1] It may have been unwarranted in the first instance, but I would think it now too late to upset so long-standing a practice."

APPEAL DISMISSED.[2]

---

[1] The distinction will disappear if proposition 4(2) of the Law Commission's Published Working Paper No. 43 is adopted. Subject to express provision to the contrary, the licensee will only be liable if he is at fault.

[2] The Court of Appeal has since accepted the principle of delegation as part of the current law (*Winson*, [1968] 1 All E.R. 197 in which leave to appeal to the House of Lords was granted but not acted upon). Also see *Howker* v. *Robinson*, [1972] 2 All E.R. 786, a case in which the principle of delegation was applied where a licensee retained control of one bar but delegated complete control of another bar to his servant who knowingly sold drinks to a boy under eighteen, an offence for which the servant as well as the licensee may be prosecuted (Licensing Act 1964, s. 169 (1)), contrast the provision with which *Vane* v. *Yiannopoulos* was concerned under which the licensee alone is liable.

BARKER v. LEVINSON
[1950] 2 All E.R. 825

A master is not liable for criminal acts committed by his servant in the course of his employment if they are outside the general scope of that employment.

Levinson was an estate agent who employed P to negotiate a tenancy. P took a premium contrary to the absolute prohibition imposed by s. 2 of the Landlord and Tenant (Rent Control) Act 1949. The magistrates found that Levinson was not guilty of any contravention of the statute, and the Divisional Court held on a case stated that they were right.

Extracts from the Judgments of the Divisional Court

Lord Goddard, C.J.—

"The principle underlying the cases which deal with the criminal responsibility of a master for the act of his servant can be stated in this way. The master is responsible for a criminal act of the servant if the act is done within the general scope of the servant's employment. In other words, if a master chooses to delegate the conduct of his business to a servant, then, if the servant, in the course of conducting the business, does an act which is absolutely prohibited, the master is liable, which is really only another way of saying that the act done must be within the general scope of the servant's employment.

. . . If, in the case now before us, the respondent had put Purkis into the position of being a general agent in respect of the flats and had left the management to him, and Purkis had done an illegal act, it may be that the respondent would have been liable. The case stated, however, shows no such finding by the justices. Purkis had no authority to negotiate the terms. He had no authority to take a premium, and what he did was an illegal act which his master had in no way, either expressly or impliedly, authorised him to do, and which, moreover the master had no means of preventing."

APPEAL DISMISSED.

FERGUSON v. WEAVING
[1951] 1 K.B. 814

The doctrine of vicarious liability does not apply on a charge of aiding and abetting the commission of an offence.

See p. 439, *supra.*

GARDNER v. AKEROYD
[1952] 2 Q.B. 743

The doctrine of vicarious liability does not apply on a charge of attempt.

See p. 370, *supra.*

INDEX

A

ABDUCTION,
mistake as defence, 29, 36–37, 38–44

ABORTION,
involuntary manslaughter, accomplice to, 416–418
procuring unlawful, 416–418

ACCESSORY. *See also* AIDING AND ABETTING
after the fact, 407
before the fact, 407–408
involuntary manslaughter, to, 416–418
knowledge of offence, 437–442

ACCOMPLICE. *See* AIDING AND ABETTING

ACCUSED,
proof, burden of, 17, 18

ACTUAL BODILY HARM,
assault occasioning, 138, 140, 142, 163
reform proposals, 174

ACTUS REUS,
duty, non-performance of legal, 1, 2–3
meaning of, 1
mens rea, relationship with, 1

AFFRAY,
definition of, 339–341, 342
public place, not in, 334, 339–341
self-defence, and, 341–343
single person, by, 341–343
unlawful assembly, comparison with, 333–334

AIDING AND ABETTING,
accessories, 407–408, 416–418, 437–442
agreement between parties, where no, 410*n.*, 413
assisting offenders, offence of, 408
buggery, 420–422
corporation, by, 124–126

AIDING AND ABETTING—*cont.*
counselling and procuring, 408–413, 416–418, 439
duress, defence of, 390–401, 421, 425
encourage, intent to aid or, 428–434
innocent agent, through, 422–426
insane, when principal offender, 418–420, 425
joint enterprise, extent of, 414–416
knowledge,
facts constituting offence, of, 432–442
imputed where delegation, whether, 439–442
mens rea, 428–434, 435–437
misdemeanour, 407–408, 409
no crime committed, where, 418–419
perpetrator,
liability as, 419–420, 422–426
where no, 420–422, 425–426
presence,
encouragement, and, 428–431
sufficient, whether, 426–428
principal in the second degree, 407–408
principal offender, acquittal of, 420–426
procuring commission of offence, 408–413, 416–418
rape, 422–426, 428–431
strict liability, where offence of, 440–441
unwilling participation, 435–437
vicarious liability, 434*n.*, 440–442, 447

ARREST,
force, use of, in, 405

ARSON,
offence, 310
penalty for, 311

ASSAULT,
actual bodily harm, occasioning, 138, 140–142, 163, 174

[448]

MURDER—*cont.*
grievous bodily harm, intent to
cause, 189–209
infanticide, defence of, 250
intention required,
objective test, 207–210
subjective test, 195, 210
intoxication of accused, 101–105,
112, 116, 118–120
malice aforethought, 189–213.
See also MALICE AFORE-
THOUGHT
mercy killing, 213–215
necessity, defence of, 401–405
reform proposals, 211–215, 401
self-defence, 183–185, 186–189
time limit on death, 212–213

MUSHROOMS,
criminal damage to, 312
theft of, 252

N

NECESSITY,
defence of, 401–405
Law Commission's reform proposals, 401

NEGLIGENCE,
contributory, 175
criminal liability, and, 15
manslaughter due to criminal, 227
beliefs of accused, 233, 249
disregard for life, 241, 244–246
driving offences, 246–248
gross negligence required, 15–
16, 227, 229, 242–246
omission, 2–3, 239–242
reform proposals, 249–250

NOXIOUS SUBSTANCE,
administering, 166

O

OBSCENITY,
Law Commission's reform proposals, 368
obscene publications, 355

OFFENCES AGAINST THE
PERSON,
assault and battery, 138–162.
See also ASSAULT
consent, 132–138
reform proposals,
assaults and wounding, 173–
174

OFFENCES AGAINST THE
PERSON—*cont.*
reform proposals—*cont.*
manslaughter, involuntary,
249–250
mercy killing, 213–215
murder, 211–215
provocation, 226–227
wounding and grievous bodily
harm, 162–174. *See also*
WOUNDING

OFFENSIVE WEAPON,
burglary, aggravated, with, 276

OMISSION,
actus reus, as, 1
manslaughter, whether amounting to, 2–3, 239–242

P

PARTICIPATION,
accessories, 407–408, 416–418,
437–442
aiding and abetting. *See* AIDING
AND ABETTING
Law Commission's reform
proposals, 408
parties to crime, 407–408
procuring. *See* PROCURING

PEACE,
breach of the. *See* BREACH OF
THE PEACE

PECUNIARY ADVANTAGE,
obtaining, by deception,
cheque, by, 285–289, 292–295
debt, evasion of, 284, 289–291,
292–298
definition, 284
hotel accomodation, 295–298
meal without payment, 289–
291

PLANTS,
criminal damage to, 312
theft of, 252

POLICE,
assault on, 138–142, 173
execution of his duty, in, 139,
146–152
mistake as defence, 147–149
execution of his duty, whether
acting in, 149–152
obstruction of, 146–147, 152–155
answer questions, failure to,
157–158

PRINTED IN GREAT BRITAIN BY OFFSET LITHOGRAPHY BY
BILLING & SONS LTD, GUILDFORD, LONDON AND WORCESTER